Sylvia Krapiwko

ADINA HOFFMAN

TILL WE HAVE BUILT JERUSALEM

Adina Hoffman is the author of *House of Windows: Portraits from a Jerusalem Neighborhood* and *My Happiness Bears No Relation to Happiness: A Poet's Life in the Palestinian Century*, named one of the Best Books of 2009 by the *Barnes & Noble Review*. She is also the author, with Peter Cole, of *Sacred Trash: The Lost and Found World of the Cairo Geniza*, which received the American Library Association's award for the Jewish book of the year. The recipient of a Guggenheim Fellowship, she was awarded one of the inaugural Windham Campbell Prizes in 2013. She divides her time between Jerusalem and New Haven, Connecticut.

ALSO BY ADINA HOFFMAN

Sacred Trash: The Lost and Found World of the Cairo Geniza
(with Peter Cole)

My Happiness Bears No Relation to Happiness:
A Poet's Life in the Palestinian Century

House of Windows: Portraits from a Jerusalem Neighborhood

TILL WE HAVE
BUILT JERUSALEM

TILL WE HAVE BUILT JERUSALEM

Architects of a New City

ADINA HOFFMAN

Farrar, Straus and Giroux   New York

Farrar, Straus and Giroux
18 West 18th Street, New York 10011

Printed in the United States of America
Published in 2016 by Farrar, Straus and Giroux
First paperback edition, 2017

An excerpt from *Till We Have Built Jerusalem* originally appeared,
in slightly different form, in *The Yale Review.*

Epigraph translated by Edmund Keeley and Philip Sherrard,
from C. P. Cavafy, *Collected Poems* (Princeton, 1975).

Illustration credits appear on pages 349–52.

The Library of Congress has cataloged the hardcover edition as follows:
Hoffman, Adina.
    Till we have built Jerusalem : architects of a new city /
Adina Hoffman. — First edition.
        pages   cm
    Includes index.
    ISBN 978-0-374-28910-2 (hardback) —
    ISBN 978-0-374-70978-5 (e-book)
    1. Jerusalem—History—20th century.   2. Architects—Jerusalem—
Biography.   3. Jerusalem—Buildings.   I. Title.

DS109.93 .H64 2016
956.94'4204—dc23

                                                2015034650

Paperback ISBN: 978-0-374-53678-7

Designed by Jonathan D. Lippincott

Our books may be purchased in bulk for promotional, educational, or
business use. Please contact your local bookseller or the Macmillan Corporate and
Premium Sales Department at 1-800-221-7945, extension 5442, or by e-mail at
MacmillanSpecialMarkets@macmillan.com.

www.fsgbooks.com
www.twitter.com/fsgbooks • www.facebook.com/fsgbooks

For M/P and D/M

You won't find a new country, won't find another shore.
This city will always pursue you . . .

C. P. Cavafy, "The City"

CONTENTS

TILL WE HAVE
BUILT JERUSALEM

BEYOND JAFFA GATE:
AN OPENING

ALMOST EVERY DAY FOR THE NEAR QUARTER CENTURY THAT I'VE lived in Jerusalem, I've walked the main street of its western half, Jaffa Road, or *the* Jaffa Road, as it was known to earlier generations.

At first a pilgrimage and camel route, then a major commercial thoroughfare, it's now a busy if bedraggled central artery that stretches from near the Old City's Jaffa Gate, cuts across the new town, curves west through hills and wadis and across a plain till eventually it reaches the port of Jaffa. From there it once extended, at least in spirit, to the boats that would carry passengers and cargo off to, and in from, various far-flung lands.

As the road opened Jerusalem to the rest of the world and brought the world to it, so the history of the new city unfurled along this street. For all its fame, and its holiness to so many, Jerusalem had been until 1867—when the Ottoman sultan ordered the construction of that packed-sand-and-stone carriage track by forcibly conscripted bands of Palestinian peasants—little more than a hilltop village contained by a wall. A cramped, dark, diseased, and by most accounts foul-smelling place whose gates were locked at night, it had prompted the visiting Herman Melville, for one, to brood in his notebook about "the insalubriousness of so small a city pent in by lofty walls obstructing ventilation, postponing the morning & hasting the unwholesome twilight."

With the presence of the toll road that stretched from the city to the sea, however, a new kind of movement into and out of those claustrophobia-inducing fortifications became possible, as did a new sort of freedom. And when a central station for carriages plying the Jaffa Road was established just beyond the Jerusalem gate that bore the same name, the city spilled forth once and for all. Greeks and Germans, Arabs and Armenians, Ashkenazi and Sephardi Jews alike opened hotels and kiosks, travel agencies and photo studios, coffeehouses, liquor stores, a telegraph office, souvenir shops, rug dealerships, a pharmacy, a bakery, outlets for carpentry and building supply, even a theater that featured tightrope walkers and performing bears. Foreign consulates, banks, post offices, and eventually the municipality itself also moved past the gate, and within a short while the crowded area just outside the walls had been transformed into a makeshift town square described by one native son as nothing less than "The City."

In 1900, in honor of the twenty-fifth year of the reign of Sultan Abd el-Hamid, the authorities erected a red-and-white candy-striped public fountain in the midst of this multilingual, multitudinous crush. An ornate stone clock tower followed seven years later. All self-respecting Ottoman cities featured such clocks in their central squares, and Jerusalem's was a point of pride to those who lived there. Forty-five feet tall, perched atop the Jaffa Gate, it was a sign of civic progress, of Ottoman patriotism; it bound Jerusalem's citizens to the other citizens of the empire, and in ways both figurative and literal it represented the arrival to this very old place of a new way of telling time. It also functioned as a kind of beacon. Soon after

it was built, the municipality strung its high outer walls with glowing gas lamps. Visible even from villages far off, the tower looked, wrote another native son, like a lighthouse.

✦

"What I see, what I see," began the Galician-born Jewish novelist Joseph Roth, using the words as a kind of mantra or incantation as he set out to describe the lazy walk he took around Berlin one May morning in 1921. Attempting to recount a walk through Jerusalem, c. 2015, one needs to vary this slightly and say: "What I see, what I don't see."

As I stroll the main street of the city I've called home for most of my adult life—a city that has held me in its grip, delighting, infuriating, bewildering, surprising me since I first encountered it—I'm considering both what meets the eye and what doesn't.

While every urban area evolves architecturally with the years, Jerusalem has a funny way of burying much of what it builds. Captured and recaptured some forty-four times by different powers throughout its long history, the city is as renowned for the structures razed there as for those it has retained. And so it is that the current town stands, as one excitable nineteenth-century commentator put it, "on 60, 80, or even 100 feet of ruins! You begin digging in the streets of Jerusalem, and you come upon house-tops at all varieties of level under ground! It is probable that we have there traces and remains of older and more numerous generations than in any other city under the sun."

But the archaeological debris isn't all ancient. Almost immediately after General Edmund Allenby dismounted his horse and marched on foot through the Jaffa Gate on December 11, 1917, declaring "Jerusalem the Blessed" subject to English martial law, for instance, the British authorities began making plans to destroy that lively Turkish town square. The squeamish, pious military governor, Ronald Storrs, found the ramshackle buildings and chaotic scene there distasteful, and he developed a particularly visceral antipathy toward the Ottoman clock and its gewgawed tower. He claimed it "disfigured" the gate, and arranged for it to be, as he put it, "bodily removed." A blockier and more plainly British sort of timepiece and tower, "shorn of the more offensive trimmings" of the earlier version, was then built at a less fraught though still central spot on the Jaffa Road, just to the northwest of Sultan Suleiman's medieval walls. The architectural equivalent of a pair of sensible shoes, this went up in 1924, two years after Britain received a formal Mandate from the League of Nations to govern Palestine, and it served both to tell the hour and to make plain who now controlled the holy city—which the British had recently declared the country's capital for the first time since the Crusades. The corner then known as Post Office Square was soon rechristened in the name of Allenby.

After a decade, that English clock tower, too, was knocked over (not because of conquest but to ease traffic flow around the curved prow of the new Barclays Bank and city hall that had just gone up on that corner), but Storrs never did manage to bulldoze the bazaar just outside the Jaffa Gate and replace it, as he'd yearned to do, with a pristine garden loop around the Old City. He left town, the British left the country, the Mandate ended, and in 1948 a high concrete and corrugated tin barrier was thrust up right beside Allenby Square, creating a crude but effective border between the new state of Israel and Jordan. That ugly wall was a finger jabbed in the eye of this once integrated and integral site. It was in fact only with the Israeli occupation  and annexation of East Jerusalem in 1967 that Storrs's half-century-old scheme for a greenbelt was realized and, declaring the city "united" under Israeli rule, the authorities demolished what the Bauhaus-trained chief planner of the project would refer to dismissively as "the dilapidated structures, shacks and rubble" and "the more visually offensive shops" around the Old City walls; a national park was set down in their place. Meanwhile, the now clockless spot opposite the walls, so recently redesigned and renamed for its conquering British hero, was redesigned once more. Today the small plaza set on the tense if invisible dividing line between the city's Jewish West and Arab East boasts a dry fountain, several squat olive trees, a line of struggling dwarf cypresses, an unremarkable set of curving stone steps, and a new name: IDF Square.

⊕

When I contemplate what I see and don't see on Jaffa Road, though, I'm thinking not only of such burials, erasures, and attempts to mark political turf by means of culturally symbolic architecture and hastily rewritten maps. I'm also musing on the multiple unrealized versions—and visions—of the city that exist and have existed in the minds of those who've felt compelled to try to build here, in all senses of that term.

At around the same time that Joseph Roth was observing the beggars and waiters, the horses and cigarette ads of the Kurfürstendamm, the British architect, town planner, and Arts and Crafts activist Charles Robert Ashbee—a disciple of William Morris and employee of Ronald Storrs—was, as Jerusalem's first-ever "civic adviser," striding the same main street that I do daily, snapping pictures and scribbling notes as he imagined a radical transformation of this area in both spatial and social terms: "*The Jaffa Road as it is*," he labeled one panoramic photograph, which shows a blur of locals in kaffiyehs, head scarves, and fezzes lolling before a pile of watermelons and a cluster of ramshackle stands and shops.

The Jaffa road as it is

He then rendered a neat pencil sketch of the same landscape, minus its saggy red-tile-roofed buildings and heaped fruit. In their place, his drawing shows an evenly staggered, spic-and-span progression of traditional domed structures, with a few neatly dressed natives marching purposefully by. This he titled *"The Jaffa Road Market as I want it to be."*

That may sound childish, perverse, or like mere wishful thinking, but Ashbee understood better than most the very steep challenges he faced in attempting to remake or reform this city according to his own romantic worldview. Although he lasted in town only briefly and, it might be argued, didn't really understand the context in which he was working, he felt as passionately aspirational about its future as so many others have who've devoted their lives to the place. Yet for all the energy he invested in its development, its civic improvement, its beautification, he also recognized the poignancy—even futility—of such efforts and the almost chronic way that Jerusalem has of frustrating hopeful expectations: "It is," he wrote, "a city unique, and before all things a city of idealists, a city moreover in which the idealists through succeeding generations have torn each other and their city to pieces."

And then there's what I *do* see:

Just a hundred yards or so from the start of Jaffa Road, the sleek, porthole-punched tower that the once celebrated German Jewish refugee Erich Mendelsohn designed as the Anglo-Palestine Bank is among the most expressive and subtle public buildings in town. When it was completed, in 1939, it was the tallest "skyscraper" in Jerusalem at a looming seven stories, but it wore then and still wears its height with unusual grace, as the soaring perpendicular of its main section is grounded dynamically by the low horizontal block at its back. As he did with all of his buildings, Mendelsohn planned this one with an acute awareness of the physical setting (a busy street that seemed to demand a building of clean, unfussy lines and a certain mute but impressive presence) and of topography (a steep incline to the rear). He also meant it—as he did all his designs—to be a bold challenge to his peers. When it opened, the bank would be the national head-quarters of the most important Jewish financial institution in Palestine, but Mendelsohn claimed inspiration for this decidedly modern and Zionistic undertaking from the shapes of local Arab buildings. He did this often, and that tack got him into frequent aesthetic and political hot water throughout his Jerusalem years.

Next door to the former bank (now an Israeli government minis-try) is the city's main post office (still a post office), another striking building that I pass by and take a certain solace from almost every day. A more monumental and symmetrical structure than Mendelsohn's, it was completed a year before the bank and was designed by the exceedingly gifted Austen St. Barbe Harrison, then the chief archi-tect of the British Mandatory Public Works Department. Private, canny, and refined, Harrison left England for the East as a young man and never looked back; his vision for his own buildings and for the city was informed by his deep knowledge of Byzantine and Islamic architecture, as well as a decidedly nonpartisan, even pacifis-tic relationship to the then already serious local ethnic strife. Though Harrison designed the post office as a proper English governmental edifice in its scale and its accoutrements, he also quietly borrowed multiple elements from those traditions he'd absorbed while living and working throughout the Levant—from the alternating light and dark stripes of Syrian-styled masonry to the geometrically ornamented panels of the massive wooden double doors. The outline of Harrison's building remains as grand as it ever was, though for some fifteen years now a certain feeling of constriction has taken hold around it, since all but one, or one-half, of those impressive sets of doors have been locked for security reasons, and visitors are funneled into the handsome old post office by means of a narrow metal detector. The same is true of Mendelsohn's former bank, the dignified doorway of which is now also cluttered with security equipment.

Not all of Jerusalem's modern buildings are so well guarded as these two prominent structures. If I walk northwest along the same road, moving toward the central area known as Zion Square, I'll soon reach yet another building the view of which somehow always startles me for its strange, almost spooky dignity—this, despite its location, opposite a large and fetid garbage compactor, usually swarming with the mangiest of stray cats. On the corner of Jaffa Road and the street formerly known as Queen Melisande Way—now named for another queen, Heleni, a first-century Iraqi convert to Judaism—this far more eclectic commercial and residential building features three stories of playfully harmonious arabesques: horseshoe arched windows, jagged crenellations, and a wide façade inset with panels of once luminous, now grime-covered tiles made by the Armenian master potter David Ohannessian, who worked in Jerusalem throughout the Mandate. A mishmash of businesses crowds the downstairs floors, changing hands and nature often (at the time of this writing, the storefronts are occupied by a popular café, a nail salon, a fluorescent-lit twenty-four-hour grocery, a nook of an old-world tailor shop, a nondescript hotel, and a self-declared "hot dog toast" take-out place with a plastic sign announcing its cryptic yet somehow appropriate name, only in lowercase English, "*after*"). Meanwhile, the dirty, graffiti-smeared foyer leads to what seem, from the sorry state of the exterior and the junk piled on its balconies, run-down apartments and hotel rooms. When it was completed in the late 1920s, the property of a well-to-do Christian Arab from the village of Beit Jala, this building was considered the height of style and was known around town as Spyro Houris House, after its architect—though that fact has long ago faded from the memory of almost all.

Who were these three very different men—Erich Mendelsohn,

Austen St. Barbe Harrison, Spyro Houris—and what led them to conceive these buildings and the other remarkable structures they designed around town? What did they see here and what did they *want* to see when they walked the dusty streets? In twenty-first-century Jerusalem, they're barely remembered, and the city or cities they had in mind are vanishing as well.

Beginning with the rocky topsoil and digging its way down, this book is an excavation in search of the traces of three Jerusalems and the singular builders who envisioned them.

I

JERUSALEMSTRASSE

1934

NO ROCOCO PALACE

ERICH MENDELSOHN WORE THICK GLASSES AND HAD ONLY ONE, weak eye—cancer forced the removal of the other when he was a young architect in Berlin, and total blindness had since been a hovering threat—but from the moment he set foot in Palestine he couldn't stop denouncing his fellow Jews for their failure to see.

The myopia he encountered there pained him. (So his wife, Luise, would write, years after his death.) He was ashamed by the ugliness of the Jewish settlements, the boxy apartment buildings, the slablike synagogues that had sprung up haphazardly throughout the land. The absence of planning also galled. Without any apparent forethought, cities had erupted, he said, like so much "wild, tropical vegetation." Even the poorest Arab villages were by comparison models of harmonious design—their dirt roads and low houses arrayed according to the shapes of the hills, each of them circling skyward toward a spiral-like crown. Luise would later report that throughout their years in Palestine he'd often stop the car by the side of the road and hop out, eager to study the lines of a favorite village on the old carriageway to Jerusalem. "A little heap of turned-up sand and rocks," it gave "the impression that it was lifted up out of the earth," and its elemental appearance fascinated him.

Meanwhile, just a short drive away, all those well-trained European architects who gathered in Tel Aviv cafés to argue and smoke as they vied for commissions and held competitions were still carrying on as though they were in Vienna, Hamburg, or Dessau—as though history and Hitler hadn't happened, as though it were possible to keep plunking down glass houses on every other corner and ignoring the climatic and cultural facts of where they'd landed: in a hot, ancient, blindingly bright, *Middle Eastern* land.

Astigmatism had not, he insisted, always been so rampant among his people. The ghetto was to blame. Over centuries of "pariah existence," he said, "their eyes had forgotten how to distinguish between good and bad. A 'better' building meant to them cement instead of wood, and 'more beautiful' meant complicated instead of simple. They had, therefore, to be trained anew to see."

To make his point more forcefully, he'd sometimes flourish an ancient ceramic vessel that he claimed demonstrated the creativity and craftsmanship that long ago characterized the Jewish people. Known as a "tear jug," this was a pitcher meant to hold the weepy runoff of its chronically saddened Semitic owners.

Mendelsohn had little patience with Jews who sniffled. He himself was less tearful than he was appalled by the "brutal disregard" of the country's singular beauty and by what he saw as the refusal of these transplanted architects to recognize that circumstances had changed, the world had changed, their materials had changed. And furthermore, "Palestine is not a virgin country insofar as architectural tradition is concerned." Though they seemed to believe they were starting from scratch, the recent arrivals had much to learn from the local Arabs who'd come to understand over centuries how best to shelter themselves from the glare, how to build with thick, cooling walls and small, carefully placed windows. It shocked him especially to see scattered along the streets of the country's raggedy Eastern cities crass imitations of his own sleek German designs—"bastard buildings," he called them, in which the steel and reinforced concrete that he'd used so dynamically in his earlier European work had been yanked out of context, used carelessly, hurriedly, on the cheap, and all in the name of settling the hordes of immigrants who—like many of the architects themselves—had just stumbled blearily onto these Mediterranean shores. With their extravagant use of glass, these buildings were, he fumed, "wholly unsuitable to the sub-tropical climate of Palestine." Such construction had "almost degenerated into a pestilence."

Erich Mendelsohn hadn't come here to make friends.

⊕

Decades later, as a widow, Luise would explain that many viewed her husband as "arrogant, impatient, contemptuous, sarcastic" but that those who knew him well and whom he trusted saw him as unstintingly generous, endlessly attentive, and, what's more, "humble . . . in the profoundest sense of a deeply religious personality—always aware of the great unknown."

But he couldn't help himself and his prophetic rages, especially once he reached Jerusalem. And then it wasn't simply scorn that he let rip in this oracular manner but a piercing, almost painful, *ambivalence* that came blasting out, as though the violent confusion of sensations he was experiencing there hurt him physically.

Taking in all he saw from the heights of Mount Scopus, for instance, the squat man with the soaring ideas was flooded by waves of mixed emotion. The colors in the distance were at once jumbled and overwhelming, with the violet-blue Judean hills stretching as far as the Dead Sea, and the Old City walls that seemed to him gray-green, covered in a glorious ancient patina. The site was (he would write Luise in excited exhaustion that night) "indescribably beautiful—yes, shattering—

"—but the present buildings are scattered about without any plan, in a terrifyingly small-minded way."

He, meanwhile, had a definite plan, or plans—for this summit, for this city, for this country as a whole. And also for himself. That was why the great Erich Mendelsohn was here, after all, traipsing around the rocky wastes of this historic hill on a blustery December day in 1934, swiveling his head and its fedora this way and that as he took in the boggling view.

Often, Mendelsohn would simply drink in a landscape or a cluster of buildings for its own sake. Just as that village on the way to Jerusalem always made him slam on the brakes and spring from the car, go scurrying out with his sketchbook and single squinting eye, whenever and wherever he was hired to build he'd apply the same thirsty observational method. But today was an official visit, not a spontaneous pit stop with his pretty wife or a solitary surveying session. Hearing of the presence in town of the well-known refugee architect—currently working in London, though for a few weeks now he'd been running a makeshift drafting office out of his room in the swank, newly built King David Hotel—the Kishinev-born, Odessa-trained director of the Hadassah Medical Organization, Chaim Yassky, had invited Mendelsohn to accompany him up the mountain.

Yassky was an eye doctor, of all things, the perfect companion for Mendelsohn as he set out on his quest to correct the Jewish people's collectively impaired vision. And although he didn't yet have the approval of his bickering building committee to hire Mendelsohn (they preferred to hold a competition), the doctor also had plans. The old Rothschild-Hadassah hospital in the heart of town on the Street of the Prophets was too small, crowded, and run-down to serve the city's rapidly expanding population. At the start of the nineteenth century, Jerusalem was home to just eight thousand, all living inside the walls; by late 1917, when the British occupied Palestine, the number of residents both within and without those medieval ramparts had swollen to fifty-four thousand. Now—seventeen years since the start of English rule and the approval of the document known as the Balfour Declaration, which pledged that His Majesty's government would use its "best endeavours" to facilitate "the establishment in Palestine of a national home for the Jewish people"—the city's populace stood near a hundred thousand and would, Yassky knew, continue to grow. With such figures and the pressing physical facts they suggested in mind, he wanted Mendelsohn to examine the more remote Mount Scopus site to the northeast of downtown and consider the prospect of designing a modern hospital and medical school on the saddle of the hill. There it would rest between those few scattered buildings of the fledgling Hebrew University and the pristine British War Cemetery, with its regiments of cross-bearing headstones standing since the Great War at perpetual attention.

The plot Yassky had selected was, as it happens, the perfect limbo-like spot on which to build in the timeless manner to which Mendelsohn aspired—poised between the promise of what would be (the new university and all it represented for the Jewish people) and what had been (that "great" war and its more universal, and devastating, meaning). The hospital's cornerstone had been laid just a few months before, and the proceedings of the ceremony broadcast by live wireless—a first—from these windy heights to the whole wide world, or at least to Cairo, London, New York, and the Wardman Park Hotel ballroom in Washington, D.C., where the fifteen hundred white-gloved delegates of the Hadassah Women's Convention assembled to hear the staticky speeches beneath a banner that proclaimed WE WILL BUILD.

As gangly and calm as Mendelsohn was soft hipped and excitable, Yassky had made his way in the world as a sober man of science, but he knew a thing or two about the sweeping rhetoric of sanctification and striving that was, at this moment, so popular in Palestine. Using the loftiest terms, he had managed to convince his endlessly wrangling committee members of the need to situate the country's new, state-of-the-art teaching hospital in the "cosmopolitan city of Jerusalem"—not homogenous Tel Aviv—where it would both serve *all* the citizens of the country, regardless of creed, and "foster . . . the progress, if not the salvation of the Jewish community of Jerusalem, which will eventually become the spiritual center of Jewish Palestine."

Such talk appealed to Mendelsohn, whose own visions, like his ambition and his scathing opinions, were hard to contain. The hospital constituted just one piece of his grand design for this Jerusalem ridge. He'd also already begun to imagine what he called "an entirely new master plan for the whole University complex"—not just a building or two but a complete network of carefully arrayed structures and roads, which would come together as a focused unity and flow naturally across the hilltop "like a proper organism." (As he conjured the image of this marvelously concentrated campus to be "executed by one hand," his own, he may also have been picturing himself strolling across its landscaped grounds, which he meant to plot personally, olive tree by olive tree; there were rumors around town that a chair of architecture at the university would be created especially for him—rumors he did nothing to dispel.) And the university was really but a single element of his gestational plan for all of Jerusalem, and for the building of Palestine as a whole. Mendelsohn wasn't alone, of course, in drawing the essential link between these different realms. Its founders hoped that the university on the hill would, when it was built, represent nothing short of a new Temple, a "House of Life," which would aid "in the quest of modern Judaism for a recovery of its soul."

No one would ever have accused Erich Mendelsohn of excess modesty, but the idea that *he* should be the one to give architectural coherence to this campus, this city, this land wasn't some megalomaniacal fantasy of his own. Among Weimar Germany's most acclaimed architects, Mendelsohn had run one of the largest and busiest practices in that country until his hasty departure just the year before. He'd long been praised, if also scorned, for his boldly expressive and trailblazing designs, almost all of them rendered for Jewish clients. One

of his earliest buildings was still his most famous—the singularly sculptural Einstein Tower, a modernist spaceship of a stucco-clad observatory and astrophysics lab created around 1920 in Potsdam, so that its soon to be Nobel-winning namesake could test the theory of relativity there. More subtle and suggestive of his work to come were the renovated offices of Rudolf Mosse, a major Berlin publishing house. That building's radically rounded, almost vehicular, corner façade caused a sensation when it was unveiled in 1923—on that city's very own Jerusalemstrasse.

"The primary element is function," he wrote breathlessly to Luise that same year, speaking of architecture in general. "But function without a sensual component remains construction."

Although he claimed inspiration from the structural logic of nature and always kept a collection of seashells and petrified wood on his worktable, he had a gut feel for the energy and rhythmic vitality of the booming twentieth-century city. On a 1924 voyage to New York, Chicago, Detroit, and other more rural American spaces, he found himself at once allured and appalled as he snapped vertiginously neck-craning pictures of towering skyscrapers, neon-

flashing billboards, and looming elevated tracks. Improbable as it
sounds, on the SS *Deutschland* sailing to the States, he'd befriended
fellow passenger Fritz Lang, then plotting his own *Metropolis*. As
Mendelsohn wrote in *Amerika*, the book of photographs and apho-
risms that documented his travels and included several images shot
by Lang—who seems to have learned a few architectural things
from his shipmate and applied them to his movie—he saw in the
United States "everything. The worst strata of Europe, abortions of
civilization, but also hopes for a new world."

It wasn't just the company he kept on the deck of the *Deutschland*.
There was something essentially cinematic about Mendelsohn's own
vision of the restless drive and flux that ruled the teeming streets.
Sometimes this took literal form. Soon after his return from the
United States, he designed a notoriously kinetic, bow-shaped movie
theater, the Universum, as part of his plan for a spacious Berlin shopping, residential, and entertainment complex. Complete with a hotel
and cabaret, it was the largest project built in that city during the
entire Weimar period, and it held all the charge and force of his
American photographs, though it converted the dizzying upward
rush he must have felt in the presence of the steep skyscrapers into
the sweep of a tremendous, forward-hurtling horizontal. "Motion is
life!" he'd proclaimed at the cinema's gala opening in 1928: "Real
life is authentic, simple and true. Hence, no posing, no sob stories.
Neither in films . . . nor in architecture . . . No rococo palace for
Buster Keaton, no wedding cake in plaster for Potemkin."

He was best known for his department stores. In his daring designs for the Herpich family's Berlin fur emporium, for instance, and in a series of audacious structures planned for the retail tycoon, cultural patron, bibliophile, and publisher Salman Schocken, curving windows and vivid signage became the most animate of immobile elements. First sketched by Mendelsohn in the middle of a Bach concert, the Schocken store in Stuttgart was, in particular, a masterpiece of stasis and fluidity played off one another in spectacular counterpoint—a steel, glass, and travertine ocean liner always gliding down the same busy street.

While it might not have been dazzling department stores, let alone fancy fur outlets, that dusty Palestine needed just yet, various Zionist leaders had singled out Mendelsohn for the highest praise and suggested that the country should be planned by "great artists" like him. He had, in fact, come here now to design a house in Rehovot for the charismatic chemist and de facto political leader of world Jewry Chaim Weizmann and his fastidious wife, Vera. Excising himself and his business affairs from Germany, Men-  delsohn's former employer Salman Schocken was also newly arrived in Palestine, and had just commissioned a villa and private library in Jerusalem. As chairman of the Hebrew University's executive committee, Schocken made clear as well his determination to have Mendelsohn plan the campus of the most important Jewish institution of higher learning in the land. Yassky too considered Mendelsohn "one of the outstanding living Jewish architects" and patiently defended him against the skepticism and even hostility of some of the sniffier members of the Hadassah building committee, who complained that he didn't understand the local conditions and bristled at his "ultra-modern style of architecture," which they deemed "not suitable for Palestine."

Yassky remained firm, however, vouching for both Mendelsohn's character and his talents. The doctor was certain that he would build in a manner appropriate to the context. Though he admitted that Mendelsohn was known as "not an easy man to work with" (Schocken had warned him), Yassky was intent on overseeing the construction of a unique building on this Jerusalem hilltop, a noble structure of the sort that Mendelsohn would surely plan—unlike various candidates whom he described as "capable architects, but . . . not above the average." He would hate, Yassky said, "to put up on Scopus another box in Tel Aviv style," an argument that seemed to stir something in the group as a whole. "This is not," agreed one formidable female member of the committee, "to be an ordinary hospital but <u>the</u> hospital of the Jewish people."

And it wasn't just the design of the hospital that would be entrusted to Mendelsohn. The very week of his scouting expedition with Yassky on Mount Scopus, he had lunch alone with Palestine's artistically inclined high commissioner, Arthur Wauchope, a friend, who promised to do what he could to put the university planning in the architect's hands as well. (Wauchope couldn't guarantee it, but he was in an excellent position to apply pressure to those making such decisions; the first high commissioner had been appointed by the British king in 1920, and since the official start of the Mandate in 1922, the man who held this post had commanded almost unchecked power as the ruler of Palestine.) A few days later, Mendelsohn found himself in a lively conversation with Wauchope's young male secretary, who enthused that he "must come here" so he "could have and do everything."

All of that said, it seemed the person Erich Mendelsohn most needed to convince that he and his practice belonged here in Jerusalem was—Erich Mendelsohn.

He regularly proclaimed his love of the land of Israel—"I . . . call myself its true child"—but the thought of actually coming to live and build there had remained a fuzzy and even fraught prospect. As early as 1920, he'd put his name on a Jewish Agency list of "engineers willing to go to Palestine." And he'd tried his architectural luck there before—both working on a plan for the country's first electrical power station in Haifa in 1923, and obsessing over designs for a business center and a tidy garden city in that same town. None of these projects took hold. Various explanations were given for this dead end, though it may well have been that his streamlined modern conceptions proved—then, as later—too much of a challenge to somewhat staid local sensibilities. According to Mendelsohn, the British high commissioner of the time declared his scheme for the power station "too European." (Ironically, the architect noted that a Berlin villa he'd constructed during this same period was deemed by a shocked German general "too Oriental.") It may, on the other hand, have been a clash of personalities between the difficult Mendelsohn and his difficult patron that halted that particular collaboration. The power station that was eventually erected was every bit as "European" as Mendelsohn's would have been; based on his initial design, it is generally considered the first "modern" structure in Palestine.

Whether or not any actual buildings resulted from Mendelsohn's initial flirtation with the country, something had shifted within him in the course of that close brush. When he'd made his first trip there that same year, the landscape had grabbed hold of his imagination. Within days of arriving, he'd sketched on a postcard a narrow Jerusalem alleyway that seemed to surge like rushing water, then swell upward toward the minaret and dome at its end—as if he were being pulled by a strong current into the view. Below the quickly rendered ink perspective, he gushed in scrawled German to an art historian friend that the experience of being there was overwhelming—far beyond his expectations—though it would "take time to settle." Once that had happened it would, as he put it, in unapologetic shades of purple, "only fortify what has long been strong. Blood and space; race and three dimensions!"

He'd paid lip service to Zionism since his student days, but the encounter with the physical fact of Palestine now seized him in the most visceral way. He spoke of being moved by two "cycles of emotion." One he called "oriental-atavistic," the other "occidental-present (of today)." They both operated within him, he insisted, the tension between them urging him on. And even at that early date, this sense of being propelled by forces at once Eastern and Western, ancient and present, made him reconsider his place in the world: "No Jew able to understand his emotions," he declared, again in rather torrid terms, "tours Palestine without the tragic touch of his own past and without the humble hope of its rebirth."

Luise accompanied her husband on the 1923 voyage and would admit, decades later, that she, too, had been "entirely unprepared" for the effect the country would have on her. In fact, her strong attraction to the East and its people—both Jews and Arabs—"almost frightened" her. An elegant, pampered European cellist, she believed herself to be of Sephardi descent but said she hadn't been conscious of being Jewish as a girl. She'd grown up spending summers in the Black Forest and surrounded by marble fireplaces, crystal chandeliers, and portraits of her female ancestors in silk dresses with low-cut neck-lines. Now this "sudden awareness of a certain belonging" was "something I could not accept easily, as it seemed to me a racial belonging." The Mendelsohns considered themselves cosmopolitans—citizens of the world—and this tribal pull appears to have at once excited and unsettled them.

But even after they'd returned to Berlin, Mendelsohn couldn't shake his newly urgent sense of his bond—as Jew and builder—with Palestine. Writing to his school friend and fellow architect Richard Kauffmann, already settled in Jerusalem and firmly established as one of the Zionist establishment's favorite planners, he explained, "Although I see my work here"—in Germany—"acknowledged, needed and appreciated by the most important people, it is without the true soil desired by my blood and my nature . . ." Mendelsohn described his wish to "come finally to the Land of Israel," though only if he could be assured commissions and good relations with Kauff-mann and his circle. "Everything else," Mendelsohn put it bluntly, "would then be a logical consequence of my own work." Was this a promise or a threat? "If these conditions are met, I would immedi-ately leave for Palestine and would inform you before my arrival."

Like the power station, the business center, and the garden city, these plans remained on paper, folded and tucked inside drawers. And though Mendelsohn continued to toy with the idea of emigration from Germany—"Reflections kept to myself," he wrote Luise in 1925, "on America—Europe—Palestine"—there was some nagging

thing holding him back, stopping him from taking the plunge toward the East. What was that thing? What nagged?

⊕

As it was, throughout the 1920s, he had the luxury of steady, high-
profile work throughout Europe and of international celebrity. He
had no pressing need to look elsewhere. In fact, beginning in 1928,
he'd even gone so far as to build and furnish a quietly spectacular
waterfront villa in a leafy Berlin suburb as an elaborate gift for
Luise.

When Am Rupenhorn was completed in the summer of 1930, its
state-of-the-art music room, carefully landscaped gardens, retracting
glass walls, self-regulating oil furnace, gymnasium, wine cellar, and
special built-in wireless cupboards had made the couple both the
glamorous toast and grumbled-about envy of Berlin society. This was
a phenomenon the architect seems actively to have exacerbated by
overseeing the publication of a photo-filled, trilingual book that
showed off to the world Am Rupenhorn—complete with Luise's
manicure kit, the miniature fold-top desk where their daughter, Esther,
did her homework, and a designer umbrella stand. In an essay published there, Le Corbusier's Puristic sidekick Amédée Ozenfant
praised and defended the "little 'palace'" in effusive terms, explaining
that "what I am particularly anxious to make clear, and what so

amazes me, is that functionalism and beauty abide here, as it were, in mutual independence." From his experience of being and working in the house, and enjoying not just its immaculate proportions but also its many subtly deployed technological innovations, Ozenfant could state, somewhat dumbstruck, that "it was as if ten mechanical guardian angels were making life easier for me." He didn't cite Le Corbusier's famous formulation of the ideal modern house as "a machine for living in," but he implied it. Am Rupenhorn was, he pronounced, "a house for a Goethe of 1930." Perhaps not surprisingly, some considered the whole display (building and book alike) unseemly, a product of the most decadent and preening sort of self-indulgence.

Whether or not it lived up to all the flamboyant flattery—or scathing criticism—heaped upon it, Am Rupenhorn was certainly a stylish birdcage for the cultural who's who of that time and place. Under specially commissioned murals by Ozenfant, a Max Pechstein portrait of the striking young Luise in a dark tilted hat, and various paintings and copper reliefs by other popular avant-garde artists of the period, including Lyonel Feininger and Ewald Mataré, the Mendelsohns regularly threw lavish dinner parties and musical evenings, attended by writers and ambassadors, publishers and princes; in the afternoons, Luise would serve mocha and petits fours from a tea cart designed by Bauhaus builder Marcel Breuer. Their neighbor along Lake Havel, Albert Einstein, often arrived at their backyard in a sailboat, his violin tucked under one arm so that he could play trios with Luise and the acclaimed Hungarian concert pianist Lili Kraus. (During such spontaneous recitals, Erich would listen closely to the music at first and then, according to Luise, tune out and start sketching.)

But the walls of their opulent home—and of their troubled homeland—were gradually closing in. Having planned Am Rupenhorn down to its last monogrammed table napkin, Mendelsohn had begun to feel uneasy about the extravagance of the house and all it represented. He sensed that alternatives might lie in some simpler existence, to the south, to the east, and in the realm of that "oriental-atavistic" impulse he felt welling up within him. After a revelatory 1931 voyage to Athens, he eagerly took other trips to Italy and the Côte d'Azure, and marveled at the light, the water, the trees, the sky,

and the "little rectangles, of clay or brick, whitewashed" that spilled down slopes and huddled in valleys throughout the region. His ecstatic descriptions of these landscapes sound like verbal watercolors, painted in a kind of sun-struck daze: "Heavens, water, the distant islands and reflected light sink into the blue, into this play of blue upon blue in eternal ease." The Mediterranean lured him with "its fullness, its tranquility," and he mused about how "the Mediter-ranean contemplates and creates, the North rouses itself and works. The Mediterranean lives, the North defends itself."

The contrast between the "eternal creative force" he felt cours-ing through these warm, bright climes and the chill of present-day Germany could not have been starker. Ironically enough, in these very years a famously nasty, racially charged architectural contro-versy had erupted when a high-profile development of boxy, state-of-the-art buildings, curated as a permanent exhibit by Mies van der Rohe in Stuttgart, was attacked by German nationalists for looking like "an Arab village" or, in fact, "a suburb of Jerusalem." The lack of properly pitched German roofs typified for the Weissen-hof's critics the "rootless" nature of its creators—a kind of modernist all-star team, featuring Bauhaus founder Walter Gropius, Le Cor-busier, pioneering Dutch architect J.J.P. Oud, leading German builders Peter Behrens, Bruno and Max Taut, Hans Scharoun, and nine other talented Europeans, including Mies himself. Distin-guished as this crew was, they were damned as "nomads of the me-tropolis," who "are not at all acquainted with the idea of the parental, let alone the ancestral home." Their flat roofs, it was hissed, "no longer keep us under German skies and on German soil, but displace us to the edge of the desert or into an oriental setting." A notorious Nazi postcard added camels and swarthy turbaned "natives" to the actually Swabian view.

While almost none of the Weissenhof architects were Jewish, the taint of "degeneracy" seemed to be catching, or leaking in through those despised flat roofs. Mendelsohn himself didn't submit a design for the Stuttgart project. (Though invited and involved, in the end he chose not to participate.) It's reasonable to think, however, that the generalized anti-Semitic animus the exhibit stirred up was a goad to him—a perverse sort of inspiration—as he contemplated his relationship to the East and the possibilities it presented for building. It's also clear he'd long understood that something was seriously rotten in Deutschland. On his return from an especially euphoric journey to Corsica, he declared to Luise that "three days in Berlin have again revealed the oppressive burden of this country condemned to fall to pieces, of this city with its false pretensions, its forced sense of merriment, and its entirely groundless hopes." All the plans and ventures being undertaken around him were, he warned, "the convulsions of feverish, sick people, who fight against their illness without knowing whether they'll suffer further, more severe attacks." He spoke of an "emptiness that cannot be filled. I feel it in my office, whose existence lacks any foundation, and in our house, whose solid existence constricts and oppresses me." Not that this sense of strangulation made the way forward clear. Even after Mendelsohn had announced to his wife the need to "free myself, which is to say *us*, from this place," he'd continued to muse about various options, zig-zagging in a single breath between the possibilities of Palestine and (remarkably) Lake Como or "who knows where?"

But the situation in Germany gradually became intolerable—and by 1933, the threat had arrived at their front door. Luise rose from bed on a gentle Berlin spring morning to the sight of a swastika-emblazoned flag moving up and down their street and the sound of schoolchildren singing "Germany awake, awake, awake; let Jewry rot, rot, rot." Soon after, one of Erich's closest companions and most trusted architectural assistants arrived late to a Bach-themed party for Mendelsohn. (The architect and his favorite composer shared a birthday, and every year he and Luise celebrated the day with friends and fugues.) Glowing with excitement, the man announced that he'd been delayed because he'd just been to see the führer in person. This friend's fascination with Hitler, Luise would later write, came as a "shattering blow" and hastened their decision to leave the country—Bach's country.

Yet when they did flee, days later, at the end of March that year—on a night train, with just a few suitcases and a treasured stamp collection—they still did not point themselves immediately in the direction of Jerusalem.

Instead they wended their way first to Holland, then almost to the south of France where, together with the Dutch architect Hendricus Theodorus Wijdeveld and Ozenfant, Mendelsohn had laid the foundations for an ambitious "European Mediterranean Academy," which might—had it ever materialized—have emerged as a kind of Bauhaus on the Riviera. Its faculty were to be the founders, along with a group of accomplished international artists including the composer Paul Hindemith, the Grozny-born designer Serge Chermayeff, and the eccentrically brilliant British typographer and stonecutter Eric Gill; its advisory committee counted among its illustrious members Einstein, Frank Lloyd Wright, Paul Valéry, Max Reinhardt, and Igor Stravinsky, and its course of study entailed both intensive hands-on work and more theoretical investigation. As Mendelsohn's section of the academy's brochure promised, the curriculum was designed to make the "young architect into a complete builder" by "unifying tradition and the desire for the expression of our own time," with an eye toward "the formation of the future."

But the future was more easily plotted in a theoretical syllabus than in the practical tangle of real life. With the uncertainty of the political situation throughout the Continent casting shadows, and tensions among the academy's founders mounting, the Mendelsohns moved on abruptly to London.

Though the architectural climate in England was far more conservative than in Germany, and his passionately iconoclastic aesthetic was generally considered distasteful by the purse-lipped British cultural establishment, Erich had been embraced by a group of the more forward-thinking local architects when he'd gone there to raise funds for the academy. They helped arrange for him to live and work in London, and at a sort of coming-out party at the Liverpool Architectural Society, in November 1933, he gave a lecture on his work, and "the famous German architect" was, according to a gushing story in *The Manchester Guardian*, "interrupted warmly and frequently by cheers." On this occasion, one of his hosts, the architect C. H. Reilly, announced to the assembled well-wishers that Mendelsohn would now practice in England. This declaration was met by great applause in public, though privately it gave way to real worry for Mendelsohn, as the decision to settle in Britain meant forgoing any hope of holding on to even a part of his substantial German savings. It also entailed the adjustment—or attempted adjustment—not just to the English language but to the imperial system of measurement, no small thing for a forty-six-year-old architectural maverick used to controlling every situation in which he found himself. (In his Berlin office he'd kept careful track of how many pencils were used; he also designed all his wife's evening gowns and insisted on accompanying her to fittings at her dressmaker's.) Although in British company he tried to blend in and now sometimes went by the Anglicized "Eric" instead of the Germanic "Erich," English tastes and manners were hard for him to fathom, and came gradually to depress him. As he'd write to an American friend, the critic Lewis Mumford, "I do not feel very happy in England. I cannot breathe in a country without spiritual tension. I cannot work where creative fight is taken as an attack against the 'common sense.'" For bureaucratic reasons, he was—as an alien—forced to enter into a partnership with Chermayeff, a British national. The younger, less experienced designer was himself sympathetic, though the collaboration grated badly against Mendelsohn's self-declared penchant for autocracy.

Yet even when faced with this difficulty and discomfort, he *still* hadn't picked up and taken himself, his wife, and his practice to the place that struck so many of his European Jewish contemporaries as the most obvious destination. As he tried to explain to a committed Zionist friend, Kurt Blumenfeld, who had questioned his chaotic and ideologically dubious itinerary, "Why not directly to Palestine? Here you touch a tender spot. All those years I envisioned Palestine built up by my hand, the entirety of its architecture brought into a unified form through my activity, its intellectual structure ordered by my organizational ability and striving toward a goal." But for all his talk of blood and space, race and their somehow cosmic link to his vocation, "Palestine did not call me." It seems he needed to be courted.

✧

By now, however, this rainy winter of 1934, a new strain of vulnerability—or was that possibility?—had crept into his tone. Having returned to Jerusalem under changed circumstances, he seemed willing to give the place a second chance.

It wasn't just that other doors had been summarily slammed in his Jewish face. Suddenly he was being offered these large local commissions by powerful people like Weizmann, Schocken, and maybe Yassky and the major institution he represented, to say nothing of the university of the Jewish people—and these jobs implied *more* jobs, which implied (Mendelsohn hoped) the realization, at long last, of that older dream of himself as Palestine's master builder, its trusted master planner. "The hotel is filling up," he scribbled to Luise, on a sheet of cream-and-blue King David stationery, "and work is bearing down on me. Here, I feel like one of the most important people in the land. But," he admitted, "without any outward signs of that importance." He almost sounded relieved—as though after all the heady, even drunken, success of the previous decade he'd suddenly sobered up.

His vision freshly focused, he seemed eager to get down to business and to reckoning with the simple thrill of the plain white page. "I am completely absorbed. I scarcely breathe, eat little." When he

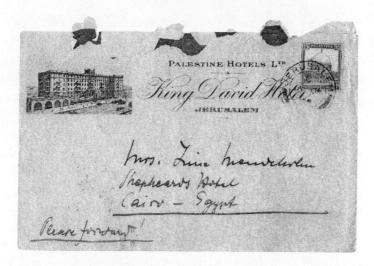

stole time to sleep, he slumbered "under buildings that are heaping up." He declared himself "wholly preoccupied." And the generic notion of high-profile employment wasn't what was driving him. The place itself had him in its grip. While plans for the Mediterranean Academy had fizzled, his renewed contact with the light and the air, the stone and the sand of these southern landscapes had rekindled his romantic conviction that Palestinian blood somehow flowed through his veins. "The Mediterranean," he'd mused just the previous year, "is a first step toward a return to that country, to that final stage where we both belong."

Belonging, of course, was directly linked in his mind to *not* belonging. Only a few months before, in October 1933, Mendelsohn had received a letter from the professional association of German architects, conveying "collegial greetings" along with official notification that, from then on, all its affiliates must be of Aryan descent. His membership was hereby terminated.

Meanwhile, even should-have-been allies and ostensible friends from his former life had turned their backs on him. Around the same time that chilling notice arrived in his Oxford Street mailbox, Walter Gropius, also living as an émigré in London, declared himself "no special friend of the Jew" and whisperingly denounced Mendelsohn to the organizers of a British exhibit on German building as "unpatriotic" and not "a pure German architect." So, too, when in February

1932 New York City's newly opened Museum of Modern Art unveiled its era-defining architectural exhibit on the International
Style, Mendelsohn and his buildings were relegated to an extremely
minor role, little more than bit players in a drama starring Gropius,
Mies, Le Corbusier, Oud, and their rigidly unadorned glass, steel,
and concrete cubes. In the introduction to the soon to be classic
book written to accompany the exhibit, Mendelsohn was described
by the museum's director, Alfred H. Barr Jr., as the man responsible
for "the bizarre Expressionist Einstein Tower" and "a ponderous department store."

One of that book's authors, a self-assured recent Harvard graduate and architectural enthusiast named Philip Johnson, had visited
Germany in 1931 to scout for the New York show and—already a
fervent fan of Mies's cool lines and well on his way to becoming a
Nazi sympathizer—decided that Mendelsohn's work was but "a poor
imitation of the style." (He judged adherence to "the style" according to a checklist of features: volume was privileged over mass,
regularity trumped absolute symmetry, and applied ornament was
eschewed. Abstract aesthetic considerations also took precedence over
all other concerns.) He was grousing specifically about Am Rupenhorn, which was built in a more angular mode than Mendelsohn's
usual rounded structures yet didn't adhere slavishly to the strict rules
associated with "the style," and so maybe seemed to Johnson to suggest the architect's faulty grasp of its principles. But the doctrinaire
young American seemed also to have been irked in a more general
way by Mendelsohn's searching and contextually variable approach.
The unabashedly sensuous presence of his buildings, their playful
sense of motion and stasis held in balance, their fluid interaction with
their surroundings—whether a busy street or a placid lake—were
perhaps just a touch too expressive, too free, maybe a little too . . .
Oriental. (It also probably didn't help that when Johnson turned up in
Berlin that summer and placed a call to Mendelsohn, the busy, testy
one-eyed architect decided he had far better things to do than waste
time chatting with this rather aggressive trend hunter whose questions he considered trite. And so he hung up.)

Was this the beginning of exile or was it the end? The once
champagne-toasted architect of neon-and-car-filled Berlin had to

wonder as he camped out in a Jerusalem hotel room and sketched round the clock. Luise had fled the "crackle of drawing paper" that "controlled the atmosphere," and swept off to Cairo for a few weeks of sightseeing before returning to England to help their daughter, Esther, plan her wedding, leaving him alone with two draftsmen to render perspectives and site plans for Weizmann and Schocken, as he also contemplated their future, their people's future.

Though he worked, he said, too much, he found time to marvel at the pair of rainbows that appeared over the Old City one day—"a mystical image," with "no present. Only past and future. Unforgettable in the gray white rainy air, edged with desert-gold sunlight." He also paused to take in the sweet scent of the winter flowers that had sprung up all around—the fragrant crocus and starlike Christ's tears. These colors, these plants, these smells moved him, and (when he managed to put down his 6B pencil and look up) he continued to circle the prospect of staying put, writing to Luise: "What obliges us to live in a northern country? . . . Isn't our place here—isn't Palestine for eighteen million . . . the only island?"

But he wasn't really asking her. Neither was the fate of all the world's Jews his primary concern. He answered himself in the same letter, mostly with himself in mind: "I am resolved to remain here. Every day I come to regard the people in the fields . . . even the European Jews who inhabit the hotel, a little more as my brothers." It seemed to take real effort for him to feel that kinship— and in fact, when he was franker with himself and with his wife, and when he admitted both his passion for the stark Jerusalem hills and his revulsion at the crude construction he saw being thrown up in slapdash fashion across them, he sounded less tentative and sentimental and more like himself: stubborn, irascible, blisteringly honest.

A few days after his initial trip to the site of the possible hospital and expanded university, Mendelsohn returned for another look, with camera, pencil, and what he called the "eye—food of the soul." Eager to frame his master plan against the backdrop of the Old City, the architect was prepared to be swept by the view, to let his excitement pour forth in a first, bold sketch.

But instead of lifting him up and inspiring him, this visit prompted from Mendelsohn nothing short of an epistolary howl:

"I have visited all the buildings on Mount Scopus. A God-given piece of country between the Dead Sea and the Mediterranean has been violated by devils' hands. A wretched, botched fruit of incompetence and *self-complacency*.

"I feel like Jeremiah—deeply depressed and wounded in my soul. And this continues and makes me obstinate, hard and insecure."

He had, in other words, decided to stay. He would need to find a more suitable office.

VISIONS, VERNACULARS

HE HAD ALWAYS EXPERIENCED WHAT HE CALLED "VISIONS." THE word appeared throughout his earliest letters to Luise, and in an unpublished memoir written much later in life she described the jolt of first meeting him when she was just sixteen and he was a twenty-three-year-old architect in training—himself something of a vision.

She felt "uneasy but captivated" at "suddenly being exposed to a very strong personality," brimming with emphatic ideas about Bach's architectonic sense of order, *The Birth of Tragedy*, and the way women's ball gowns flow. He wore strange clothes—a specially made suit that he had himself designed, with "trousers . . . tight and cut in the way sailors wear them." Looking back across the century she'd remember them as "what are now called bell-bottom[s]." He had long hair, combed back, those ever-present spectacles, a large nose, "energetic chin," and what she considered a beautiful mouth: "Everything about him was unusual. He seemed to me to be someone from an entirely unknown world."

If he was a kind of Prussian Martian, these visions that gripped him were like radio transmissions from that far-off planet. They seized him at odd moments and seemed to take control, to possess him. Luise would later recount how, soon after the outbreak of World War I, he'd called her to come see him, "as something of fundamental importance had happened to him during the last days. The first sketches of an architecture in steel and concrete had overcome him. In the middle of war cries, terrible events in Belgium, invasion of the Russians in his homeland, the flight of his family to Berlin, he was sitting there, bent over his drafting table, obsessed by the impact of visions which would not leave him for a moment."

During the war, he was posted to the Russian Front, where he sketched furiously, living, as he put it, "among incessant visions." He slept little, drew feverishly, and arranged with his commanding officer to take nighttime guard duty in order to devote himself to rendering these imaginary buildings—towering silos, mammoth factories, monumental water towers. These weren't intended for actual construction, but he needed somehow to fix them on the page in all their elastic, massive grandeur. Tracing paper was in short supply, so—huddled in the cold and dark dugout, men dying nearby—he drew tiny versions of these enormous edifices (one inch equaled a thousand feet) and sent the phantasmagorical miniatures to his new bride, writing her that "the visions are once more behind every ring of light and every corpuscle in my closed eye. Masses standing there in their ripeness flash past in a moment and slip away." In the trenches, as he'd later put it, "my architectural dreams are the only reality."

Such single-minded concentration would serve him well in Jerusalem. No matter the tumult taking place all around him—strikes, curfews, explosions, people massing in the streets—he could be found alone in a pool of lamplight, his face almost touching the paper on which he was working. A good deal had changed, however, since he reckoned with those architectural apparitions in the trenches. Now renowned as a planner of actual (not imaginary) buildings, he had a lengthy CV, a business partner, many assistants, elegant sans-serif letterhead, and a style for which he was widely known and that was often imitated.

He'd also had ample chance to consider the danger of such unchecked visions, which often gave way to delusion. Solid as all those buildings and his reputation so recently seemed, he'd become acutely aware of the fragility of these constructions, the shakiness of the ground on which they stood. Who could blame him if—just as he once imagined beams and walls, windows and bricks being raised high in Stuttgart and Berlin, Chemnitz and Cologne—he kept picturing them tumbling down, reduced in an instant to a mere heap of German dust?

❖

However black his musings were, he was by nature compelled to create. To be an architect is, almost by definition, to imagine what still *could be.* And in his case, that meant not just envisioning a bright new future but reckoning with the lessons of the past, in all their darkness and complication. "Although my pessimism has always unsettled you . . . ," he wrote to Luise, "I feel as if, at important moments, I carry an infallible seismograph inside me, which is responsible for my absolutism, for the optimism of my political and artistic convictions."

Old-new Jerusalem seemed especially ripe for his canny syntheses of what had been and what might be, and within days of visiting Mount Scopus with Yassky, he'd poured onto paper a series of remarkably embodied preliminary sketches for several major projects to be built throughout the city—an important university building, the villa and library for Schocken—while the Hadassah complex, a bank on the Jaffa Road, and the master plan for the whole Mount Scopus ridge were already taking dramatic shape in his mind. So were plans for the fresh start he'd resolved to make with Luise in Palestine. "If possible," he wrote her from an airplane high above the clouds, "it will be England and the East for us at the same time." To this letter, written in German, he appended an English aside: *"What a life!"*

In April of that next year, 1935, he returned to Jerusalem to establish an office and found himself at once fueled and frayed by the impatient rhythms of the place: "In Berlin it took me twenty years, in London two years: here—or at least that is what my clients demand—it must not take more than two months." No sooner had he checked back into the King David Hotel than "the rush begins."

The local tendency toward a kind of barely controlled chaos wasn't at all what he was used to, but he claimed to revel in the intuitive challenges the place posed. "The Orient," he declared to a friend, "resists the order of civilization, being itself bound to the order of nature." Yet this was why "I am so strongly attached to it, trying to achieve a union between Prussianism and the life-cycle of the Muezzin. Between anti-nature and harmony with nature."

Idealized as it may have been (the term "orientalism" wasn't yet considered pejorative), his desire for East-West fusion found expression most tangibly in the form of the Jerusalem building with which he fell in love the moment he saw it during his first week back. Located on the fringes of the new neighborhood called Rehavia, a five-minute walk from downtown, this sparely furnished, wood-cupola-capped windmill would serve as his office and his home with Luise for as long as they lived in the city. Initially they negotiated what he called "a life between poles," making the three-day-long trip by plane to London every few months; later, Jerusalem would be their only home.

When he wrote her to tell her he'd rented the bladeless mill, he praised its proportions but didn't mention the fact— which Luise herself would note with a shiver in her memoir— that it bore an uncanny resemblance to his first building, the Einstein Tower. It was as if, more than fifteen years in advance and a world away, he'd somehow conjured it. Meanwhile the mill was in every respect the opposite of another of his earlier architectural visions, that other dream house, Am Rupenhorn.

Gone were the designer tea trays, the retracting glass walls, the mechanical guardian angels. Gone was the Purism. The mill was constructed simply, in the local style, with thick walls of rough-hewn Jerusalem stone. An enormous fig tree shaded the rambling grounds and dropped seedy-sweet fruit everywhere. A basic outdoor staircase led to an attached wing of low domes and a roof terrace, whose uneven, undulating outline seemed to belong more to a Palestinian peasant house than to the contemporary, decidedly bourgeois "European" neighborhood on whose outskirts the building sat. Rehavia occupied an area once known by the Arabic name of Janziria, and comprised a large tract purchased in 1922 by the settlement arm of the Zionist movement from the cash-strapped Greek Orthodox Church. Designed as a garden suburb by Mendelsohn's Munich classmate Richard Kauffmann well before Mendelsohn arrived in town, Rehavia had already emerged along its orderly grid, but its houses were still taking stylish shape one by one. Donkeys hauling stones and tools traipsed by every day, in fact, kicking up billows of dust. Though this expanse had until recently been mostly rocky fields and olive groves, some fifty years before Kauffmann began drafting his street and park plans, the Greek Church had built the windmill, and it stood on the edge of the modern Jewish quarter as a silent reminder of other, older forms.

But Eastern as its foundations were, the building was now also swept by strong Western winds. Erich hired another Erich, Kempinski, a highly experienced German-born civil engineer, to run the office. And Kempinski in turn hired assistants—another engineer (Naftali) and four architects (Wolfgang, Gunther, Hans, and Jarost)—who spread out their neatly rendered floor plans and worked downstairs in a large octagonal space surrounded by several small rooms, "monks' cells," one of which became Mendelsohn's private architectural retreat. A Dr. Wolfgang Ehrlich was employed as the firm's secretary and occupied another of the cells. There he filed blueprints and correspondence and kept the accounts; a young woman named Lilly typed letters in several languages on Mendelsohn's new stationery, which listed English, Arabic, and Hebrew addresses in both Soho's Pantheon and Rehavia's windmill. The sounds of rustling papers and German murmuring filled the air.

Upstairs, Luise decorated their living quarters in a deliberately, almost defiantly, rustic manner, covering the floors with straw mats and the sofa with white canvas, scattering baskets of fruit and vases filled with flowers across the deep windowsills. A huge bed and voluminous mosquito net took up almost all the space in the upper room. The only concessions to their former brand of luxury were the curtains of Damascus silk and the continued employment of the housekeeper, Melli (also German), who, as Luise put it, "came with the mill." Melli's face was sweet but she was round as a dumpling, and ever-opinionated Erich couldn't "bear ugly, old or fat women," so Luise promised "to dress her in such a way that she would look like part of the windmill." As if Melli were an oversized doll left by the previous tenants, Luise outfitted her with a little white cap so she appeared "something out of a fairy tale, like the good mother in Cinderella." The former Berlin socialite seemed to enjoy playing a game of Palestinian village house.

The mill had no refrigerator, no running water. Water was scarce throughout town, and most of what the Mendelsohns had of it, they chose to use on the oleander and cypress they placed in barrels ranged across the terrace. They also filled the garden to spilling with jasmine, cactus, and a deceptively plain-looking Queen of the Night, which waited until dark to drench the whole compound with its fragrance. Wildflowers proliferated.

The windmill was—as Luise would pronounce it decades later—"perfect." By which she seemed to mean both that they felt more buoyant there than ever before and that she enjoyed the slightly scandalized attitude of some of their Berlin-Jerusalem acquaintances, who "were not able to understand" how she "who in their eyes was so spoiled, would prefer to live in a primitive windmill than in one of the newly built apartment houses."

Erich was less concerned with social niceties. He seemed grateful simply to have found such a refuge, such freedom, such possibility—to be able to spend his days working inside such a structure. Eager to absorb its dimensions, he wanted to learn the local vernacular, so to speak, by actually living inside it. Both by choice and by necessity, here in Jerusalem he would begin a new, more humble architectural chapter of the literal bildungsroman that was his life, and in a way the mill would be his teacher.

"I am," he wrote that year, "building the country and rebuilding myself. Here I am a peasant and an artist—instinct and intellect—animal and human being."

In fact, all kinds of building and rebuilding were taking place, closer to home. One day, resting on their gigantic bed and staring up at the ceiling, Luise noticed a trapdoor, which she discovered led to a tiny, hidden room at the very top of the house. A "dark and dirty dome" guarded by a glint-eyed owl and filled with the cracking wheel and rusting chains of the mill's old grinding apparatus—now "dangerously deteriorated and capable of breaking loose at any moment"—it seemed almost to hold the building's unconscious, the suppressed memory of the floury function it once performed. It scared her.

Erich, meanwhile, had a knack for turning such darkness to light. He meant to render the long-forgotten hutch functional again and soon converted it into a private aerie, building a staircase toward it and cutting a window to let in the breeze. The space had just enough room for his drawing board, a chair, and a gramophone. He listened to Bach while he worked late into the night, and the music—Luise would one day write—made the whole mill sing.

❖

As Mendelsohn looked hard and learned from the mill—studying its scale, the thickness of its walls, the nature of its stone construction— he wanted his employees to do the same: to perceive where they were with a vengeance.

Inviting Julius Posener, a younger architect who once worked in his Berlin office, to take up a job with him in Jerusalem, Mendelsohn forbade him from traveling by boat straight from Marseille or Trieste to Haifa. Posener didn't "know the Orient," so Mendelsohn ordered him to go slowly and follow the land route, starting at the Bosphorus. He wanted him to soak up the topography, take in the foliage, contemplate the buildings of Constantinople, of Asia Minor, of Syria. "Otherwise," according to Posener, later in life, "I'd be of no use to him."

Disobeying the master, Posener soon reported for duty at the windmill fresh off the Marseille boat, and Mendelsohn greeted him by asking what he had seen on his journey.

The young man had to admit, sheepishly, that he'd seen nothing at all.

Finding this an unsatisfactory answer, Mendelsohn ordered him to start work with a two-week vacation and commanded him to go out and observe all he could of the country—preferably on foot.

These demands were a matter of principle. Mendelsohn believed fiercely in the need to absorb the local landscape through both the eye and the soles of one's solid European shoes. He insisted architecture shouldn't change abruptly at passport control, though each local setting had its own strict demands: Jerusalem's severity wasn't the same as "the lighthearted character of the plains" around Rehovot, near the coast. But each of these settings shared essential characteristics with others, well beyond the country's borders. "No one," he'd write while on a brief 1937 trip to Capri, "ought to build in Palestine who has not first studied the rural buildings of the Mediterranean." And for Mendelsohn, that Mediterranean was not just the site of pretty whitewashed Greek villages or of imposing Roman ruins, but an *Arab* place, a *living* place as well. "Will Palestine develop an architecture of its own?" he'd ask elsewhere, at around the same time. "Certainly, and as an integral part of its very nationhood. Will it be Western? Of course not. Palestine is in the Orient, of the Orient."

Mild as that sounds, it was a view considered suspect—even somehow treasonous—by many of his colleagues, especially those who'd banded together in Tel Aviv to plot what one of the most prominent of them gleefully called "architectural revolt." Modeling themselves on the Berlin "Ring" of modernist architects (to which Mendelsohn himself had belonged), and given to the not so new *Neue Sachlichkeit*, or New Objectivity, recently celebrated by forward-thinking architects throughout Europe, they referred to themselves (in Hebrew) as "the Circle," but they added a combative twist, in honor of the Palestinian target on which they'd set their sights. They saw themselves as soldiers of an architectural sort, conquering the land and wielding as their weapons wet cement and silicate blocks, brise-soleils and *pilotis*. They weren't violent people, but when he later described their activities, one of the Circle's leaders, Polish kib-butznik and Bauhaus graduate Aryeh Sharon—who would go on to become *the* architect of the fledgling state of Israel, author of the country's first master plan and head of a "brigade of planners" under the command of David Ben-Gurion—casually adopted the rhetoric of battle. One architect was remembered as "a courageous fighter for pure building cubes"; they were credited with "infiltrating into the well-established architects' and engineers' association." They presented "a common front" and "dared to attack sharply and openly the existing conventional attitudes," and so on. Eager to banish all trace of the old, the sentimental, the "primitive," and—worst of all—the "Oriental," they meant, it seems, to vanquish both their own humbling diasporic history and the more recent (Arab) history of this country. Posener himself would eventually join this group and—taking up a slightly gentler tack—praise this new breed of European-born Jewish architects for "freeing their dwellings from the memories of the past."

Warlike or willed as their forgetting was, they were, to be fair, also serious people and some of them quite gifted. Trained like Sha-ron at the Bauhaus, or schooled in the style of Le Corbusier or by Mendelsohn himself (several of these architects besides Posener got their start in his Berlin office), they were devoutly committed to their work, to socialism, and to the Land of Israel. As firmly as Mendelsohn believed, they believed. They believed in cooperative housing estates and kibbutz dining halls; they believed in trade unions and in the Workers' Health Fund. They believed in chicken coops, the melon crop, Dead Sea potash, and the General Federation of Jewish Labor. They believed in their city, Tel Aviv, and many of them designed buildings there of striking intelligence and modest grace. Their Hebrew was fluent, or getting there. Many of them viewed Mendelsohn as a foreigner and as a snob—and he did little to persuade them otherwise. Though proud to be a Jew, he called himself an *English* architect. He considered himself an artist, not a soldier, and certainly no Socialist. He built villas for rich and powerful men, not housing for the workers. He never (*ever*) sat in cafés; he considered the only worthwhile circle the kind he traced with his pencil and compass. He'd chosen to live and build in the antiquity-obsessed city of Jerusalem, to their minds a moldering and unnervingly Eastern place. There he had not only turned his back on concrete (their material of choice), he'd embraced the use of local limestone, whose various types and dressing styles—*tubzeh, taltish, musamsam*—didn't even have names in Hebrew. In the raw parlance of the native-born quarry workers, the hardest grade is actually called *mizzi yahudi*, for the legendary toughness of the *yahudi*, the Jew.

He had a schoolboy's knowledge of the language of his fathers, those tough Jews, but didn't bother to try to speak it in the street. Instead he carried on in German and in his oddball new English. He said he saw political hope for the Jews of Palestine only in "close collaboration with the Arabs." His wife was often abroad, in London or on one of her regular vacations in Zurich, at the Salzburg festival, in Milan, in St. Moritz. And not only did he himself jet in and out of the country every few months—sometimes bearing for Luise a bouquet of fresh-picked wildflowers, which he entrusted to the stewardess for proper inflight storage—he enjoyed frequent private dinners with Wauchope at Government House. On these occasions, duly noted in the "Social and Personal" column of the English-language *Palestine Post*, the high commissioner served champagne; he and Erich admired the view of the Old City walls and listened to Bach records together.

When, soon after his arrival, the Circle asked Mendelsohn to send them "a few of his impressions" of Palestine for publication in their Tel Aviv journal, he was curt. "The principal hope of the Jewish people is the building of its national home in Palestine," he started predictably, then continued in a sharper key: "A great part of this building is of an economical character. The world, however, will not judge us by the amount of citrus fruit exported, but by the spiritual value of our spiritual contributions."

But perhaps the truth about the world's judgment rested somewhere between *their* well-stacked orange crates and *his* lofty metaphysical aspirations, a compromise Mendelsohn—for all his vaunted vision—could not see. He wasn't, though, wrong to worry about the aggressively amnesiac thrust of much of the building taking place around him. "We have," he mused from his windmill perch, "a lot of rethinking yet to do in Palestine."

HOMING

HE COULD, IT'S TRUE, SOUND OVERLY ROMANTIC ABOUT THE allure of "towns and villages in oneness with the flowers of their fields, the hues of their skies." Had he merely replaced the fantasy of the dazzling, driving Weimar street with the fantasy of a rosy return to some Middle Eastern Eden?

But the exacting Mendelsohn wasn't lolling dreamily in those poppy-filled Palestinian fields and gawking at cloud formations. Still every bit the Germanic taskmaster—a man of unflagging ambition and scalding opinions—he had long (and only half-jokingly) called himself the "Oriental from East Prussia," and now the old nickname made special sense. Hans Schiller, one of those younger architects newly hired by Kempinski for the Jerusalem office, would recount later that Mendelsohn pushed his assistants "mercilessly in the pursuit of perfection," though he pushed himself harder. "Every detail had to bear the imprint of his hand: 'There is but one designer in this office and that is Erich Mendelsohn.'" Yet for all his Teutonic tyranny, he was, according to Schiller, inspiring in his doggedness and even his difficulty, "a man of exuberant vitality, dynamic impatience, [who] drove toward ever higher goals: 'I never tire until the job is done.' There was always a job to be done. He worked relentlessly." Posener would describe him as "authoritarian" and remember the antipathy his staff felt toward him, along with the gratitude and admiration. "He was one of the most lovable people I ever met—and at the same time one of the most unpleasant."

When his assistants arrived at the windmill in the morning, Mendelsohn was already sequestered in one of the small cells off the main room, but they found his sketches for the day's projects waiting on their drawing boards. They were expected to convert these visions into working plans. At midmorning he'd emerge from his lair— wearing a cardigan and smoking a clay pipe filled with lemon leaves— and engage them in detailed conversation, overseeing each stage of the transformation of these fluid pencil emanations into sections, elevations, designs for air ducts and piping circuits. He did so with what Posener described as "almost painful meticulousness."

He meant to design not just the finest buildings that modern Jerusalem had ever known but also the gardens that surrounded them and the furniture within—something that would require constant struggle with his merely mortal clients. He dubbed interior decorators "interior desecrators" and would soon lock horns with Vera Weizmann, who had no patience with the sleek tables and stiff-armed chairs he'd designed for her house in Rehovot. She decided to forgo these stylish pieces in favor of cozy, if not downright frumpy, Edwardian stuff more to her liking. As she would recount their showdown: " 'But you will ruin everything,' he protested. 'Probably,' I answered, 'but I have to live in the house, not you!' "

Generally, however, he knew it was better to try to satisfy his clients. Frau Schocken didn't care a whit about the rural buildings of the Mediterranean. She wanted her Jerusalem villa to be arrayed according to the gracious proportions of Am Rupenhorn, which was, Erich confided to Luise, "more unforgettable to her than to me . . . ," though this time he obliged his stern patron's wife and her wishes. Lake Havel might not flow through Jerusalem, but Mendelsohn searched for a way to adapt that waterside Berlin building's classical shapes to the banks of a dry, curving street in Rehavia. The Schockens and Mendelsohns would be neighbors there, and he wanted them to be happy.

For months before both men arrived in town, letters had passed between a rented cottage in Stoke Poges, England, and a five-star spa-hotel in Marienbad, between Mendelsohn's London office and Schocken's on Berlin's Jerusalemstrasse. In clipped but warm German terms, they'd discussed the architect's pending "decision" about Palestine and the possibility that he'd build a house in Jerusalem for his longtime employer.

Besides offering the prospect of a lucrative contract with a client whose visual tastes dovetailed so neatly with his own, it seemed the idea of planning Schocken's dwelling appealed strongly to Mendelsohn since it might bring him a step closer to calling the country home. Having worked together for years in Germany and in a very real way helped to make each other's fortunes, their fates appeared somehow cosmically linked. ("It's strange," Mendelsohn had mused in May 1934, "that all our old friends who are living in England . . . tell me that, in relation to Palestine, my time has not yet come. I tend not to believe them, especially since you yourself have chosen to live there.") Given their intertwined history and what he hoped would be their intertwined future, this was a job he was eager to have, and Schocken was eager for him to have it. Schocken actually considered himself something of a builder—albeit one without a drafting board. "I am," he'd once declared, "a force that creates order, and my art . . . is architecture, even though I am not yet building anything." Mendelsohn would do that for him, and Schocken's vision of his own place in Jerusalem hinged critically on his ability to conceive elaborate projects in the style to which he'd become accustomed. Buying up various parcels of land from individuals and the Greek Orthodox Church, the bibliophile-businessman had gradually cobbled together a sizable plot, planted with olive trees in the adjacent areas known as Nikephoria and Karm ar-Ruhban, or the Monks' Vineyard—on the vague border between the mostly Christian Arab neighborhood of Talbiyeh and mostly Jewish Rehavia—and as soon as Mendelsohn reached Palestine in December and had a chance to survey the site, the plans began to take shape.

They quickly became "free and light" and what he deemed "very beautiful." The Schockens themselves were, he reported to Luise, quite pleased with his sketches—even "delighted" with what he had dreamed up. And this despite considerable challenges. Besides their demands that he scale back the size of the proposed building, he'd need to reckon with the difficult pitch of the plot, on a low rise of landfill that was the highest point in the immediate vicinity. The house was also the first structure he'd build of Jerusalem stone, or really two layers of Jerusalem stone poured full of concrete and reinforced with iron girders, the whole some fifteen inches thick.

There was something at once inspired and insane about Mendelsohn's attitude toward this house, which he seemed to view as both a natural extension of the rocky local terrain and as a model haut-bourgeois home, appointed with all the latest European creature comforts. While he had devised the building with an almost didactic eye toward climatic conditions, with rooftop pergolas that provided needed shade, and the careful positioning of windows to block the bright sun, he had no reservations whatsoever about planning a sumptuous mini-estate that boldly defied its *social* setting and featured amenities unheard of in poor, parched, recently Ottoman Jerusalem, including a swimming pool, central heating, a garage, and outbuildings to house the caretaker and the chauffeur.

Having left glamorous Am Rupenhorn and the entirety of their savings behind for the rustic Jerusalem windmill and all the simplicity and even frugality it entailed, the Mendelsohns themselves had entered a period of relative austerity. They tried their best to warm the mill with small, portable kerosene stoves and to keep their food cool in a zinc-lined box filled with ice sold by a man on a donkey. Luise shopped in the Old City markets for what she'd later describe as "native things rather than what they called 'Hollywood exquisiteness,'" and she boasted of avoiding, for instance, the fashionable beauty parlor favored by the gossiping Jewish women of her background and class. Instead she preferred a perfume-and-paper-flower-filled Arab-run establishment, where she couldn't understand a word of the chitchat and they had no running water, but she enjoyed the way a small boy in a caftan climbed up on a stool and washed her long dark hair with a watering can.

But Erich didn't hesitate to provide his powerful employer and his family with the very best foreign things (Schocken's) money could buy; in fact, the architect seemed to get a vicarious thrill from ordering up the most lavish indulgences on behalf of his patron—so, perhaps, hanging on to this fraying remnant of his own former life.

He was also keen to integrate into his plans the various European luxuries—the grand piano, good crystal, and world-class art collection—that Schocken planned to import. For now, a Swiss bank vault held the two Cézannes and three Renoirs, the Van Gogh and Manet, the Chagall and the two Pissarros. As soon as walls existed on which to hang them, they'd be packed up with the greatest care and shipped to Rehavia. Together with a whole carefully kept inventory of Kollwitzes, Kokoschkas, and Daumiers, these works and all they represented were never far from Mendelsohn's mind, and in fact it appeared he meant for the house to serve at once as a kind of elegant display case and itself an objet d'art. So it was that he mapped every doorframe and pipe, each vine and rosebush that would make up the organically integrated villa and garden compound, issuing in the process stringent instructions for everyone from the glaziers to the wall tilers to the plasterers to the insulation workers.

His demands were cast—and remain in the archive—in the form of a dry legal document (an agreement with the contractor), but they also have about them the ring of a credo: "*The materials, articles, and workmanship shall be of the best quality and execution. The word 'best' as applied to materials, articles and workmanship shall mean that in the opinion of the Architect there is no superior material or article on the market and no better class of workmanship.*" In the dozens and dozens of typed pages that follow, each of these materials and articles is described in exhaustive detail: "*Reinforcement (rods and bars) will be wrought of iron having a safe tensile stress of 1200 kilograms per square inch . . . The ends of all tension bars shall be bent into a U form or otherwise anchored in a manner approved in writing by the Architect. If any bend shows signs of brittleness or cracking, the rod or bar shall be removed immediately from the site . . .*"

Little was left to chance—not even irregularity. And in this sense he didn't stop at issuing commands to the workers: "The trees to be chosen for [replanting in] the front yard of the house . . . should be the most crooked and planted slanting toward the west," he explained in a letter to Schocken himself. "It will thus give a fine contrast to the straight and regular lines of the building." Later, once the house was built, he'd take this tack to inadvertently comical extremes, and provide Herr and Frau Schocken with precise instructions for the way they should push their dining room chairs back under the table at the completion of each meal.

Erich Mendelsohn had always been obsessed with maintaining the strictest control, and in this respect, he and the domineering Salman Schocken were cut from the same tightly woven cloth. In many ways, this made them something of an architectural cliché, no different from other demanding designers of houses and their demanding clients the world over. But in the messy Middle Eastern context in which they now found themselves, the exactitude of the architect's technical specifications took on a new sort of urgency. Not only did his orders seem a frantic defense against the lax local attitude to building, they also revealed a barely masked terror at the gaping uncertainty before him.

Through no plan, no blueprint of his own, after all, his life had been completely and utterly turned upside down these last few years, and such commands seem Mendelsohn's slightly desperate attempt to exert power over something, anything—whether the proper placement of the cabinets in the Schockens' pantry or the alignment of tiles on the staircase, which *"from the Ground floor to the 1st Floor [are] to be of cream Jerusalem marble, eggshell polish. Risers to be 2 cms. and the treads 3 cms. thick. Treads to project 2½ cms. over risers rounded on edge . . ."*

For reasons less sentimental than practical, Schocken had decided to transport to Jerusalem all he could of the world they'd left behind. This was in part a function of taste and habit, though in a colder and more calculating sense, it served his financial interests to do so.

Because of the severe monetary restrictions placed by the German government on Jewish émigrés, he could protect his fortune only by bringing it out of the country in the form of building materials, which he'd then import to the Rehavia plot. This maneuver was made possible by a controversial agreement between the Nazi government and the Jewish Agency, the official representative of the Jews of Palestine. Considered mutually beneficial to these sworn enemies by its supporters—including much of the Labor Zionist leadership and the movement's rank and file—the arrangement was known as the Ha'avarah, or Transfer. Which is to say that it was designed to transfer Jews from Germany to Palestine as it fed the German economy and channeled capital in the form of export goods to the Jewish state in the making.

For Salman Schocken, this was a business arrangement. For Erich Mendelsohn, it was a great irony—or, one could say, a compromise that landed squarely in the darkest part of the one-eyed visionary's blind spot. Because for all his talk of the need to reckon with native materials and forms and to evolve a fusion of "Prussianism and the life-cycle of the Muezzin," he seemed not to mind at all that— Jerusalem stone and local labor aside—the house and library were both distinctly MADE IN GERMANY. Everything from door handles to sink units, wall tiles to insulation, asbestos, cement, kitchen appliances, and white shag carpet—even tulip bulbs—had been purchased in the country from which they'd just fled, then packed up by Schocken's Zwickau construction office and placed on a Haifa-bound boat.

While Mendelsohn had little choice in the matter, he also didn't protest. The Palestinian equivalent of these high-quality European goods was far inferior (if it existed at all), and the regular arrival of the German shipments meant that, though he'd set out to build now in a strange land, he was for the most part working with familiar stuff. He never commented in writing on this arrangement, so we can't know how he felt about it. Maybe it pleased him, maybe it irked. In either case, it seems bureaucratic necessity had made possible the wishful fusion of here and there, Muezzin and Prussian, that he'd really meant all along. The house would be the example, in microcosm, of the fanciful alloy he envisioned for the city and country as a whole, a kind of architectural *West-East Diwan*, poised in some imagined space between the Middle East and Mitteleuropa.

Whatever reservations he may have harbored in private, he threw himself headlong into the project of creating a palazzo befitting Schocken's position as a kind of twentieth-century Jerusalem Medici—patron of the greatest Jewish cultural figures of the age, including Hebrew novelist and Nobel Prize winner in the making S. Y. Agnon, Kabbalah scholar Gershom (né Gerhard) Scholem, Vienna-born philosopher Martin Buber . . . and Mendelsohn himself, who didn't mind at all being thought of as a kind of latter-day Semitic Brunelleschi. If his feelings toward Palestine were rooted in ambivalence, this building would at least embody with the greatest possible gusto the various contradictions the architect felt welling up inside him.

In order to build and furnish this masterpiece, Mendelsohn spared no expense, hiring the eminent London landscape architect Geoffrey Jellicoe's firm to advise on the deployment of shrubs and roses across the grounds. The job was given to one of Jellicoe's assistants, the soon to be acclaimed English gardener Russell Page, who took Mendelsohn's initial sketch and mapped the pittosporum, acacia, salvia, and dahlia, the oleander and rosemary, the flaming sword iris, the salmon zinnia, and yellow lupins with a precision that was at once almost surgical and somehow tender. ("N.B.," reads a note on the side of one especially intricate handwritten plan. "Plant white narcissi in drifts through plumbago, and in clumps of about 25 along paths, and in odd corners.")

Indoors and outdoors were charted in careful relation. At one point Mendelsohn even took a trip to Damascus to see an exquisite, huge, nearly five-hundred-year-old carpet that he heard had been put up for sale. This antique was in excellent condition and was, he decided, perfectly suited to the Schockens' living room: "It brings the same vividness into the interior . . . that the garden will bring to the austere exterior, once it is finished," he assured Schocken, promising that it would carry into the entire space "the stern monumentality" and "complex colors" of the Van Gogh painting *Cypresses*, slated to hang on one wall. He arranged for the Syrian dealer to journey with the rug all the way to Jerusalem so that Schocken could see its weave and shades for himself, and in situ.

A long bargaining session unfolded after the rug did, as Schocken examined the threads with a magnifying glass and studied the back and bargained some more—then, unimpressed, sent the Damascene and his carpet packing, leaving the marble floors of the room chilly and bare.

Even as they continued to wrangle over the possible purchase of the carpet—with Mendelsohn assuring Schocken that its presence would "fill the house with the irresistible command of great art," and his employer countering that such a fine old piece was "not suitable for a private home" (a strange claim coming from someone who drank his coffee and read his newspaper each morning in the sumptuous midst of a museum-worthy art collection)—both architect and client seemed oddly oblivious to the context in which they now found themselves living and working. Neither was ready to acknowledge just how perverse such a purchase would have appeared in this town at this moment. Though Jerusalem was rapidly changing and expanding, and it had its share of native-born aristocrats who also lived in gracious and elegantly appointed homes, the city was for the most part still a humble place, a traditional place. Most of its residents lived simply and without ostentation, in modest apartments, small houses, or (in the case of the needy, who filled crowded slums) hovels of various tin, stucco, or crumbling stone sorts. Refugees were arriving from Europe with not much more than the clothes on their backs, while much of the veteran local population—Arab and Jewish, Greek and Armenian alike—had precious little to begin with.

But Schocken was a rich and rigid man, unapologetically fixed in his ways and unwilling to bend to suit new circumstances. The longer he lived in Palestine, in fact, the more German he seemed—as though he believed he could, by sheer force of will, turn this rough corner of Jerusalem into one of the poshest suburbs of Weimar Berlin. He insisted that his staff file daily typed reports of their activities, and that alphabetized guest lists for the regular salons and teas he and his wife hosted be drawn up according to category—with an actual A-list of cultural and political figures and other distinguished acquaintances, followed by D for Deutsch (the "German Circle"), L for Literature, R for Rabbis, U for University, and so on. He ran his office like an army regiment. In later years, Hannah Arendt would come to call him the "Jewish Bismarck."

Meanwhile, Mendelsohn, for all his managerial rigidity, prided himself on his creative openness, his ability to adapt his art to varied settings, and even to take pleasure in doing so. (This seems a stretch, but decades after his death Luise would insist that her husband's personality had been bacchanalian. To dance with him at a party, for instance, meant "to follow his rhythms and swirls . . . [and] forget oneself entirely. This love for dancing . . . was like an outlet of a dionysic urge. He would sweep with one beautiful girl after another in his arms through all the dancers—forgetting everything around him. A raving madness!") More than that, he'd been downright dogmatic throughout his working life about the need to truly *see* one's surroundings and build according to what one has seen. As the case of Posener and the Marseille boat make clear, since arriving in Jerusalem, Mendelsohn had fashioned an ideology of tending fiercely to the climate and contours of Palestine.

Such transformations, though, don't happen overnight. Alert as he tried to be to the environment in which he was working, Mendelsohn was still Mendelsohn—architect of the swooping line, the busy street, the grand gesture. As early as 1936, he admitted in a letter to Luise that "when I am rested, I can see myself returning to daring structures . . . industrial buildings, large spaces, large constructions, large tensions in steel." Engaged as he felt in Jerusalem, "I need the world—not for the world's sake but for its big scale. One can reduce the world for the sake of the world, but one can't reduce one's . . . own scale. Judea is heavenly—but too small for me."

That said, as the Schocken house neared completion that very same month, he pronounced it "very good. It is becoming classic in spirit," and it did in fact mark a new beginning of distinct, and distinctly restrained, sorts. All the flamboyantly propulsive forward motion that characterized his German buildings was now set aside for something more subdued in its dynamism, more turned in on itself, though no less rooted in the topography of its site or somehow alive to the possibilities presented by its materials. The pale pocked stone may not have had the tensile qualities of his once-beloved reinforced concrete, but in his hands and in these plans, it appeared to breathe, punctuated as it was by little windows, a recessed balcony that ran the length of the second story, and a rhythmically spaced series of doors below. These opened out from the long, airy living room and onto a narrow veranda that swept around at its end into a subtle yet dramatic bend—designed to provide the

Schockens with a private box at the outdoor opera that was the ever-shifting spectacle of the Jerusalem landscape. Closest by were the fluidly terraced gardens that he'd designed so that they'd swirl greenly all around the house; in the distance, the Judean desert and mountains of Moab glowed. Within the compound, meanwhile, the oval swimming pool echoed the curve at the other end of the veranda as did the rounded balcony that seemed at once to match, or really rhyme with, the rounded bay window of the Schocken Library that Mendelsohn was also building, just across the street.

He called it his "Rembrandt window," for the soft, diffused bands of painterly light it would filter into the reading room at the library's heart. The villa's balcony and library's window also seemed meant to serve, together, as a hushed nod to the extravagant curvilinear corners that were the trademark of the department stores Mendelsohn had built for Schocken in Germany. This small detail seemed a kind of whispered confession on the architect's part: *I know very well where*

I am. While almost everything else about the men's lives had changed since the construction of those dazzling temples to commerce and cosmopolitanism, the shape remained in miniature, a shadowy memento.

BAUMEISTERS

RARELY DID MENDELSOHN DESIGN A STRUCTURE IN STRICT ISO-
lation; some larger plot or grander purpose was almost always implied. Planned the very same December 1934 week he first sketched
the villa, and clearly meant to stand in expressive relation to it, the
library was intended to be much more than a mere repository for
Salman Schocken's books, though it would of course provide shelter
suitably solid and elegant for his sixty thousand–odd volumes. These
included precious incunabula, valuable first editions in German and
Hebrew, and one of the most important private collections of Jewish
manuscripts anywhere in the world. While Mendelsohn and his draftsmen and the stonecutters, plasterers, and plumbers worked on the
house and the library—the latter located on the dirt way then known
as the Talbiyeh Road, later to be paved and renamed for Balfour and
his Declaration—all of these bibliographic treasures were piled in
crates in a rented Rehavia apartment next door to the one where the
Schockens were temporarily living, on nearby Ramban Street.

So, too, the library building would house Schocken's latest major
undertaking, the Institute for the Study of Hebrew Poetry. Intent on
spearheading a renaissance of Jewish literature by plucking—or hiring
a team of scholars to pluck—his people's poetic history from the
would-be trash heap of history, Schocken had founded the institute in
Berlin just four years before. Now he needed to rescue it and move it
to Palestine.

But the intellectually ambitious tycoon imagined an institution that would not just save—it would *surpass*—what he'd created in Germany, which was why the project so appealed to Mendelsohn. Like the medical center Dr. Yassky envisioned him erecting on Mount Scopus, and the university campus that Schocken and Wauchope wanted him to design, the library had been conceived by patron and planner alike as nothing less than one of the spiritual cornerstones of the Jewish national home that both were intent on constructing.

In more immediate and earthly terms, Schocken and Mendelsohn envisioned the library as the pivot around which the future cultural life of Jerusalem would spin. While the villa was a purely personal undertaking, the library would be what Schocken dubbed a "half private, half public setting," which would make "a place for itself in the breathing life of the city" by serving the needs of a wider, though still highly select, group of "intellectual workers," who would, if all went according to plan, create a vital, secular Hebrew culture that would flow out to the world from the new city of Jerusalem.

Grand as such goals were, Mendelsohn was soon caught up in the hundreds of far less lofty particulars that such a project inevitably entails. He'd taken a site he deemed "absurd" and created plans for it that he said had "spirit and something of Palladio." A clean-edged, jagged T-shape, to be fashioned of the ubiquitous chalky Jerusalem stone, the building would have a slightly floating quality about it, with windows that hovered just a little lower than the eye expected, as though the library itself were one of Schocken's scholars, his gaze turned toward his book. Add to that the softening flourish of the rounded Rembrandtesque oriel, and it would, when completed, exude a strong inner calm. Such stately proportions suited a structure that, as Schocken saw it, would "be an extension of the great National Library" at the university on Mount Scopus. He wanted to fashion, he declared, "something that will allow this city to thrive." Though Jerusalem lies "at the center of the world and represents the central cultural place for Jews," it had little but tumbledown study houses and old synagogues to its physical credit. The city needed, he believed, a building more worthy of its stature—an edifice about which "someday someone should be able to say, 'there was once a man who created this.' " The question, of course, was just who that Solomonic-sounding man would be: the far-sighted publisher and patron Salman Schocken, or Erich Mendelsohn, the far-sighted architect?

But there were many such building contests taking place—literally—on all sides. At the same time he was laboring over the plans for the villa and library, Mendelsohn was asked by the wealthy Egyptian Jewish Aghion family to consider designing them a house on the plot they'd bought, smack-dab between the two Schocken buildings. As Erich would report to Luise in September 1935, the Aghions, of Alexandria, "are enthusiastic . . . but too careful" to make an immediate decision. Refusing to provide sketches without payment or a definite commitment, he declined the chance to vie for the job—which instead went to his old friend and sometime rival Richard Kauffmann, who in turn fashioned an elegantly angular two-story structure whose most notable feature was a flamboyantly curved, window-fronted, and very "Mendelsohnian" entryway that must have seemed at the time of its construction equal parts homage and challenge.

Years after both architects had exited the scene, the Aghion House would come to dominate Balfour Street as the official residence of a series of Israeli prime ministers. Never mind the competitive relationship between the two former Munich classmates and the way it once played out in the interactions between their various buildings. By the second decade of the twenty-first century, such subtle, even good-natured, architectural jousting will have been forgotten, as Kauffmann's smart and simple building has been almost completely swallowed by an aggressive scramble of bulletproof glass, high security walls, heavy gates, lookout towers, two-way mirrors, and multiple security cameras, and the street on which it sits has been closed to all but pedestrian traffic. Renovated almost beyond recognition, threatened with demolition by developers, and caught for years in legal limbo, the former Schocken Villa next door is now a trash-strewn ruin, its windows shattered or filled with concrete blocks.

Meanwhile, in order to visit the Schocken Library—and work at the archive that holds the voluminous correspondence between the patron and architect about its very construction—one must, I must, ford a pacing platoon of jumpy young guards wielding Uzis and pistols. Tense as things are all around it, though, the building itself holds an older kind of poise. As I open its heavy bronze-handled door and enter its cool, pale foyer, essentially unchanged since its completion, the library has ways of quietly making it known: There was once a man who created this.

While Schocken and Mendelsohn were joined, as the architect himself described it, by "our common experiences and our mutual conceptions," they were very often at odds. As part of his carefully orchestrated Transfer deal, for instance, Schocken insisted on bringing the head of his Zwickau office, the non-Jewish Baumeister, or Master Builder, Willy Heinze, to Palestine to supervise work on the villa and library, a fact that enraged Mendelsohn. The offense taken was both personal and cultural. "I know that you value me as an artist," Mendelsohn vented to Schocken in early 1936, "but I sense you do not trust me to oversee construction." The reason for this, he wrote, "lies somewhere in the past," but "I am trying to figure out: why this mistrust from you of all people who, as you yourself feel, are tightly bound to me not only as an understanding client to his architect but as human being and as Jew?" And it wasn't just that Heinze understood (Mendelsohn complained) nothing of human relations in Palestine, but that in light of "what has happened in Germany" his presence in Jerusalem was nothing less than "an injury to the Jewish sense of solidarity and an obvious insult to me."

Mendelsohn may have been overly sensitive—flinching at the mere perception of a social or aesthetic slight. But Schocken himself could be downright cruel. For several years, as construction proceeded on his house and library and he expressed his satisfaction with their progress, he refused to grant Mendelsohn the full sums that the architect said were owed him for his work and that he needed to pay his office bills and the salaries of his employees. For all his generosity as a literary and scholarly patron, Schocken could be a serious skinflint in both emotional and monetary terms. As one who had managed by various means to preserve much of his German wealth, he appeared to have little sympathy for others less fortunate or financially adept. So Mendelsohn was forced to spend hours tallying columns of numbers and arguing his case in countless exacting letters dispatched to Schocken's secretaries and accountants, to whom the rich man had coolly delegated the task of bargaining with his old friend.

They'd always enjoyed strong disagreements, but in Jerusalem this predilection for conflict reached absurd new heights, as when, in Luise's eventual telling, her neighbor Mrs. Schocken invited her to stop by for a visit at the newly built house. "Suddenly she asked me to look at a wall, separating the staircase from the utility wing, and asked me whether I could see anything disturbing." Understanding that this was a test, Luise became uncomfortable, "being aware of the consequences my comment could have." However, try as she might, she couldn't see anything especially disturbing. "There you are," Mrs. Schocken said, "and Erich Mendelsohn wants us to tear down the whole wall because the door is placed one inch too much to the left." Luise was, she writes, "upset, because after she had drawn my attention to this 'mistake,' I felt at once how disturbing it must have been" for Erich, who eventually demolished and rebuilt the wall at his own expense.

Not that the men's stand-offs stopped them from also being close; if anything, such tension appeared to draw them into an even tighter bond. On the occasion of Mendelsohn's fiftieth birthday, in March 1937—in the midst of their most bitter financial feud—Schocken would host a party in his honor at the newly completed library. After depositing their coats, hats, and umbrellas downstairs, on the custom-made chrome hooks and hallway-long rack (the latter complete with a special drain to accommodate pooling rainwater), after they made their way up the angular staircase with its curving bronze banister, two-story-high vertical windows, and glowing eggcup-like sconces, the guests wandered into the immaculate reading room, all marble, lemonwood, glass, and exquisitely bound books. There they were welcomed in German by Schocken.

Reading from several neatly typed pages, he thanked his architect for finding the proper form for this building that would, he assured the assembled group, be given over to "practical, serious work for the future of this country." Although he took the opportunity to de-

clare the architectural profession "an impossibility" that "inevitably produces conflict, with the architect himself, and certainly with his surroundings," since the artist must translate dreams into actual stone and iron, he also found room in his birthday toast for high praise. "I have," he proclaimed, "never fought with anyone as much as I have fought with Erich Mendelsohn." He said it with the deepest admiration.

It wasn't just squabbles with his old patron that occupied—and preoccupied—Mendelsohn. Nothing in this city happened without a fight.

At first, having broken free of the constraints he felt chaining him in Europe, he insisted he found this pugnaciousness invigorating, declaring jubilantly that "here every act is a struggle. Visible, necessary, open, offensive struggle," while "there everything is concealed, clandestine, on the defensive."

However combative he was by nature, though, it felt strange and slightly unsettling to find himself in a place where he wasn't the only one given to confrontation—*everyone* was busy battling, as if for the battle's own sake. When it came to the plans for the future of Mount Scopus, in particular, there was almost no subject that didn't unleash a clash. And now—because these were public buildings he was being asked to design, on closely guarded budgets—decisions had to be made by entire skeptical and even hostile committees, after lengthy discussions whose every minor rhetorical detour would be detailed in pages and pages of typed minutes. Such drawn-out collective caviling may have made him long for the cozy, almost marital predictability of his quarrels with Schocken.

Well before Chaim Yassky managed to persuade the Hadassah officials that Mendelsohn was the man to build their hospital and medical school, prolonged wrangling on the subject of his possible hiring took up their regular meetings. Though Mendelsohn himself wasn't present for these squalls, he knew very well their tone, which tended to veer from the melodramatic to the nitpicking, as, for instance, when one of his more entrenched detractors insisted that it would be "dangerous at this time to select an architect who is entirely new to this country." Shouldn't the job go to "a Palestinian"? But "are there any really Palestinian architects?" another board member countered. The other architects they'd been considering—all European-born—were "not really Palestinians. Mr. Mendelsohn is merely a newer importation." This tail-chasing semantic debate dragged on for several meetings.

While qualms arose about Mendelsohn's alleged financial extravagance and his infamous ego, much of the concern centered on the well-worn topic of his aesthetic sense and its suitability to the setting. The committee, in the words of one member, "had the feeling that his architectural style might be too modernistic," while another "[admired] him as a pioneer in his type of architecture [but] . . . expressed doubts as to whether Mr. Mendelsohn would be flexible enough to create a new form for Palestine."

A general wariness hovered over his appointment. A New York expert whom Hadassah consulted questioned Mendelsohn's knowledge of hospital design, stiffly warning that architectural experimentation must be put aside in the interest of the "functional procedure of the institution itself as a piece of working machinery." While this specialist recognized "the worthiness of Mr. Mendelsohn and his difficult position as an exile from Germany," he could, he wrote, "hardly conscientiously recommend his employment." And when the American president of the whole Hadassah organization, Rose Jacobs, journeyed to Jerusalem and met with Mendelsohn in the summer of 1935, she, too, seemed suspicious. "I tried to emphasize," she reported to yet another committee, back in New York, "that we are looking for a building that will be a monumental contribution to Palestine." Back coiled as a cat's, he wasted no time in squaring off with her, "[putting] me through an examination as to what I meant by a 'monumental' building." She answered that they were "not looking for Grecian designs with columns and ornate figures, but that what we want is perhaps more difficult to achieve—beauty achieved through simplicity." Efficiency was the organization's main concern, she explained, as was posterity. They wanted a hospital "so well constructed that Palestine would have it for eternity, always using it and developing it." At which point Mendelsohn launched into a full-throttle interrogation, grilling Mrs. Jacobs for her opinions of various other structures recently erected throughout the city.

Though generally strong-willed, she conceded this contest and retreated into self-deprecating feminine apology. ("Poor Hadassah," she wrote to the committee, "if it should have to depend on my understanding of and reaction to things artistic!") But the more free-floating skepticism about Mendelsohn's style hardly let up once she and her colleagues approved his candidacy. Certain American supporters of Hadassah disliked his bold brand of sensual functionalism, or functional sensuality. Later, even after they'd accepted his design and construction had begun, one especially testy American Jewish commentator asked rhetorically if the hospital complex "must . . . be built as if it were a cross between a Berlin department store and a Passaic silk factory." Mendelsohn's plans should, according to this critic, "be swiftly and pitilessly redrawn."

Lucky for Mendelsohn, the gently forceful Chaim Yassky remained rocklike in his support, and he recruited Schocken to serve as character witness. And ironically enough, the architect's most devoted sparring partner proved in this context his greatest advocate: "In his opinion," according to the minutes of a late January 1936 meeting between Yassky, Schocken, and one Dr. J. J. Golub, expert in joint diseases and medical buildings, sent from New York by Hadassah to advise on the plans, "there is no one to compare with Mr. Mendelsohn among Jewish architects all over the world." Furthermore, Schocken assured them that the building Mendelsohn would design would be "one distinguished for beauty and renowned far and wide." He took, meanwhile, the same occasion to caution that "there are few architects who tire out those who give them their commissions as does Mr. Mendelsohn," since his "fine artistic taste and his power as an artist" made life difficult; he was "independent and not at all cautious in his relations with people, and for this reason creates dislike for himself." That said, Schocken defended Mendelsohn's integrity as "above suspicion" and simply suggested that a paragraph be added to the contract that limited the architect's responsibility "particularly in regard to the execution of the work."

But the contract itself was really just the start of a very familiar story. No sooner had Mendelsohn signed it and traveled with Yassky and Golub to Alexandria to inspect that city's hospitals than the monetary and legal wrestling began, with Mendelsohn declaring himself "rather aggrieved" at the allowance he'd been given to employ technical consultants. Because of the low figure, he might be compelled, he warned, to hire some "who are not first rate." The bean counters in the New York office weren't especially interested in such refined distinctions and were intent on scrimping wherever possible. They begrudged Mendelsohn every cent, which meant that he had to plead for the most basic things, from funds to order a scale model (to check the buildings in relation to the extremely uneven terrain of Mount Scopus) to an advance on his fees, without which, once again, he couldn't pay his staff.

Mendelsohn was certainly difficult, but he seemed to have more than met his match in the penny-pinching Coordinating Committee to whom he was forced to report in Jerusalem and which, faced with a deficit, continually demanded that he cut costs—whether by making small adjustments, like replacing cork floors with linoleum, eliminating harmonica doors and shutters on windows not directly exposed to the sun, or by tampering with much more essential structural matters. They proposed, for instance, "simplifying the construction" by reducing the amount of cement in the foundations, even lopping off whole floors and canceling entire departments. Given how much time and effort he had already invested in this project, he had little choice but to negotiate, trying to hold on to as much as he could of his original conception. "Even my enemies' illusion of the 'expensive master builder' is gradually fading away," he joked ruefully, "and I am already dreading the moment when I have only 'friends' left." The committee seemed to believe there was always another corner to cut, or price to be haggled over.

They may have saved a few hundred pounds here and there, but these compromises came at a cost that wasn't calculable by any bank clerk. Even before ground was broken at the building site, Mendelsohn sounded exhausted. Working yet another sixteen-hour day, he dashed off a note to Luise, then in Zurich: "All is one turbulent hither-and-thither, everyone demanding satisfaction." Even for a dyed-in-the-wool pugilist, the romance of the nonstop showdown was beginning to wane.

UPRISINGS

SUCH TUSSLING ONLY SERVED AS A PRELUDE TO ACTUAL, PHYSICAL warfare. In April 1936, the bickering and bargaining of the various committees were all but drowned out by far louder and more ominous noises—gunshots, explosions, sirens.

Angered by British policy regarding the political status of Palestine and alarmed by the number of Jewish immigrants who'd flooded the ports since Hitler's rise (the country's Jewish population had more than doubled in the past five years), many local Arabs were profoundly concerned by both the present situation and the future they saw unraveling before them. Over the course of just a few days in the middle of the month, a string of murders and murderous reprisals—Arabs killing Jews, Jews killing Arabs—gave way to angry demonstrations, attacks by vengeful mobs, and harsh police reaction. The Arab leadership then declared a general strike, and low-grade but very real violence erupted throughout the country, with stabbings and stonings, explosions and arson becoming regular occurrences. As a result of the events—which the Jews and the British described as "the riots" or "disturbances" and the Arabs would come to call "the revolt"—modern Jerusalem split for the first time in its history into something like two, with Arab-owned shops in the Old City and nearby neighborhoods shuttered, as residents of the mostly Jewish quarters tried to pretend that everything was normal. Jews avoided the Arab areas, and Arabs skirted the more pervasively Jewish zones.

The uprising, meanwhile, landed right on Hadassah's front step, and Chaim Yassky found himself running a kind of urban field hospital out of the cramped old building on the Street of the Prophets. Although a few Arab outpatients still received treatment at the radium institute there, they didn't stay on the wards—"owing to the lack of vacant beds," according to Yassky—and for now he'd have to put off his dream of directing a broadly ecumenical institution that would serve as a medical haven for all the people of this very mixed city. Instead, Hadassah evolved into a charged symbol of *Jewish* Jerusalem during this period, its "nerves," in the words of one American eyewitness, "drawn tight as a fiddle string." Extra beds were squeezed into the hospital, doctors placed on twenty-four-hour call, and the nursing staff was expanded. The wounded were rushed in for treatment, the dead hauled straight to the morgue; Jewish refugees from the Old City and Hebron lived in squalor in camps around town, and nurses from the hospital were sent to care for them. The beleaguered medical workers reckoned with cases that ranged from the mundane but potentially fatal (as, for instance, when ptomaine poisoning "caused by eating decayed foods" broke out among the refugees and the hospital suddenly teemed with patients) to the extreme and gory. A Jewish professor of Arabic was shot dead while working at home at his desk, the bullet exploding inside his head, resulting in wounds the usually restrained Yassky described in his report on the incident as "horrible . . . Part of the brain and the skin of the skull were found on the walls and the floor."

But even as Yassky and his staff tried to get on with the grisly work of tending to the injured and to the dead, and of helping the police investigate each incident, they were also saddled with the difficult task of, as one local journalist put it, "sooth[ing] the seething crowd." Every time an Arab killed a Jew, large throngs massed outside the building's gates, demanding some kind of catharsis. In the instance of the professor's brutal murder, according to Yassky, "Despite my objections, the District Officer (a Jew) arranged that the funeral orations be held in the courtyard of the hospital, and the whole crowd tried to push its way into the hospital grounds."

On another occasion, three people—including one Polish-born doctor who worked at the hospital—were shot dead on their way out

of a screening at the Edison Cinema, just a few streets away. Ironically enough, Yassky had given himself a rare Saturday night off and
was there to see the early show of a Russian film called *Happy Is the
Day*. Instead he wound up treating gunshot wounds and riding the
short distance back to work in an ambulance. Again he had to prevent
an angry mob from storming the hospital grounds and now ordered
extra gatekeepers to block the crowd from surging into the building
itself. The next day, the Jewish parts of town shut down completely for
the tripartite funeral: workshops and stores closed, offices and schools
let out early, the university canceled classes, and an enormous horde—
estimates ranged up to thirty thousand—gathered before the balcony
of the hospital, where the corpses were laid out, wrapped in prayer
shawls. As the politicians gave their speeches ("Innocent blood has
once more been spilled on the stones of Jerusalem . . ."), the "hysterical weeping" of one of the widows could be heard from inside
the ward where she was being treated for shock.

All of which is to say that the hospital had, as one Hebrew newspaper account put it, "unwittingly become the depot of the sadness
and pain of the entire city." And while Yassky and his staff experienced real depression as they reckoned with the most tangible aspects
of the often abstract struggle that had now seized hold of the land,
he attempted to keep things as ordinary as possible: "Purposely," he
wrote, "because of the high tension in Jerusalem, I called meetings
of the building committee and medical advisory committee, and not
only urgent problems but even the smallest detail of daily routine was
attended to." When asked by a reporter about "news with regard to
the erection of the healing center on Scopus," Yassky answered that
"even during the riots we are not discontinuing our preparations for
one moment."

" 'When will building operations be begun?'
'At the end of July, or early in August, at the latest.'
And the work goes on . . ."

Much of that work went on in London, to which Mendelsohn happened to return just before the mayhem set in, and at the Rehavia
windmill in his absence. Even as the local rhetoric was cranked up

several notches ("I need hardly attempt a description of the pall of excitement and grief which hangs over the city," wrote one Hadassah official in Jerusalem to her counterpart in New York that May, "nor need I tell you that any attempt at routine work is merely a brave show"), he and Kempinski and their assistants labored over the specifics of the new hospital. During this time they drew up a structural system, mapped rooms, began to render the final plans to scale, calculated preliminary stresses, and met with various consultants, quarry representatives, and building firms to discuss possible contracts.

Was it really just a brave show? In fact, Mendelsohn himself seemed basically undaunted. "The work was interrupted by the present disturbances in Palestine," he wrote crisply in a report composed that same month, "only in so far as negotiations with the special firms are concerned."

And it wasn't just his distance from the anger and gore that made this possible. When he returned to Palestine in early July, he hardly missed a beat, enthusing to Luise about the "fresh and delicious" air that blew even at midnight, his first back in Jerusalem. He wrote her of the smooth functioning of the office and the now routine wrangling with the Hadassah committees—mentioning the more general troubles only telegraphically and parenthetically: "Schocken is in a good temper. I was all day yesterday at his construction sites, and in the evening (curfew pass) at his house until after midnight." The completion of the Schocken house had been delayed because stone deliveries had stopped with the closure of the quarries.

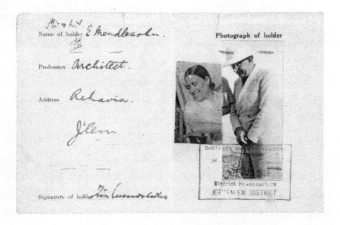

The violence itself went almost unmentioned as he described the state in which he found his various projects. Incomplete though it may have been, the Schocken house pleased him especially. It was "still a naked babe without the frills and ruffles of greenery but already it stretches out above the three amphitheater-like terraces of the great slope . . . Everything is very beautiful and generous in scale." And a trip to the Mount Scopus site at long last exhilarated him. The medical complex existed so far only on paper, but he could already see it standing sublimely on its hill. "The chief building seems to stretch from Jerusalem to Saudi Arabia—so long does it appear. The maternity section lies close by the Arab village on the slope down to the Dead Sea. The view," he wrote, "is timeless. He who dies here has not far to travel." He'd also been having "exciting days," sketching the Anglo-Palestine Bank, slated for a central spot downtown, on the Jaffa Road, beside the new post office, which was currently under construction.

For all his architectural enthusiasm, however, Mendelsohn was hardly oblivious to what was happening around him. The next few years would, he knew, be "lean and uncertain." Recent events had taken a severe monetary toll on Hadassah, and Yassky had warned him that the hospital project "must be executed at minimum cost." Otherwise, the entire building program would be scrapped. The problem wasn't just the strain on local resources, but the difficulty of fund-raising abroad in the midst of such a crisis. Though Yassky didn't tell Mendelsohn this, he confided to several of his Hadassah colleagues that collecting American donations had become extremely difficult of late, since "certain elements of Jewry in the Diaspora are becoming apprehensive with regard to the Zionist undertaking."

The bank plans also remained up in the air. Within weeks of his return, Mendelsohn found himself in the painful position of having to give his assistants at the windmill notice that if the major projects on which they were now working weren't built, he'd be forced to lay them all off. Nothing these days was sure.

Beyond absorbing the effect on his business interests, Mendelsohn's inner seismograph certainly also registered the political tremors right underfoot. The troubles rattling Palestine, though, seemed to him a set of fainter aftershocks from the quakes that rocked the wider world. In his letters of these months, he made no more than glancing reference to the bloody local situation and instead worried aloud about Spain and England, Hitler and Lenin, tyranny and freedom, the last great war, and the next. "We thought that after the initial burst of gunfire, the world war was already the resolution, the culmination," he wrote Luise in August. "Today we know that these were only the cracks showing before the collapse. How difficult it will be to clear away the rubble heap, to begin to rebuild the foundations." Mendelsohn wasn't one to use architectural metaphors lightly, and—faced with the crumbling edifice of a whole continent—he seemed to know of no other option than to apply himself to the construction of actual buildings here, on another.

At 8:30 a.m. on October 21, 1936, Erich Mendelsohn and Chaim Yassky led a tour of some hundred dignitaries, reporters, university officials, and Hadassah representatives around the Scopus site, where the outlines of the hospital, the nursing school, and the medical school had been marked in chalk. A handkerchief in his breast pocket, fedora tilted slightly, Mendelsohn excitedly outlined his plans for the whole complex. A pickaxe was hoisted, soil turned, and the building begun.

Yassky may not have confided in him the difficulty of fund-raising in these turbulent times, but Mendelsohn didn't need to be told. He could see for himself the effect that financial and political pressures were having on the breathless way the cityscape piled up, and on his own plans as they emerged from his mind and his pencil. Try as he might to concentrate on the matter at hand, those concerns weighed heavily on him, and he had to fight to keep a certain contraction of ambition, a blurring of vision, from taking hold.

To its idealistic American sponsors, the new and improved Hadassah hospital meant much more than spacious wards, state-of-the art labs, and surgical departments for the ill. It served as a symbol made of stone, and they intended its construction to demonstrate the strength and resolve—the robust health, in fact—of the country's

Jewish population, to promote in the most pointed way Jewish industry, and to employ as many Jewish laborers as possible. As originally planned, some five hundred were slated to be hired to work at the building site over the course of several years, and materials— from the Gasoconcrete floor insulation to the 15,000 square meters of tilework, 50,000 sacks of cement, the Oil-O-Matic heating apparatus, the 260 beds, and all the bathroom fixtures—were to be ordered from Palestinian Jewish firms. Articles extolling this fact would be published in the country's Hebrew and English press, where the decision to buy locally and Jewishly would be declared, for instance, "a source of great satisfaction to the public." Unlike Schocken, who'd ordered the materials for his house and library packed neatly into those German shipping containers and sent to Jerusalem, Hadassah demanded that its contractors provide written assurances that they weren't using any German goods at all. If they were found to be doing so, they'd be forced to pay a fine. Never mind the quality of the stuff in question. What mattered most was that it wouldn't be German; it wouldn't be Arab; it would be guaranteed Made by Jews in the Land of Israel.

Aesthetic considerations of the sort that tended to obsess Erich Mendelsohn were, in other words, a very low priority here. To even suggest such a subject in the context of the rampant unemployment, seeping bloodshed, and social instability that currently plagued

Palestine was to seem somehow detached or indulgent, swayed by suspiciously effete foreign concerns.

In a state of emergency—which most of the Jews of Palestine believed that this was and would inevitably continue to be—who had time for such niceties?

✦

A few weeks after that pickaxe was first wielded at the hospital site, a royal commission arrived from London "to ascertain the underlying causes of the disturbances." The general strike had just ended, but the violence throughout Palestine persisted, and the king had sent this group of serious men in three-piece suits to determine whether "either the Arabs or the Jews have any legitimate grievances" against the British Mandate, and, if so, to make recommendations.

In order to do that, the commission—an earl, a baronet, a bevy of lords—set up their headquarters in the ballroom of Jerusalem's prematurely bedraggled Palace Hotel. Perhaps it was coincidence, but the derelict condition of this large hall and the once sumptuously appointed building that held it seemed to indicate something more general about the declining state of things both physical and fraternal in Palestine. The hotel's establishment in the late 1920s had itself been a product of the increasingly charged atmosphere surrounding construction in Jerusalem. Commissioned by Palestine's main Islamic governing body, the Supreme Muslim Council, under the leadership of the mufti, Hajj Amin al-Husseini, the building had first been designed as a luxury apartment house by a well-known Turkish architect and staunch Ottoman nationalist named Ahmet Kemalettin, who'd been invited to Palestine by the council in 1922 to renovate the al-Aqsa Mosque. That apartment house never materialized, and when Kemalettin left town and eventually died in Ankara in 1927, the plans were placed in the hands of his assistant, one Mehmed Nihad, who was asked to refashion the design as a grand hotel, conceived in the same lavish neo-Suleimanic style that his mentor had envisioned. Stretching a full city block, it was set on the edge of the flourishing commercial neighborhood known as Mamilla, just beyond the busy area outside the Jaffa Gate, and it featured an impressive battery of Eastern flourishes. With wide horseshoe-arched windows, decorative rosettes, and stalactite-shaped carvings arrayed across its façade, the Palace was clearly designed to make both an architectural and a political statement. Meant to draw tourists from the wider Arab and Muslim world to Palestine, the hotel was also intended to pose a defiant stone challenge to certain major Zionist-sponsored buildings then being erected around the city. And if the fact of the structure itself didn't make that plain, the symbolism would be literally spelled out in a flowing Arabic inscription, placed high above the entrance. This consisted of a few lines from a carefully chosen seventh-century poem—"*We will build as our ancestors built and act as they acted.*"

The irony is that, for all the nationalistic muscle flexing surrounding the idea of the hotel—and though building took place during an especially tumultuous period in the country's history—the actual construction of the Palace constituted a genuinely collaborative project, fruit of the wary coexistence that still prevailed in the city. The mufti himself had employed as contractors—and eventually befriended—two Jews (one of them Chaim Weizmann's son-in-law) and a Christian Arab, and he would later hire them to build his own house. Though the mufti had stipulated that the contractors should favor Arab workers when hiring, the crews who labored at the site were made up of both Arabs and Jews. And when the hotel's festive opening took place in late 1929, a British official had raised a toast to the Supreme Muslim Council, to the Turkish architect Nihad Bey, and to George Barsky, the establishment's Jewish proprietor, while the mufti had heaped public praise on his non-Muslim contractors. Described in the local press as providing "at last . . . a meeting place for people of all creeds and races," the Palace was also

the most luxurious new hotel in the Middle East. Offering its guests what advertisements called "EVERY COMFORT OF A DISTINGUISHED HOTEL-DE-LUXE," it featured not only extravagant al-Asqa–meets–Art Deco ornamentation, but all the latest amenities—including central heating, hot and cold running water, three elevators, and more than sixty telephones.

Distinguished and deluxe though it may have been, the Palace went bankrupt after just a few years, when the still more luxurious King David Hotel opened down the street. Financed and owned by Egyptian Jews, planned and managed by Swiss Christians, it was, according to its Zurich-trained architect, Emil Vogt, meant to "evoke the memory of the ancient Semitic style and the atmosphere of the glorious period of King David." It had a massive symmetrical façade fashioned of both smoothly cut and heavily rusticated stone, and, playing on that First Temple theme, its interiors featured darkly stained cedar, rich marble floors, elaborate fluted columns, and stylized "biblical" decorations—a fanciful mishmash of "Phoenician," "Hebrew," and "Assyrian" motifs, swirled through with painted grapevines and pomegranates. Although the King David wasn't technically a Zionist establishment—neither its owners nor architect were Palestinian Jews and it had been constructed at the urging of various British officials, who felt the country needed a hotel of the posh class they'd enjoyed during their postings in Egypt—its grand opening right on the heels of the Palace's own did add an unfortunate architectural dimension to the national struggle then seizing hold of the city. More than a contest between a couple of high-end modern hotels, the showdown between the Palace and the King David seemed to pit two of Jerusalem's most beloved and sacred ancient structures against one another—a fantasia on the al-Aqsa Mosque vs. a fantasia on Solomon's Temple.

That said, for all the heavily scriptural symbolism of its design, the King David did in fact function throughout most of the Mandate as a swank private club of sorts for well-heeled Arabs, Jews, Englishmen, and foreigners alike—"the great meeting place of the city," according to one British army officer who used to drink at its bar and lounge in its garden. The top floors of the hotel would also go on to become the headquarters of the British Secretariat and military command, and an imposing emblem of foreign rule: In July 1946, the King David would famously be bombed by the armed right-wing Jewish underground, the Irgun—one whole wing demolished, ninety-one people killed. But even amid the violence, it would continue to serve, and still serves today, as one of the city's most exclusive hotels, albeit one where the guests are almost entirely Jewish and/or foreign.

With the closure of the Palace, meanwhile, *that* building took on a much bleaker, more functional look as the British government leased it and moved some of its offices there. Rooms were divided with concrete blocks. Graphs and maps hung on the walls.

In preparation for the London commission's arrival (its members would be staying in style at, of all places, the King David), the high arabesque-entwined marble columns that framed the octagonal lobby of the Palace had been given a clean coat of white paint, the ballroom aired out, and a large semicircular table dragged in. Here, over the course of several months in the late fall of 1936 and winter of 1937, the British dignitaries would hear detailed evidence from expert witnesses—English, Jewish, Arab—about everything from population growth to hygienic conditions to water supply to European anti-Semitism to the export of olive-oil soap to the high rate of taxation among the Arab fellaheen . . . as they tried to find a way to make sense of what they'd call in their report the "present problem of Palestine." No other "problem of our time is rooted so deeply in the past," though the real question was the future, which weighed heavily under the flowery ceiling and ornate chandeliers, remnants of the earlier, more hopeful life of the Palace Hotel.

Beyond the ever escalating conflict between Arabs and Jews, the Jews themselves were increasingly at each other's throats. Soon after building began on Mount Scopus, gangs of Jewish activists from Ze'ev Jabotinsky's militantly nationalistic Revisionist party who believed their workers had been shut out of the project by the left-leaning authorities stormed the construction site and the Hadassah offices on the Street of the Prophets. In the course of one such rampage, they smashed furniture, ripped doors from their hinges, scattered files, and even assaulted several nurses; on another occasion, a brawl broke out around the concrete mixers and newly dug foundation pits on Mount Scopus, with the Revisionist laborers charging the Socialists and starting a fistfight.

The battle was both physical and rhetorical, as an official from the Revisionist movement wrote angrily to Hadassah's American headquarters, claiming that "the Socialist . . . groups terrorized the Hadassah Building Committee" and threatened to declare a strike if the Revisionist workers were employed. The Revisionists insisted that *they* were the ones who were attacked and that "the report about the demolishment of the Hadassah offices is a deliberate distortion of the facts by the Leftist controlled news agency." Yassky, for his already overworked part, was forced to take time out from treating patients, running the hospital, managing budgets, and overseeing the complicated building project to defend Hadassah's local hiring practices. In a telegram to New York, he recounted: VIOLENT DEMONSTRATIONS OF REVISIONIST WORKERS HAVE TAKEN PLACE . . . THEY ARE BELIEVED TO BE EXPLOITING MATTER FOR POLITICAL PURPOSES STOP. The contractors were willing to hire laborers from the full range of Zionist streams but EVEN IF CONSENT GIVEN BY ALL CONCERNED TO THIS PRINCIPLE WE DO NOT BELIEVE THEY WILL BE SATISFIED SINCE THEY DEMAND ALLOCATION OF WORK BEYOND ALL PROPORTION AND SEEK POLITICAL PROPAGANDA STOP.

And there in the midst of it all was Erich Mendelsohn, pondering the placement of the hospital's telephone wires, oil paint vs. whitewash for the hallways, and whether steel or wooden window frames would serve as a better shield from the severe wind and rain that batter Mount Scopus in the winter. According to the minutes of yet another meeting, held in the grimmest midst of the country's current strife, "Mr. Mendelsohn pointed out . . . that on steel windows there must be precise workmanship which, he believes cannot be obtained in Palestine for the price Hadassah is willing to pay. For that reason, he felt that it would be preferable to use wood windows. He mentioned also that Palestinian carpenters are now making excellent windows of wood."

The hospital's planners were not just confronting the political forest fires that had been deliberately set on all sides; they were also reckoning with incompetence on the part of the quarry, which had been

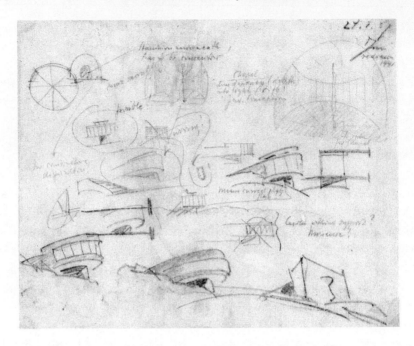

hired solely for ideological reasons: This was the only functioning Jewish stonecutting company in the area, and in the words of one Hadassah official, "There can be no thought of using Arab quarries." At a certain stage Mendelsohn found himself in the bizarre position of having to defend the very use of stone on this major Jerusalem building.

Even after construction had started, such basic architectural decisions remained up for grabs, and he had to explain patiently that—as municipal regulations dictated—he had designed the hospital expressly with stone in mind. He had in fact been the one to put forth the cost-saving idea of using machine-cut stone for the first time ever in Palestine. But since the quarry had so far proved incapable of delivering even a fraction of the fifteen thousand square meters they had promised, the planners needed quickly to consider other options. Traditionally chiseled *taltish* stone was mentioned, and dismissed ("apart from the question of expense involved, . . . Jewish quarries could not possibly provide so much hand-cut stone in time"). Then concrete was proposed, forcing Mendelsohn to insist that "the appearance of a long building with many windows at regular intervals faced in concrete would be deplorable."

Despite his rigid reputation, he was clearly trying his hardest to be flexible, to mind his manners, to concede as much to his employers as possible without losing sight of his own plan: "Stone," he informed them, sounding wearier than ever, "gives such a building the life which is its beauty." Understanding the bureaucratic situation, however, he mostly kept his argument practical. Not only would the last-minute switch to this other building material require the construction of coping and sills, but concrete "very quickly shows cracks and stains, and is very expensive to maintain in good order." Pipes and fittings would be much harder to mask, and the move to concrete would require his office to draw up an entirely new set of plans, for which—given all the delays that had already plagued the project—there was simply no time.

Bending over backward to make his designs viable, he went so far as to suggest they consider the use of *artificial* stone, actually a mixture of concrete and stone chippings, "the very idea" of which, he admitted, "sounds at first ridiculous in Jerusalem which abounds in stone." But it had "many advantages. It could be manufactured to look exactly like natural stone and," critically, "it is cheaper."

Much discussion on the subject of artificial stone ensued, with Mendelsohn showing the committee various samples, and someone suggesting that a new (more euphemistic?) term be found to describe the ersatz item. Perhaps "composite stone" would be better. All agreed on the need for secrecy, since if word got out that they were considering buying this other material in quantity, it might force the quarry into bankruptcy and so "the last chance of Jewish stone being produced in Jerusalem would disappear."

At a certain point Rose Jacobs threatened to halt building entirely unless natural stone was used, and Erich Mendelsohn continued to try his hardest to sound cheerful as he vouched for the physical properties of composite stone. It was, he insisted, "less porous and more durable" than the real thing—as perhaps he was trying to prove himself in the course of all these meetings.

In the end, because of "permanent difficulties" with the quarries—the workers had gone on strike, the gang-saw malfunctioned, and the whole operation been subject to temporary closure after it was placed in receivership and all the machinery taken as security—Mendelsohn and the committees decided to cover parts of the hospital's inner courtyard walls with composite stone.

But more than a year later, with the dramatic horizontals of the hospital rising skeletally on the ridge, they were still wrangling about the situation just next door, and what material would best suit the exterior of the medical school. If left "unfaced for some time . . . [it] will make a very bad impression on American tourists."

As it was discussed at these interminable meetings, meanwhile, the national state of emergency by now sounded like an almost hum-drum feature of the local landscape—as if the rocky political situation in Palestine were just another God-given fact to be reckoned with, like the gusting winds and uneven terrain that made building on Mount Scopus so complicated. Stating frankly that "it seems probable that the situation, bad as it now is, will grow worse," in July 1937 the royal commission had finally offered its conclusions and recommended partitioning the country between Arabs and Jews, explaining that as a "peculiarly English proverb" puts it, "half a loaf of bread is better than no bread . . . There is little moral value in maintaining the political unity of Palestine at the cost of perpetual hatred, strife, and bloodshed."

Though the idea of partition proved popular among most of the liberal Jews Mendelsohn knew, it depressed him, great believer that he was in organic unity. The working class's "dream of a socialist state with the capital in Tel Aviv is being fulfilled," he wrote darkly to Luise. Meanwhile Jerusalem—slated to be part of a special British enclave—would be "decapitated" from the rest of the body that was Palestine, and then "commanded to live." Such an arrangement meant, he told her, "creating a ghetto by political concessions. You take away the ideal, the idea, the dream, the future." His own heartfelt if slightly hazy thinking about the prospect of Arab-Jewish synthesis seemed more wishful than ever.

That said, he could shift in an instant from despondency in the face of the general situation to delight in the specifics of all he was building. As the whole Hadassah complex took gradual shape, Mendelsohn came to sound amazed by "the grand scope of the long

parallel buildings—enthroned between the steep desert slope and Jerusalem." An understated yet almost topographical force emanated
from the hospital's outline, with its low domes echoing the domes of
the Arab villages just below. (The workmen, Mendelsohn said, "in
biblical style call them the 'breasts of the building.'") And this sleek,
quietly curvaceous building bound it to both the landscape and the
other buildings in the complex, which, he wrote with a kind of wonder to Luise, "express . . . freedom, with proportions that sing and
have that unaffected simplicity, the logic of which I have been seeking from my early days, and which is my goal."

Sometimes, after they threw a dinner party or held an impromptu
late-night chamber music concert under the windmill's huge fig
tree, they'd pile with their guests into a few cars and make their way
up the winding road to Mount Scopus, where they'd wander in the
moonlight over the building site. Then—"deeply moved" and overcome by "a mood of reverence and gratefulness" (as Luise would
report of one particularly charmed predawn outing)—watch the sun
rise over the city.

ACTUAL AND POSSIBLE

SUCH CALM CAME OVER MENDELSOHN ONLY IN CERTAIN CONTEXTS. As accommodating as he tried to be with the committees, and rhapsodic as he may have waxed with his wife and tipsy dinner guests about the buildings' progress, he remained, in the bright light of day and in select company, just as defiant as ever.

If anything, standing in the busy midst of the workers and donkeys and cement mixers in the noontime glare on Mount Scopus, he'd be swept by an even stronger sense of possibility—and of indignation—than that which washed over him when he'd first toured the site with Yassky back on that windy winter day in 1934.

The hospital and other medical buildings were, after all, still just one part of his grand design for the entire ridge, about which he'd come to feel unabashedly proprietary. The stakes were much higher than they'd been when he first arrived. Now he and his buildings formed part of this view, and the mapping of the university "in accordance with a unified plan" he declared "my special mission in the development of the country."

Aside from his own desire to see this scheme through, he was, he believed, answering a call that had been put to him by those in power. His first job in this context was to design the so-called Rosenbloom Building, which would house the all-important Institute of Jewish Studies, described at its 1924 opening by the university's chancellor, American rabbi Judah Magnes, as "a holy place, a sanctuary in which to learn and teach." Temporarily housed in a rented Ottoman-era khan, the institute would, Magnes proclaimed, set out to answer no less than the question: "What is Judaism?"

But central and maybe even sacred as this branch of the university may have been, Mendelsohn considered the institute's ground plans a kind of architectural down payment. He knew that there had been talk for years about entrusting the whole campus to him. And as soon as he'd opened that makeshift office at the King David Hotel in late 1934, the university had been, he'd written then, "already waiting" for him to put forth "an offering" for "an entirely new master plan." As chairman of the university's executive committee, Schocken had clearly been influential in urging the administration "to profit from the presence of . . . [this] well-known architect, formerly of Berlin." And Magnes had also been eager to hire him, writing excitedly at the start of 1935 that "he [Mendelsohn] is going to give us a real conception of a university and I hope that we shall be able to employ him right along in connection with our buildings."

In a way, everything Mendelsohn had come to Jerusalem for seemed to be waiting on this mountaintop. While his other local projects had entailed one compromise after another, he meant to make this campus unmistakably his own, to render it an ultimate statement about his vision of Palestine's future. The plotting of this site struck him in fact as a dream commission—the embodiment of all his grand plans both for this landscape and for himself.

At least where the university was concerned, such plans were long overdue. On the occasion of its grand opening in 1925, one journalistic booster had announced the dawn of "a new epoch in Jewish history," but so far the physical facts lagged badly behind the rhetoric. They amounted, as it happens, to little more than a few scattered structures.

This motley mix consisted, first, of a late nineteenth-century summerhouse, built for a philosemitic Protestant lawyer from Liverpool and his painter wife, in the simple, stately style of rural villas owned by local Arab aristocrats. Purchased by the fledgling university in 1914, it had recently been renovated with various Art Deco touches by Fritz Kornberg, another German Jewish émigré, and it now held the chemistry institute and a microbiology wing. The villa's stables served as administrative offices. There were also blocky new structures for math and physics, as well as the palatial national library, designed of heavy masonry with multiple arched windows and a large Byzantine-styled dome by the pioneering Scottish town planner, sociological maverick, and Christian Zionist Patrick Geddes and his son-in-law, Frank Mears. They'd worked together on the library with Benjamin Chaikin, a British Jewish architect who'd arrived in Palestine in 1920 and was often hired by foreign firms to oversee their local building projects. (He had performed this service for, among others, Vogt, the Swiss architect of the King David Hotel.) Finally, on the very southeastern edge of the hill, facing out toward a spectacular view of the Dead Sea, sat an amphitheater, also designed by Kornberg in a sort of nouveau-Mesopotamian manner and later adjusted by Chaikin, who seemed eager to add yet another style to the scramble already confusing the ridge and so threw in a few neoclassical columns.

Various plans for the whole university had been put forward over the years. Most famously, Geddes and Mears drew up a flamingly symbolic one in 1919. They had been invited to render a town plan (the report they eventually offered the British military governor was titled, modestly, "Jerusalem Actual and Possible"), and their design for the campus was integrally connected to their vision of the "renewed Jerusalem," which "is the undying hope of Israel." According to this elaborate scheme, the entire city would somehow radiate from or turn up toward the university's perch on Mount Scopus, as if it were a latter-day Temple Mount, anchored at its pinnacle by a "Great Hall" to be constructed on a massive scale and in the shape of a Star of David. Not only did Geddes picture the "coming of the Palestinian people at various occasions of the year" to celebrate their seasonal festivals in this vast pavilion, he also dreamed of the way the various humanistic and scientific disciplines of the university might all converge there, so bringing—as he put it, in his typically wafting terminology— "fuller co-operative synergies, and these [moving] increasingly towards Synergy . . . even increasingly toward Synthesis itself."

And just to underline the link between this Mount and that other

Mount on the opposite ridge, site of the absent ancient Jewish Temple, Geddes planned—and Mears sketched—an enormous "floating dome" made of ferroconcrete. Meant to be the world's largest structure of its kind, it would be placed atop the Great Hall and mirror the iconic seventh-century Dome of the Rock, the oldest Islamic edifice on earth, which Geddes deemed "the very best of all the buildings upon the whole sky-line." This university he imagined would serve as "something more than . . . classrooms and laboratories." It would be, in a way, a miniature version of the whole New Jerusalem—actual *and* possible—and would "in its distant completed form" become "a spacious City of Dreams."

This scheme had been scrapped in 1929, with Magnes somewhat hyperbolically telling Mears that "there has not been a single person of whatever profession or from whatever country to whom your plans have been submitted who has liked them."

In fact, all kinds of power struggles were taking place behind the scenes, and though these had nothing to do with architecture, the plans became part of that fight. Certain university representatives had, meanwhile, made a point of featuring a drawing of the Great Hall in drives for both international money and sympathy. It appeared on postcards, framed by hovering cameo-like portraits of Weizmann and Einstein; a gigantic sketch of the building turned up behind Einstein himself when on his first visit to New York in 1921

כִּי מָלְאָה הָאָרֶץ דֵּעָה

HEBREW UNIVERSITY
JERUSALEM, PALESTINE

he addressed a Waldorf-Astoria ballroom packed full of American doctors and appealed for cash to fund the Jerusalem medical school. And their design had its architectural champions as well. These included Geddes's protégé Lewis Mumford, who praised it in print as "the intellectual masterpiece of a sociologist who is also an artist." British psychoanalyst David Eder, Weizmann's liaison to the university, defended it too and wrote frankly to Magnes that "I have the impression that you . . . regard architecture as one of the futile arts, and are not interested in considerations of beauty and strength being expressed in building form." Although Geddes and Mears had been hired by the Zionist Commission to conceive these ideas, Geddes himself wondered if the problem was that he and his son-in-law weren't Jewish, and complained to Mumford that they'd been "unscrupulously 'chunked.'"

Whatever the real reason for that plan's rejection, more modest later schemes for the university met a similar fate. At the time of Mendelsohn's arrival in the country, the campus still lacked an overarching design. And so, taking Magnes and Schocken's enthusiasm as an invitation to proceed, he had gotten right down to work.

As early as March 1935, he had rendered a preliminary set of sketches—"I am," he wrote Luise as he started drawing, "bewitched by what I see and hope to capture"—and by May 1936, he'd completed a full block plan for the campus and medical center. Forgoing anything like the heavy symbolism of Geddes's design, he'd let the swells and dips of the landscape guide him. Inspired by the shapes of those gently stepped Arab villages he so admired, he had found a subtle way of balancing the heights of the buildings that already existed and those still to be constructed, so that they at once corresponded to the uneven terrain and related to each other as masses.

Bearing in mind the harsh and extremely variable climatic conditions of the site, he had created a new east-west axis that ran perpendicular to the narrow ridge and that would, he said, allow the sun to warm the buildings in winter and in the summer capture "the cooling west winds." The various structures would be linked by means of careful landscaping, bringing the whole hill together as that "proper organism" he loved to invoke. He wasn't inventing new forms but taking his cues from a building tradition much older than himself, rooted deeply in the region. "Look," he wrote, of his vision for the Mount Scopus compound, "at the villages of the Mediterranean like Amalfi in the Bay of Naples, Megara on the Road from Eleasis to Corinth, the Nile villages of Upper Egypt and the mountain villages of Judaea." Consider, he suggested, "an ordinary Arab village."

He elaborated: "Generally speaking, the peasant everywhere has mastered the problems of nature better than anyone else, and it is this adaptation to natural conditions that has inspired architects through the ages to the most important examples of town planning." The play of sun on the buildings' unbroken façades, the "shady, terraced gardens," the courtyards with fountains and pergolas—all came together in a kind of sublime hush, and it was this feeling he hoped to capture with the block plan. Meanwhile, though his designs for the complex would strive to "follow the fundamental principles, i.e. the principles of Mediterranean tradition, the concrete realization of these principles must be in harmony with the spirit of our own epoch. The creative form only is permanent; all stylish imitation is dead from the outset."

The spirit of our own epoch, the principles of Mediterranean tradition, the creative form—such high-minded considerations were very far indeed from the thoughts of the university administrators, who were particularly skittish at the moment. And it wasn't just Mendelsohn's inflated terminology that unnerved them. Whatever their initial excitement about his work, they had recently and radically changed their tune, now sounding anxious at the prospect of committing to a long-term plan, *any* long-term plan. They preferred to raise money and to order up buildings piecemeal, in accordance with the wishes of those writing the checks. Although they'd hired Mendelsohn to design another building, a student center known as the university clubhouse, they seemed unwilling to think beyond that and appeared especially desperate to please the Rosenbloom family, of Pittsburgh.

The solidly Middle American Rosenblooms, for their part, were no great fans of Erich Mendelsohn's expressive yet refined neo-Mediterranean lines, and they had little patience with all his avant-garde architectural talk. Their 1926 gift to the university came with the provision that the building bear both the name of their late patriarch, a banker and philanthropist called Sol, and a lintel-inscription of a verse from Isaiah: "For out of Zion shall go forth the law and the word of God from Jerusalem."

Their decidedly staid architectural preferences, meanwhile, found institutional support in one L. Green, honorary technical adviser to the Hebrew University and, as it happens, by far the most outspokenly anti-Mendelsohnian participant in Yassky's building committee meetings. Green, a civil engineer, objected from the outset to the architect's involvement with the design of the hospital and complained that Mendelsohn "stands at the head of a school of architecture, the adherents of which identify themselves with the ultra-modern style of architecture—a style which [is] . . . not suitable for Palestine." In the case of Mendelsohn's design for the Rosenbloom Building, Green asserted, somewhat vaguely, that "a long narrow one story building is not likely to prove aesthetic."

With or without Green goading them on, the Rosenblooms were, anyway, fickle. It seems they may have played a role in sacking Geddes and Mears and had also vetoed another set of blueprints for the building that would bear their family name. They'd first hired a different architect, an École des Beaux-Arts–trained American who'd designed a grandiose domed structure to stand, like a large pseudo-oriental Reform temple, vying with the library for attention, as it dominated the whole campus and Mount Scopus ridge. This plan was turned down for financial reasons, and a "reduced" version prepared by Chaikin, then rejected by the family, also vaguely, as "unsatisfactory." Green himself had adjusted those plans to "harmoniz[e] the appearance . . . with the style of the neighboring library building"—a move criticized by the administration. (Magnes and Schocken felt that "as the [National] Library building was not a success aesthetically, it was undesirable to repeat its style in the Rosenbloom building.") The family, though, seemed keen on this more ostentatious plan, and, when faced now with Mendelsohn's far sparer designs—several carefully staggered blocks, meant to blend into the hilly landscape, as part of his terrain-conscious design for the campus—they again announced their displeasure, using as fodder a highly critical report on the plan by the not exactly objective Mr. Green: "We are very much dissatisfied," complained the son, Charles, himself a philanthropically minded collector of prints and rare books. "The building has the appearance of"—yet again—"a modern factory building . . . It has no individuality whatsoever, particularly for a Memorial Building."

At first, Magnes (by this time university president) backed up Mendelsohn and tried to exert gentle pressure on the donors to accept his design, insisting that it was "a splendid, practical, and beautiful conception." But money eventually talked, and by the summer of 1936, the Rosenblooms had formalized their distaste for Mendelsohn's plans—to which they were reported to be "completely opposed . . . Under no circumstances will they accept them." Instead they had independently hired yet another architect, a Joseph Weiss, of New York. At this, the bottom-line-minded Schocken, Mendelsohn's great patron, absolutely rolled over and declared in a letter to Mrs. Rosenbloom how pleased the administration was with this choice, even writing to Weiss himself to enthuse about how lucky the university was in their choice of an architect.

This situation, understandably, sent Mendelsohn into another of his rages, and in an especially furious July letter to Schocken he vented at "the deep depression which we must feel as Jews, when we see the noble lines of [this] unique landscape belittled and disfigured by buildings without scale or coherence." The Rosenbloom Building was probably a lost cause, and one for which Mendelsohn didn't seem inclined to fight. But the design of the whole university was something else altogether, and the administration's capitulation to the Rosenblooms' middlebrow tastes was, he felt strongly, indicative of a much more sweeping problem.

He'd hoped and expected that Schocken, as one of those "who trust their eyes more than their brains," would have put an end on Mount Scopus to "the irresponsible boorishness" that determined so much of the building taking place throughout the land. "Want and speculation" were driving development, as "the comprehensive plan" was "to be sacrificed to the individual wishes of the donor, who understands no better." It was, he insisted, "thanks to this point of view that the only Jewish university acquired the appearance which it has today . . . Never before has a university been built with so small an awareness of the fact that the concept of a university demands more architecturally than a heap of souvenirs of somebody's charity."

Though his wounded pride clearly played a role in unleashing this diatribe, he was, of course, also speaking of something larger than himself and his hurt feelings. Just as his plans for the university represented the pinnacle of all he believed Palestine could be, so the scattershot facts on the ground pointed downhill, to the nadir.

Such jeremiads were nothing new. Mendelsohn's early visits to Mount Scopus also made him livid. This time, however, he had decided not just to howl to the heavens (or to Schocken), but had, he wrote Luise, "called in the Romans—for the sake of an ideal."

As he plotted his block plan he had, in other words, been surveying more than the topography of Scopus; he'd also been charting the political lay of the land and had decided to use his social connections to the high commissioner and other British authorities to reach what he called "a secret agreement" to bypass both the university officials and the donors. According to this arrangement, his designs for the top of Mount Scopus would be considered part of an "integrated town planning scheme . . . [to] be built or executed by one hand." Jerusalem's British town planner, Henry Kendall, sent an official letter to the university, warning against "piecemeal building" and requesting the submission of such a development plan.

Mendelsohn's scheme worked initially, at least in part. The Town Planning Commission declared at an August 1936 meeting that "in view of the unique site and the importance of the University as a future cultural centre," the plans for development of the area "to form one harmonious whole" should be "drawn up by one architect for all future buildings." Mendelsohn himself might have written this document, so closely did it hew to his vocabulary and vision: "In order further to achieve this organic unity the person preparing the plan should either be architect for all future buildings, or if impracticable in certain cases, the buildings should be erected in direct consultation with him. It would then be possible to ensure the unity which was so essential in a town planning scheme of this magnitude." Stone was specified as the building material to be used and the city engineer obliged to submit his plans for a diverted ring road around the site after examination on the ground with the town planner and "the Architect Mr. E. Mendelsohn."

This resolution was the result of a calculated campaign waged both by Mendelsohn and the Mandatory administration. Just days before the commission convened, Mendelsohn met with Wauchope, who not only offered him an additional job—to design the government hospital in Haifa—but also made it clear that, as Erich wrote to Luise, "he would not like to lose me—us." But that was a matter of friendship; the high commissioner was also ideologically and politically committed to aid in the construction of Jewish Palestine, and he had singled out Mendelsohn as the best candidate to oversee its physical design. "Of modern architects," he explained in one confidential letter to London, "I imagine he stands about first." Employing architects like him would not only help to placate Jewish demands for work but would also satisfy what Wauchope perceived somewhat paternalistically as a pressing emotional need: "In the National Homeland the Jews feel they must have opportunities to express themselves not only in tilling the soil but also in such realms as those of art and music."

Or as Mendelsohn described his conversation with Wauchope to Luise: "He said the National Home will exist as long as England exists and he wishes me to guide it architecturally—to build, as he said, all the important buildings." A few days later, Sir Arthur even sent him a confidential letter, alerting him to expect a formal invitation from London to build the Haifa hospital and declaring that "it would be one of the few joys of 1936, if you do this for us, and we secure unity of your design on Mount Scopus." To Mendelsohn, this was "one of the most friendly invitations I have ever received in all my practice . . . How different from the others—full of trust."

By calling in the Romans, though, Mendelsohn may also have gone too far for some of his Zionist patrons, who preferred to keep things within the tribe and who considered such a resort to outside power a basic betrayal. (In his angry letter to Schocken, he'd written contemptuously of the university's shameless pandering to donors like

Mrs. Rosenbloom and her son and how it "must carry the blame for a great part of the hostile attitude displayed by the non-Jewish intelligentsia of the country . . . towards Jewish urban development.") His reputation in certain Jewish circles was already murky; his arrogance was notorious, and he probably only made matters worse when he held forth in public about how, for instance, "the layout and architecture of the new buildings on Mount Scopus are bound to disappoint the layman who expects either England's domestic and baronial splendor or America's ambitious and imposing verticals." On the other hand, "no one will be disappointed who regards it in the light of the monumental austerity and serenity of the greatest spiritual creations of this part of the world—the Bible, the New Testament, and the Koran."

It wasn't just his exalted sense of himself that got him in trouble with his fellow Jews. The suspicions that surrounded him derived in large part from the unabashed warmth he displayed for both British patronage and Arab building. Bad enough that he was so chummy with the high commissioner, whom—as the revolt dragged on— many Jews had come to blame personally for not crushing "the disturbances" completely. What hardworking, flag-waving Zionist wanted to be instructed to marvel at the climatic wisdom of the Palestinian village house in the middle of an armed conflict with the very peasants who lived in the same? Or so the logic would seem from the often snide Jewish reactions to Mendelsohn's buildings and being.

In the fall of 1936, the popular Tel Aviv poet Natan Alterman put forth a mean-spirited bit of Hebrew doggerel in, of all places, *Haaretz*, the newspaper Salman Schocken himself had recently purchased. The poem summed up this attitude: "Day after day, an event takes place, a gathering, or '*reception*'—as it's called in the diaspora. / We have an ancient windmill here, a fortress for the children of Europe in Asia. / Its wings are clipped, no flour's ground there, but if there's no flour, there's fantasia . . ." And so on for another few caustic column inches, which broadly mock the "master of the reception" for attempting to embellish "our life in this country" with "English snobbism and the Orient's enchantments." And worse. In Alterman's lines, the Jewish escapists in the windmill are served by a waiter named Mahmud, "polite, civilized" who smiles at them with "a five o'clock smile," behind which lurk "1936 and 1929," years of wide-spread Arab violence toward Jews.

He didn't name the subject of his daggerlike satire, but he didn't need to.

❖

Conceived as an emphatically plain stone rectangle, meant to harmonize with the other structures to come on Mount Scopus, its single flourish a wide, roofed terrace facing out toward the Old City, Mendelsohn's streamlined university clubhouse opened officially in late January 1937. That same year, foundations were poured for the medical school; the hospital began to evolve from beams and joists to actual walls and roofs; and a scale model of his block plan for Scopus went on display at the Paris World's Fair—in the very odd company of both Picasso's *Guernica* and a towering eagle-and-swastika-capped monument to "German pride and achievement" designed by Hitler's architect, Albert Speer.

But the idea of actually building the university according to Mendelsohn's plans had, it seems, been pronounced dead. Or maybe it never lived at all. The university officials appeared more interested in the sway he was thought to hold with the British authorities than with his visual (not to mention visionary) sense of what this place could be. In order to secure permits from the Town Planning Commission to build Weiss's version of the Rosenbloom Building, they needed to show a plan, and Mendelsohn had conveniently rendered such a plan—though as Schocken himself admitted in a 1938 letter to a colleague, this had been a "sheer fantasy of Mr. Mendelsohn's, which nobody ever seriously thought to be a real plan for the future building work of the University in accordance with its real needs."

Magnes, meanwhile, had done a complete about-face with regard to Mendelsohn. He denounced the spare clubhouse as "a singularly unsuccessful building" and said the medical center "strikes ever so many persons as inappropriate for Mount Scopus." More than that, he declared himself "absolutely opposed" to Mendelsohn's appointment as consulting architect and now stepped up to defend the judgment of the chronically naysaying Mr. Green, whose work, Magnes reported in an exasperated letter to Schocken, "has been sound and solid and has saved the University thousands of pounds." High art, in other words, was hardly what was called for in times like these, and the presence of a diva like Mendelsohn had only been a drain. "I do not think the University should be put into the hands of any architect as a permanent consultant, no matter who he may be."

Magnes's problem with Mendelsohn wasn't political so much as personal. If anything, the rabbi's ardently pacifist vision of a binational Palestine was much closer to Mendelsohn's idea of Arab-Jewish synthesis than that of perhaps anyone else involved in this conversation. He simply disliked and mistrusted the architect in what seemed an almost visceral way and was, he wrote to Schocken, "astonished" to hear him defending Mendelsohn at a recent meeting as "the first Jew in two thousand years who is really building." (And what, he asked, "about the great synagogue at Toledo?") In Magnes's opinion, Mendelsohn was highly suspect, "first . . . because his style has aroused such violent and widespread opposition among many different types of person . . . And second, because it seems to be the unanimous opinion that Mr. Mendelsohn is an exceedingly difficult man to deal with. You yourself characterized him once to me as 'ein gefährlicher Mensch' "—a dangerous man.

But Magnes did have a certain tendency to overstate his case. And Mendelsohn's demanding personality seemed the least of the

dangers lurking. Threats ranged from the "bomb of a very dangerous type" that Yassky reported was found in a concrete mixer on the
hospital building site one autumn day in 1938 (it was discovered
before it detonated, though as he wrote to Hadassah's New York office, "We must . . . envisage the possibility of the Arabs making a
large scale attempt to destroy the buildings by bombs, dynamite,
etc.") to the far more sinister rumblings of war that could be heard
all the way from England, Germany, and the Sudetenland.

"The political events have taken our breath away here," Erich
wrote Luise from Jerusalem that same month. (This time, she'd traveled to Wales.) Even though Europe was far off, "this land is full of
its own dangers. But the fate of the Jews is so bound up with the fate
of the world in general that we cannot distance ourselves." Although
newspapers had been hard to come by, he'd managed to get to a
friend's radio to listen to Chamberlain's speech about his conciliatory
talks with "Herr Hitler" in Munich, and it seemed to him "the pro-
logue to a tragedy, the course of which had become unstoppable."

Afterward, he told her, he lay awake all night, obsessing about
what to do—flee Palestine, without staying to see his buildings'
completion, or hold on, risk conscription in the British army and
"separation from you for who knows how long and under what
circumstances?"

At first, he'd resigned himself to being carried along by events.
But the next morning, he asked about flights, "debating whether it
was advisable to remain where I was or to take my chances of getting
shot down over the Mediterranean." It was a cruel twist on his old
fascination. The sea that once enchanted him so, with its "play of blue
upon blue in eternal ease," now seemed ominously cold and dark, a
kind of liquid tomb.

CITY OF REFUGEES

"INSTEAD OF PRAYING—" HE WROTE LUISE ON YOM KIPPUR, THE
Day of Atonement, October 1938, "I have piled my table high with
garden plans for all the buildings, color particulars, arrangements,
surrounding walls, interior rooms, new sketches for chandeliers and
the bronze doors for the bank." He'd spent hours walking the Hadassah site the day before and sounded excited yet not quite satisfied—
irritated at having been denied money for extra flowers and trees,
which he needed in order to soften the lines of the bare buildings.
These funds were instead used "so that the machinery in the hospital should look shiny and luxurious and should hit the Americans
in the eye." If the whole complex were built right now, he boasted,
"even the bourgeois would hold their tongues."

Like so much about his life at the time, this letter swung pendu-
lously between light and shadow. One minute, he was marveling at
the clarity of the sky, the blissful sunshine of Jerusalem that autumn,
and the next he was spiraling down into the darkest despair. He
hadn't been seeing anyone, he told her. He was disgusted by small
talk. He knew he'd be "uprooted, probably for the rest of my life . . .
I feel lost in a world that has lost itself."

These drastic shifts of tone might be chalked up to his strong
feeling for counterpoint. "Rehavia is full of unrest," he wrote her
earlier that year. "All one can do is play Bach, Wagner, and Mozart—
with the windows open—and try to dream one's way out of the

present." Such ecstatic oscillation had, however, by now given way to something much less musical, and more painful. His sense of drift was palpable. Commuting between Jerusalem and London at first seemed to afford him the best of several distinct worlds. But recently his commissions in England—never plentiful—had completely dried up, and in Palestine each project was fraught with extreme, extra-architectural difficulty. In both cases, his buildings had met severe public ambivalence, or worse. Though his British work had been praised in certain circles, his fluid forms were still considered by most Englishmen to be, like himself, "alien" to that landscape. In Palestine, many of his Zionist patrons seemed more devoted to the cause of building a homeland than to the intricacies of actual build-ing. His work there may also have been, ironically, somehow *too* bound to the "native" landscape for popular tastes. All this—combined with the tense atmosphere that permeated both cities that fall, with needy refugees here and needy refugees there, bombs exploding here and the threat of bombs dropping there—seemed to have brought about in him something of a crisis.

Much as Luise understood the causes of his depression, she'd later admit that his black mood during this period startled her. And it was no longer merely a personal matter or internal tug-of-war. As he knew, and others were telling him with growing impatience, the time had come for him to decide once and for all where he planned to live and work, and to make that decision public. "You need," warned his old Berlin friend Kurt Blumenfeld, now settled in Pales-tine and an important figure in the institutional life of the Jewish state in the making, "to choose between Jerusalem and London. The situation as it stands is untenable." Mendelsohn had further opportu-nities in Palestine, but his continued absence complicated matters, as did the extremely mixed messages he'd been sending about his role there: Was he coming or going? Guest or resident? Blumenfeld was sure, he wrote, that if Mendelsohn were to declare his unchecked commitment to Palestine, the general attitude toward him would change.

And Chaim Yassky—who'd been one of his most patient and un-wavering supporters over the years—recounted for Mendelsohn a long conversation he'd had with Schocken, during which they discussed

his "problem." And here Yassky echoed Blumenfeld almost verba-
tim, explaining that while he believed "every effort should be made
by responsible Jewish bodies to enable you to continue your work in
Palestine . . . you must make up your mind to make your home in
this country and to do your share toward its upbuilding together
with the rest of us." The doctor was not one to mince words, and his
diagnosis sounded if not quite fatal, then final: "By acting like a
'Prima donna,' you will be unable to attain that end since the only
recognized prima donna here is Palestine itself."

If his friends' admonitions and the pressure building up in his own
chest weren't enough to sway him one way or another, history itself
soon forced him to pitch his old penchant for dialectics and at last
make a firm decision.

Erich and Luise became British citizens in August 1938, and now
the rampaging mobs of November had shattered both Jewish shop
windows throughout Germany and any last illusion the Mendelsohns
might have had about the future of that country. They used their
brand-new English passports to do whatever they could to yank her
mother, their sisters, their sisters' husbands and children from the
jaws of near-certain death. Erich had made his way back to London
that same month as he and Luise scrambled to secure visas for their
families. The process took several agonizing months and required
them to provide bank-certified pledges that they would assume full
financial responsibility for each of their asylum-seeking relatives.
During this time, Erich was besieged by other refugees, acquaintances and strangers alike, who had heard of his "success." Once
powerful and well-connected bankers, scientists, civil servants, they
were now unemployed, impoverished, and reduced to pleading for
his help. He did what he could for them, which wasn't much. Soon
the Mendelsohns' relatives began to make their way to London
and gradually filled their cramped Mayfair apartment or sought out
rooms for rent in nearby boardinghouses, where Erich paid their bills.
Though he and Luise had little money to spare, there was for once no
question of what they must do.

However tight their living quarters and budget had become of
late, their situation was still a good deal better than that of most of

those around them. In February 1939, the Royal Institute of British
Architects unanimously voted to make Erich Mendelsohn a fellow.
He seemed to have arrived at long last on the English architectural
scene, though—true to wavering form—the very same month of
that arrival, he began plotting their next flight.

England wasn't far enough from Germany, and, in February 1939,
he insisted that Luise accompany him to Jerusalem. When they
reached Palestine after a grueling three-day air and car trip that took
them from Croydon Airport to Marseille to Corfu to Athens to the
Greek island of Kastellorizo to Tripoli to Beirut to Tel Aviv, the options before them seemed starker than ever. This inching journey
had only sharpened, in fact, the contrast between their two worlds.
England's foggy darkness behind them, they touched down in the
bright light of the Palestinian spring, and everything seemed clearer.

Now it was just a matter of time before he made the decision final.
When he returned alone to London a few months later, he wrote
that "the aggravating situation here" had simplified matters, and he
worked quickly to pack up their belongings, arrange housing for their
families, and close his British office. The tension in England was stifling. Building conditions were "reactionary," and he smelled both
nationalism and anti-Semitism in the air. Oswald Mosley and his Fas-
cists were drawing large crowds to their meetings; there was almost
no construction taking place that wasn't connected to war, and what
work there was went to architects "of British parentage." On top of
that, the weather was bad: "not one bit of sunshine, cold and unpleasant." As he absorbed all this, "bombs explode . . . I feel strongly the
entire atmosphere—unreal and pregnant with disaster. Just as it was
in 1914 before the outbreak of the war. Only this time it will be
worldwide."

Back in Jerusalem, meanwhile, the flowers were blooming; Luise
walked the Rehavia streets and heard live Beethoven quartets spilling over stone walls . . .

And so—jarringly—their most peaceful period in Jerusalem began, with the world poised on the edge of war. It's odd, perhaps, that
the city should have seemed to them so placid during these days of
all days. Objectively speaking, tensions were high. Massive British

troop reinforcements had poured into the country to squelch what remained of the revolt. In an attempt to win the allegiance of the Arabs to the Allies, the British government had published a White Paper that strictly limited Jewish immigration and land-purchasing rights. Nixing earlier proposals for partition, it declared plans to establish "within ten years an independent Palestine State . . . in which Arabs and Jews share in government in such a way as to ensure that the essential interests of each community are safeguarded." The official Zionist bodies denounced this as a "Black Paper," nothing less than the "liquidation of the National Home," and demonstrations both peaceful and violent broke out throughout the land; the Irgun launched a terror campaign against British and Arab targets. Yet somehow, for Erich and Luise and their neighbors in Rehavia, life hummed along at a relatively low pitch. Compared to the situation in Europe, after all, the situation in Palestine seemed nearly pacific. At the same time, after years in transit, the Mendelsohns had finally come to rest in one spot, the downstairs of their beloved windmill. With less work lately for his assistants, and a much more urgent need for income, they moved into the office space below and rented the top floors to a friend.

Refugees were everywhere now in Jerusalem. Out-of-work German Jews still grasped their good leather briefcases and hurried along officiously, as if late for important meetings. One Austrian journalist the Mendelsohns knew arrived in Jerusalem with nothing to wear but embroidered lederhosen and a Tyrol hat. Decked out in this absurd Alpine outfit, he greeted every passerby with a beaming "Shalom."

The woman Gottfried Benn would one day call "the greatest lyric poet Germany ever had," Else Lasker-Schüler, also surfaced in town, almost starving. Looking more than slightly lunatic, with her unwashed blue caftan and flowing black skirt, her hair wild and dyed in red patches underneath a leopard-skin cap, she was seventy years old and penniless. Having hastily fled Nazi Berlin in 1933, she'd made her way to Switzerland, and now to Palestine, where she was planning only to visit, but, trapped by the threat of war and by Swiss paperwork, she wound up living in a tiny unheated room with no bed. With her haggard yet somehow ageless bearing, "the whole of her seemed," one acquaintance from this period would later remember, "as if carved from a mandrake root." The Mendelsohns' friend and Rehavia neighbor, Vienna-born architect and painter Leopold Krakauer, enlisted Luise's help in arranging to provide for the once heralded, now tormented poet.

Krakauer had come to the right place. Though they'd never met, Luise had been "deeply impressed" by Lasker-Schüler's work and her flamboyant bearing since the poet trawled the cafés of Berlin in the teens and twenties, and now Luise found herself enchanted by her "fiery black" eyes, her "beautiful deep voice," and her hyperbolic imagination, from which would often pour forth the most elaborate orientalist effusions. Acclaimed in Germany since before the Great War, her "Hebrew Ballads" color the stories of various Old Testament figures with an entire expressionist's paint box of bold flourishes and shadowy flecks—cloaks of gold and silvery goats and monkey bites and lanternless nights. Together these "Hebraic" lyrics constitute what the poet would later pronounce, without a trace of irony, her contribution "to the building of Palestine." And her fascination with a phantasmagorical East extended well beyond written verse. For years she'd toyed with various mythical personae—Jussuf the Prince of Thebes, Tino of Baghdad, the Black Swan of Israel, whether dressing up and playing these parts or rendering quirky drawings of her exotic alter egos bedecked in turbans and pointy slippers. Perhaps not surprisingly, Jerusalem brought out the most outlandishly theatrical, or delusional, in her.

When she first visited the city in 1934, Gershom Scholem—yet another Rehavia neighbor—wrote his old friend Walter Benjamin, then in Paris, to report on the presence in town of the poet, "a really bewildering figure . . . who would fit in better in any other country in the world than in the real Orient." He described how she'd claimed to have conducted a thirty-minute conference with King David "about which she now demands kabbalistic edification from me," though a few days later Scholem abandoned his perplexity for pity. She was, he wrote Benjamin, "a ruin, more haunted than inhabited by madness." That said, she was one endlessly *inventive* ruin. On returning to Zurich after that first trip, she wrote a highly eccentric prose poem of an illustrated travelogue, *The Land of the Hebrews*, that drew more from her own wishful thinking and psalm-fueled fantasies than anything she could possibly have encountered in that land itself. "Arab children play with Hebrew children on the side streets of the Jaffa Road," she gushed. "Why not the people of all lands?" The idea of the earthly Jerusalem as being somehow heavenly—both pure and purifying—enthralled her. "Every guest who enters this city," she rhapsodized, "exchanges his clothes for holy garments. This pious transformation obliges all to behave solemnly and courteously, so as not to startle the devout spirit of the exquisite, exalted city . . . I have never," she raved on, "heard an excessively loud word or a shrill sound in Jerusalem."

She must not have been listening—or looking, for that matter. One Jerusalem acquaintance would later describe *The Land of the Hebrews* as "a terrifying muddle of grotesque errors and magnificent insights, an extravagant, incoherent, moody book marked by utter irresponsibility toward the actual facts of the reality which she had seen and fled." Contemplating her drawings of Jerusalem, as a "wonderful fairy city," complete with Greek monks dressed as Roman noblemen, "wonder rabbis clad in costly garments of gold paper," a Mexican wizard named Komma of Cairo, as well as dervishes and bagpipers, promenading together on the Jaffa Road, another commentator would pronounce it "a pity that the . . . spectacles she wears cannot be purchased at the opticians."

Or, as Luise—whom Lasker-Schüler had taken to calling "Athena"—would put it, more simply but with a note of gentle envy: "She lived entirely in her own world. She had no connection at all to reality." At one point, soon after her return to the city in 1939, the poet proposed to Salman Schocken that he "throw away all the books" and that they instead band together to build an enormous fairground at the center of Rehavia. In this way, "we'll reconcile the Jewish people and the Arabs." She herself planned to lead the children in rousing rounds of Hebrew and Arabic folk songs and "solve the Jewish-Arab problem" by erecting collapsible stalls, a simple wooden carousel hung with colorful glass beads, and "also a waffle stand."

Her schemes for conflict-erasing carnivals aside, Lasker-Schüler's blithe disregard for the gritty facts of life in present-day Palestine may have been more willful than her critics claimed. For all her published descriptions of Jerusalem as "the healing bath of the soul" and "God's chosen bride in the land of Palestine," she had in fact been shocked by her encounter with the city and—as early as her 1934 visit—confessed to a friend that the experience had been so unsettling, "I can no longer maintain my one-time belief in the greatness of the Jews." Now stranded in a dingy room at the none-too-Viennese Hotel Vienna, she felt miserably lonely and out of place—not unlike Erich Mendelsohn, in fact, lost in a world that had lost itself. "The Dimdumim begin," she'd write Schocken, in a far less festive mood, planting the Hebrew word for dusk in the middle of her German letter. "The twilight that is just as sad as I am. I imagined existence in Jerusalem differently. I am so deeply disappointed . . . I am sinking into myself and will die of sadness here."

As she may or may not have realized, she was also the butt of jokes among those Luise described as "young pioneers," who had "no patience, no sympathy for a person living in a dream world." The children made fun of her as well, following her down the streets of Jerusalem and taunting her, calling her a witch. Drawn to "this exceptional woman," Luise defended her, as she seized on the cause—making Lasker-Schüler's rescue her personal mission. All her years rallying behind Erich the often misunderstood artist, Erich the Oriental from East Prussia, Erich the stubborn visionary seem to have prepared Luise well for this far more extreme case, and she convinced Schocken and the Jewish Agency to provide Lasker-Schüler with a small stipend—much of which the poet wound up spending on bird food. Once described as a "solitary, exotic night bird" herself, and someone whose hands resembled a hawk's talons, she seemed happiest on a park bench dispensing bread crumbs to the pigeons and sparrows.

In the meantime, Luise and Krakauer arranged for her to give a reading in the windmill. This would be a benefit, and, as Luise explained, "the entrance tickets would have to be quite expensive."

When she arrived to inspect the mill, the poet seemed at first suspicious and then "more and more fascinated" until she erupted in a rapturous cry that, as Luise would quote her, "This is where I belong; this is part of a Jerusalem I dreamed of and could not find so far. Here I will read my Biblical poems." As Luise led her around and showed her the garden, she continued to effuse: "All the people who

will come to my reading have to come on camels, and those beautiful animals must find shelter under this fig tree."

In the end, the windmill proved too small—as Lasker-Schüler
reported excitedly to a friend the day before the big event, more than
twenty-five people had bought tickets—so Luise proposed that they
move the proceedings just around the block, to a more spacious
venue, Erich's very own Schocken Library.

And there, on a Monday evening in late June 1939, in the austere
lemonwood reading room on the second floor of one of the finest new
buildings in the new Jerusalem, Jussuf the Prince of Thebes appeared
in her usual blue caftan and leopard-skin cap. Facing a temperature-
controlled wall of glass-fronted, bronze-rimmed shelves filled with
the former department store magnate's rare German and Hebrew
first editions, she took her place at a small table, framed by two candles and placed inside Mendelsohn's signature Rembrandt window.
Though he'd designed it several years earlier, before Lasker-Schüler's
arrival in town, he seemed somehow to have anticipated this unlikely occasion and conceived the rounded glass enclosure precisely
with it, and her, in mind.

But it was more than the window that marked the peculiar inevi-
tability of the gathering. It was almost as though the room had been
awaiting the performance of this rite, a kind of consecration. Perhaps
the architect's most immaculate Jerusalem construction of all, the space
had always suggested a modern, secular holy of holies—the very
heart of this bookish building at the heart of this city of the Building
and the Book. These were strange, dark days, and now, in a somehow
suitably strange and dark way, the great broken poet filled the role of
high priest(ess) as she rang the tiny bells strung around her wrists and
intoned her "biblical" poems to a rapt crowd of learned refugees. Her
German words echoed against the walls and floor, the ceiling and
shelves, the glass panes of that oriel window that Erich Mendelsohn
himself had built here in the would-be land of the Hebrews. And
for a single night, all the world's woes were pushed aside as the
exiles were restored to what it was they'd lost—a place they used to
call home.

PALESTINE AND
THE WORLD OF TOMORROW

NOW THAT MENDELSOHN HAD FINALLY MADE UP HIS MIND TO BE
here and only here, in Jerusalem, there was very little for him to do.
War seemed imminent, and in a matter of months he'd put the finishing touches on all the major projects that had consumed him for
the last several years.

Declared "A Record of Speed and Efficiency" by *The Palestine
Post*, the construction of his government hospital in Haifa took place
in a relative flash. Commissioned in August 1936, it opened its doors
in December 1938. Although Mendelsohn spoke proudly of the way it
"follows the sweep of the blue bay and the tender contour of Mount
Carmel—the real one," the design of the hospital had also made him
extremely uneasy. His first and only government commission in Palestine had required him to follow British Colonial Office regulations
and separate the wards into those for "white people" (English citizens and soldiers) and "natives" (Arabs and Jews). It was, he'd write
a few years later, as the tensions in Palestine continued to mount, "a
policy which does not seem to be producing amity in Haifa at the
moment." In fact, the only patients to use the hospital were English
and Arab. Because of British policies in general—and segregation
at the hospital in particular—Jews would boycott the hospital until 1948.

Troubles, though, loomed all around, and they tended to over-
shadow Mendelsohn's ostensible architectural triumphs—or throw

into very curious relief the festivities that surrounded them. Against what had often seemed insurmountable odds, building at the medical center on Mount Scopus finally came to a close in May 1939, though this fact was relegated to a small second-page item in the local newspapers, pushed to the side by the endless anxious coverage of the immigration-restricting White Paper, which would be announced and loudly denounced that very same month. Again Yassky and Mendelsohn led a large group of journalists and dignitaries around the Scopus site. This time, however, the tour was a subdued affair, "as, under present circumstances," according to one report, "it was not thought proper to hold a large-scale celebration, but to go ahead with the work on hand in a quiet and business-like fashion."

In fact, some celebrating did take place, but it did so behind closed doors. On the occasion of the Hadassah inauguration, the Schockens held an "at home" for a hundred carefully selected invitees. (After praising the project and its various patrons and planners, the host offered a toast to Mendelsohn, the medical center's architect, and, as it happens, architect of the very room where the guests milled and sipped their drinks.) And Erich and Luise themselves threw a reception to mark the buildings' completion and the arrival in Palestine of the exiled German conductor Hermann Scherchen, an old friend. He had come to lead the Palestine Symphony Orchestra in multiple concerts over several months. His first appearance in Jerusalem was dedicated to Bach, Busoni, and Bruckner, and after various speeches in the maestro's honor, as one newspaper account had it, "dancing in the floodlit Windmill continued until dawn, when Mr. Mendelsohn conducted a party over the newly completed building of the Hadassah University Medical Centre of which he was the architect."

But it was hard to keep dancing as the bombs went off. Hours after the White Paper became official, the Irgun detonated a car battery packed with explosives at the Department of Immigration on Queen Melisande Way, and the next day peaceful protests in Jerusalem devolved into rioting, with Jewish mobs smashing shop windows near the government buildings downtown and shooting to death a British policeman. The battle between the stone-throwing throng and the baton-wielding police raged on for three hours, and when the crowds at last dispersed, barricades of stone, large pieces of corrugated iron, wood from a telephone booth, iron girders, and box springs lay scattered across the road. Since the stampeding hordes had gone to the trouble of destroying all the streetlamps in the area, the city center would remain submerged in darkness for weeks.

In the ensuing May days, large nonviolent demonstrations continued, though within a month two more bombs exploded at an Arab-owned movie house on nearby Princess Mary Avenue (later renamed for a Jewish queen, Shlomzion), shattering every pane of glass in the building, blowing the doors from their hinges, blasting a crater in the floor, and injuring eighteen audience members, most of them Arabs. "WRECKAGE AT THE REX" screamed the headlines.

After that particular bombing, all the Jewish cinemas and cafés in town were ordered closed by military order and "as a punishment for the firing by Jews upon Arab buses," certain Jewish buses were grounded as well. But a homicidal sort of routine had already taken hold, as the Irgun planted four more bombs near the Jaffa Gate, killing five Arabs and injuring nineteen; a young Jewish woman tried to sneak a bomb in a picnic basket into the middle of a crowd of Arabs who'd come to visit their relatives at the Central Prison on a Friday afternoon. Several days later the Irgun targeted the brand-new general post office a few streets away and planted three gelig-nite packages there, including one that detonated in the face of the very same British sapper who'd managed to defuse the bomb at the prison.

He was killed instantly and an enormous hole blown in the counter, its place taken by shattered glass, mangled steel supports, and broken blocks of concrete. Large chunks of ceiling had collapsed and now lay strewn across the marble floors of the main hall, completed with fanfare just a year before.

But construction and destruction were—are—bound together in this city to an almost perverse degree. The week the post office bombs exploded, Mendelsohn's newest building opened right beside it on the Jaffa Road, and the same newspaper whose pages were otherwise filled with accounts of "wanton sabotage and tragic loss of life" proclaimed that "today another monument in stone may be hailed as evidence of past achievement and hope of future progress." Even as the rubble from the post office blast was being cleared, the seven-story perpendicular and low attached block that together formed Mendelsohn's Anglo-Palestine Bank admitted customers for the very first time.

Long before all hell broke loose next door and the newly built bank tower provided troops of the British Black Watch with a con-venient perch from which to patrol the riots, he'd conceived this two-part structure as a way of reckon-ing with both the highly uneven terrain and strict town-planning bylaws. The horizontal in the back kept to permitted height while the tall, clean-edged portion that faced the busier street called to mind, he hoped, the "stark verticals" of the traditional buildings of Hebron. All in all, he meant the bank's variable levels to invoke, once more, the gently stepped villages of the Judean countryside. Curved

window grilles, the narrow strip of a long, mounted flagpole, the massive embossed bronze doors, and dozens of slender torch-shaped sconces all punctuated the imposing yet unfussy façade in terms that Mendelsohn himself described in typically elevated fashion. In a newspaper article meant to introduce the bank building and explain yet again his architectural approach to a probably distracted and/or skeptical public, he wrote that "he who knows the Mediterranean Sea—not only from Tel Aviv—who remembers the coloured stone fronts of Venice and Damascus and at the same time the button-like bronze ornaments of the Florentine Palazzi and the contrast-ing colour scheme of Jaffa's mosque will recognize the interchange of naked and ornamental stone walls as the true nature of the house of a nobleman or an important business firm."

Reading his words now, three-quarters of a century later, there seems something overly solicitous in these attempts to articulate the power and dignity that he meant to convey with his building. He didn't need to sound quite so defensive. As he and all his readers knew, the bank represented a major Zionist institution. It was also the most centrally located building he'd designed for the city so far, occupying as it did—and still does, all these years later—a pivotal spot on the modern town's main street.

Yet Mendelsohn seemed to realize better than anyone just how little his grand ideas about bronze ornaments and contrasting color schemes, to say nothing of Florentine palazzi and the stone fronts of Damascus, really mattered to most of those who'd deposit checks and arrange for loans at this bank. What counted right now were political symbols, facts on the ground, ideological bottom lines. And though it went completely unmentioned in his article, published a mere week after the explosion, the bombing next door seemed to have rattled him, as in his very opening paragraph he made a point of describing his bank in relation to the post office, which was "the most frequented public building [in the city]" and one whose "architectural importance is of a great artistic value."

It shouldn't have come as a surprise that the terrorists had set their sights on the post office. The largest and costliest government building constructed by the British in Palestine, it stood as an obvious emblem of Mandatory rule, and for those enraged at the White Paper and violently opposed to all it represented, the building seemed an ideal target.

What the terrorists didn't and couldn't see, however, and what Erich Mendelsohn himself was painfully aware of was that while the post office was certainly meant to be a substantial, formal, and very *English* structure in all ways, it also bore the subtle private stamp of its builder, the veteran British government architect Austen St. Barbe Harrison. A highly refined and reclusive lifelong expatriate whose work and temperament drew him out of England and to the East as a young man and whose extensive knowledge of Islamic and Byzantine building informed even his most stately colonial structures, Harrison had lived and worked in Palestine for fifteen years, beginning in 1922. The post office, his final finished project in the country, was also his final statement about the possibilities of building there. With its neatly staggered blocks of hand-cut stone from the quarries of the nearby Arab village of Beit Safafa, its arched windows and ornamented wooden doors, its Syrian-styled stripes of alternating black basalt and pale gray *ablaq* masonry, the post office was and would remain a structure that—like Mendelsohn's own throughout the city—draws from traditions both Eastern and Western, local and foreign, ancient and modern, and fuses them all into a somehow dynamic and logical whole.

But why, really, should the bomb-wielding brigades of England-loathing Revisionists have cared about any of that? Harrison was neither a Jew nor a Zionist, and if anything, all his fine feeling for "Arab" architecture made him doubly suspect in the eyes of those determined to forge a Jewish state in blood and fire. In the brutal new context of national score settling that had seized hold of Palestine these past few years, there was no place left for a sensibility as singular and circumspect as Harrison's, a fact he himself had grasped and taken to heart. By the time the high commissioner snipped a ceremonial ribbon, stood to the strains of "God Save the King," and proclaimed the post office open for business the previous summer, Harrison had vanished from Palestine and the Colonial Service both, tiptoeing away as quickly and quietly as he could.

While the Anglo-Palestine Bank building itself was unlikely to be the target of Jewish terrorists—the first part of its name aside, the bank was more or less the financial arm of the Jewish state in the making, working to acquire land, develop agricultural settlements, and plan urban neighborhoods of a distinctly Zionistic sort—Mendelsohn felt the need to defend Harrison and his building, for reasons at once political and aesthetic. Of course he was, in a very real sense, also defending *himself* and the vision of a cosmopolitan Jerusalem that both he and Harrison had aspired to create. As he did so, he was, too, standing up for a way of being in the world and with other human beings—not only other Jewish human beings—and of living outside the mental ghetto that this place was quickly becoming. Connected through friendship to Mendelsohn's old Mediterranean Academy colleague, the sculptor and typographer Eric Gill, the two had sometimes socialized. (Gill had visited Palestine twice in the last several years, working on a series of bas-reliefs for Harrison's Palestine Archaeological Museum and a rounded "tree of life" for the side of Mendelsohn's Haifa hospital.) Though they weren't exactly close, and their personal and architectural styles were quite distinct, they seemed, during Harrison's time in Palestine, kindred spirits. Before his departure, in fact, Harrison was perhaps the only other architect working in Palestine whom the highly critical and none-too-modest Mendelsohn considered his peer and equal.

With Harrison's hasty exit from the Jerusalem stage, Mendelsohn was even more alone than before: "Your leaving Palestine for good has greatly affected me," he wrote the British architect in early January 1938, c/o Cook's Travelling Office, Cairo, "because I always felt and emphasized that your works are of the highest value to Palestine and should stand for ever as examples of your great mastership of bridging the past and the times to come."

But Mendelsohn's work, too, spanned centuries. And on Jaffa Road, the stone walls of his bank and Harrison's post office remain poised in charged conversation—with each other, with the street where they stand—even now, long after their builders have gone.

Around the time that Harrison fled Palestine, Mendelsohn's friend and patron Arthur Wauchope also announced his resignation, and a different high commissioner replaced him—one far less inclined to sip champagne, listen to Bach, and arrange for architectural commissions with a freethinking Jewish free agent like him. Under the new regime at Government House (another of Harrison's slyly ageless buildings, built just a few years before), "the book shelves no longer housed the poets," according to one British eyewitness, "but cheap editions of crime novels." While the dandyish Sir Arthur had played host to a nearly nonstop salon throughout his years in Palestine—with concerts, cocktail parties, and art all around—his replacement, Sir Harold MacMichael, had other, more basic tastes and counted as his "hobbies" "maps, reading detective stories, collecting semi-precious stones and cutting down trees."

Soon after, Salman Schocken also started preparing to leave. A gradual process, which began with extended trips abroad to raise funds for the Hebrew University, it would end when he decamped in October 1940 on one of those junkets and simply didn't return. Although he had recently transplanted his eponymous publishing house to Tel Aviv from Berlin—where it had been looted by Nazi gangs in the wake of Kristallnacht and was eventually forced to close—he'd been eyeing the exits from Palestine for some time now.

Like Mendelsohn, he'd found himself increasingly at odds with this rough-and-tumble setting. Before Hitler's rise to power, he felt, he said, "in the mix" in Germany. Here in Palestine he was outside any such a mix. The politicians saw him, he complained, as someone who just gave money; they didn't turn to him for advice. Although he had invested seriously in the revival of secular Hebrew intellectual culture, he hadn't ever really learned the language, and despite his ostensibly powerful position as publisher of one of the country's leading newspapers and head of the university's board of trustees, he lived on the cultural margins, which is to say in the very villa that Mendelsohn had built according to his exacting Prussian specifications. While the house once provided shelter from the harsh context in which it was constructed, its marble floors, lavish gardens, and elegant swimming pool now seemed only to underscore the fact that he did not belong here. There was a certain irony in this belated realization. The Schockens had wanted a sleek little palace just like Am Rupenhorn. Mendelsohn had provided it. And as with the dream house Erich built for Luise on the shores of Lake Havel, the Schockens abandoned this Palestinian version after a few scant years.

With Schocken's going, a part of Mendelsohn went, too.

In Europe war had finally erupted, and this far-off conflagration had in a way banked the local fires. It wasn't that Palestine's problems had gone away, of course, but that they'd been temporarily muffled. "We are still in the midst of peace which the outbreak of the war has made—a contradiction in itself—a real one," wrote Erich to a British friend at the start of 1940. "Internal strife has completely stopped and we enjoy again the beauty of the country's first spring: the cover of fresh green, an abundance of flowers and oranges with which even the most greedy ones cannot cope."

Besides eating all that plentiful citrus, though, Erich didn't have much to do. He'd recently wound up work on a cavernous research laboratory that Chaim Weizmann entrusted to him at his institute in Rehovot, and he had completed a commission for an agricultural college in the same town. But in the frustrating absence of other old allies and new commissions, he felt isolated and idle, and so turned his thoughts to rendering plans for a different kind of structure, one for which he'd be both patron and architect: an edifice made of words.

"Palestine and the World of Tomorrow" was, for Mendelsohn, an unusually rickety construction—a slender yet unwieldy pamphlet, written in his awkward and often overblown and misspelled English and privately printed in Jerusalem, February 1940. Whatever it lacked of his usual architectonic grace and control, however, the short essay more than made up for by way of passion, ambition, and—that old obsession—*vision*. More directly than ever before, in fact, it set forth his most vatic prescription for the political and cultural future of the land, and in a way what he wrote there brought him full circle, back to those "explosions of imagination" he was so desperate to capture on small slips of paper while stationed as a young soldier on the Russian Front. Whether or not anyone would actually *build* what he planned was, in other words, almost beside the point. Convinced of the worth and originality of his ideas, he was determined now to fix them on the page for their own sake.

Urgent manifesto, rambling disquisition, fervent plea—the pamphlet begins by offering a sweeping view of no less than six thousand years of Mediterranean history, from Egypt's invention of the alphabet to the Phoenicians' creation of coinage to Judaism's formulation of "the moral law," and so on, through Roman civics to Greek philosophy and dramatic poetry. For centuries, he writes, "the Mediterranean basin retained its place as the master of the world," and Palestine functioned as "a perpetual highway for the nations ruling the Mediterranean. Its history is tied up with the fate of those great empires." Meanwhile the "remains of its Architecture and Art" he writes, capitalizing his nouns in Germanic fashion, "reflect these manifold invasions and their influence upon its civilization."

At its heart, the architectural legacy of these empires is syncretic. He finds traces in the destroyed Jewish Temple of "a culture moulded by Babylon, Egypt, and Minoan Crete," and sees everywhere the remains of Rome, early Christianity, and Islam. Such glories, though, belong to the distant past, and just as the whole region gradually fell into decline, so did Palestine become little more than "an unimportant trade route to the Far East."

He blames the sorry state of things on the Industrial Revolution as much as on geography or Turkish rule, and after a protracted woolly ramble over the ensuing centuries and some convoluted sloganeering, Mendelsohn comes around to the actual subject—and point—of the pamphlet, which isn't really about architecture at all but the chaotic condition of the cosmos right *now*, and the possibilities this crisis offers, both for the world and for the Jewish people.

With the Emancipation, the Jews of Europe believed they might become part of the societies in which they lived, but "the nationalist and racist hatreds of the last decades" showed this hope to be misguided. Given their "national feeling, based on an undying belief in the prophecies of the Bible," Palestine was the only answer. After he waxes rhapsodic about "the return of the Jews to . . . the country of their historic origin," praising the idealism of the early settlers and the "epic battle" waged during the first five decades of "Zionist colonization," he abruptly shifts gears. In light of current events, the idea of an independent state is, he says, too narrow.

"Palestine is not an uninhabited country. On the contrary, it forms a part of the Arabian world."

And here he bursts forth into his most explicit call for action: Jews must "become a cell" of what he calls "the future Semitic commonwealth." This new entity should take its cues from the culture that found expression when the Arab empire was at its height and Arabs and Jews were the "torchbearers of world enlightenment." While Europe languished in the Dark Ages and the Jews there huddled in ghettos, the Jews of the Arab world rose to powerful political positions and created lasting works of art.

Once again, he proclaims, the time has come to bring about a "reunion of matter and spirit." The Jews, he says, "return to Palestine neither as conquerors nor as refugees. That is why they realize that the rebuilding of the country cannot be done except in communion with the original Arab population." Surveying the tumultuous years of British rule, he declares that the Mandate has run its course and that a new model is necessary.

"The gate to the Semitic world," Palestine today symbolizes "the union between the most modern civilization and the most antique culture. It is the place where intellect and vision—matter and spirit meet. In the arrangement commanded by this union both Arabs and Jews . . . should be equally interested. On its solution depends the fate of Palestine to become a part of the New-World which is going to replace the world that has gone."

"Genesis," he ends with a roll of rhetorical thunder, "repeats itself."

Or does it? Although cast in the soaring terms of a collective credo, "Palestine and the World of Tomorrow" seems in many ways a last-ditch display of willfully wishful thinking on Mendelsohn's part—an oracular howl, or cri de broken coeur. Given all that he'd witnessed in the past several years, he knew very well just how unrealistic this vision was. Obsessed as he'd been with absorbing the physical and climatic details of the place, he seemed to have given himself over one last time to the most airborne sort of illusion, as if he could pretend that all he had long imagined for Palestine were in fact the case. "The Jews," he writes in bizarrely sanguine fashion, "seem to grasp the fact that Palestine can only be built up in close collaboration with the Arabs and that she can become a place of well-being only in case both peoples come to an understanding." His rousing call for a peaceful and artful Semitic Commonwealth isn't so very far in the end from Else Lasker-Schüler's plan for a conflict-resolving waffle stand and Arab-Jewish amusement park.

On the other hand, even as he held forth publicly about his great hopes for the land and the world of tomorrow, he was also privately mired in the same old doubts and even despair, to say nothing of restlessness. "I think that Palestine must necessarily be a center for the Jews . . . ," he wrote Lewis Mumford at around this time, but "the scale of the land is very small, and its population is divided into two camps—politically and intellectually. There is no opportunity for me as architect to propagate the ideal values of my work . . . And so I often wonder whether America could not be my field of activity."

Choosing to leave Jerusalem was far less dramatic than deciding to stay.

Because of the constant delays brought about by the "disturbances," and Hadassah's regular demands for revision of his plans, the Mount Scopus commission had cost him a great deal of extra time and money, and now that it was complete, he wrote Yassky in the spirit of their "close and harmonious collaboration" to ask if—as he said had been promised him by a gentleman's agreement at the project's outset—they might now offer him additional payment: "Even the most malevolent could not claim that your Architect has been paid according to his abilities, faithfulness, and achievements."

Yassky agreed and tried to intervene with the board. And though he praised Mendelsohn's conscientious work and described the "rather precarious" state of the architect's finances, those in charge of the checkbooks were unmoved. Rose Halprin, chair of the Palestine Committee, could offer only a primly maddening letter in which she informed Mendelsohn that Hadassah had decided not to pay him any more, though "we need hardly point out that in no wise is this a lack of appreciation of the great achievement for which all thanks are due you." Payment, after all, was secondary, as "we know how much gratification you have derived from serving Palestine through the erection of the Medical Centre. We are happy that public acknowl-edgment has come to you for your share in the work . . ." and so on. This cheerful brush-off was enough to send Mendelsohn into an apoplectic fit. He shot back that he had "for years devoted" his "technical and artistical ability to Hadassah's work without thinking of the disastrous financial clauses of a contract" he'd been "persuaded to accept." They had given him a promise in which he'd trusted.

"Your letter, dear Mrs. Halprin, has shattered my confidence and I must leave it at that, if Hadassah does not find her way to do justice to my cause. Words of praise and promises for the future cannot change my attitude."

He'd continued to take on piecemeal work for the university— completing designs for a modest gym and nearby playing field in 1939 and, together with Schocken, judging an architectural com-petition for a small museum there. But it was now perfectly clear that with Schocken gone and Magnes hostile to him, he wouldn't be planning the campus as a whole. He asked for the return of his scale model for his "collection of unrealized projects" and in turn the university asked him—without a hint of shame—for a cash dona-tion. While there were again murmurings about arranging for him to teach architecture on Mount Scopus, with Weizmann even tele-graphing Schocken at his new perch in New York's Delmonico Hotel, SORRY HEAR MENDELSOHN MAY BE LEAVING PALESTINE . . . SUGGEST TRY UTMOST CREATE CHAIR FOR HIM AT JERUSALEM SO AS SECURE HIS SERVICES FOR COUNTRY—nothing came of that. In Wau-chope's absence, talk of entrusting him with "guiding" the country architecturally and planning "all the important buildings" had also evaporated.

"Palestine and the World of Tomorrow" had, meanwhile, only confirmed his most scornful critics in their sense of him as a de-tached snob and dangerous fantasist, if not an outright traitor. "He made himself very unpopular in Palestine with this brochure," Luise would later write, "but . . . Eric was not a diplomat and it was his whole personality to say what he thought was right. It did not make life easier for him, or for me."

All of these disappointments ached internally. There were,

however, other, outer reasons why Erich and Luise began to consider packing their bags yet again. In September 1940, Italian bombs struck Tel Aviv and the surrounding Arab villages and killed 137 people. Rommel and his troops were soon in Libya, creeping closer, and, as Luise would explain, "It seemed clear to us that when they would reach Palestine, a terrible slaughter of the Jews would occur. We had not escaped the fury of Hitler to be delivered to his fury in Palestine."

And yet . . . while all of these factors contributed to their eventual departure in March 1941, none of them alone satisfactorily explains it. If anything, Mendelsohn had come full circle, returning to the same sense that gripped him, back in 1933, that "Palestine did not call me." He was still waiting to be called. And perhaps not surprisingly, even after they'd gone—making their way first to New York and finally to San Francisco, where he found his practice confined mostly to the design of suburban American synagogues and his mood increasingly melancholy—the decision to leave was never quite final.

Over an ocean and the course of several years, he and Yassky continued to correspond warmly, though when in 1945 Mendelsohn suggested the possibility of returning to Jerusalem, should the proper commissions present themselves, Yassky sounded like he'd reached the frayed end of one very long rope: "It is up to you to reconcile those two parties, namely, Jewish Palestine and Mendelsohn. You realize that this reconciliation cannot take the form of Palestine's inviting Mendelsohn to come here. The reconciliation may take place when Mendelsohn humbly comes to Palestine as many thousands have done before and many thousands dream of doing now . . . I should be extremely sorry to see that what I mistook for your sincere desire to return to Palestine was conditioned by the number of projects which you might or might not be asked to undertake. That, my dear Eric, is a peculiar Zionism with which I personally can have nothing to do."

This letter pained Mendelsohn deeply, and he responded, "I left Palestine financially poorer than when I arrived . . . I have never looked at Palestine as a source of fortune as I haven't become an architect to be a rich man. I left Palestine when the outbreak of the war stopped every building activity without which . . . I would have become humiliatingly dependent. I have never deserted Palestine nor will I ever desert her ideals."

In fact, he'd never return in body, though in a very real way, he'd remain there, or his singular eye would, and will: Circles and cycles abound. On the mountain where the two men squinted out at the astonishing view together on that windy day in 1934, his hospital would continue to stand, long after both of them did. In it, Else Lasker-Schüler would draw her last breaths in January 1945. Driving up in an armored convoy toward it, Chaim Yassky and seventy-seven doctors, nurses, patients, orderlies, and others would be slaughtered in a notoriously grisly attack by Arab forces in April 1948, four days after Jewish forces slaughtered in a notoriously grisly attack some hundred Arab residents of the nearby village of Deir Yassin and a month before Israel declared itself a state.

"If I had the chance, I would begin again," Erich Mendelsohn wrote a friend in March 1953, "letting my earliest sketches guide me, considering all I have done since a preparation for a final, newly creative period." The next month, his doctors would discover a tumor in his thyroid gland (a different cancer from the one that took his eye three decades before), and after he died quietly that September at San Francisco's Mount Zion Hospital, his ashes were scattered to the California wind.

II

BEAUTIFUL THINGS
ARE DIFFICULT

1923

IN THE GARDEN

HAPPY TO BE ALONE IN HIS LEDGE-LIKE LITTLE GARDEN, WHICH commanded a sweeping view of the Old City walls and the flat, stepped roofs of the village he knew by the biblical name of Siloam, Austen St. Barbe Harrison sat and sketched. He was only thirty-two years old and already the reluctant veteran of several war zones, a fundamentally peaceful person whom peace seemed chronically to elude. But here in the Jerusalem neighborhood of Abu Tor—under a cypress, with his white dog, Bogie, sleeping beside him, the door to his small wallflower-laced stone house propped open to let in the breeze—the chief architect of Palestine's Public Works Department appeared to have found, or created, a quality very much like it.

The most private of public servants, Harrison knew precisely what he enjoyed and possessed an almost otherworldly ability to order the space and hours around him so that he might gently but firmly obtain that. On this particular occasion, in late October 1923, for instance, he'd requested a four-day furlough from his government-issued drafting table because he wanted to stay home and draw the village below. This leave was, he wrote his younger sister Ena, back in England, "most grudgingly agreed to by the new Director of Public Works," the kind of man "who can get no kick from anything in life" outside of the office. "He almost had a fit when I told him how I intended spending my time."

Though he led what he himself called "rather an Eremetical Existence," Harrison insisted that "I am really a sociable person despite appearances. Only I must be able to get away from society which suffocates me." Luise Mendelsohn would later describe him as a friend to her and Erich and "a very sensitive artist," though she'd add, pointedly, that "He did not like women and when I asked him to a cocktail party at the windmill he answered my invitation by saying that he never went to Cock or Hen parties."

Partygoer or no, he was devoted to his friends—several formidable females among them. (The adventurer, Arabist, and travel writer Freya Stark would become a confidante and regular correspondent after the two met in Cairo in 1940.) And later in life, Lawrence Durrell would dedicate *Bitter Lemons*, his memoir of the turbulent years he spent in Cyprus, to Harrison, his neighbor and regular companion there in the 1950s. Although Durrell quotes yet another English friend, Harrison's architectural partner in Cyprus, Pearce Hubbard, as calling him "an awful recluse . . . one wouldn't come so far from the haunts of man if one were a gregarious or clubby type," the author of *The Alexandria Quartet* understood the role that sustained friendships played in Harrison's quiet existence. "For him too," writes Durrell, of Harrison, "the island life was only made endurable" by visitors from beyond and so he had "built himself a khan or caravanserai on one of the main highways of the world" into which he welcomed these widely wandering kindred spirits.

Jerusalem may be dry and landlocked, but it's also an island, and many of the aesthetic ideals that Harrison would eventually bring to bear on his secluded Cypriot life he'd taught himself while residing in this simple three-room house in Abu Tor. For Harrison, though, it really didn't require much study, since many of these habits came to him naturally. Durrell would later remember him as representing "that forgotten world where style was not only a literary imperative but an inherent method of approaching the world of books, roses, statues and landscapes." In Cyprus, Harrison would transform a stable-like hovel into his home "with a tenderness and discretion" that made "the whole composition sing." The house seemed to Durrell "a perfect illustration of the man," with its book-lined walls and glowing icons, its point-arched loggia and lily pond that served as more than a mere function of good taste and instead embodied "an illustration of philosophic principles—an illustration of how the good life might, and how it should, be lived."

So it was in Jerusalem as well, where, working with his typical patient resolve, he'd made every inch of this unpretentious house's vaulted ceilings and stone floors his own. He'd scattered carpets and hung woodcuts on the whitewashed walls, lowered a piano into a pit in the main room, and carefully arranged a large blue-velvet-covered couch, a few oil lamps with muted orange shades, candles for reading, several armchairs, and other chairs of rush and painted wood. He'd also set his beloved gramophone into a deep window niche, from which at all hours Couperin, Bach, and Puccini spilled into the Palestinian night.

As he ordered his home and its simple yet precisely chosen and placed furnishings, so would Harrison order each building he planned in Jerusalem. From the angular ornamentation of the ventilation slits at Government House to the shady cloisters at the archaeological museum and the square carvings on the wooden doors at the central post office on the Jaffa Road, each architectural element was an expression of his keenly absorptive sensibility and of those philosophic principles Durrell describes. Having internalized the airy yet compact feel of his house in Abu Tor, he'd set out to replicate something of its cavernous, thick-walled quality in almost all his Jerusalem plans. "There is a particular kind of rubble vaulting peculiar to this country which not long before the war was everywhere employed and today is still employed outside the cities," he wrote in one official memo concerning the design of a major government building. "This vaulting merely whitewashed or painted is so pleasing to the eye that any kind of decoration or 'finish' becomes superfluous." Ironically enough, given his taxpayer-funded position and the ostensibly impersonal nature of his Palestine commissions, the unfussy symmetries and clean proportions of his humble peasant-built dwelling in Abu Tor would serve as silent inspiration for almost all the public buildings he'd leave behind him there. And so, in the most essential way, would his composure, his solitary nature, and his unflagging capacity for perspective, in every sense of the word.

While he has been forgotten by most of those who today pass

through and use his Jerusalem buildings, each remains a "perfect illustration of the man"—part of his archive, and of the city's own.

Besides providing him architectural inspiration, the Abu Tor house
served as a refuge—not just from the chatty distractions of tea parties
and receptions but also from the grueling job he'd taken up the year
before.

Fresh from planning the reconstruction of towns and buildings
in the war-devastated regions of Macedonia and then in Thrace,
and around the area of the Gallipoli battlefields, where his work
plotting settlements for refugees was abruptly cut off by the outbreak
of yet another war (this one Greco-Turkish), he'd answered a call put
forth in 1921 by the first high commissioner of Palestine, Herbert
Samuel. In code, Samuel had telegraphed the secretary of state for
the colonies, Winston Churchill, and demanded EARLY SELECTION
AND DESPATCH of FULLY QUALIFIED ARCHITECT FOR SERVICE WITH
PUBLIC WORKS DEPARTMENT JERUSALEM. The appropriate candidate
would be PRACTICAL ENERGETIC MAN PREFERABLY WITH SOME
EXPERIENCE OF BUILDING WORK ABROAD IN CLIMATES OR COUN-
TRIES SIMILAR TO PALESTINE . . . POSITION CONSIDERED BEST
SUITED FOR UNMARRIED MAN BETWEEN THIRTY AND THIRTY
FIVE . . .

With his experience of building work abroad in climates similar to Palestine, the eminently practical, energetic, and most unmarried Harrison, age thirty that year, fit Samuel's description to an uncanny T. Although he was essentially, even implacably, British—he counted Jane Austen as an ancestor and himself as her namesake, took tea, smoked a pipe, and ate porridge for breakfast till the end of his days—he had turned his back on England as a young man and had no desire to return. With the exception of a few months in 1922, engaged in what he called "Delhi work" at Sir Edwin Lutyens's London architectural office (where he assisted with plans for the imperial Indian capital as he beefed up his colonial CV) and a short stint in the late '30s designing the buildings of Oxford's Nuffield College (his original spare, flat-roofed plans for which were rejected by the donor as "un-English" and later adapted resignedly by Harrison "on the lines of Cotswold domestic architecture"), he would spend most of his life far to the southeast of it. In the process, he became a kind of honorary Levantine as he rooted himself in a series of modest but elegantly appointed dwellings in Palestine, Egypt, Malta, Cyprus, and Greece. However British Harrison may have been, the much-modified Nuffield commission was his single attempt at building in Britain. And for all the respect he'd come to command as an architect in Palestine and among a small circle of English architects, he'd remain mostly unknown—then and now—in his native land.

Some of the discomfort he felt among his countrymen was social: "I admire English people so much provided I am not mingled with them," he wrote. "When too close in the mass they bring out my worst instincts." But his attraction to warm foreign lands derived not so much from the urge to flee England as from his strong feeling for the spirit of each of these olive-eating places, taken singly and as a region. At one point, contemplating the fact that he might be compelled to live and work in the country of his birth, "a cold shiver" ran down his back. "How can I be happy," he mused, "in a place where the sun does not always shine."

The landscapes of the Mediterranean had riveted him from the first moment he encountered them as a recent veteran of various dressing stations and bivouacs on the Western Front. Having refused to apply for the officer's commission that was nearly a given for young men of his class, he served as a stretcher bearer in some of the grislier battles of the war, dragging bodies through mud and tending to the wounded. It was "the only job in the army I can undertake with a good conscience," he wrote in the midst of the fighting to his worried mother—though even then he wondered aloud "whether I would not have been more honest if I had simply claimed to be, what I really am, a 'conscientious objector' and gone to prison."

Perhaps it was the memory of these scenes of modern devastation he'd recently witnessed around the European trenches that made the ancient ruins he encountered in the Mediterranean seem so vital, and so achingly familiar. For a man devoted to a life of construction, he had a distinct fascination with wreckage. In letters from the front, he'd described, for instance, the "abject desolation" surrounding one famous battlefield—unnamed, it seems, because of the censor: "Everywhere were trenches, barbed wire and acres and acres of shelled ground now partly hidden by rank grass and made bright with poppies and cornflowers." Nearby, a French village whose "name was once on everyone's lips" was now "only a mass of bricks."

On his first trip to Greece, in 1919, a certain melancholy echo was audible as he described being alone in nature with "the awful silence, the uncanny stillness" and wandering "among the massive walls of old Eion, now but an isle in a morass." Sometimes the links between these haunted vistas were more direct: "Curiously enough," he wrote of a late-afternoon walk on a mountaintop near Salonika, "the wood at the summit with the clouds entangled in the branches of its trees brought back to my mind that eventful day three years ago when at dawn we searched Louzy Wood [Bois de Leuze] in the Somme, enveloped in fog, for the wounded of the Division we had that night relieved." The same way the weird hush had marked a lull in the battlefield bombardments, this Macedonian reverie soon faded ominously as he "watched the sun sink into the sea turning its customary blue into golden shimmer." Dusk descended quickly in these parts, and hurrying down the mountain, he wondered whether he'd reach Salonika before nightfall. "I quickly lost sight of the mule track which I had hoped to follow and stumbling over rocks and bushes drew close, as luck would have it, to one of the many flocks of sheep and goats that wander about the mountain. A stranger in the twilight hours is not welcome to shepherds so the guardian of these sheep did not recall his dogs who, as soon as they saw me began to howl. I threw stones at them but that only made them fiercer and for a few minutes I quite expected to be bitten. I put on a bold face and doubling my pace left them still howling and growling behind me."

The difference now was that—angry canines aside—he was in love with what he was seeing. Setting out on foot or donkey to survey possible building sites, or "crawl[ing] up and down" the streets of Salonika "noting and measuring bits of churches and walls and watching the people in the gay and busy bazaars," he declared that he'd "never . . . in all my life been so consciously happy." He seemed to have felt himself newly alive, delivered from the horrors of war and sprung free from the various strictures that bound him back in England. He was also, critically, drawn to the "irregularities of Byzantine construction," which he found remarkable; in Constantinople Hagia Sophia's proportions and immensity dazzled him. The countless mosques he visited there awed him as well, and he described the markets of that city as "a wonder. Imagine a number of connected streets of great length covered by barrel-vaults and lined with four thousand booths." Village inns, stone fountains, minarets, crumbling monasteries, sheikhs' tombs, caravanserais, old Turkish and Venetian forts, half-buried Doric columns, and fading inscriptions on the floors of ancient temples also fascinated him, even as their presence stoked his romantic conviction that joy and beauty were more poignant for being so fleeting: "This sense of exquisite pleasure cannot of course last; who indeed would want it to last," he asked rhetorically in the midst of one of these idylls.

But architecture almost always gave way in this landscape to archaeology. Asked by the Macedonian director of antiquities to sketch a prehistoric dwelling he'd uncovered in one of the tumuli of Salonika, Harrison found himself contemplating the shattered vases, ornamented gold leaf, and human teeth that emerged from the cemetery of what appeared to be the buried town of Therma. On another outing with the same official, he visited the locked fourth-century church of Saint Demetrius, in the part of Salonika that had burned in the fire that swept the city in 1917. The church was still standing, but its marble revetments were badly damaged, and the roof had tumbled to the floor. Its elaborate mosaics "calcined and wrecked" by the flames that raged there just two years before, the devastated building might as well have been the scene of some ancient sack or conflagration, gradually reverting to nature and now property of the rooks who nested noisily within its blackened walls.

❖

When in Greece, Harrison had set his sights on finding further work there or in the Near East. Even as he'd been drawing up plans for the repair of various "destroyed cities" in Thrace and Macedonia, he'd installed himself at the British School in Athens, where he lived after leaving Salonika and, in his free time, devoured every book and article he could find about Byzantine and early Muslim building. This new Eastern obsession didn't, meanwhile, dampen his abiding passion for classical construction—not surprising for an architect whose training had centered on the monumentally rational Beaux Arts style in vogue when he was studying first as a college student in Canada and then in London.

But analyzing such stately symmetries in a classroom was one thing; experiencing them viscerally for himself was another. On a 1920 trip through Rome, he was smitten by the city and the buildings that so grandly constituted it: "I had become a little tired of Italy as presented in the thousand and one architectural text-books which I have been obliged to study . . . ," he wrote in a letter to his father. "This very expression 'Eternal City' and phrases such as 'See Rome and die,' 'All roads lead to Rome' etc., made Rome seem commonplace to me. Now I know that they are true. Rome is truly marvelous . . . See Rome and Live would be more appropriate. Since the War material interests have made great inroads in me; but now I am once more wildly enthusiastic about Architecture. I have been rushing about, sketch book in hand, seeing hundreds of buildings and it is useless to catalogue them."

Oddly enough, in light of the prodigious imagination, time, and care that Harrison would pour into Jerusalem—all of his major work would take place there in the course of the fifteen years he'd spend in the city, and he would eventually come to be viewed by local architectural historians as *the* representative builder of the British Mandate, "almost the sole author" of its official designs—he'd leave no such record of his initial encounter with the place. Much later, having left it, he'd look back wistfully and describe "descend[ing] the stepped suk which leads from the citadel of Jerusalem to the Great Mosque and stand[ing] for the first time on the threshold of the Haram ash Sherif" as "one of those experiences that a man of sensibility treasures all the days of his life." The contrasts between the "religious calm" of the space and the "secular bustle" all around, as well as the beauty of the Dome of the Rock and the "thought provoked by passive contemplation of this historic and holy ground" combined in a way that was "so absorbing that he is likely to be reduced to awed silence."

Perhaps this hushed sense of wonder accounted for his taciturnity on arrival. Of his letters that would survive into the next century, the first postmarked from the city was written in July 1922. Addressed to his mother, it mostly contains chitchat about the weather, the terrible food included as part of his room and board at the Old City's Austrian Hospice, the government's panicked reaction to a strike by local Arabs against the impending Mandate—they'd called in extra troops who "march through the streets every day, blowing their bugles. This is intended to impress the Arabs who respect the British but hate the growing ascendency of their Israelite cousins"—and the fact that his dress suit and sports coat were missing from his luggage.

Or maybe he had expended his store of lavish adjectives on those lands where he was just stopping over. Now he was ready to hunker down to sustained work in one spot, applying all the lessons he'd learned about Byzantine buttresses, four-square Turkish reception halls, and water-burbling Andalusian courtyards to a city capacious and world-weary enough to take them all in.

FALLEN WALLS

HARRISON'S PASTORAL, STAY-AT-HOME SKETCHING SESSION WAS hardly typical of how he spent his early days in Jerusalem. From the outset, he found himself overwhelmed with work, most of it far from inspiring. In fact, the gap between his architectural ideals and the very real drudgery of his position couldn't have been more yawning.

His talents were certainly recognized by his superiors. A confidential dossier that would one day be filed among the yellowing papers of the by then defunct British Colonial Office provides the report-card-like estimation that in 1924, Palestine's director of public works considered A. St. B. Harrison a "very capable officer and a skilled architect both in design and the preparation of quantities and estimates," while no less than the chief secretary of all the land had "formed a high opinion of this officer's capacity." Harrison was, in clipped English sum, "the right man in the right place." A range of substantive architectural prospects were, accordingly, dangled before him: Ronald Storrs, the governor of Jerusalem, announced himself eager to appoint him to the still only hypothetical position of chief architect of the city; the director of antiquities appreciated his knowledge of archaeology and wanted him to transfer to that department; "vague rumours" circulated about a "gift of £10,000 for a Museum" that he might be asked to design; and it seemed he might be entrusted with planning a costly countrywide system of police barracks and outposts.

But meetings swallowed much of his time, as did writing and rewriting official letters and humoring small-minded administrators like his supervisor, who may have enthused about Harrison's skills in his confidential reports but in person nitpicked relentlessly, apparently for nitpicking's own sake: "When I give him a draft letter he reads the first paragraph and begins to criticize it saying that I have omitted this that and the other," Harrison fumed to his sister Ena. "When he has blown off steam and has tried to give me the impression that only he has the foresight to remember these factors he reads on and finds them all duly noted in the later paragraphs. Then he does not apologize—he never does this—but looks annoyed." And it wasn't just his boss who irritated Harrison. Most of what went on in the office was, he declared, "pure humbug. At a committee meeting they will rush business because they have another committee to attend; and when it is concluded they forget all about it and sit about wasting time sipping tea and talking drivel until they are ejected."

Even though the Mandate was brand-new, it was already creaky as a colonial arthritic. Political and budgetary constraints made productive, creative thought seem slightly futile. "A general feeling of uncertainty and pessimism," he wrote, hovered over the government offices, and with the need for an official government architect being constantly questioned for financial reasons, he was forced to protect his position by adding to it the role of town planning adviser for the entire country. "This will bring," he sighed to his sister, "a lot of niggling uninteresting work which I would rather not do." And indeed he soon found himself a "little overawed by the immensity of the task" he had undertaken in "launching forth into the sea of Town Planning. I don't know where it will end: there is no shore within sight." The job was, he wrote, "Herculean," since "the towns are a mess and the committee of pots haven't an idea what to do. I am not sure that I can improve the position very much seeing there is no budget voted. I may be useful as the Committee's scapegoat." He'd much rather be at home, drawing. (He planned, he wrote, to transfer some of his sketches to wood, for engraving.) In the meantime, he was learning about the intricacies of building in Palestine the cold and wet way. The first rains had begun to fall, and everyone was scrambling to mend their roofs. His own ceiling "shows patches of damp in places so that I am not without anxiety." But worrying seemed to be part of his job description.

Between stabilizing Jerusalem's newly unearthed pre-Jebusite wall and planning a school in Tulkarem, a market in Tiberias, a police station in the town of Madjal, and a police post in the village of Lajjun, Harrison had his hands full—if full of what he called "hack work." Among other things, he'd been ordered to design the Palestine Pavilion for the so-called British Empire Exhibition to be staged on a massive fairground at Wembley in suburban London.

With its miniature Taj Mahal, Burmese Chin-long players, and butter sculpture of the Prince of Wales decked out by Canadian dairy farmers in full Native American headdress, this colonial lollapalooza had other things on its mind besides Palestine's plain block of a whitewashed, black-striped, Muslim-mausoleum-like pavilion, which by the time it was complete Harrison said was, anyway, "ruined by a committee." He had poured himself wholeheartedly into the plans for a "characteristic" local building, but after endless wrangling at meetings, all that remained of what he'd proposed were "the two terminal domes." Those in charge had, he wrote his father "so modified it, cut it about that I refuse to recognize it as my baby, or

rather I cannot. I long for a Maecenas instead of a Committee so that I can do something worthwhile."

The extravagant Wembley opening ceremony in April 1924 was, meanwhile, attended by 110,000 rapt spectators and presided over by King George V himself. Multiple military bands and a grander-than-gala performance by a choir of 3,000 capped off the proceedings. Conducted by "Pomp and Circumstance" composer Sir Edward Elgar, this vast assemblage of white-surpliced singers belted out William Blake's fiery words, broadcast to ten million radio listeners all over the world:

> I will not cease from mental fight
> Nor shall my sword sleep in my hand
> Till we have built Jerusalem
> In England's green and pleasant land.

Not everyone was as ecstatic about the fair and its prophetic visions. The lavish but wholly willed and self-satisfied exhibition prompted one visitor among the hordes who made their way there during its first few weeks, a skeptical Virginia Woolf, to describe the windstorm that swept the concourse the day she wandered its pathways as somehow presaging the end of an era and the demise of a certain British way of being. "Pagodas are dissolving in dust," she'd write, conjuring her vision of an oddly welcome sort of apocalypse: "Ferro-concrete is fallible . . . The Empire is perishing; the bands are playing; the Exhibition is in ruins . . ."

Harrison may have had similar premonitions about the fallibility of ferroconcrete. As a paid employee of that same empire, however, he had little choice but to keep on working—in the actual Jerusalem. (In December of that same year, one of the city's central avenues was christened with King George V's name, the occasion marked by a ceremony that was modest light-years away from all the pageantry at Wembley: a banner was hung and a small ceremonial arch erected. A trilingual cornerstone commemorating the event still rests at the intersection of Jaffa Road.) With the arrival in Palestine during the summer of 1925 of a new high commissioner, the much decorated and extremely mustachioed Field Marshal Lord Plumer, there was talk of Harrison's being asked to plan several large post offices, a central prison, the museum, and even the main government compound. His position remained wobbly as that ancient city wall, though, and he felt he must take each commission, small or large, odd or end, as it came to him.

So it was that in a single month that fall he submitted for approval plans and estimates for the house of the British chief representative in Amman and designed the new Palestinian coinage, the first since the English took control of the country. "I don't relish this job because I have to drive a tandem—a Hebrew and an Arab scribe, neither of whom are likely to have much respect for my ideas and I have to satisfy too many masters: the Colonial Office, the High Commissioner, the British mint and George Rex." His drawings for the coins would eventually be approved, though the official communications described them as "somewhat austere" (the chief secretary insisted he liked "Mr. Harrison's austerity"), while Harrison himself was scornful of his own handiwork, which he had "reason to believe is horrid. I am not a medallist and the sculptor has not appreciated my intentions. Moreover I know neither the Arab nor the Hebrew script so perhaps the result was inevitable."

More meaningful than his first (and last) stab at numismatics was his first attempt at a substantial local building. English and unsurprising though the Amman residence was meant to be, with its drawing room, study, garage, playroom, and so on, all set forth in a strictly outlined "schedule of accommodations" approved in London, he meant to design a structure that suited its setting in both climatic and cultural terms. Explaining that "the house must be as habitable in the hot dry months of midsummer as in the chilly wet ones of winter," Harrison conceived the building according to the airy symmetries of the Ottoman-era urban mansions he knew from his travels throughout Egypt, Syria, and Palestine. As in many of these subtly capacious homes, the living quarters would consist of an array of rooms radiating around a cavernous central enclosure. In particular, he'd taken to architectural heart the floor plan of the grand Çinili Kiosk, the "tiled kiosk," built "in a Persian mode" by an anonymous fifteenth-century architect on the grounds of the Topkapi Palace in Constantinople. With its quartet of high, vaulted chambers, or iwans, surrounding a domed, cruciform hall, this garden pavilion was the only remaining one of three, built at the command of Mehmet the Conqueror. Each stood for a far-flung kingdom the sultan had vanquished and made part of his sprawling empire. All of which rendered the kiosk, in slyly scaled-back form, an excellent model for the home of yet another representative of yet another empire on which its leaders claimed the sun would never set.

For Harrison, though, the symbolic assertion of Britain's global political reach was a good deal less interesting than the progress that the kaffiyeh-wearing workers were making on his first major building in this Middle Eastern mode. Now they'd started blasting rock for the cisterns; now they'd finished the ground-floor windows; now "the stone vaulting (my first) will soon begin," he reported with his usual understated excitement to his parents. The wife of the chief representative was "unfortunately . . . only just beginning to understand what it is she is being given." When she imagined her properly British and bourgeois abode, Harrison's variation on a Turkish pleasure palace was perhaps not what she'd had in mind.

As he worked, he walked and looked, and he was always working, walking, looking—sketching, scribbling, roaming wadis and rooftops and back alleys on his days off. He often did this alone, as on the weekend when he trekked some forty miles from Jaffa to Caesarea on foot, or the Sunday he walked by himself for hours from Ramallah to Jericho and almost collapsed in the heat. And he sometimes set out on longer journeys—with just a driver and his own thoughts—traveling to Nazareth and Gaza, from Beirut to Baalbek.

But for all his reclusiveness, he also liked company on such outings. When Ena came for an extended stay in the spring of 1925, they explored closer to home as they scrambled over rocks and hills and took cameras down into Siloam, or Silwan, that ancient village just below his house. Over the course of her several months in Palestine, they hiked to Bethlehem, rode donkeys to the pools of Ain Farah, drove all around the Dead Sea. Another guest, Patrick Geddes's son-in-law, the architect Frank Mears, arrived in town the next year to work on the plans for the Hebrew University and the national library and wound up staying with him in his Abu Tor house. "A clever modest fellow . . . ," according to Harrison, "he is very much older than I am and I am learning much from him." They visited "interesting buildings together," as Harrison wrote his father. "This I particularly enjoy as never before have I found anyone who cares to do this kind of thing." They'd just been to Nablus and hoped soon to explore Hebron.

His traveling companions were, in other words, helping him to better see the place where he'd landed and where he was starting to build. And these sociable surveying excursions weren't confined to Palestine. One of his closest friends in Jerusalem was the English ar-chaeologist and architect George Horsfield, then excavating and working to preserve the ruins of the Roman city of Jerash in Trans-jordan. When Harrison went to spend "a glorious ten days in the broiling sun" there with Horsfield around the time of Ena's visit, he rendered plans of one of its ancient amphitheaters and found himself contemplating the startling sight "after a motor run of six hours from Jerusalem" when "you come suddenly upon a great triumphal arch standing in the middle of a wide plain. Then, as you proceed, one after another there appear the ruins of two temples, two theatres, two baths, a colonnaded forum and half a dozen colonnaded streets. The whole is surrounded by the fallen walls of the city which is about a mile square . . . The cemeteries without the walls are of enormous extent." With its crumbling fortifications and vast stretches of graves, Jerash sounded strangely like a depopulated version of Jerusalem.

This abandoned Roman town was hardly the only derelict impe-rial relic through which he had occasion to ramble. On another trip to Transjordan—with Palestine's director of antiquities and head of the British School in Jerusalem, John Garstang, who kept urging Harrison to transfer to his department—they wound up making their way out of Amman and toward Qasr Amra, where a bathhouse was all that remained of the best-known of the so-called desert castles. Built in the early eighth century by a pleasure-loving Umayyad ca-liph from Damascus, the small, plain, vaulted structure stood alone in the middle of a desolate expanse. All around, Harrison wrote, were "graves of nomads and in one of the rooms was a corpse which had been deposited there by passing nomads." Flies abounded, as did frescoes teeming with fading zodiacs, flowers, animals, and "girls doing salome dances and men playing pipes and flutes." However vivid, these traces seemed haunted: the chipping wall paintings, the dead body, the flies, "a wide-mouthed well . . . but this well is now dry."

Harrison didn't really need to venture so far, though, to absorb the local landscape in excellent company. Of all the Jerusalem friends and visitors who taught him to see more sharply where he was, the one from whom he learned the most—"certainly much more than from anyone else in Palestine," as he'd put it years later—he met just outside his very own garden in the moonlight. On that particular dazzling night, he mistook David Bomberg for a chimney.

The squat British painter in the soft hat might have chosen to pitch his easel anywhere in the bright Jerusalem dark, so it seems almost fated that he'd picked this spot, right beside Austen Harrison's Abu Tor home. The two didn't yet know each other, and Bomberg had gravitated to this perch because of the wide-open angle it afforded him onto the slopes of Mount Zion, the Old City walls, and the funnel-shaped roof of the Dormition Abbey. New to Jerusalem, he and his wife, Alice—a free-spirited convert to Judaism and a divorcée some ten years his senior—had just moved into half a rented house immediately below Harrison's.

Their bearings and biographies were so wildly at odds, it's hard to imagine the men tolerating, let alone enjoying, one another. The calm, reserved, politely Protestant Harrison was descended from what he called "undistinguished country gentry" in Kent, and although he was living in relative rusticity here in Palestine, he hadn't shed all the genteel trappings of his old British life. He employed an Arab servant, Yacoub, to keep house, and he found money to pay for both Greek and singing lessons. He liked to be alone; his letters that have survived into this century are entirely silent on the subject of romantic or sexual attachment.

The depressive, aggressive, and very Jewish Bomberg, meanwhile, was raised in the impoverished East End of London, one of eleven children born to a temperamental Polish immigrant father and a doting if harried mother. His marriage to Alice was tempestuous in the extreme; one acquaintance from their Jerusalem years reported in her diary that "they can behave like wild cats and quarrel fiercely." Usually living from meal to meal and painting to painting, he was ferocious about his art, and his work was fueled by a gnawing restlessness, a constant need to upend his own and others' conceptions. He both craved the attention of his peers and scorned it, refusing to sign their manifestos or appear in their magazines. A childhood friend would later recount that "pugnacious is too mild a word" to describe him as a young man. "He wanted to dynamite the whole of English painting."

By the time he planted his canvas on that hillside in Abu Tor, he was thirty-three years old; his explosive relation to the tradition had been severely tempered and darkened by his harrowing experiences in the Great War's trenches and by the loss of several close friends in the fighting. He was also troubled by his increasingly marginal status in the English art world, and by the paralyzing sense that he had exhausted the possibilities of painterly abstraction. Understanding that Bomberg had reached something of a crisis in his work, the Scottish etcher Muirhead Bone had intervened and encouraged him to take up a more realistic tack. At the same time, Bone had lobbied the Zionist leadership to hire the painter, since the work of a talented artist working in situ in Palestine would lend, Bone suggested, "more variety to their propaganda and . . . strike the minds of thoughtful imaginative people to whom photographs make little or no appeal." He should be, in Bone's unfortunate animal-trainer-like terminology, the Zionists' "tame artist."

So it was that Bomberg's and Alice's boat tickets were paid for by Keren Hayesod, or the Palestine Foundation Fund, in exchange for paintings of the "Zionist reconstruction work"—swamp draining, settlement building—that its leaders were eager for him to get down to producing for use on their posters. But when he and Alice visited the Jewish settlements, "David got no inspiration from them," as she'd later report. "They seemed to be untidy and shiftless and to lack a sense of order." Instead of the "heroic pictures" the Zionists had ordered, he found himself drawn instinctively to rendering the shapes of Jerusalem's minarets and city walls, its domes and church spires, whose most minute details he became possessed with the idea of re-creating on canvas. He was, as Harrison would one day put it, "the most intense painter I've ever known. He could be elated or depressed; and when he finished a painting, he would claim it to be either a masterpiece or a total failure."

Unlikely as a friendship between them seemed, Harrison scraped together the money to buy one of the first paintings that Bomberg completed in and of Jerusalem (*Siloam and the Mount of Olives*, a more accomplished variation on the drawing that he himself had been attempting while sitting in his garden on his days off), and they grew extremely close, bound by the numerous traits and fascinations that, for all their differences, they shared. Both were highly gifted visual artists, obsessed with their work and unrelentingly critical of their own creations; both had experienced hallucinatory visions of death and destruction during the war. Both had broken free of England and its stifling manners; both came alive in the open air of Palestine, while both held themselves aloof from society there. As awkward as Harrison felt among groups of Englishmen, Bomberg seemed uncomfortable at gatherings of Palestinian Jews.

Both responded strongly to the light of the place. Bomberg set out in his paintings to try to capture it baldly and in all its parched starkness (or moonlit calm), while Harrison worked his hardest to create in the cloisters and courtyards of his buildings cool pockets of much-needed shade. Although Bomberg had veered from the pure abstraction of his earlier work, he was still propelled by what he called "a *Sense of Form*"—as was Harrison. Both aimed to strip away all "irrelevant matter" from their creations. As their work evolved in this setting, it evolved in tandem. The logic, restraint, and complex placidity of Harrison's architecture were mirrored in the eerily vacant, controlled cityscapes of Bomberg's Jerusalem paintings and drawings, which show a town nearly empty of people but still alive with stark edges, looming uprights, gentle curves.

Both were introverts who relished friendship and serious, frank conversation: "We talked of everything . . . ," Harrison would remember, decades after Bomberg's death. "No subject was taboo not even Zionism, Jews, imperialists, civil servants round which subjects most Christians & Jews skirted in those days. But above all we talked about art . . . I learned so much from him . . . He was so patient with my ignorance & innocence."

He was being overly modest, since they both taught each other—Bomberg would later insist as much—and if anything, Bomberg's newly naturalistic, precise, and emphatically *architectural* paintings of Jerusalem seemed to reflect the city as the men came to view it together. Even after Bomberg and Alice moved to a room at the top of the Banco di Roma building inside the Jaffa Gate, the painter spent long days and nights intent at his easel in Harrison's garden. All his most vivid landscapes of the Jerusalem rooftops are seen from this, his friend's, angle.

⊕

For better or worse, the men were also bound by their relationship to what Harrison wearily called "propaganda." Both were skeptical individualists working for political bodies whose ideological certainties unnerved them—though to varying degrees they did what they must in order to eat. Harrison proved more skillful at this than the fiercely uncompromising Bomberg.

The architect would later recall one of the early pictures of "Palestine Development" that Bomberg rendered in his role as dutiful hired hand. This was a grim, blurred set of huddled gray and black forms, meant to represent workers laboring in a quarry, and not surprisingly his Zionist handlers found it "void of propaganda value & refused it. I remember what a state David got into . . . trying at one & the same time to please his masters & preserve his integrity." He might as well have been describing himself—though Harrison's temperament was much more controlled and he'd made his peace with this state of affairs in ways that the chronically agitated Bomberg never would.

When Plumer took up the high commissioner's post, Harrison knew the demands on him would change, "as I expect I shall find it less easy to avoid Government House functions. I have contrived so far to attend none." He'd even had to order a dress suit from the Army and Navy stores "just in case I am commanded to attend." Annoyed as he was by this expense—he'd rather have spent his money on Bomberg's paintings and gramophone records—when he finally did make his way to Government House for lunch, Plumer impressed him; he was "very gracious and had obviously informed himself about me." The new high commissioner had plans for the government architect, and for the country at large. He "hates the house in which he is obliged to live"—the drafty and fortresslike Augusta Victoria Hospice built in a heavy German style at the behest of the kaiser on the Mount of Olives at the start of the century and used as German military headquarters during the war—and was eager to replace it. He was also eager for the Public Works Department to step up construction of the various police buildings, post offices, and quarantine stations that a properly functioning British territory demanded.

Plumer may have been a war hero whose chest was thick with military medals, but he prided himself on his common sense and his matter-of-fact, nonpartisan approach to maintaining law and order—as though by means of firm will and good manners one could rule Palestine like a sleepy English village. Never mind all the violently competing claims to every inch of land in the land. He himself had, he asserted, "no personal policy." His policy was "that of His Majesty's Government." He ordered his district commissioners to stop issuing their regular political reports because, as he insisted, "There is no political situation—don't create one!"

Harrison had no such illusions about the politics of Palestine. "Everything is propaganda," he repeated, ruefully, several times in one 1925 letter to his father. He had been asked to weigh in, for example, on what he called "the great University scheme," the plans that Geddes and Mears had drawn up for the campus on Mount Scopus. Much as he appreciated both architects personally (his affection for Mears was plain, and he'd later call Geddes "that unappreciated genius"), over the course of eighteen months he'd pored over and discussed the design with Magnes and other officials, and discovered that "the whole thing was based on pious hopes and little cash . . . The Geddes dream was propaganda." And it wasn't just Jewish or Zionist intentions that he doubted. He was also wary of various Englishmen in authority. "For a second time I have been pressed (by Sir Ronald Storrs) to give up my Government job and become City Architect of Jerusalem. I was asked to state my own terms. I have categorically refused because I believe the proposal only propaganda for Storrs."

But for all his wariness, he was eager to get down to more serious work, and Plumer's presence made that possible. In October 1926 he wrote his mother to say that "everything is now settled as regards Government House." While the secretary of state had offered to "send a 'competent' architect from England to do it," his superiors wanted Harrison to render the plans. Noting that he was "somewhat of an expert on the historic side of near Eastern architecture," one of them scribbled in the Colonial Office file that "I have always heard very high accounts of Mr. Harrison, the only criticism being that his artistic tastes were of too high an order to be wasted on the erection of police barracks & public lavatories. Government House should give him better scope."

And as Harrison himself summed up the situation, "To cap it all Lord Plumer, of whom everybody is a little frightened, said that 'even if Mr Harrison was not in Palestine but in England he is the man I would wish to build the House and I would send for him to do it.' So that's that." He hoped to be relieved of the hackwork he had complained of "so that I can concentrate on the design of important buildings."

TECTONICS

IT REGISTERED FIRST AS A THUNDERING, QUEASINESS, THE SOUND
of rocks splitting loudly apart—"a tremendous noise as though a mine
had exploded, or as though one was being run down by a fleet of
heavy lorries. The ground may have swayed for I felt slightly sick," as
Harrison described it, still reeling two days later. Or as another English official who found himself sitting in his Old City house on that
stiflingly hot Jerusalem afternoon would recall it across the years: "a
heavy rumble followed by a crash . . . The walls began to shake and
one, a metre thick, opened up, and I saw daylight through it." He,
too, would say he felt "sea-sick." Nearby, Alice Bomberg had dozed
off when she "was awakened by the door rattling furiously and I
thought it was David trying to get in, but I had no memory of locking the door, and it was the shaking of an earthquake."

As soon as the ground beneath them stopped shifting, panicked
crowds spilled into the streets. Black plumes of dust rose, and with
them the sound of women wailing. The devastation wrought over just
fifteen seconds that July day in 1927 was severe: Houses and markets,
churches, mosques, and synagogues had collapsed into heaps. Hundreds were crushed to death, many more injured. Thousands were
suddenly homeless.

Harrison happened to be right near the epicenter, in Nablus,
when the earth opened up. Returning home from a trip to visit the
excavations at, of all places, the biblical Megiddo, or Armageddon,

he was sitting in a hotel garden, watching water spew from a fountain while his companions took midafternoon naps. Then the reverberations began. As he'd try to reconstruct the quake soon after for his mother, it seemed "like the cracking of great whips as the rocks and buildings cracked." Realizing what was happening, he sprang away from the three-story stone structure. "Not far from me was a man whose face was as white as his kuffiyeh. He went off his rocker and behaved as I used to when, to annoy you, I pretended I was mad. His eyes rolled, his head lolled and he seemed to chase invisible flies with his hands. I pushed him towards the road. When the quaking ceased the noise of tumbling buildings could be heard."

After being sent to examine those tumbled buildings in the devastated old city of Nablus, he returned to Jerusalem and had to scramble to assess the wreckage there. A twelfth-century dome at the Church of the Holy Sepulcher had been smashed; Geddes and Mears's national library on Mount Scopus was "badly cracked," while the roof of the university's chemistry department had collapsed and much of its machinery been ruined; on the Mount of Olives, a minaret had fallen and killed a praying sheikh; the buildings of the new Jewish suburb of Talpiot were severely damaged. The top of the Tower of David's minaret had broken off, and the Old City had "the appearance of having passed through a military siege," and so on and on. As Harrison would write an American correspondent, "I suppose in the world's view it was nothing prodigious or abnormal, but it has shaken up this little land physically & mentally."

It had especially shaken David Bomberg, who had been painting on the roof of a building near the Western Wall and left his post just a few minutes before the tremors began. He was safe, but—as Alice would later report—the next day they walked past the house where he'd been working and saw it reduced to a mound of stones, "and then he got the shock—that if he had not left when he did he would have been in that heap of rubble too, and he got the horror of it . . . And so he got the idea that he must get away from Jerusalem as he could not paint anymore among the ruins." They'd scrounge money to buy him boat-deck fare to France, Alice would sew him a sleeping bag out of two cotton quilts, and he'd flee Palestine and their rickety marriage soon after, never to return.

Throughout it all, Harrison remained calm. "The earthquake has," he wrote, "brought one blessing to me. I now sleep regularly in my garden. The top of the mosquito net keeps the dew off me and I am very comfortable." As always, he managed to breathe deeply in the midst of mayhem.

✜

Besides toppling walls, wrecking roofs, and killing many people, the quake that struck the Holy Land brought the usual local talk of signs and wonders. The Orthodox declared the fact that no Jewish casualties were reported a miracle, and as one newspaper related, "The rabbis of Jerusalem have issued a proclamation calling upon their people to assemble in the synagogues to offer thanksgiving for their deliverance and pray that the disaster will not recur."

It was also considered by some a divine sign that while Augusta Victoria was among the hardest hit of all the structures in the city, and the high commissioner's private rooms were badly damaged, Lord and Lady Plumer had been on vacation in England when the quake struck. (Less lucky was the Russian maid working at the house in their absence—killed by collapsing masonry.) Meanwhile, one awe-struck journalist reported that a chunk of the building's tower had tumbled and fallen through the chapel roof, "destroying a picture of the former German Emperor in biblical robes." Or as another still more supernaturally suggestive account had it, when the "huge stone . . . burst through the Chapel roof [it] obliterated the blasphemous mural of Wilhelm, and finally became motionless below [an] unscathed portrait of Jehovah."

Actual act of God or no, the quake caused the evacuation of Augusta Victoria, now deemed unsafe for habitation. On his return from England, Plumer and his retinue moved first to the convent of Tantur, on the way to Bethlehem, and then into a house on the Street of the Prophets, and Harrison was ordered to speed up his work planning the new residence—a building whose function would be as symbolic as it was practical. Even before the portrait of the kaiser met its violent end, the fact that the official residence of the high commissioner was rented by the British from "a German Institution" seemed to wound the pride of the Englishmen filing reports at the

Colonial Office, and now this unexpected seismic turn of events had made more urgent than ever the need to replace the cumbersome old Teutonic compound with an appropriately modern British structure.

Haggling about the proper scale, cost, and placement of Government House had dragged on for several years prior to the quake, as had polite though pointed argument about whether Harrison should be given the job at all. "There is," he wrote his mother, "almost no precedent for the architect on the spot being entrusted with so important a building and many important architects may well be fishing for it." (Various local Jewish architects were also pushing for a competition.) Because of the political weight of the commission, the idea of awarding it to a relative unknown appeared to make the decision makers in London uneasy. The secretary of state himself took an interest and suggested that "it would be well worth while to get hold of Herbert Baker"—among the most famous architects in England and Lutyens's partner in planning the extravagant colonial stage set that was Imperial Delhi—"even if it cost a little more."

As memorandum after memorandum was issued and filed and commented on, quibbled over, debated on Downing Street, Harrison had meanwhile kept his head down in Jerusalem and kept working— intent on designing a building that would be explicitly "suited to its environment," as he put it in a 1926 letter to the head of the Public Works Department. It was, he explained, "undesirable to add to the number of buildings in Jerusalem which have been erected to plans made abroad by architects following their various national styles." Instead, he meant to "make sensible use of available materials" and "avoid flouting local tradition." After rendering several sketches for buildings at various provisional sites, he'd offered his first full-fledged set of plans for the house in March of that year. A substantial addition to the Greek Orthodox monastery of St. Simeon in the neighborhood of Katamon, this version of the residence suggested a kind of all-in-one church-state compound, with the late nineteenth-century monastery itself serving as the high commissioner's private chapel.

After these drawings were rejected a bit vaguely, due to "financial and religious considerations," another plot of land, farther out of town on the Bethlehem Road, was selected, and Harrison was sent back quite literally to the drawing board, from which he soon offered up a design for another variation on a theme. With a wide veranda, a cloister, and a spacious reception hall, these plans were dismissed by the functionaries in Westminster as too lavish—not suited to a territory the size of Palestine, and also unwise, from the point of view of colonial protocol. "If the H.C.'s house is too large," wrote one official, through a yawn, "it will not only cost a lot to build & maintain in repair, but the H.C. will be deprived of the best of excuses for not offering to put up tourists who are—or think they are—of importance—viz. 'sorry—no room for you.' Jerusalem is not," he went on, "like some Colonial capitals—a place with no hotels in which a white visitor can stay even for a few days." The technical officers of His Majesty's Office of Works were also skeptical about the scheme, "conceived on monumental lines in a grand manner," with too much corridor space and "a large area devoted purely to architectural effect." Their decision to turn down the plans, they insisted, constituted "no reflection on Mr. Harrison's work," though they did send a revision of those plans, which Harrison privately called "rotten in every respect."

Unwilling to see his thoughtful work mangled in this way, he'd fought back—explaining in a carefully worded though quietly passionate response that what looked to British eyes like a design produced in the grand manner was in fact the opposite. The criticism of the plans as ostentatious was, he wrote, "I believe based on a misunderstanding, due, in part, to the fact that the critics are unacquainted with Palestinian conditions." While the plans might appear to an English architect without experience in this context "bizarre and gratuitously extravagant," they were actually "much simpler than they seem." The vaulted spaces would be whitewashed plainly in the style of Palestinian village houses, which meant that the various costly additions that "ordinary modern rooms" call for—"plaster cornices, dadoes, friezes, paneling, etc."—would be unnecessary. Furthermore, they'd get the best of local craftsmanship. Rubble vaulting could be built cheaply and well in Palestine, while "untraditional" craftsmanship there was expensive and "lamentably poor."

By now, though, the Bethlehem Road site had proved a problem as well—a quarry was slated to open next door, as was a municipal sewage drain—and in the aftermath of the earthquake the need to find a new plot of land and get on with the building had become imperative. Besides working to scale back the number of rooms, Harrison scouted a suitable spot. By late autumn of 1927 he'd found it, not far from his own house in Abu Tor, and "after mature consideration" a committee appointed by the chief secretary had decided unanimously that the most suitable location was a secluded ridge some two miles from the center of town, known as Jabel Mukabber.

A still more staggering iteration of the already staggering view from his very own garden, this rise offered a dramatically sweeping panorama of Mount Zion, the walled city and Dome of the Rock, Gethsemane, the Dead Sea, the Judean hills, and the gently stacked houses of the village of Silwan—the perfect position, in short, for a structure that "cannot be overlooked nor can it be built around." The term was never mentioned in the course of their meetings, but the site where the house would eventually stand was, and is, also known to some as the Hill of Evil Counsel.

Which details will be remembered? Which will fade with time? Which disappear?

When in the summer of 1928 Austen Harrison sat at his Jerusalem drawing table and dreamed up (by his own count) a *fifth* set of plans for Government House, he couldn't pause to contemplate such things, which might give way to futility or to despair. To linger on them might have meant to consider the possibility that less than a hundred years from that very month, the officials who'd pass their days in the high-vaulted rooms of this stately, somehow ghostly building— with its cubic tower and domed porte cochère, its wide, rounded terrace, its gardens, grotto, and covered walkways—would barely recall that the British had ruled here or that this had once been the home of the high commissioner for Palestine.

Too much history will have intervened by then. "Palestine" will mean other things. There will be no high commissioner.

On a December day well into the twenty-first century, after I'm handed a pass at the security gate and granted permission to tour the building and grounds, no one I speak to knows Harrison's name. Off-limits to the public, this peculiar no-man's-land of a compound now serves as headquarters of the United Nations Truce Supervision Organization and various other UN bodies with hard-to-retain acronyms. The structure that once was Government House is still an audacious and singularly concentrated set of conjoined blocks and domes. These shapes suggest at once the hard-edged clarity of their architect's structural thinking and his penchant for a kind of playful abstraction, the outlines of a modest Palestinian peasant house fused with contours far grander and stranger. By now, though, certain things about the building have changed. The mihrab-like tiled fireplace, coffered ceiling, and oak parquet dance floor of the ballroom Harrison so carefully designed are a clean but slightly bedraggled-looking "hall of flags," where a smiling toy Santa Claus–and–reindeer set is arrayed across a table.

The high commissioner's elegant though austere dining room is now a coffee bar. Weirdly deserted this winter morning, the cavernous main drawing room around which the house seems meant to revolve leads to the vaulted side chambers that Harrison planned meticulously and again according to the design of an urban Ottoman mansion. What once were the "smoke room" and "His Excellency's study" have been converted to drab offices, with fluorescent lights and plastic heating units affixed to the whitewashed walls. Smoking is now prohibited, and the names of all His Excellencies—like that of the building's architect—have been forgotten. So, thankfully, has the fact of the separate quarters he designed for the "native" and "European" servants. There are no more servants.

I'm shown around the oddly charmed, somehow enigmatic house and grounds by a gracious young American peace-process function-ary in a well-cut foreign suit. He seems genuinely curious to know more about that long-gone British architect and his building plans, though as we wander together through the hallways and gardens in search of an official who reportedly knows of "an archive" concern-ing the compound, we find no trace of him or it.

We pause to admire the raggedy pet cemetery that now occupies the lower level of Harrison's carefully plotted "sunk garden." In a peculiar way the makeshift tombstones of "Boots," "Phyllis the Cat," and "Rudi" make the memory of their four-legged presence more lasting than that of many others who've passed through over the de-cades. One friendly if slightly dazed-looking African deputy we meet beside a temporary outbuilding squints in the thin sun and of-fers that, if he is not mistaken, the British left the country in 1952—or maybe it was 1950 . . . which is to say that even the most basic, undisputed facts about this place have proved less durable than the building's solid blocks of *mizzi hilu*, drawn from a quarry opened off the Bethlehem Road just for the purposes of building this house and nicknamed by the laborers "*mizzi Harrison*," for the man they all knew had specially selected this fine grade of hard white stone.

No—though Harrison had spent more than enough time con-templating the remains of other, older civilizations to know how quickly whole empires sink into the sand, he couldn't concern him-self with such rueful brooding. He was, instead, too busy drawing up plans for Government House and explaining to the impatient new high commissioner, John Chancellor—who arrived six months after the ailing Plumer's departure in July 1928—that though the basic design was spare, "a house is not like a factory or office build-ing, where much of the detail is repeated. Almost every room and every fitting calls for separate detailing." But Chancellor had no time for aesthetics. He was anxious to move out of the improvised official residence where he and his wife and staff were camped out; expect-ing the Prince of Wales to travel to Palestine in 1930, he also wanted to be sure the new Government House would be ready for this important state visit.

Harrison, for his part, was working as quickly as possible on one of his first major projects in Palestine, which for obvious reasons he wanted to get right. Aside from the need to prove himself capable of such an undertaking, the much-celebrated Herbert Baker still lurked in the architectural wings, and Lady Chancellor had taken it upon herself to privately show the great man Harrison's plans, which he somewhat cryptically announced had "radical defects"—chief among which may have been the fact that they were not rendered by Herbert Baker.

But there was nothing slow or indulgent about Harrison's approach. This was just how he worked and just the attention that such

work demanded. And though his plans may not have required the addition of all those fussy English cornices and dadoes, he needed to use his pencil to think his way through each geometric ornament on every portal and cabinet. Spareness, too, required care. In the dining room, for example, the large stone fireplace would be flanked by two niches, one for coal and the other for wood, which would each be equipped with painted doors whose

quasi-Islamic decoration—four simple yet somehow intricate intersecting straight lines, in a whirling, pinwheel pattern—seems meant to echo and reflect the quasi-Islamic decorations and their simple yet somehow intricate intersecting lines that appear on the other painted doors and windowpanes throughout the house. The wooden tracery that would front the galleries in the main rooms needed to be plotted, as did the designs to be stenciled on the colored ceilings in each of these jewel-
box-like upper spaces; the octagonal stars that would be cut high into the whitewashed stone walls and low into the flagstone patio floor also each needed to be mapped . . .

As he supervised a team of draftsmen who labored over final plans for each room and every decorative touch, and consulted closely with craftsmen like the Armenian master potter David Ohannessian, who was specially fashioning in his Via Dolorosa workshop the tiles for the Topkapiesque ballroom fireplace, Harrison worked patiently to draw up exacting specifications for the building's furnishings. Maniacal as these directives may have seemed, they stood as a statement of the philosophical principles that Lawrence Durrell would one day praise him for. He would, in other words, exert the same care selecting the cushions and bolsters, the drapes and the lamps of the most "representative" house in the land that he would for his own home. The political symbolism of the house was, as it happens, far less important to him than was the expression of that more universal "Sense of Form." He imagined a structure that would be firmly grounded in the materials, building methods, landscape, and visual vocabulary of this Eastern place, even as it existed somehow outside of time and the precise moment of its construction.

The walls should be, he wrote, "plastered and distempered in ivory white," with the only real color coming from the furniture and hangings. This plainness made the colors of those decorative elements critical. They ought to be, he explained in one report, "bold, bright (probably primary)" and "too much attention cannot be directed to the effect of electric light" on these tints since "important use will be made of the rooms at night." He suggested that in the central drawing room the furniture covers should be blue and the wall hangings predominantly orange, though "the orange should not be too red." (He didn't mention it in the report, of course, but the main room of his own whitewash-walled Abu Tor house was arrayed in the same colors.) While the preponderance of vaults "tends to suggest that a mediaeval effect is being aimed at in this house . . . this is not the case and no furniture smacking of any 'period' should be purchased. Interest should depend entirely on clear structural lines and clean colours."

He went on to specify the precise nature of, for instance, the reading lamp to be placed in the entrance hall at a desk table for the visitors' book. This should be the sort typically used on church lecterns "but to rest on and not be affixed to [the] table. Material: pottery, rustless metal (not brass) or lacquered or ebonized wood."

The drapes in the dining room should be made of velvet, velveteen, or another silky-sheened fabric while those in Lady Chancellor's room might be "of chintz or cretonne with a lively pattern." And here, again, "as it is very desirable that no 'period' furniture should appear I suggest that firms which ordinarily specialize in period furnishing should not be approached in the matter."

Try as he might, though, to unmoor the building and its décor from a specific set of historical associations—and to strip the various shapes and colors back to a kind of impartial, eternal, even platonic essence—it wasn't so easy to avoid the period in which he was living and building, or to sidestep the politics that surrounded his every choice of carpet and candelabra.

In the months just after the foundations were poured and the frame of the house began to take striking shape on the bare ridge of Jabel Mukabber, John Chancellor and most of Palestine were consumed by other, more basic concerns. Despite the former high commissioner Plumer's stubborn insistence that there was "no political situation" to speak of, after his departure the Palestinian Arab leadership had come together with unusual unity to demand, as they had before, the establishment of a representative assembly. This would make way for the country's self-government in a number of years and would establish a parliamentary democracy in Palestine, based on proportional representation. Chancellor agreed to consider the possibility. A standoffish and generally suspicious veteran of colonial postings in places as far-flung as Trinidad, Tobago, and Southern Rhodesia, he was new to the Middle East and no particular ally of either the Arabs or the Jews. But he had quickly come to realize that unless something changed in the administration of Palestine, "there is reason to think that political agitation against the government may assume an objectionable and even dangerous character." So he traveled to London that summer of 1929 to discuss the idea of the representative assembly with the Colonial Office, and in his absence, tensions mounted in Jerusalem and a series of bloody confrontations erupted.

Ostensibly the cause of the clashes was disputed sovereignty over one of the most charged of all local sites and symbols, known variously as the Wailing Wall or Western Wall (considered by Jews to be the retaining wall of the otherwise-destroyed Second Temple) and as al-Buraq (according to Islamic tradition, the place where Muhammad tethered his winged horse, also named al-Buraq, when he arrived in Jerusalem from Mecca on his miraculous night journey). In fact, the entirety of Palestine seemed what was really at stake. Loud, angry marches by Zionist youth groups gave way to louder, angrier demonstrations by Muslim worshippers who descended on the Wall after Friday prayers at al-Aqsa one day in August and burned Jewish prayer books. This affront prompted strident rhetoric on all sides, and the verbally tense situation soon exploded into serious Arab violence—looting, assaults, then murderous riots. The small Mandatory police force did little to contain the escalating chaos, and by the time the rampaging ceased, 133 Jews were dead at the hands of their Arab neighbors; 116 Arabs were dead, mostly at the hands of British troops; and many more (Jewish and Arab alike) were wounded. Long-standing Jewish communities in Hebron and Safed were devastated. Six Jewish colonies were destroyed, as was any shred of trust that might once have existed between local Arabs and Jews, Arabs and Englishmen, Englishmen and Jews. As one of Harrison's British neighbors, Palestine's director of education, Humphrey Bowman, summed it up in gloomily architectural terms, "We have built for 10 years, & it has crumbled to pieces in 10 days."

For all his careful instructions about the "possibly vermilion or light red" color of the leather or leather-substitute couches in the smoke room of Government House, in other words, there was only so much Austen Harrison could control or keep at bay. The earthquake of the summer of 1927 had given way to the riots of the summer of 1929, which in their way also exerted what one historian of the period would later refer to as "a seismic effect" on the attitudes of everyone "involved in the Palestine conflict." And even those, like Harrison, who would have preferred to remain *uninvolved* had no choice but to brace themselves as the ground opened under their feet.

By the time the latest commission of inquiry had come and gone, and John Chancellor and his entourage moved into the finished house in late March 1931, Harrison's insistence on his building's sublime timelessness seemed wishful thinking at best—and it wasn't just the messy modern Middle East that he was now forced to reckon with, as his creation was admired and inevitable historical analogies were drawn. One flattering review in a British architectural journal dubbed the new Government House "a Crusaders' Castle of To-Day" and proclaimed that "this house represents the fulfilment, at long last, of a dream that set the mediaeval world aflame." The construction of such a building had been, according to the article's author, the ideal of everyone from Peter the Hermit

to Godfrey de Bouillon, Richard the Lionhearted, and "a host of knights and nameless foot-sloggers from every village and forest and castle of the Gothic North." While the new Government House is "frankly twentieth century," it "appeals to our northern imagination because the architect, consciously or unconsciously, has made its general form remind us of the Holy Land of the Crusades, not of the Roman province of Judea nor, by some flight of fancy, of Solomon's palace."

While a second upbeat magazine feature offered a sunny photograph of a clean-shaven Jew in a straw hat and khaki shorts and a bearded Arab in a traditional robe and skullcap working "in harmony on this building using local stone and many native methods of construction," yet another newspaper account came closer to speaking the truth about the house, its context, and all it represented: "The solid building stands out for all to see, the suggestion of fortification in its appearance being, perhaps, symbolic of the role which the logic of circumstances is forcing upon the Mandatory Power."

Deliberately or not, Harrison had built a citadel on a far-off hill, a citadel worthy of the Crusader Kingdom of Jerusalem—which as he of all people knew had lasted almost two hundred whole years.

ABOVE, BELOW

AT THE SAME TIME HE WAS PLANNING GOVERNMENT HOUSE, Harrison nursed an architectural secret—"a real secret not to be spoken," as he confided to his mother six months before the quake. Even in the days just after the earth shuddered, and he described to her the widespread destruction brought on by the shifting of the local ground, his thoughts remained fixed on the building he wanted more than any other to construct, though the particulars were still "highly confidential."

Since coming to Palestine, he'd learned all kinds of things that fascinated him—about rubble, twig, and packed-mud vaulting; about the various grades and colors of Jerusalem stone and the different styles of its chiseling; about the *madafeh* (reception room) and the *mastabeh* (living space) of the traditional peasant home; about modern art and ancient relics, Armenian tiles, and the alternating light and dark masonry stripes known as *ablaq*. He had also learned much more than he would care to know about politics and pettiness and about what he continued to refer to as "propaganda": "How heartily sick I am of political propaganda vested as aesthetical criticism," he'd write a close friend in a moment of especially pronounced disgust. In this top secret case he was well aware that "all kinds of strings will be pulled to prevent me from doing this big job." Ever a master of scale, he had measured the situation correctly.

It *was* a big job, the biggest he'd reckoned with so far. Declaring that "the past of Palestine is more important to the world than the past of any other country, and there are no monuments more precious than those which reveal to us the past of this land toward which all civilized people turn with reverence," the American philanthropist John D. Rockefeller Jr. had confidentially pledged $2 million to build an archaeological museum in Jerusalem. Rockefeller had been persuaded by the highly enterprising, small-town-Illinois-born, Yale-and-Berlin-educated Egyptologist, archaeologist, philologist, and founder (with Rockefeller's funds) of the Oriental Institute at the University of Chicago, James Henry Breasted, that the holy city— and indeed all of humanity—was in desperate need of a new museum. The building that then held many of Palestine's most important artifacts was a poorly lit, run-down, and overcrowded three-room house, while countless other precious relics simply lay outdoors, exposed to the elements and at risk of damage or theft. And beyond the need to rescue all these local objects and provide them with a proper home, Breasted was intent on establishing a center in the Near East where he might further realize his own lifelong dream of a "historical laboratory," devoted to the study of no less than "the Origin and Development of Civilization."

Breasted tended to think in grand if not grandiose terms. The first American ever to receive a Ph.D. in Egyptology, he'd coined and popularized the term "Fertile Crescent" to refer to the semicircular sweep of land that runs from the Nile to the Mediterranean to the Euphrates and was, in his words, "the earliest home of men." And his scheme for a Palestinian museum and research institute dedicated to the analysis and display of Near Eastern artifacts was in fact a severely scaled-back version of the thwarted scheme that he and Rockefeller and Rockefeller's Beaux Arts–inclined architect, William Welles Bosworth, had outlined for Egypt's King Fuad several years before, in the form of floor plans and a comprehensive program for a $10 million museum and archaeological institute in Cairo.

As described in the appeal they offered up with great pomp to the Egyptian monarch in 1925, this investment would be "a gesture of friendliness and appreciation from a citizen of the great Democracy of the West, profoundly interested in that remote spiritual ancestry which is common both to your Majesty's subjects and to the

American nation." Bosworth's previous work included the restoration of the Palaces of Versailles and Fontainebleau, as well as the design of the neoclassical Cambridge campus of MIT and the formal gardens of Rockefeller's Westchester county estate. And again in the Egyptian case his patrons encouraged the architect to think in majestically massive terms. The sumptuous structure he meant to erect on the banks of the Nile was intended, according to Breasted, its intellectual mastermind, to be "perhaps the most magnificent museum in modern times." Its exterior would be built of solid ashlar masonry, with a portico held aloft by a dozen forty-five-foot-high columns "which it is hoped may be monolithic shafts of granite from the same Assuan quarries whence the ancient Egyptian architects hewed their granite, from the days of the first pyramids to the vast obelisks of Luxor and Karnak."

These fanciful plans for the celebration of ancient Egyptian artifacts, though, hadn't taken into account the needs or desires of modern Egyptian human beings, and when King Fuad and his prime minister actually absorbed the details of the "gift" the wealthy American and his ambitious house Egyptologist were offering, they declared the conditions "absolutely unacceptable" since "they infringe upon the sovereignty of Egypt!" They had a point. According to Breasted and Rockefeller's terms, the museum was slated to be directed for thirty years by a commission made up largely of American, British, and French "men of science" and not by Egyptians themselves. Europeans and Americans would administer the endowment that would support the museum and institute—possibly forever. At a time when the king was reckoning with a serious popular nationalistic movement and threats to his authority, they were essentially asking him to cede control of Egypt's antiquities to a group of Western interlopers. They were also strongly suggesting he agree to the version of history they planned to put forth in foreign-tourist-friendly exhibits that would outline what their prospectus called "human development" as it proceeded "from primitive savagery" to "a highly refined culture . . . through a magnificent culmination to a decline which eventually resulted in European supremacy and . . . in European leadership of civilization."

Breasted's condescending attitude toward the present-day place and its people extended to Fuad as well, whom he considered "a vain and self-conscious Oriental." He hoped "to intoxicate" the king by donning a top hat and full evening dress and presenting him with an elaborate color brochure outlining the project. The vision put forth in this lavish watercolor-illustrated publication would, Breasted assumed, "give him such a pipe-dream of Arabian Nights possibilities" that "we shall be able to stampede him." His Highness was, in the end, not so easily stampeded, and the idea of Rockefeller's Egyptian museum came crashing down with all the force of one of those huge Karnak-worthy shafts of granite.

In the wake of the collapse of these flamboyantly neopharaonic plans—and in keeping with the far humbler Palestinian setting—the Jerusalem museum was meant to be a much simpler affair, and at first Breasted proceeded cautiously, securing a $20,000 grant from Rockefeller to pay for initial sketches and an option on the eight-acre plot of land that Harrison and his friend John Garstang, the department of antiquities director, had scouted, just to the northeast of the Old City walls, in the area known as Karm ash-Sheikh. Harrison's first designs for the Rockefeller-funded museum were all drawn up in secret in the spring of 1927 and approved enthusiastically by the Americans. They praised his approach to "fundamental matters of circulation, lighting, and external architecture," and came around to agreeing with his own sense that the site required an asymmetrical building, as opposed to the symmetrical structure he had first designed.

Breasted had sent him a pile of floor plans of various American museums built in an imposing Beaux Arts mode—from New York's Metropolitan to the Field Museum in Chicago and the Cleveland Museum of Art, each with its Grecian columns, sweeping marble staircases, and grand rotunda or great hall, designed to dazzle. But Harrison had his own distinctly earthbound sense of what form he thought the Jerusalem museum should take: "the Romanesque such as one finds in Sicily. Not that there is any reason that Sicily should be followed except that there as here in Palestine East meets West & in both countries building materials are alike." He had also included a boxy tower as part of his design, since—as he wrote in neat longhand to his Chicago correspondent—"it is traditional here to give important buildings towers, as you know." Without it, the building would be somewhat hidden from the new parts of town; a tower would also provide excellent views of the Old City. Breasted agreed, and friendly discussion ensued about the precise shape of the tower, the angle of the museum's façade in relation to the Old City walls, and so on and cordially on, with Harrison declaring in his typically self-critical way "how pleased I am that you have discovered some merit in my scheme. Its defects are so glaring that I missed the merits."

But as they entered into sustained conversation about all the geometrical, topographical, and stylistic possibilities ("I am writing this letter, in order that you may not receive a shock when you see the plans I have now in hand," Harrison cautioned Breasted in September 1927, after substantially revising his preliminary design, "for I have returned once again from asymmetry to symmetry . . ."), and even after Rockefeller agreed to devote a full $2 million to the project, they kept the proposal for the museum under wraps for diplomatic reasons. Though the budget for this structure was appreciably smaller than that for the Egyptian museum, the terms that Rockefeller and Breasted were offering the Mandatory authorities were also appreciably more respectful than those presented to King Fuad. The government of Palestine would need to agree to expropriate and contribute the Karm ash-Sheikh site and to remove the slaughterhouse and municipal incinerator located nearby, but there was no mention of foreign archaeologists assuming control of local antiquities. According to the terms of Rockefeller's gift, the museum itself would be explicitly given to "the Palestine Government for all future time without any conditions whatever as to its future management." As one SECRET AND CONFIDENTIAL letter from Breasted to Plumer had it: "The reason for this arrangement is, of course, obvious: the proposed Palestine Museum is to remain in English hands." Or, as one of Rockefeller's other advisers put it in a blunter and more gleeful note to his boss, "What a satisfaction it is to deal with the English after trying to deal with other races!"

Breasted certainly seemed to consider Harrison his cultural equal. When the architect came back around to a symmetrical plan, for instance, the Illinois Egyptologist appeared delighted—as much by Harrison's straight-shooting English character as by his structural

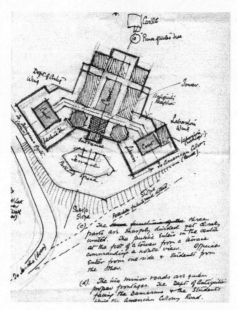

savvy. "The man who has the courage to change his opinions more than once if he is sure that they are each time based on the facts," he proclaimed, "is the only man for me." He sounded relieved to have at long last found someone in this dusty, sunbaked part of the world who spoke his language.

Beyond the lofty geopolitical reasons for discretion about the museum plans, closer to the ground, Palestinian politics also played a role in the secrecy that first surrounded the project. Once Rockefeller's grant was made known, Harrison realized there would again be "a howl and suggestions that there should be a competition" to choose the architect, just as a howl went up when he was appointed to build Government House. The country's many newly arrived Jewish architects in particular were upset that they hadn't been considered for the work. But he did at least have the trust of Plumer (who hadn't yet announced his imminent retirement); the high commissioner told him that "despite the clause in the letter covering the gift to the effect that the architect shall be one of eminence," the job was his. And this made way for an unusual admission by Harrison of his own superior expertise. "Without any prejudice,"

he confided to his mother in November 1927, "I think he is not wrong in making this decision. I feel I know more about building in Palestine than any other man and what I don't know about museum design is something I can learn."

No sooner had he pronounced what sounds uncharacteristically like a boast, though, than his usual skepticism and self-deprecation kicked in: "That is what has been decided but . . . I may, after all, not get the Job. Why Lord Plumer has such faith in me I cannot imagine."

He was, it turns out, at once right and wrong. On the one hand, he was wrong to doubt himself so, since he did finally get the Job—a Job for which it seemed he'd been preparing since his earliest days as an architect of the archaeological, or archaeologist of the architectural. His friend Garstang had resigned as director of antiquities in 1926, and late the next year, his successor, Ernest Tatham Richmond— himself an architect and a specialist in Islamic building with a long and complicated connection to Palestinian politics and planning— reported that Harrison had "happily gained the confidence of the authorities both in America and in Palestine [and] is thoroughly qualified to undertake this work." At around the same time, ample correspondence crossed the ocean to this effect, with Breasted declaring his great satisfaction with Harrison to Plumer and Plumer declaring to Breasted the same. Once the job was definitively Harrison's and the veil of silence had been lifted, he was ordered to travel to London where he hired three assistants to help him plan the museum.

But he was very right about the howling that ensued as soon as all this became public, since his trip prompted what he called "a rather vicious campaign in the Jewish press here" attacking the authorities for importing British architects and for not holding a competition. "They say I was sent to England because I know nothing whatever about museums and that I recruited men who did." He had, he added, also received letters "from more than one Jew apologizing for this campaign." But it was a distracting way to work.

There were, meanwhile, other distractions—and other diplomatic dances that also needed to be performed, since in this context the placement of every stone wall and clerestory window became a political two-step. Though Harrison's plans had been approved in prin-

ciple, Richmond and the other members of the local committee
charged with overseeing the museum's construction now began to
question the presence in his design of a tower. As Richmond wrote
in a January 1928 letter to Breasted, many of the committee members considered it an unnecessary expense. Moreover "on the aesthetic
side it is, as I am sure you will agree, desirable to regard the design
not only as an isolated architectural unit, but also in relation to its
surroundings, which include to the immediate south the Holy City
itself."

Benign as the complaint sounds and friendly as Harrison and
Richmond generally were with one another, this appears a perfect
instance of the "political propaganda vested as aesthetical criticism" that made Harrison so "heartily sick." Given the fact that
the museum, and with it the offices of the Palestine Department of
Antiquities, would be built on a slight rise above the Old City, the
committee felt that the tower threatened to dominate. Such a suggestion would, Richmond wrote, "surely be unfortunate; it might
even be looked upon as a breach of architectural good manners, for
the Museum will be the servant, as it were, of the great historical and
archaeological interests symbolised by the Holy City, outside the
walls of which, it should, I suggest, stand certainly with dignity, but
also with becoming modesty." In a more personal aside, Richmond—a
recent and very devout convert to Catholicism—admitted that in
his opinion "Jerusalem has enough towers already." It would be, he
believed, "a pity to add to them, or to appear to join in a competition for unnecessarily attracting attention." (Looking back, it's worth
noting that Richmond was registering his distaste for such structures
at the very same time that the American architect Arthur Loomis
Harmon—whose New York firm was then also busy designing the
Empire State Building—was drawing up and getting approval for
plans to build Jerusalem's fanciful new orientalist extravaganza of a
YMCA, whose most prominent feature was its 150-foot-high "Jesus
Tower," by far the tallest structure in town. Located across the street
from the King David Hotel on the road then known as Julian's Way,
and funded primarily by a wealthy family from Montclair, New
Jersey, that building was also constructed with money donated by
Rockefeller.)

According to Richmond, Harrison was willing to reconsider the museum's tower, though shortly after returning to Jerusalem from his trip to London, Harrison wrote a bit grumpily to his mother to describe how he was "fighting the local committee" about it and to complain that they'd gone directly to Breasted without consulting him: "They don't like to oppose outright for they are not sure of themselves and they fear to place themselves in opposition to the donor so they wriggle. I am wriggling too."

But Breasted—at the safe remove of Chicago and not nearly so entwined in Jerusalem's sticky webs of political and religious intrigue— strongly defended Harrison to the committee and insisted that "the self consistency of Harrison's designs as a whole should be the determining consideration, rather than whether Jerusalem already possesses a sufficient number of towers." Furthermore, without a vertical like the one that Harrison had planned, the long low outline of the rest of the building would seem "extremely tenuous, depressed and totally lacking in any uplift." Harrison had deliberately "given his building very reserved and austere lines, exclusively structural in character. Hence the need for something more." Perhaps, Breasted suggested, they could reach a compromise by simply lowering the height of the tower instead of removing it entirely.

Off the record and in response to Breasted's defense, Harrison thanked him for "all the pleasant things you have found it possible to say about the plans." For now he preferred not to comment on the tower question "as it is sub judice," but he would, he wrote, "like to congratulate you on having so fully comprehended what is at stake. I have given a great deal of thought to the matter and am still doing so."

Yet even as they were all busy peering upward, and imagining the tower and its effect on the sacred skyline, Harrison was also forced to lower his gaze and contemplate the facts already on the ground, and beneath it.

No lot in Jerusalem is ever really empty. Karm ash-Sheikh certainly wasn't, and if anything, the architectural challenges posed by this small swatch of land made it (and still make it) a fraught microcosm of the entire fraught town.

In addition to the rocky contours that swelled below it, the irregularly curved roads that ran alongside it, and its close proximity to one of the world's most famous city walls—as well as many of the holiest spaces and structures anywhere on earth—Harrison's museum would need to delicately work around a building that had long existed on the site. This was a crumbling two-story villa built in the early eighteenth century by the aristocratic religious scholar and leader Sheikh Muhammad al-Khalili when he came from Hebron and planted his land with a vineyard and an orchard of fig, olive, almond, and apricot, and which Breasted and the antiquities authorities insisted on calling "the Crusader Castle." (It seems Godfrey de Boullion and his troops did camp out in this area before they took Jerusalem in 1099, though they had nothing to do with the construction of the gracious if slightly ramshackle stone building that now sat upon it and that was known to the locals as Qasr ash-Sheikh, the Castle of the Sheikh.) A massive pine tree also marked the spot, and legend had it that more than two hundred years before, when al-Khalili arrived there, he brought its seedling in his turban. Fixed on a slightly different cast of historical characters, the English knew the pine as the "Prince of Wales Tree" since the soon to be King Edward VII pitched his tent beneath it when he visited Jerusalem in 1862.

Whatever the villa and pine were called, both were literally central to Harrison's decision to revert to a symmetrical plan, since "by Mr. Rockefeller's special request" the tree must be "retained in an organic relation to the Museum," according to one account, and the tree itself seemed already to exist in organic relation to the *qasr*. While Harrison warned Breasted that "I do feel that it would be easy to pay to these objects too great a respect," he had a very clear idea of how he'd like his design to interact with these elements that predated it. The old building "externally is so modest that I think reverence rather than apotheosis is indicated." And "the life of a tree is limited alas & I do not think that the future of this building ought to be too greatly influenced by this one. I propose," he wrote, "simply to honour it by placing my axis so that it passes through it." Seasoned gardener that he was, he'd be proved right when some sixty years later the tree would die and be cut down—though as long as Harrison's building stands, the central line of his museum plan will preserve its memory like that of a phantom limb.

More difficult to design around than these visible traces of former lives planted on the site were the hidden traces of the former lives that lay beneath it. In late June 1928, Harrison was overseeing the digging of trial pits in preparation for the laying of the museum's foundations when the workers unearthed an expansive Roman and Byzantine graveyard.

The cemetery wasn't a total surprise. As early as 1874, the French archaeologist and orientalist Charles Clermont-Ganneau had commented on and published his description of this "group of sepulchers, cut in the rock," complete with a map. ("There have been found in them . . . ," he wrote, "quantities of bones, broken pottery, 'boxes' in soft stone, and an ear-ring in gold . . .") His words were reproduced in the widely circulated *Survey of Western Palestine*, published ten years later, and the citation dutifully copied out in various letters between Breasted and the antiquities authorities as early as 1927, though their presence seems not to have been considered a problem when the site was chosen for the museum. Now, though, as the workers started to dig, those few bones and broken pots quickly multiplied and soon gave way to a vast trove of objects and skeletons. "We

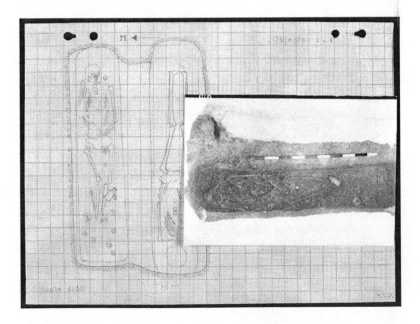

have," Harrison reported to Richmond just a day into this procedure, sounding at once frustrated and awed by the way the ghostlike
past had again wafted up to haunt the present, "found a grave in practically every pit dug." Within a week, the workers had filled baskets
with tens, then hundreds of pins and beads, potsherds and lamps,
"skulls and many human bones," in the words of one antiquities
inspector, "with the arm bones crossed diagonally and the skulls between, evidence of careful burial." And just as carefully as they were
set in the tombs all those centuries ago, these remains would now
need to be exhumed with exacting attention.

So extensive was this field of scarabs and skeletons that a month
after the digging began, Harrison called a halt to the foundation work
"pending further investigations." As is often the case in Jerusalem,
the dead had overwhelmed the living. It would take almost a year for
the excavating to resume and another nine months before he could
report to his mother that "the foundations of the Museum are well
in hand," though "a heavy downfall of rain has not been helpful."
Other developments also slowed the work: Plumer had left and Chancellor arrived and impatiently awaited the construction of the new
Government House, which the authorities gave political priority over
the museum. Because of the riots of 1929, work in Harrison's office
had ground to a halt for several months, and it took some time for
things to return to a kind of normal.

Against this backdrop of bones and bloodletting, Harrison was
meanwhile in the peculiar position of creating his very own remains,
in stone and on paper. The latter will require excavation as well,
buried as their traces eventually are in the archive of the museum
built over the graves.

No trowels or baskets are necessary. Years later, perched on a
plastic chair before a laptop computer, I open a fraying folder and
read a letter dated February 1, 1929, from A. St. B. Harrison to
Mr. Richmond: "*There is a matter about which I intended to speak to you
when last I saw you. It is possible—I am afraid probable—that someone will
have to lay a foundation stone. God knows I would much rather this were
avoided. I must however be ready for any emergency.*"

It's odd and more than slightly eerie to be thumbing through
these pages while sitting in the space labeled "Record Room" on
Harrison's floor plans. As he penciled in those letters, had he ever

imagined that *his* records might one day be deposited in this very room? *"The position for such a stone I have already considered. I ought however to search for a suitable stone (possibly a piece of Hoptonwood from England) & have it carefully lettered. I cannot do anything, however, until I know what is to be inscribed. Brevity is very desirable. We don't want to emulate the inscriptions in London public conveniences."*

Whatever his vision for the future of the building, he can't possibly have conceived that the same room would become world-renowned in the 1950s as "the Scrollery," the long, light, and airy Jordanian chamber in which the Dead Sea Scrolls would first be pored over and parsed. The ancient past would have a famous future here, even as his own modern moment would already be fading from view. *"What I am afraid of is that one day someone from the Secretariat or elsewhere will have a brilliant idea & I shall be asked to have a stone ready within twenty-four hours or less & as I am rather sensitive about lettering, I should consider this disastrous."*

He might not even recognize his architectural handiwork in what would become the cubicle-and-tin-shelf-crowded Israeli office where, more than another half century after the fragments of the scrolls are arrayed under glass across long tables here, I find myself typing his words into a computer file to the sound of Hebrew telephone chit-chat and the synthetically sweet smell of hot instant coffee.

Which details will be remembered? Which will fade? Disappear?

RELATIVE RELICS

THAT THE MUSEUM FILLED WITH RELICS WOULD ONE DAY ALSO BE a relic may or may not have occurred to the fez-, fedora-, and turban-wearing guests seated before the raised wooden platform at the ceremonial laying of that foundation stone in the summer of 1930. Or perhaps the assembled dignitaries, under all their varied hats, truly believed that the building's importance would endure for ages—together with the British Empire and Palestine itself. Posterity was certainly on the minds of those in charge. Why else the emphatic fanfare of the carved inscription?

THIS STONE WAS LAID BY LIEUTENANT-COLONEL
SIR JOHN ROBERT CHANCELLOR. G.C.M.G. G.C.V.O. D.S.O.
HIS BRITANNIC MAJESTY'S HIGH COMMISSIONER AND
COMMANDER-IN-CHIEF IN PALESTINE, ON THE 19TH DAY
OF JUNE IN THE YEAR OF OUR LORD MCMXXX

Why else set down with inching exactitude and why later store the plans for every stage of the so-called Order of Procedure, from the instant when His Excellency mounts the platform by the north steps to the speech by the director of antiquities and its translation, to the speech by His Excellency and its translation to the point when the director of public works hands the lead box filled with "Palestine coins" to His Excellency, His Excellency places the box in the cavity, the director of public works hands the trowel to His Excellency . . . and so on and on, exceedingly stiffly, until that moment of high if not exactly spontaneous climax when His Excellency taps the stone, the director of public works hands the level to His Excellency, His Excellency levels and declares the stone truly laid, and (after yet another translation) leaves the platform by the south steps?

Why else preserve Rockefeller's Western Union telegram to Chancellor offering CORDIAL CONGRATULATIONS and wishing FOR THE MUSEUM A LONG LIFE OF USEFUL SERVICE? Why record and retain the list of those invited to celebrate this burial that follows all the exhumations? *Dr. Albright, Signor A. Barluzzi, Dr. E. L. Sukenik, Dr. & Mrs. Canaan, Mr. D. C. Baramki, Dr. L. A. Mayer, Miss Garrod, the Archminadrite Kallistos, Jacob Spafford, Adil Eff. Jabre* . . . Was there, in the urge to keep and catalog these piles of inky ephemera, some flickering awareness of just how fleeting the moment was? In all their ethnic, religious, and linguistic variety, the guests represented a hybrid and relatively peaceful Jerusalem that may already have seemed to some of them—given the violent explosions of the previous summer— to be dangerously fragile if not under serious threat. Though if they were anxious, they didn't show it. The photographs of the crowd that had gathered on folding chairs before the Old City walls that sunny Thursday afternoon convey an air of almost drowsy calm.

Whether later glued into Harrison's personal photo album or sent

on with captions to Breasted in Chicago for preservation at the Oriental Institute archive or mailed to Rockefeller's Manhattan office in the Standard Oil building for his secretaries to deposit in fine wooden cabinets—all the black-and-white pictures will fix in time, as in amber, that sense of the day's overwhelming placidity, even boredom. The professors and priests, the judges and journalists, the mufti, the mayor, the Jewish Agency representatives, the Arab Executive representatives, the bishops under their pointed hoods, the women in their cloches and chic high-heeled shoes (they are wives, secretaries, one formidable schoolmistress, a pioneering archaeologist or two): all sit side by side and turn their faces upward, smiling faintly as His Excellency proclaims it—according to the typed copy of his remarks, later filed neatly on several continents—"a great privilege to be present today to lay the Foundation Stone of the Palestine Archaeological Museum."

Everyone, that is, except Harrison, who detested official functions but who apparently couldn't avoid this occasion, meant to honor the construction of what Chancellor assured the crowd in the same speech would be "this beautiful building." In the photos of the ceremony that will be so carefully held for decades to come in those far-flung albums and archival boxes, the architect's tall, lanky frame and close-cropped head appear in fragmentary profile at the very back corner of the platform. Averting his gaze as the speeches are made and the stone is lowered on its winch, he stares off to the side or down at the floor and looks intensely uncomfortable, as though he'd rather be almost anywhere but here.

If the ceremony made him miserable, it was no reflection on the museum itself, which—thinking back after its completion and his hushed 1937 flight from Jerusalem—he'd describe as "the one work in Palestine with which I was connected which has given me some measure of satisfaction."

Understatement aside, he'd been waiting for years to build such a thing, more than any other of his designs the product of his very own time-traveling, quietly kaleidoscopic imagination and forceful will, and one whose funding by a wealthy private foreign investor had protected it from some of the grosser compromises he felt had been foisted on him in other, bureaucracy-bitten, government-sponsored contexts. As it emerged in his final plans and in the small ceramic model placed on display beside the platform at the June ceremony— as well as in the finished building itself—the museum would be, in a subtle though palpable sense, the pale stone embodiment of all the architecture he had absorbed in this part of the world, and of all the architecture he most admired. With its curved barbican and squat octagonal tower, its arrow-slit windows and wider, arched windows, its cave-like cloisters, sun-bleached courtyards, staggered rooftops, and multiple low-domed cubes, his design borrows elements from Islamic tombs and Crusader forts, Byzantine churches, Palestinian peasant houses, and even the Alhambra. In the process, it makes a mysterious if somehow inevitable whole of these disparate parts, both suggesting and transcending the cultural context of each squinch and every column. It's almost as though Harrison had drifted to sleep and *dreamed* this building, which, for all its gravity, also conveys a certain sly and even sphinxlike wit. The building seems to be symmetrical but isn't, quite. Its careful geometries give the illusion of matching one another, but discreet differences proliferate throughout, as architectural half rhymes. With its play of light and shadow, its strict lines giving way to gentle arcs and rounded vaults, its hidden nooks and wide-open spaces, it takes shape as a kind of whispered riddle— somehow akin to Jerusalem itself.

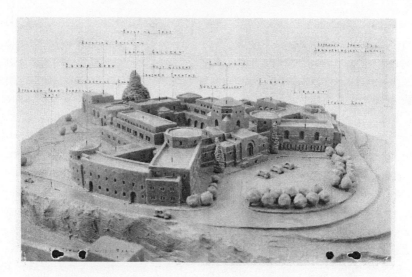

More than paying homage to any one tradition or style of building, the museum soundlessly echoes the ramparts and domes of the Old City right beside it, but it transforms the chaotic, competing turrets and towers of the actual jumbled and often angry landscape into a single harmonious whole. The museum isn't exactly utopian—of *no* place—since its rubble vaults and lemony stone mark it absolutely of *this* place. But the building is, in a way, aspirational, as it suggests Harrison's own private vision of the city—not exactly as it was, but as it might, in a better world, be.

He knew as well as anyone, of course, that in order to build such an immaculately serene structure, with its shades of the heavenly Jerusalem, he'd need to reckon with the demands of an all-too-earthly town. Delays were by now so commonplace he barely bothered to note them in letters, though Breasted had to keep careful track, since Rockefeller's grant was due to expire if it wasn't used by the first of January 1931, so he and more than one high commissioner needed to politely and repeatedly ask the patron for extensions. (The 1929 stock market crash had also added a newly nervous dimension to Rockefeller's participation, as his own fortune, though still substantial, was badly hit.) Just a few months after moving into Harrison's brand-new Government House that year, Chancellor left Palestine and was replaced by Sir Arthur Wauchope, an old friend of Breasted's, who was, the Egyptologist insisted, "in no way whatever to blame" for the slowness of the building's progress. Besides the discovery of the graves and the 1929 "outbreak . . . wherein the Arabs massacred the Jews at many points in Palestine," construction had been further bogged down by the difficulty of finding a sufficient quantity of acceptable stone. Although Harrison and the highly cultured Scottish Wauchope would seem temperamentally poised to become natural allies, the architect sounded both wary and weary at the prospect of having to learn to please yet another high commissioner—the fourth to have ruled Palestine since his arrival. "I hope only that he is not a Tartar," Harrison wrote his mother, a few weeks before His latest Excellency took over. "He is a bachelor . . . He is said to be musical and artistic. But I have learned that this may mean many things. He is said to have a passion for enjoying his house. This too may mean many things." And in fact the slight Scotsman with the silver hair and the fine taste would soon gain a reputation around town for ranging all too widely. Much as Erich Mendelsohn admired Wauchope, he'd be remembered later by one British official for "his intolerance, his charm, his bursts of temper, his calculated shrewdness, his inconsistencies, . . . [his] many kindnesses . . . [He] was a living example of Dr. Jekyll and Mr. Hyde."

But before reckoning with the high commissioner's seemingly split personality, Harrison had to contend with the shortage of quality stone. First he managed to piece together small lots from seventeen different sources, then the government opened a quarry near Nablus specifically for this project, and he and his assistants had to modify their drawings to make the best use of that supply. As always, the all-American Breasted also blamed cultural difference for the "astonishing amount of time required for . . . construction," offering that "it is not a usual thing to put up a building of this character in a country as primitive as is the case here . . . [so] some delay might have been expected." Moreover, "our British friends in Palestine are, like all their countrymen, slower and more deliberate than we are."

Harrison had in fact been working doggedly—as had a crew of some seven hundred local laborers who'd managed by June 1932 to make use of three thousand square meters of walling stone, a thousand tons of cement, and two thousand five hundred cubic meters of sand. According to one of Harrison's progress reports, filed that month, they'd almost completed the lower floor, and work on the upper ground floor was proceeding "rapidly," with some of the vaults already in place. He was eager to oversee the completion of the building's carcass by January 1934, with the "major part of the finishing trades" wrapping up their additions by the middle of that year. With this in mind, a "considerable quantity of Walnut has already been selected in Syria and brought to the site, where it is now being cut and stacked."

Unmentioned in all these crisply worded accounts of the precise amount of stone, wood, and cement required to erect and properly outfit the museum were calculations of a less architectural, more flesh-and-blood sort: namely, which population would finally outnumber the other in Palestine?
These days Jews from Germany and Austria were entering the country in droves, much to the dismay of the native-born Arabs. Even though the government had established certain immigration quotas, in late October 1933, further demonstrations protesting the arrival of so many Jews gave way to further violence. A deputation of local Arab leaders arranged to meet with Wauchope to air their complaints and again
demand a representative government. According to one newspaper account, they "stated that the basic fear in the Arab mind was that the Jews would obtain supremacy in Palestine to which Sir Arthur replied that there was no need to fear since he was ruling the country with equity." The next month, Harrison adopted the same breezily dismissive tone as he assured his mother that "there is no cause at all for anxiety. The rebellion is over. I had neither so amusing, nor so exciting a time as in 1929. In the last troubles, you will remember, I was the target of Jews; in this, of the Arabs. They ambushed five of us in a car and fired at us: but luckily missed. Once again I had to search my elderly landlord for arms." Politics, meanwhile,

now permeated every stage of the building process, from the appointment of architects to the hiring of laborers. The relatively pastoral Eastern backwater where Harrison had first begun work as a young architect was now the epicenter of one of the world's most relentless life-and-death national struggles—a struggle in which he himself had no particular stake, though staying detached was itself, he'd come to realize, a highly dubious prospect. Fairness of the basic sort in which he believed seemed challenged at every turn.

Not only was ethnic tension mounting daily, so was Harrison's strong sense that Wauchope did not value his work. ("As usual, he gives me credit for nothing," he wrote Ena, "and finds everything I do amiss.") The high commissioner was also exerting pressure on him to produce as quickly and cheaply as possible plans for a host of other buildings, including a large government complex on Julian's Way, near the King David Hotel and the YMCA, meant to hold the as yet only theoretical legislative assembly. Despite all these distractions, however, Harrison remained determined not to take sides or cut corners but to see into being his syncretic masterpiece. So it was that he closely supervised the same Italian contractors responsible for Government House, E. di A. De Farro & Co. of Alexandria, Cairo, Jerusalem, and London, who managed the large crews of Arab and Jewish workers, craftsmen, and technicians. Cork tiles, rolling shutters, electric light fixtures, door fittings, and locks would be shipped from England, along with most of the rest of the museum's equipment—from fire extinguishers to electric clocks to display cases with adjustable bronze feet. The apparatus for the so-called Optical Lantern Room would come from Switzerland, while the terrazzo work and cement tiling would be produced by a Jewish firm in Jaffa. And again Harrison arranged with the ceramicist David Ohannessian to create several vivid pieces to punctuate the building's otherwise muted palette. The first was an elaborate turquoise, blue, black, and cream effusion of Andalusian-styled *cuerda seca* ceramics that would cover the walls and ceiling of the intricately domed pavilion at one end of the cloistered central courtyard. The other was a plainer installation of small black-and-white tiles that together formed blocky Greek letters and sent a line from Plato running in a ribbon around the upper walls of the circular Archaeological Advisory boardroom like a length of antique tickertape.

Harrison chose the phrase ostensibly because it contains the first-ever use of the Greek word *archaiologia*, or the study of antiquity—THEY ARE VERY FOND OF HEARING ABOUT THE GENEOLOGIES OF HEROES AND MEN, SOCRATES, AND THE FOUNDATION OF CITIES IN ANCIENT TIMES AND, IN SHORT ABOUT ANTIQUITY [ARCHAEOLO-GIA] IN GENERAL—though this may be one of the building's dry inside jokes, since as Harrison of all people knew, this dialogue, *Hippias Major*, is not so much concerned with antiquity as it is with beauty, and the question of just what *that* is. A pretty girl? Gold? To be rich and respected? Or is beauty what is appropriate? That which is useful? Favorable? The pleasure that comes from seeing and hearing?

Socrates and his fellow philosopher Hippias don't resolve the question in the course of their dialogue. But in its final words Socrates tartly tells Hippias how much he has benefited from their conversation: "*For I think I know the meaning of the proverb 'beautiful things are difficult.'*" In a way, this writing, too, was on the wall.

At around the same time that the latest riots broke out, Harrison invited Eric Gill to travel to Jerusalem to carve a set of ten bas-reliefs for the museum courtyard. The idea he'd proposed to the maverick Catholic craftsman wasn't explicitly political, but it might as well have been, sitting as it did at such stubborn odds with the aggressive nationalistic tug-of-war now playing out around him. He wanted Gill to create a set of carvings that would line the walls of the court and represent "the various civilizations which have formed the cultures of the land of Palestine."

Although the scheme was essentially backward looking and maybe even a bit staid, there was, too, a more pressing dimension to the design. Set at even intervals between the cloisters' columns, each relief would be placed in equal relation to the others, with no single culture dominating but all of them coexisting in the bright calm of the museum's inner sanctum. While Harrison was far too politically reticent to ever make of his architecture an outright argument, the space he had conceived as the building's heart does seem to express a kind of bottled-up, unspoken desire for the strife just to *stop*, or at least to subside temporarily as he hoped it would within the placid realm of this enclosure, with its lily-pad-dotted, goldfish-filled reflecting pool and wide-open view of the sky.

The vision of such a peaceful oasis in mind, Harrison sent Gill a list of "ancient nations" for him to consider carving, and the sculptor agreed to take on the Jerusalem assignment—which would constitute for him both a practical stonecutting job and profound religious pilgrimage, or vice versa. Different as Harrison and Gill were in so many basic respects—the former intensely private, even-tempered, monkish, deliberate, skeptical; the latter charismatic, vatic, voraciously sexual, spontaneous, devout—their dedication to the notion that "art embraces all making" bound them in an essential way, as did an unwavering, DNA-level Englishness. Gill prided himself on his vehement nonconformism and ability to shock, but he'd also rendered public sculptures for some of the stodgiest institutions of the English establishment: the Stations of the Cross at Westminster Cathedral, the reliefs of three of the four winds that face the headquarters of the London Underground, Ariel and Prospero on the front of the BBC's Broadcasting House, and so on. One of Gill's protégés, the poet, painter, and engraver David Jones—who would spend several weeks with him in Jerusalem while he carved at the museum and walked the actual Stations of the Cross—would describe his friend and mentor after his death as "absolutely colossally English. I don't think I've ever met anybody who was so terribly English," something that was often said of Harrison, despite all his years abroad. Consciously or not, his decision to bring Gill to Jerusalem at this particular moment in his life and the life of the country seemed almost a way of buttressing his own British sense of self and of the fundamental Britishness of even his most Palestinian buildings. Besides all the ancient nations the Palestine Archaeological Museum was meant to represent, in other words, the civilization this compound would ultimately come to stand for above all others was that of Britain and the British Mandate. It was an artifact in the making.

After consulting in early February 1934 with Harrison's old friend the archaeologist George Horsfield, Gill rendered quick sketches for each of the reliefs and sent them to Harrison, together with a note in his spiky yet flowing hand: "I hope," he wrote, "you won't think the figures look too stumpy & clumsy & comic. You see in such small panels . . . it's not possible to retain naturalistic or academic proportions." Gill's trademark blend of sincerity and playfulness does indeed give the blocky figures an almost cartoonish look—though the approach works well to leaven what might otherwise be a ponderous assignment. The pencil sketches come complete with scrawled picture-book-styled captions that summarize in a single phrase the contribution to Palestine of each civilization. These wouldn't appear in the final carvings but seemed to serve as conceptual goads: *"The Chaldeans brought agriculture," "Egypt brought the rule of Kings," "The Phoenicians came in ships," "Israel brought the Law,"* and so on, through what was brought by the Greeks (Humanism), the Persians ("Strange Rites"), Islam (the Koran), and the Crusaders (Building). The Byzantines "found the true cross," and Rome, which "conquered nature (i.e. took Bull by the horns or wolf by the teats)," is the most childlike of all the somehow defiantly childlike images, and shows the kneeling, naked Romulus and Remus suckling hungrily from their canine wet nurse, Lupa.

"Also I hope," Gill wrote Harrison, anticipating the response to such stylized images, "there will not be too much criticism on archaeological lines—the exact shape of the Phoenician galley or of a crusader's helmet. I'll go to the British Museum & the V&A this week but I'm sending these sketches without delay so that you may see what I propose."

By late March, Gill and his assistant, Laurie Cribb, had made their way by boat then train to Jerusalem, where they met and immediately liked Harrison. "Suffice it to say that he's a very nice man indeed & most kind and enthusiastic. (Age 42)," Gill reported in one of his brisk letters to his wife, back in England. Gill was visually alert, but he confined himself in a matter-of-fact and cheerful way to the most imprecise of physical descriptions: "Clean shaven, typical architect's face," whatever that might mean. As soon as they arrived at the train station they were whisked off to have a "splendid" breakfast and hot baths at Harrison's "beautiful" house, then were driven to see the museum, deposited their tools there, installed themselves at St. Étienne's Dominican convent outside the Damascus Gate, and—by the next day—were already hard at work.

"We've started the job. V. difficult to get started. It's v. hot here already & v. glaring and dusty. But lovely beyond words—incredibly lovely." Performing the Middle Eastern equivalent of bringing coals to Newcastle, Gill had shipped a supply of Derbyshire-quarried Hoptonwood stone all the way to stony Jerusalem, and—as though it were just another day back in his workshop in Buckinghamshire—started "roughing out" work in a small shed near the museum. Once the stones were fixed on the wall, he'd begin carving, and after a week he'd be able to report that "all is well & we are well . . . The work is going on but I have been delayed by having to make new designs for three of the panels (owing to

The Sculptor at work

criticism by local pundits)." He and Harrison had been given, he wrote in another letter, "a lot of bother" from various archaeologists about the details of the panels, "but eventually we decided, having got all we wanted out of them, to leave the archaeology behind— they said it was archaeology, the others (me & H) . . . said nay, it's nought but very nearly complete nonsense."

Having switched his usual stonemason's smock and felt hat for a specially ordered gold-and-black-striped robe, along with a tradi- tional Palestinian kaffiyeh and 'igal to keep the sun off his neck, he was carving long, hard days, from 7:30 a.m. to 5:30 p.m., in the bright light on a wooden scaffold. "Up to the present," he wrote at

the end of April, now finished with five of the ten panels, "I've been working all on the shady side of the courtyard . . . But to-morrow I start on the sunny side & then I shall know what it is really like. It's very hot here now—you can hardly pick up the chisels if you leave them in the sun."

Once he'd completed the reliefs, Gill would also carve a tympanum over the museum's entrance—as he put it, "a half circle representing MAN! (i.e., man from the point of view of museum curators)." Though an early sketch shows a carpenter sawing wood and a farmer threshing wheat under a tree, the carving that he'd finally render— while suffering from a severe toothache—shows two blank-faced soldiers, swords at their sides as they kneel and raise their arms in peace or surrender before a leafy tree. Meant to symbolize the meet- ing of AFRICA and ASIA in Palestine, they may be Assyrians, they may be Crusaders, but either way, "I am," Gill would write Harrison afterward, "v. miserable about the main door. I was ill when I finished it. It shows."

Despite his abscessed tooth and the somewhat thick symbolism of these various carvings, Gill also managed to bring a light touch to the smaller objects and multiple signs that punctuate Harrison's building and give it—for all its Eastern monumentality—a certain gentle English whimsy. He fashioned, for instance, a toylike gargoyle that would spew water gently into the courtyard fountain and designed the clear, somehow good-natured English, Hebrew, and Arabic lettering that Cribb would cut into the stone and paint a vibrant red all around the museum:

WAY IN $\rightarrow$ SOUTH GALLERY   CLOAKS

The letters on the signs, from EARLY BRONZE AGE 3000–2000 B.C. to DRINKING WATER, are all treated with the same unfussy respect, as is the warning to

placed like another ancient relic near the Roman altars and Byzantine lintels that fill the courtyard cloisters.

When they weren't carving, Gill and Cribb spent hours with Harrison, walking and talking and taking in the Christian sites—to which Gill as a fierce believer was especially drawn. He and Harrison became quite close during this period. (Gill would later "affectionately dedicate" his *Palestine Diary*—a collection of letters to his wife from this journey—"to his friend Austen St B. Harrison.") And in later years, Gill would look back rhapsodically on his time in Jerusalem and call Palestine "the last of the revelations vouchsafed to me."

"Far . . . from finding disappointment in Palestine I found only good," he'd insist, sounding a little like a plainspoken British Else Lasker-Schüler—who was as it happens visiting the city for the first time that same month, though the two Jerusalem-entranced caftan wearers never met. "For Palestine is the Holy Land . . . the antithesis of everything our England stands for." On top of that, "I never saw or imagined anything more lovely than the Holy Land . . . so also I never saw anything less corrupted by human pride and sin"—words that sit oddly in relation to the far messier shifts between rapture and revulsion that he set down in real time. In one especially raw moment, Gill wrote his wife that it's "impossible to convey Jerusalem to you in a letter. Its marvelous loneliness & its confusion. I am so . . . torn asunder between love & hatred & so worried by the job in hand and its futility . . . I am so sorry." It must have been something in the chalky water: "The city is fundamentally depressing—tragic, confused, divided, surging with suppressed hatreds & conflicting cultures—the only peace the peace preserved by English policemen & why do they trouble to possess it?"

It was in many ways the question that Harrison had been asking himself with growing anxiousness of late, and even as the museum neared completion and he labored to finish as speedily as possible plans for a range of other buildings—the Jerusalem post office; the massive block of government buildings with its legislative assembly; an uncharacteristically sleek, whitewashed, almost Mendelsohnian government printing press; among others—the politics of his office, and of the country in general, weighed on him more and more.

"To have almost finished the Museum is for me to feel a great sense of relief—a great load lifted off my shoulders," he wrote to his mother in October 1935. "It might have been something more than this had I not been working under a cloud here." The building wouldn't open to the public for another three years, as the exhibits and library books and laboratory equipment were moved in and unpacked. But other architects had already praised its design in the strongest terms: Frank Mears—"a man not given to enthusiasm . . . who knows

some of the problems with which I have had to wrestle from having worked in this country"—wrote to tell Harrison that the museum was "an object lesson to all of us on the virtues of simplicity and restraint." An article by Lotte Baerwald, widow of the German Jewish architect Alexander Baerwald, who had built several major buildings in Palestine, appeared in a Berlin Jewish newspaper that same year. Under the headline "Ein Großer Architekt: Harrison," she declared, "Palestine may count itself happy to possess as its chief architect Harrison, a great artist. Where he has a hand, there rises a masterpiece. But," she wrote, "who knows Harrison? Who speaks of him?"

For all of this adulation, though, he felt anything but buoyed up. "It would," he brooded, "take a lot to turn my head: I am much too conscious of my ineptitudes and failures." And even as he was praised in grand terms from afar, the strain at close range had intensified. "My difficulties increase so that I am beginning to wonder whether I shall be forced to get out. For if only I could weather the storm there is much interesting work still to do in Palestine. Wauchope is so hounding me," he wrote in exhaustion to his mother, "that I feel almost that he hopes I will resign. This must sound silly to you, for he is such a big man and I am such a little one."

That storm was, as always, political but this time it brewed in the grayest, coldest, most bureaucratic sense. While Harrison's artistry may have been appreciated in the big wide world, back in the cramped confines of the Public Works Department there were, according to one observer, "terrible rows going on." Jobs had been given to private architects, which was "rather a smack in the eyes for Harrison . . . as he is supposed to do all Government buildings, but there is stacks to do, and Harrison is an artist and a dreamer." His friend George Horsfield even wrote to Harrison's mother to confide his concern about Austen, who "takes life hard. The creative spirit is strong in him and he suffers accordingly."

Politics of a more national sort also affected him directly. Not only did Wauchope seem personally unimpressed by Harrison's designs, he had made a point of seeking out Jewish architects and giving them work. "We are," he explained, "a Mandatory Power and I think where possible we should employ Palestinians, more especially where they can leave their mark on the land in such a way as architecture lends itself." By Palestinian, he meant Jewish: "There are," he wrote, "no Arab architects of proved capacity." Although the government's assignment of architectural commissions was hardly the cause of the Arab Revolt that exploded in April 1936, the perception of such economic and political favoritism was partly what had prompted the latest—and by far the most sustained—blast of local violence to date. (Chaim Yassky was now running his makeshift field hospital out of the old Hadassah building on the Street of the Prophets; Erich Mendelsohn was hard at work on plans for the new medical complex on Mount Scopus.)

By August 1937, Harrison had endured quite enough of the never-ending ethnic and personal agon, to say nothing of the way each new crisis affected his architectural work. "I am very, very tired—" he wrote to a friend in England that same month, "the result of two years with nothing fruitful to do. Job after job has been transferred to private architects & those left to me have been abandoned. Mendelsohn got my Haifa Hospital after I had prepared sketch plans & estimates . . . I am taking advantage of the obscure political situation to try & get out . . . I have got into such a state mentally that I can stay only at the risk of going off my head. I ought of course now to be doing my best work—I am 45. If I go I must, I suppose, give up architecture. I am thinking of living in Greece or on the Bosphorus . . ." He was considering, he said, "wandering" for half a year or more, "to recover my mental equilibrium. I don't think I could live in England longer than a month."

"You don't," he asked, "know a Maharajah, a sultan or other oriental potentate who wants the services for ten years or less of an architect saturated with Near Eastern traditions do you? I should make a good court architect & should be careful not to design anything so perfect that my lord should be tempted to cut off my head." He was, it would seem, joking.

◈

And then it was over. He had "escaped."

He felt "like a convict escaped," he wrote Ena, repeating and apparently savoring that word, "from some penal settlement in South America."

After waiting exactly fifteen years and a day since he started work in Palestine—the minimum required to receive a government pension—he fled in secret, telling only a few close friends and his assistants; all the furniture and rugs in his Abu Tor house were sold off in his absence. After he left, he received letters from various admirers and acquaintances, surprised by and sorry for his departure: "Good luck in your care free future," wrote the chief of police, a friend. "I regret that for the moment we cannot build aesthetically beautiful police stations but only grim loop-holed buildings to withstand the concentrated anger of a population driven to despair by a policy which might have been carried out with a minimum of mental and physical suffering and which even now might have been carried into happier channels."

Back in England, Eric Gill sounded cheered by the news of his leaving: "Thank goodness you are now free. It is jolly fine I may say in a manner of speaking no longer to have to think of you languishing like a suppressed volcano at Jerusalem . . . You must have had some bad moments when you were packing up at Deir Abu Tor and it's horrid to think of those rooms thus desolated—the first room I entered in Jerusalem. If it comes to that I can't bear to think of Jerusalem & no Austen groaning in the wilderness."

He escaped before the museum's grand opening in January 1938—canceled at the last minute when the English archaeologist J. L. Starkey was ambushed and murdered on his way to the ceremony by what one newspaper account called "a party of Arabs in circumstances of shocking brutality." He escaped before his Jerusalem post office was finished and feted, its counter promptly blown to bits and that British sapper killed by the Irgun and their Zionistically charged gelignite packages. He escaped well before the British Mandate limped to a close in mid–May 1948. That same week one prominent English architectural journal would publish an article complete with photographs of his plans for the government compound which, the write-up explained, became "obsolete" with the 1947 UN resolution to partition the country between Arabs and Jews. There was no longer a need for a general assembly where all the legislators could sit together. And now, even though "this partition scheme has been abandoned, . . . even if some central government emerges from the present chaos it is unlikely that this project will ever be realized."

It wasn't just the unbuilt structures whose fate was foggy. In December 1947, right after the UN approved partition and civil war erupted, the Mandatory authorities would move the Jewish employees of the Palestine Archaeological Museum, together with a card index of objects and various files and books, across town to a temporary branch office in Mendelsohn's Schocken Library. The British curator, Arab employees, and most of the museum's holdings would stay behind, though by November of the next year, on a stopover in London between trips to Cyprus and Egypt, as war in the new state of Israel raged, Harrison would write to a close Jewish friend back in Jerusalem that "I am expecting to hear anyday that the Palestine Archaeological building—the only building I have designed for which I have some respect—has been blown sky high. It presents a sorry appearance. I believe it is occupied by some of Abdullah's men."

In fact the building would continue to stand, largely unscathed, remaining under the control of an international board until 1966, when Jordan's King Hussein briefly nationalized it. After 1967 and Israel's occupation of East Jerusalem, the Israeli Department of Antiquities and many blue-and-white flags would be installed there. The new administration would peel back the sticky tape that hid

Gill's Hebrew letters for a period after 1948 and repaint them the same old red . . . though the Arabic inscription indicating

would remain pointedly colorless. The building would soon be absorbed into the Israel Museum and come to be known as "the Rockefeller"; the department itself would later evolve into the so-called Israel Antiquities Authority.

For all the disgust he evinced at his departure, Harrison would in fact slip back for a few brief visits, before 1948 and after it, to the city's Jordanian side. In the mid-1940s he even designed a compound for the British Council in Jerusalem, as well as a warden's lodge for the Ophthalmic Hospital of the Order of St. John—the plans for both of which were eventually scrapped. ("I am," he wrote a friend from Cairo in late 1946, "extremely busy planning buildings which will never be constructed.") But with the years, he tried to distance himself from the place and to obliterate in uncharacteristically extreme fashion the traces of his time in the city; he burned most of his personal papers and preserved just a weathered sheaf of retyped and, it seems, redacted correspondence. For whatever reasons—professional, political, sexual?—his last two years in the country would completely disappear from his private written record. But he couldn't erase the lingering fact of his presence in Jerusalem.

He's there on a hot July day well into the next century, for instance, when I weave my way through the teeming streets of East Jerusalem and pass through a metal detector and under the hard gaze of several Russian-accented, pistol-packing Israeli security guards. They're especially suspicious of those (very few) who arrive on foot at the gate of this fortresslike Israeli institution in the middle of a busy Palestinian neighborhood. But no matter which government claims control of this highly sensitive piece of property, it's still somehow Harrison's museum.

Or so I tell myself as I move around the smoothly curved wall of the barbican, now a kosher cafeteria, thread around the employees' crookedly parked cars, up the steps, and through the cool and cooling entrance, under Gill's kneeling soldiers and their truce-inducing tree. No matter its besieged-seeming current state, this remains one of my favorite buildings in the whole city—an island of calm and focus—and after I make my way through the empty and echoing tower hall and down a long, vaulted corridor, I enter a room to one side. There, I open a cardboard box filled with sketch pads, postcards, press clippings, telegrams, and gardening notebooks, and pull out that fading typescript with its handwritten title, "Some Letters of Mine," the "some" a wry provocation to the would-be biographer.

These are the letters he spared from the fire—those that, for all his strictly guarded privacy, he wanted someone, or ones, to read: a papery time capsule. After wandering with him from Egypt to Cyprus to the Greek island of Evia and to Athens, where he lived for years, died at age eighty-six, and was buried, they've made their unlikely way back to Jerusalem and to this space of his own design, the former British Record Room, the onetime Jordanian Scrollery, the present-day Israel Antiquities Authority Archive, which will soon serve some other purpose altogether, as yet unspecified.

In a few years, this archive, and with it Austen Harrison's written traces, will also be moved—into a sprawling new archaeological campus designed by Moshe Safdie, the most renowned and would-be Herodian of contemporary Israeli architects. If Harrison, "the" architect of the British Mandate, favored modesty, proportion, and understatement, Safdie, "the" architect of post-1967 Israel, has no such preferences. His ostentatious plan for the campus— which will sit near the Knesset and Prime Minister's Office and, it is said, hold two million relics, fifteen thousand pieces of the Dead Sea Scrolls, and the largest archaeological library in the whole Middle East—features a massive concave glass-and-polymer fabric canopy, held aloft by soaring tensile cables and modeled in the most literal fashion on the tents used on local archaeological digs. Aggressively symbolic in more than that sense, it also seems meant to invoke an engorged variation on the biblical tabernacle, and so to demonstrate the Jewish state's God-given rights to both the ancient relics belowground and the country's built future.

But all that is yet to come. Contemplating the layers of what the older museum's builder has left behind, I can only dig, and keep digging, here and now.

III

WHERE THE GREAT
CITY STANDS

2014 / 1914

SIGNS

I've set out this summer in search of a ghost.

Throughout hot July, during burning August, I find myself walking the streets of Jerusalem compulsively, as if I thought I could track a ghost's footprints. I seem, in particular, weirdly drawn to the same stretch of Jaffa Road, opposite Zion Square. Years ago this was the ghost's part of town. It's said that he built it and that his office was here. He must have strolled something like this same route every day. Would he recognize it now?

Pale stone construction aside, the row of balcony-studded buildings that define the commercial core of twenty-first-century West Jerusalem do still suggest a chic street in Athens, circa 1925. The basic structures have an unapologetically pretty solidity, with arched openings for shops and cafés below; above, those multiple small balconies are framed by elaborate Art Deco–ish ironwork grilles and held aloft by variously curved or notched corbels.

It takes some work to register this essential elegance, since these days the buildings' storefronts are cluttered with gaudy awnings, rusting air conditioners, Israeli flags, security cameras, tangled electrical cords, and loud plastic signage in a scramble of English, Hebrew, and basic cookbook Italian:

SICILIANO PIZZA PASTA KOSHER

LorD KitscH

WELCOME TO HAVE A LOOK!! JERUSALEM HOSTEL AND HOTEL FROM 250 NIS

CHANGE

Shai Kong unique clothing

AROMA espresso kosher

LOTTO
7 million shekels

BURGERSBAR since 1999

47 SHEKEL BUSINESS LUNCH

JOSEF SHOES AND BAGS SALE SALE SALE SALE SALE

INTIMA

A L D O gelateria

A Spoonful of Italian Love kosher

HAIR CITY the Israeli Center for Stimulating Follicles: extensions
& Japanese straightening—Quality Prestige Style

Once, the Zion Cinema that borrowed its name from the nearby mount and in turn loaned the square its name sat at the heart of the new city. After the movie house was demolished in 1979, a defiantly ugly eleven-story double shaft of a bank building was rammed into its place—a stone-and-glass stake driven into that heart—and a void created, though a few businesses (a bookshop, a pharmacy, one old-world jewelry store) have held on across the street for years. With their plain exteriors and simple placards, also plastic, they're hardly enticing to look at, but their no-frills presence at least serves as a constant in this uncertain landscape. Most of the nearby hamburger joints and polyester-clothing outlets, meanwhile, seem fleeting almost by flimsy design and would fit better in the food court or airless lower level of a seedy suburban shopping mall than in Jerusalem's once gracious downtown.

The reasons for this sad state of affairs are various. Expansionist post-1967 government policies designed to encourage Jewish suburban sprawl, poverty, a deep-seated cultural indifference to physical beauty, terrorist bombings, the long-delayed completion of the new light-rail line, which for nearly a decade left this area a dusty, barely passable construction site—all have taken a serious toll on the center of the city.

Just a few blocks from Erich Mendelsohn's bank building (now rented to a government ministry by a group of entrepreneurs who, news reports say, plan to "unify the building's height" by adding multiple floors to the back and turning it into a luxury hotel) and Austen Harrison's post office (still intact but looking a little the worse for wear), that signature row of Zion Square buildings was sandblasted clean just a few years ago, to coincide with the light rail's overdue opening. Several ten-ants have since tried to spruce up their surroundings by add-ing geraniums in plastic boxes and painting their balcony trim. On the whole, though, and despite their efforts, an inexorable air of dilapidation persists. A layer of streaky grime has already returned to coat the pink stone; someone has sprayed nonsensical graffiti above a length of hand-carved molding. The lambent blue and turquoise Armenian tiles set into the arched windows and angular doorframes of the grandest façade are especially filthy, in places almost black with grit.  On their second and third floors, some of the offices and apartments retain the long-ago-modish, now decaying robin's-egg blue wooden doors that must be as old as the walls themselves. Others sport dirty modern aluminum casements. Floor rags and plastic tarps droop from rooftops and laundry lines. While a pair of stone columns lends a modest gravitas to the glinting displays at the entrance to that old-world jewelry store, on the top floor of the same building a large hole has been punched in one pane and left to gape—a raw, untended wound.

Such violent contrasts are everywhere here this summer—a

hundred years since the start of the Great War and a few weeks into Israel's latest petty but punishing "military operation." Terminology notwithstanding, it is war, all-out and brutal. If the former shaped the modern Middle East, the latter seems yet another of its cruel aftershocks, one in an almost countless series of conflicts and crises that have rocked this place over the last century. Maybe it's all just a single, long war? In Jerusalem, you can't see the fighting this time around, but signs of its proximity crowd in. Literally. Across the front of the newish city hall, for instance, hangs an enormous Hebrew banner proclaiming with a certain cuddly aggression that JERUSALEM HUGS THE SOLDIERS OF THE I.D.F.

And far off as the bomb-dropping F-16s may be, the pretext for this latest showdown took shape nearby at the end of June, when a gang of Palestinians shot dead three Israeli teenagers on the West Bank and then, in a forest on the outskirts of town, a gang of Israelis forced a Palestinian teenager to drink gasoline and burned him alive in "revenge." Since that night, Jewish mobs run wild through Jerusalem's streets, in search of Arab prey. I haven't witnessed any of this, though in the bright sunshine there are hints of what has happened, what may happen, come darkness. One day, for instance, following my usual path past Zion Square I notice a trio of high-school-age girls in skinny jeans and tank tops laughing and prancing as they wave construction-paper placards and chant. In some other context, they might be raising money for their prom or plugging for a car wash, but in this relentlessly antagonistic setting their Magic Marker scrawls—and taunting calls—declare THE PEOPLE DEMAND REVENGE and RABBI KAHANE WAS RIGHT! ✿. The American-born Jewish Fascist Meir Kahane was once banned from the Knesset for his outspokenly racist views, but by now his attitudes are so commonplace that no one pays the happy-go-lucky teenagers much attention.

Not every local protest, though, meets such apathy. On another afternoon, a crowd gathers at the same spot to shout insults at a young man who's silently holding his own Magic Marker–scrawled Hebrew poster. One must draw close to read the words that are causing such outrage:

I AM A JEW WHO DOESN'T HATE ARABS.

And I am searching for a ghost. Searching for a ghost who may have no place any longer in this angry town square, or in this bellicose ghetto.

Throughout hot July, during burning August, as I move with my notebook and camera back and forth and back again past both the protesters and the row of once proud pinkish buildings that give downtown its spine, I'm looking for him, as I'm looking for clues. Clues to what it is I've lost, to what the city's lost or is rapidly losing: some sense of itself as a place more multitudinous, more heterogeneous, more generous than the "eternal united capital" of a single battered and battering people. Clues to the origin of these buildings, and for signs of the architect who imagined them here, as a backdrop to these dramas he could never have conceived.

It may already be too late. He is, after all, no more than a ghost. But he's a ghost whose traces I've become somehow desperate to find before they disappear completely, as if by doing so I might hold him here—hold something of his city and its waning worldliness here—a bit longer. Though even as those words take shape, I realize that it may well be *myself* I am trying to keep from vanishing from this landscape.

For now, I'm still here, and I believe the ghost is too. And so it is that in the midst of the never-ending war, and the heat, I set out in search of Spyro Houris.

WHO?

By now, his name has almost been forgotten, though during the period of the British Mandate he was, according to local architectural historian David Kroyanker, "one of the best-known architects in Jerusalem" and "among the most outstanding Arab architects."

Kroyanker knows more about the modern city's built past than almost anyone. Born in genteel, largely German-speaking Jewish Rehavia in 1939, he studied architecture in London and—while working as a planner for the municipality under Mayor Teddy Kollek in the 1970s—played a central role in importing the foreign idea of

architectural conservation to a city that was well on its way to oblit-
erating much of its recent architectural history. In his many popular
Hebrew books on Jerusalem's neighborhoods and buildings, he ascribes different designs to Spyro Houris—from this central row of
buildings on Jaffa Road to the most lavish mansion in all of East
Jerusalem, the richly tile-fronted villa that was once the home of the
important Palestinian writer and intellectual Is'af al-Nashashibi, to
several palatial structures in the once mostly Christian Arab, now
Jewish, neighborhoods of Talbiyeh and Ba'qa. At the other end of
Jaffa Road, one of the most ornate—and currently most dilapidated—
Mandate-era buildings in the whole city stands dwarfed by the mon-
strous new central bus station. The ornate building features reddish
and pink *ablaq* masonry, toothy carved stone crenellation, and further
floral Armenian tiles, as well as calligraphed Koranic inscriptions that
declare, for instance, "*Peace be to You; you have led good lives. Enter
Paradise and dwell in it forever.*" This building, says Kroyanker, is also
one of Houris's.

It's hard, in fact, to know much for certain on this front. Kroyanker
describes what he calls "the ethnic aspect of architecture," and he
categorizes building styles according to this slightly slippery rubric.
While he found ample documentation for his books about late nine-
teenth- and early twentieth-century Jewish neighborhoods and
public buildings and for his volumes about "European" (i.e., church)
architecture from the same period and for the Mandatory (British
governmental or Zionist) building that came later, he was forced to
reckon with the archival black hole that surrounds the history of private construction over the past century and a half—which is to say
residential and commercial buildings erected by anyone who wasn't
Jewish. The official record of such projects is notoriously scant. The
Ottoman authorities who ruled before 1918 left few written traces
behind them, and Kroyanker goes so far as to state in a 1985 volume
devoted to "Arab Building Outside the Old City Walls" that for the
period of English rule "no documentary material exists," by which
he means that "as the result of an error"—unspecified—"the permit
files of Mandate-era buildings were burned in the municipality's
storerooms in 1948."

That same year also marked a dark dividing line in the city's living memory. Those who made their homes in many of these buildings and remembered their construction had vanished from the local landscape and had taken that history with them. By the time Kroyanker came around asking questions decades later, there were few Jerusalemites who recalled any such specifics at all, and he was left, as he writes, to gather shards and broken bits of information from the few witnesses who remained. Kroyanker is far too mild in his manner and his politics to mention the *willful* forgetting that also seized the Jews of Jerusalem during these years, though he would probably be the first to admit that for most present-day Israeli Jews, the term "Arab house" mostly implies high real estate values: a handsome, solidly built, and now pricey old structure with certain characteristic architectural features, including large rooms, thick walls, colorful tiled floors, arched windows, high ceilings. The actual Arabs who built and once lived in such a house rarely enter the conversation. In a decidedly nonconfrontational and even sepia-tinted way, Kroyanker has set out to recount certain aspects of the human side of this architectural story. Doing so has not been easy. He says that in the book about "Arab architecture" he attempted to assemble a kind of mosaic, but the results are, he admits, fragmentary, and in many cases the details are unverifiable. This work was, he explains in rather melancholy terms, "connected in many instances to an unpreventable race with death."

So it is that Kroyanker's attributions to Houris are often couched as "maybe" or "possibly" or "it would seem." Sometimes he ascribes to him a shadowy partner he refers to just as "Petassis." Sometimes he does not. (Houris and Petassis may have worked together to design that row of Jaffa Road buildings near Zion Square.) But in book after book he repeatedly credits the architect with "most of the ceramic houses" in the city—by which he means the dozen or so grand private twentieth-century residences whose façades are ornamented with the vibrant tiles of the Armenian ceramicist David Ohannessian, whose work also figures so centrally in the interiors of Austen Harrison's Government House and museum and either on or in several other British-built structures from around the same time. Although a few buildings in Tel Aviv are decorated with heavily figurative, Zionistically symbolic tiles from the 1920s—all shepherds, reapers, camels, and pregnant biblical quotation—the more abstractly floral and richly patterned ceramics of the sort that adorn Houris's buildings exist nowhere else in the country and are considered by natives and tourists alike to represent the quintessence of Jerusalem. Which is to say that whether anyone but David Kroyanker and me and a small scattering of others know the name Spyro Houris, his architecture has become a symbol of the city itself.

Kroyanker's colorfully illustrated, anecdote-filled books are meant to be informative, pleasant, and intellectually unthreatening. They're designed to sit on coffee tables or be packed in satchels and taken on edifying weekend walks through Jerusalem's leafiest back streets. Such walks are, as it happens, an Israeli institution, and for certain aging, educated Ashkenazi Jews who set out on these instructive strolls, usually in safe, chatty groups, Kroyanker's books are equipment as de rigueur as solid shoes, a good sun hat, and a bottle of drinking water. Perhaps not surprisingly, given their intended use, the books' footnotes are minimal or nonexistent. But now that I've become fascinated by, even slightly obsessed with, the mysterious Spyro Houris, I'd like to follow out these bread-crumb trails. Kroyanker identifies various buildings as the architect's but provides minimal information beyond that. He writes that Houris studied in Athens, sometimes worked with "Petassis," and had close connections to the Greek Orthodox Church. That he was "an Arab" and that his buildings typify a certain "Arab" style. He often uses "A Thousand and One Nights" as a catchall term to describe this eclectically ornamental look.

I want, though, to know more—about both the architect and how Kroyanker knows what he knows about him. He has assembled the largest archive in the world that documents Jerusalem's urban fabric, and I imagine that—given all that he's written on the subject—he must have a thick file on Spyro Houris. Realizing that I risk seeming like a nudnik or a brat, I call him to talk.

Which is to say that I call a number in Tel Aviv. Irony of ironies, after a lifetime in Jerusalem, Kroyanker, his wife, and their 120 cartons of documents about the city (between 140,000 and 200,000 individual pieces, according to one estimate) have recently decamped for the coastal plain—not, he has said in various newspaper interviews, because they are fleeing but to be near their daughters and grandchildren, who, like so many younger secular people, have left Jerusalem for good. Public statements to the contrary, one wonders if he, too, quietly felt he'd had enough of the increasingly powerful and proliferating ultra-Orthodox, the constant political tension, the dirt. Kroyanker has often described his love-hate relationship with the town of his birth—"a ragged city . . . A very extreme place"— and has offered various damning assessments, including, for instance, the 2005 observation that "I don't believe that anywhere in the advanced Western world, which we presume to be a part of, there is a main street that compares to Jaffa [Road] in terms of urban degeneration and neglect."

He is gracious when we speak, though he sounds a bit distracted. Or maybe—despite his insistence that, no matter his new Tel Aviv address, he'll continue to research and write about Jerusalem—he's just grown tired of the subject, a feeling I understand all too well. Even as I pepper him with questions about Spyro Houris, I feel myself wilting slightly, exhausted by my own perplexing fixation on this city and its many buried layers. He's sorry, he says, but he knows nothing more than what he wrote in his books. Neither does he remember where he got most of his information: People told him things, certain facts were once well-known, many people have died. As for the few biographical snippets about Houris that he mentioned, maybe they came from that Hebrew book called the lexicon of something or other. He can't remember the exact title; I should check his bibliographies. It has been a long time.

I have, as it happens, already checked his bibliographies and checked them again. So I try a different tack: A striking photograph of Houris appears in several of his books. (The first book has no photo credit, the second book cites the first book.) Does he know where he found that? No. He doesn't want to discourage me, he sighs, but he doubts there's anything more to be learned about Houris. He wishes me the best of luck . . . And here the conversation shifts into a livelier and sharper key as we turn to the subject of his childhood neighbor, Erich Mendelsohn—about whom he has *plenty* to say that he hasn't written in his books, which praise Mendelsohn's work and call him, for instance, "among the greatest architects of the twentieth century and one of the fathers of the International Style." But now—sounding almost impatient at my admiration and affection for this defiantly uncategorizable, patently diasporic figure—he changes his tune and his tone. "There were," he informs me, a bit sternly, "other architects here who were just as talented." Mendelsohn expected to have the whole country handed to him on a plate. He was arrogant; he didn't care about this place, about this culture. (Kroyanker doesn't utter the word "Zionism," but Mendelsohn's refusal to subjugate his artistic ambition to its demands is strongly implied in this critique. The architect was no team player.) "It's good that he left."

While certain pieces of this city's recent history have already evaporated into the dusty air, old grudges die hard around here. Highly knowledgeable, prize-winning seventy-something-year-old architectural expert though Kroyanker is, I can almost hear the echo of certain catty conversations he must have overheard the grown-ups whispering in Rehavia, circa 1947.

But what of the fading memory of Spyro Houris? Contrary to common computer-age wisdom, there are those who are absent from Google, from Facebook, even from the unsettlingly vast digitized archives of the Church of Jesus Christ of Latter-day Saints. Whole categories of human existence hover under those radars. After I thank Kroyanker and we hang up, I go back to studying the evidence at hand.

THE EVIDENCE, AT HAND

His buildings themselves offer the most solid proof of his former presence in town, and it is of course those buildings that have sent me scrambling to find his traces.

This is an admittedly peculiar quest. There were better-known architects who worked in Jerusalem at the same time that he did, and it would be wrong to argue that he was a world-class figure like the defiantly visionary Erich Mendelsohn or the quietly inspired Austen Harrison. He designed on a more modest scale and appears to have been willing to bend his style to suit the needs and tastes of a wide range of clients. That said, it seems to me that the far less celebrated, far more protean Houris managed to infuse each of his very different buildings with qualities of wonder, complexity, and—for lack of a better word—humanity that are at once unique and wholly suited to their setting, scrambling as they do elements of East and West, grand and intimate, old and new. There's something about the freedom, warmth, and sheer variety of Houris's designs that strikes me as oddly poignant, as his work encapsulates the category blending and border blurring that are, or have historically been, part and parcel of Jerusalem itself. As I set out to find whatever I can about him, I am trying to put the puzzle pieces together and to discover: Who was the man who made this hodgepodge make sense?

Three highly distinct Jerusalem mansions offer up matching calling cards on their cornerstones, the most solid evidence we have that the architect existed and that he built here:

These inscriptions are more than signs of his authorship. They also bear, or so it seems to me, coded messages from beyond the grave.

The whole thing is, for starters, carved in Latin, not Arabic, characters. *Spyro*: the first name is Greek. *G.*: an odd flourish in local terms, where middle initials don't tend to matter. *Houris*: the family name is common in Arabic and is usually written in English as "Khoury" or "Khouri" (meaning "priest"); but for whatever reason this Houris didn't want to be a Khoury and so ordered the craftsmen to chip it *this* somehow alien way into the stone. In the Greek pronunciation the final *s* drops away. And if that weren't foreign enough, there's that last touch—*Architecte*. Was the choice of French a mere affectation (his clientele were wealthy, worldly people), or does it tell us something more essential about Spyro Houris and the language he dreamed in?

Just as important as the verbal substance of this stone signature is the very fact of such an inscription at all. To my knowledge, no other Jerusalem buildings of the period bear the names of their designers this way. (A handful of houses do include the Hebrew name of an engineer or builder, but the gesture is rare in these parts.) Aside from the fact that the practice seems to be, again, imported, it's striking that Spyro G. Houris, Architecte, wanted others to notice what he had created. Of course, the very *presence* of his name on those three buildings begs the question of its *absence* on the others usually ascribed to him. If he signed some buildings, why didn't he sign them all?

For now, I set this riddle aside and make my way to the National Library of Israel. This is a dignified if slightly worn-at-the-edges building from the late 1950s that may or may not be modeled on Le Corbusier's Villa Savoye and that sits on the spacious green Givat Ram (post-1948, pre-1967) campus of the Hebrew University. Soon the library will be replaced by a brand-new, state-of-the-art Swiss-designed structure located not far from the brand-new pseudo-tabernacle of the Israel Antiquities Authority campus, as well as the recently built Supreme Court, the Prime Minister's Office, the Bank of Israel, the Foreign Ministry, and the aptly named National Parking Lot. In his day, Houris would have known the area now occupied by the literal corridors of Israeli power as the Arab village of Sheikh Badr.

Spyro G. Houris, Architecte: Seated at one of the long green Formica tables in the airy general reading room, I pore over all the Mandate-era business directories that have survived the years, in search of those spectral words. *The Directory of Arab Trade, Industries, Crafts and Professions in Palestine and Trans-Jordan, 1937–1938*, for example, was published in English, Arabic, and French by the Arab Chamber of Commerce in Jerusalem, and it contains, at least in verbal form, the mercantile artifacts of an entire lost world, listing as it does every sort of Arab enterprise in town—from Asphalt and Bitumen to Dentists to Newspaper Correspondents to Silk Yarn. It features ads for Lind & Halaby's Goodyear Tyres and Tubes, the Ottoman Bank, and Edward Said's father Wadie Said's Palestine Educational Co., founded 1910 ("Books & Periodicals of every description, Stationery of all Kinds, Office and School Supplies, Account Books, National Loose Leaf Books . . .") as well as full-page exhortations to "BUY ARAB NATIONAL PRODUCTS: ENCOURAGE ARAB ENTERPRISES. If you are in doubt where to shop REFER TO THIS DIRECTORY."

The names of the officers of the Association of Arab Architects and Engineers in Jerusalem also appear here—and one Adib Khoury is described as the group's secretary. This Khoury advertises himself as a "Licensed Land Surveyor, Supervisor of Building Construction." Could it be that Spyro Houris sometimes went by this other, more explicitly "Arab" name? While it's true that in Arabic the word for "architect" and "engineer" is the same—*muhandis*—and the categories often bleed into one another in this context, I wonder if a licensed land surveyor and supervisor of building construction would dare dub himself an *architecte* and inscribe it on the side of a mansion. The discrepancies are too great here: Adib Khoury must be someone else. The entire lost world this directory contains does not seem to include Spyro Houris.

When I scour the Jerusalem section of "Engineers and Architects" in the *Palestine Directory and Handbook* of 1932, meanwhile—issued in English and Hebrew by the Tel Aviv organizers of that year's so-called Levant Fair, designed to promote Zionist industry and commerce—I recognize various familiar names, most of them Jewish and spelled a little strangely (Kaufman, Kracover). Here and there several of the city's other leading Arab architects appear (Sheiber, Baramki) as does one "Pefasis" on HaSolel Street and an engineer called "Fatasis," also on HaSolel Street. (Are they both the same enigmatic Petassis? A history book provides this mystery man with the first name "Nikephoros.") But Houris seems, again, to be absent, or perhaps in hiding. Why? Running my finger down the page one last time before I close the book for good and with a mounting sense of bewilderment, another entry jumps out at me: "Koris-Sapiro, G.," which must be Houris, Spyro G. It seems the directory's Jewish editors were so flummoxed by this particular array of alien syllables (Greek?

Arabic?), they simply assigned him a new—almost Eastern European and barely recognizable—handle.

And the name game goes on as, in the next directory I check, the alphabetical listings include one "Spyro, G., Arch." In Hebrew it's rendered "Shapiro." I am, at once, finding him and *not* finding him. A digitized search of old newspapers offers yet another version, which in some ways both alleviates my sense that I'm chasing a shadow and only adds to the mystery as, on November 17, 1919, the Jerusalem newspaper *Doar Hayom* features an unobtrusive ad for SPIROS HOURIS, ARCHITECTE, then, "architectural office, preparation of plans, surveying, price estimates, work tenders of all kinds"—in, of all languages, Hebrew.

אדריכל ספירוס חורי
ירושלם
SPIROS HOURIS, ARCHITECTE
משרד לאדריכלות, הכנת תכניות, מדידה,
קביעת־מחירים, הצעת־מלאכות מכל המינים,
P.O.B. 257 Jerusalem

Now I know this much: His telephone number was 427. His mailing address was P.O.B. 257, Jerusalem. In 1932, his office was located on "Jaffa St."

But who *was* Spyro Houris?

A PICTURE'S WORTH

The photograph that Kroyanker reproduces in several of his books is a classic period piece, a formal studio portrait of a young man with cat-like eyes and a brushy mustache, a wide, unwrinkled brow, and a dark suit whose breast pocket is punctuated by the corner of a soft white handkerchief. There's a certain softness about him in general. His skin is slightly pale and his cheeks are smooth; he has broad shoulders and looks like he might be tall—an athlete?—though it's hard to say for sure, since he is sitting, his hands folded in his lap, legs crossed. Leaning a bit uncomfortably at an angle against the wooden back of an elaborately carved throne of a chair, whose one visible arm curls into the head of a lion, or dragon, he looks, for lack of a better term, *European*—though perhaps this is simply the way Palestinian Arab men of his class and background dressed and posed for studio photos in this era (the 1910s?). Or maybe it says something else, something more specific about where he came from and who he considered himself to be.

But his demeanor and this décor are in a way familiar. Another, more frequently reproduced photograph from what must be around the same time—this one is usually dated c. 1920—shows the famously charismatic intellectual, educator, and political maverick Khalil al-Sakakini and several of his friends and fellow members of a literary circle known around town as the Party of the Vagabonds. (Many of them were also his colleagues at the progressive Dusturiyyah, or Constitutional, School that he founded in Jerusalem a decade earlier.) Posing in the same stiff way as Houris, they all sport similar mustaches, suits, and ties, and don't look like they know where, precisely, to place their hands while the photographer does his slow work. Staring intently at the camera, Sakakini sits to the side of the dapper journalist Achille Seikaly, who leans against the wooden back of an elaborately carved throne of a chair, the arms of which also curl into the head of a lion, or dragon. It may well be the same chair, the same studio where Spyro Houris sat for his own portrait.

If Houris left behind few words that might serve as clues to his biography, Sakakini was the opposite: a highly verbal public figure who systematically documented his life and times, and who meant the record of his doings to endure and stand as testimony for later generations. A devoted father and teacher, as well as an ardent modern, he was a man with his gaze fixed unwaveringly on the future. In keen detail recorded in voluminous Arabic diaries and letters, Sakakini related not only four and a half decades' worth of his private daily routine (multiple entries begin "After bathing, exercise, and breakfast I . . .") and explored his sometimes agonized passions—for both certain close male companions and his childhood next-door neighbor, distant relative, and eventual wife, Sultana—but also charted his engagement with the most tumultuous events of his day. For some thirty-four hundred handwritten pages, beginning in 1907, his diaries track his fluid allegiances to various causes, groups, and identities. Soon after his 1953 death—in exile, in Cairo—one of Sakakini's daughters, Hala, published a heavily edited version of the journals; more recently, eight unexpurgated volumes have emerged in elegant Arabic paperback editions.

Since his words first appeared in print, even in Hala's more primly truncated version, scholars have been poring over and drawing from them a portrait of the period in general and of this singular individual in particular. While certain readers have chosen to see him solely as a characteristic type ("whose diary . . . affords striking evidence of the state of mind of the educated class of his community and generation"), most commentators understand that Sakakini was at once an articulate representative of the various political moments and movements that defined the Middle Eastern age, and utterly his own man. He was born Greek Orthodox in Jerusalem in 1878, considered himself at different points a proudly secular Ottoman subject, a committed proponent of "Greater Syria," an Arab linguistic nationalist, a Palestinian patriot, a self-celebrating voluptuary, and a freethinking citizen of the world. His business card announced "Khalil al-Sakakini, human being, God Willing," and while he felt deeply tied to the Greek Orthodox community—then the largest Christian denomination in Palestine by a long shot—he was an outspoken atheist who at one point proposed replacing the Lord's Prayer in the liturgy with lines by the great pre-Islamic poet Imru' al-Qays. His contempt for the Greek patriarchate was, meanwhile, as political as it was theological. Like many local Arab Orthodox, he fiercely objected to the foreign control of the church's hierarchy. Though in 1909 Arabic speakers constituted 85 percent of the church's membership in Palestine, its leadership came from an entirely Greek-born monastic order known as the Brotherhood of the Holy Sepulcher. This brotherhood was, as Sakakini and his fellow reformers believed, both crooked and oblivious to the needs of the local community, and he declared his desire to "cleanse" the Jerusalem church by pushing for the expulsion of the brotherhood from Palestine. "My aim," he wrote in his journal, "is to bring to an end Greek tyranny."

When in 1913 Sakakini wrote a pamphlet called "The Orthodox Renaissance in Palestine," which strongly condemned the brotherhood's "Hellenizing" influence as it extolled the notion of Arab Orthodox reform, he was promptly excommunicated. (The ban was, it seems, mutual: "I can't live under the leadership of these corrupt priests," Sakakini raged to his diary later that same year, after one especially tense encounter at the Jerusalem patriarchate. "I can't be a part of this denomination . . . After today I am not Orthodox . . . I am not Orthodox. I am not Orthodox.") But for all his disgust at the church leadership, and his devotion to the Arab people and to his own Arabness—at one point he named each room in his Jerusalem house for a different Arab capital, so moving in the course of a day from Sana'a to Damascus to Córdoba to Cairo—Greek was also in his blood. He felt profoundly bound to the culture of his paternal grandmother, who was, as he called her, "Greek of the Greeks of Constantinople." He loved Greek philosophy, poetry, and art. That said, it was—Sakakini was, we all are—complicated, and in a basic way, none of these pat ethnic labels could really account for the complex and evolving individual he felt himself to be. As he declared in an often-quoted 1915 diary entry, "I'm neither Christian nor Buddhist, Muslim nor Jewish, just as I am not Arab, not British, not French, not German, not Russian, or Turkish. I am just one among humankind."

And who did Spyro Houris consider himself to be? Did *he* keep a diary? If so, did he write there of his breakfasts and his baths, of his buildings? In Arabic, or in Greek? In French? Did he, too, consider what record, what words, what wisdom he wanted to leave his children? Did he *have* children? I can ask and ask all I want. His photo stares back in silence.

PLOTS, PRIESTS, PATRIARCHS

A much-enlarged version of the same photograph keeps staring, still silent, when one July afternoon I enter a simple three-room house at the edge of the Jerusalem neighborhood known as the Greek Colony (beside the far better-known German Colony) and find it hanging on the wall. With its irregular geometrical panels, the wooden front door to the house has been unlocked for me by Anastas Damianos, the official head of the once substantial, now severely shrunken Greek community of West Jerusalem. At its height in the midst of the Mandate, this consisted of some seven thousand members. Now, as the (Orthodox Christian) Damianos jokes halfheartedly, "We have enough for a minyan." A modest and unassuming man in his seventies, he can't help but wield the large, old-fashioned skeleton key with a certain inadvertent ceremony.

Though I'm speaking Hebrew with Damianos, I am, for once in this city—it happens very rarely—pleasantly confused about his ethnicity and his mother tongue. He's slight and dark skinned, with wire-framed glasses, a light gait and gentle manner, and his fluent Hebrew is accented in an unfamiliar way. As he'll eventually explain when I ask, his was the only Greek family in their Galilee village—his ancestors arrived in Palestine from Monastir in Macedonia before 1850—so as a child he spoke Greek at home and Arabic outside it. He has lived in Jerusalem for more than fifty years and, now retired, worked for decades as an official in the Arabic-language section at the largely Hebrew-speaking Israeli Ministry of Education. He collects icons; his children live in Greece and Spain. He has agreed to show me the building, which has recently been renovated by the energetic Greek-Israeli-Jewish, American-trained architect Elias Messinas and now serves as a humble museum of the history of Jerusalem's Greek community, though it is mostly locked and shuttered—unless one arranges to have coffee and a long, lively talk with Messinas, who in turn passes on the cell phone number of Damianos . . . I am, I told Damianos when I called him, eager to see the interior of a house built by Spyro Houris.

Or *seems*—yet again—to have been built by Spyro Houris. The usual air of uncertainty hovers over this attribution, as it does over the cluster of buildings that make up the heart of the orderly neighborhood, which Houris himself is thought to have planned before the First World War. A "Greek architect" was responsible. Kroyanker speculates that he was the one, as do several other Israeli historians and geographers. Damianos himself is not so sure; the dates don't make complete sense (I agree), and the style of most of these structures seems distinct from that of Houris's other buildings, the materials and construction cruder. But it does appear that Houris was responsible for planning at least some of the buildings in the neighborhood, including this house, where his picture now hangs on the wall.

As the story is usually told, at the end of the nineteenth century, a forward-looking Greek archimandrite named Efthimios took it upon himself to buy up some 1,000 dunams, or 250 acres, of farmland in the south of Jerusalem. Having formed a building association, he proceeded to arrange a lottery for these coveted plots, on which the winners would be responsible for constructing their own homes. First a community center and four adjoining houses were erected. Then, at some point between 1902—the date inscribed on the community center's lintel—and the moment sixteen years later when in the midst of the Great War German air force planes swooped over the city and snapped a series of remarkably sharp aerial photographs, Houris (or someone) built another sixteen houses along the same tidy grid.

While the enterprising archimandrite may genuinely have been interested in alleviating congestion within the Old City walls, where most of the community then lived in severely cramped conditions, his goals were also—as is almost always the case in Jerusalem—political. It appears he was eager to create a strong Greek presence beyond those walls, and the establishment of this upscale residential neighborhood was just part of his plan. With the bursting coffers of the patriarchate available to him—pilgrims had been bringing gifts and making donations for centuries—he began to buy land elsewhere as well. He established a row of shops in the booming Turkish town square outside the Jaffa Gate, built a grand new hotel (called, as it happens, the Grand New Hotel) right inside it, and purchased a large Crusader-era market known as the Mauristan in the Christian Quarter. Part of that suk now bears his name.

When the war began, the pilgrims stopped coming, the money ran dry, and the church was forced to sell off or lease certain properties, including large tracts in that area known as Nikephoria, where the King David Hotel and the YMCA would eventually be built. But it was in large part due to Efthimios and other entrepreneurial ecclesiastics like him that the Greek Church became what it is today, one of the most powerful landholders in the entire country, owner of more real estate in Israel than any single entity besides the state itself. The fact that the church still lays claim to such vast and sensitive tracts of land makes its history much more than the object of dusty antiquarian curiosity. The most pressing present-tense power struggles revolve around these holdings, as, for instance, in 2005 when the patriarch was ousted by the local Arab community. Demoted to the rank of monk, he was, he claimed, forcibly locked inside the church compound for several years, his groceries hoisted up to him on a rope. Allegedly he'd conspired to sell Efthimios's Jaffa Gate hotel and the land around it to a group of Jewish settlers, and so to shore up his standing with the Israeli authorities by helping to "Judaize" Jerusalem.

I am, though, getting ahead of myself, and far ahead of Spyro Houris, who may not have lived to witness such sordid struggles but whose plan for the Greek Colony—if it was indeed his plan—does indicate his close ties to priests and to power. Whether or not he built the whole neighborhood, his links to the church are more than a matter of mere speculation: In the course of my digital wanderings, I've happened upon a small item from *The Palestine Bulletin*, July 16, 1930, announcing that "the honour of Commander of the Order of the Saint of the Sepulchre has been conferred on Mr. Spiro G. Khuri by his Beatitude, the Greek Orthodox Patriarch, for presenting the plans of restoring a convent near Jericho, which was destroyed during the earthquake of 1927." Whatever his religious beliefs, he clearly didn't share Khalil Sakakini's contempt for the church's Greek-speaking hierarchy and if anything seems to have made his living in part from his connections to it. "They say," writes Kroyanker, "that the representatives of the Greek Orthodox Church . . . would oblige those who bought land from them to hire the professional services of the Greek Orthodox architects Houris and Petassis."

Is it so? Looking around the plain main room of the house in the Greek Colony—with its whitewashed walls, high ceilings, and simple wooden window frames, now painted a pale lemon shade—it is not ecclesiastical plotting and prodding that I am thinking about. Rather, I'm trying to imagine Spyro Houris first imagining this house. I am trying to imagine Spyro Houris imagining a house for his beloved.

THE GREEK DOCTOR'S DAUGHTER

I'm also trying my hardest to find hard facts—to follow paper trails and architectural patterns, to unearth old photos and yellowing maps—but the saga of Houris's connection to the Efklides family, for whom this house was built and to whom it belonged until the last of its elderly occupants died there in the 1990s, is far less solid than that. It has about it the air of a legend or fable and can't be proved, exactly, though the details that emerge from various historical sources, and from the memories of those, like Damianos, who knew at least some of the cast of characters personally, may be pieced together like a kind of half-remembered dream, somehow spookier for its faintness. Where a ghost is concerned, there will be ghost stories. So:

Once upon a time (in 1891, to be exact) the twenty-seven-year-old Dr. Photios Efklides—a Turkish Greek, born in Brousa, now Boursa, recent graduate of the medical faculty at the university in Constantinople—arrived in Jerusalem. Recruited by the Ottoman authorities to direct the new municipal hospital there, he soon settled into several rooms near the Greek patriarchate in the Old City and started work in one of the grandest buildings on the Jaffa Road, which was commonly believed to be haunted.

One account said that the wealthy man who'd built it as his home had died soon after he moved in, and that the next year his son died, and then another relative died . . . and by this point no one wanted to draw near the house, since a curse clearly hung over the imposing structure with its substantial stone gate and its two deep cisterns. According to another often-repeated and more hyperbolically Gothic version of events, the building had been planned as a home for a well-to-do young Arab Catholic couple who were engaged to be married. When the groom died before the wedding, the guests propped his corpse in a chair and led in his lovely young bride, outfitted in her brocade dress, jewels, and veil. Necrophiliac nuptials of a sort ensued, as ululation accompanied the traditional dance performed with lighted candles by the mother of the groom, who then, it was reported by one contemporary memoirist, "tore her clothes, gave a terrible death cry, and snatched the veil from the bride's face." This "violent demonstration of grief evidently killed the mother." After her death, the building sat derelict for a decade.

Whether such ghoulish rites had really occurred, by the time Efklides arrived in Jerusalem, the authorities had decided to put an end to all the talk of corpses and curses and had assumed control of the abandoned mansion, added the sultan's intricate seal to the façade, and turned the place into a free hospital for the poor of all races. And within a few years the good doctor had established both himself and the institution as friendly fixtures in town. He became known all around as Dr. Photios, or the Greek Doctor, and the building, too, took on various nicknames—al-Mustashfa ("the Hospital"), al-Baladiyyeh ("Municipal [Hospi-tal]"), or as-Sihiyyeh, from the Arabic word for "health," the very salubrious sound of which implied that Efklides had finally managed to dispel the belief that evil spirits wafted through its hallways. He soon married Maria Samptopolo, a tall, beautiful pilgrim from a village in the Dardanelles, and she gave birth to three small, beautiful children: Alexander, Heleni, and Clio.

Besides running the hospital and a day clinic for peasants from the surrounding countryside, Efklides was now appointed the chief physician of Jerusalem, a role that seems to have entailed a constant shifting of registers. On the one hand, he performed the unglamor-ous and often exhausting work of a glorified village doctor. While theoretically the hospital was open to all, its patients were primarily poor and Muslim, and the hospital's resources were meager, with two thermometers and one syringe shared on a twelve-bed ward. On the other hand, as a high-ranking Ottoman official, he took part in much of the peacocky pageantry that marked the last years of the old regime, before the Young Turks came to power in 1908. On state occasions, Dr. Photios would don an intricately embroidered uni-form, complete with filigreed silver buckles that anchored his elab-orate sleeves, and adorn himself with the multiple medals he'd been awarded by both the Greeks and the Turks. In 1901, the sultan him-self bestowed on Dr. Photios a firman, a special recognition of his service to the empire. As befitted a man of such standing—a man with such a beautiful wife and beautiful children, such elaborate sleeves, and such imperial honors pinned to his chest and floridly calligraphed on a scroll in his own name—the doctor needed an appropriately impressive house in which to show it all off. So it was that sometime before the Great War broke out, he contracted an architect to build him a house in the new neighborhood that had sprung up outside the Jaffa Gate, near an ancient pool and the most important Muslim graveyard in Palestine, all of it known as Mamilla or Ma'man Allah, the Shelter of God.

In his 1985 book on "Arab architecture," David Kroyanker writes that in 1912 or '13, Spyro Houris designed a house at 25 Mamilla Road for "the Efkitedes family"—which another historian, who interviewed Heleni Efklides on her ninetieth birthday, May 25, 1986, corrects as he confirms that it was the *Efklides* house. By now, one can no longer visit the building (to say nothing of Heleni), since the Mamilla Dr. Photios and his children knew—once a thriving and decidedly messy and mixed Arab, Jewish, Greek, Turkish, German, British, French, Armenian commercial, industrial, and residential district—has been bulldozed. Between 1948 and 1967, No Man's Land and a mostly Kurdish Jewish slum sprang up there, along the Jordanian border. After Israel annexed East Jerusalem in the wake of the 1967 war, the concrete wall came down and the residents were "cleared" from their homes.

Now—after more than forty years of planning, razing, digging, more planning, delays, construction, and further delays, brought about in part by the discovery of extensive First Temple–period and/or Byzantine graves and the violent protests by ultra-Orthodox Jewish groups that followed—the same area is occupied by a flashy $400 million commercial development. This compound includes a lavish yet antiseptic apartment complex whose units are mostly used as holiday homes by wealthy foreign Jews, an outsized luxury hotel with a predictably bombastic biblical name, and a glitzy Miami-meets-the-Middle-East shopping mall—all of it designed, yet again, with the trademark aggressively symbolic touch of Moshe Safdie.

The construction of this swank compound was apparently meant to erase both the memory of the difficult period of Jerusalem's history just after 1948 and the seam between Arab East and Jewish West

Jerusalem, so attempting to "unify" the still fundamentally divided city. While a certain welcome melding of populations does in fact take place there—as young women in hijabs stroll past young women in head scarves—the presence in this setting of such opulence and such high-end consumerism only underscores other divisions: "In Israel's poorest city," writes the clear-eyed, sharp-tongued architecture critic Esther Zandberg, "this colossal project is a stone-clad memorial to the sin of hubris."

And for all the talk of "unifying" the parts and people of Jerusalem, the very Israeli Mamilla complex is hardly neutral or common ground in political terms. While the developers took great pains to dismantle and then reconstruct, stone by numbered stone, the house in which Theodor Herzl once spent the night (this is now occupied by a café called Herzl, catty-corner from the Rolex store), the reconfigured façade of the Efklides residence—unmarked—is all that remains of what may be Spyro Houris's first building in Jerusalem. The inside has been razed and replaced by a darkly cavernous pop-music-blasting atrium occupied by a blur of chain stores, among them the Gap, Bug Computers, American Eagle, and a lingerie store called Whispers.

Other erasures have also taken place, as Kroyanker has since published a thick, glossy Hebrew album of a book about the history of the neighborhood and its "renewal"—commissioned by the project's Tel Aviv–based developer—in which he leaves out all mention of the Efklides building and of Houris. Meanwhile, down the street, and near what once was the mufti's Palace Hotel (now an elaborately refurbished and rather garishly decorated Waldorf Astoria that caters to well-heeled religious Jews from abroad), the Los Angeles–based Simon Wiesenthal Center is currently constructing what may be the ultimate stone-clad memorial to the sin of hubris, a $250 million Museum of so-called Tolerance, built directly over a large part of the cemetery of Ma'man Allah, which tradition holds dates to the seventh century and contains both the remains of several companions of the Prophet Muhammad and the twelfth-century graves of thousands of Saladin's soldiers. The area continued to serve as a burial place for some of Jerusalem's most distinguished Muslim families right until 1948.

No less renowned an architect than Frank Gehry (né Goldberg) was first hired to plan the museum, and—thinking in the monumentally swooping, metallic terms of LA's Walt Disney Concert Hall or the Bilbao Guggenheim but not, it seems, in terms of all those dusty old skeletons buried in the Jerusalem earth—he designed one of his characteristically chaotic and commanding structures. Complete with sixteen undulating titanium "Pillars of Tolerance," which would have held the 118-foot-tall building aloft and, according to the museum's sponsors, "be seen from miles away," the building would also have featured a bulbous Grand Hall, which Gehry described as symbolizing the "living room" of Jerusalem, "because of its openness on all sides." (A peculiar conceit for a museum built in a city that the Israeli powers that be have blocked off from the West Bank and its Palestinian population by means of a snaking twenty-five-foot-high concrete wall and multiple corral-like checkpoints.) For reasons that may have had more to do with budgets than politics and the international uproar that arose with the announcement of the plans to build an institution dedicated to tolerance right on top of this major Muslim graveyard, Gehry eventually dropped out—insisting all the while that he continued to consider the project "vitally important." In an official statement, he proclaimed his admiration for the idea of the museum, which "will serve as the embodiment of human respect and compassion." He was replaced with a far less famous husband-and-wife team of Tel Aviv architects, who rendered plans for a very different (and more restrained) sort of building—though whatever one may or may not say about the relative merits of their design, the museum's charged location and goals didn't shift in the slightest with Gehry's departure. According to news reports, the prominent American rabbi in charge of the whole perverse production has explained that one section of this self-proclaimed "Center for Human Dignity" will "deal with the question of 'How did the Jews survive for 3,500 years?'" while the other will "confront Israel's issues as they are today, domestic and international issues, but not the Middle East peace process . . . It's not," he has explained, "about the experience of the Palestinian people . . . When they have a state, they'll have their own museum."

Shopping malls and cultural centers may, in other words, be just as haunted as houses. Built over graves of all ages and sorts, the whole neighborhood seems to me teeming with phantoms.

But while the Efklides house in Mamilla is gone, another exists—the simple structure in the Greek Colony, where, along with the picture of Spyro Houris and that elaborately carved wooden chair, Anastas Damianos now shows me Dr. Photios's framed Greek-language Ottoman medical license and his ornate swirl of gold-lettered firman.

The circumstances that led to the construction of this building are also vague, though at some point it seems Efklides's fortunes turned. Maybe the curse of the hospital building had attached itself to the Greek doctor; maybe he was just unlucky, but first his marriage to the beautiful Maria Samptopolo had curdled, and they separated. Then, in May 1916, in the midst of the war, as a typhus epidemic swept the city and sent him scrambling to try to save as many lives as he could, Dr. Photios himself succumbed to the illness. He was fifty-two years old, and his funeral was, according to one eyewitness, "truly a demonstration of sorrow," an embodiment of all the grief then washing over the town, together with the dread disease. The hospital lost not just its director during this infectious interlude, but its pharmacist, secretary, and three nurses. Dr. Photios's demise was a major event. One Hebrew newspaper reported that "The Doctor Is Dead" and described how his "geniality and fine character" had drawn a "large and impressive" crowd to his burial. Dignitaries and doctors, consuls and clerks, army officers and eminent people "of all the communities of our city" assembled to lead him to his grave in the Greek Orthodox cemetery on Mount Zion.

In a last will and testament drawn up just a month before his death—and, it would seem, in sober awareness of the very real dangers he faced as he labored on the typhus ward—Dr. Photios left his fortune to his three children, together with a small provision for his estranged wife, various shops and buildings to the Greek community of which he'd been such an upstanding member, and all his books to the Greek hospital inside the Old City. As he requested in plain terms that his children not live with their mother, it seems he may also have left an unwritten directive for Spyro Houris to plan for them that small house in the Greek Colony. While the house is often described as having been built at the start of the century, when the doctor was still alive, the photographs snapped by those German air force planes in 1918 show an empty lot where the house stands today. Subsequent maps—from 1925, 1926, and 1927—reveal the same blank spot, though by 1929, the government cartographers had taken care to ink in a little box of a house on that corner.

Whenever it was that the walls of the building were constructed, the Efklides siblings eventually found themselves living in close quarters there. Though their home was modest and the money their father left them dwindling, they somehow still carried themselves as the privileged children of the great doctor, whose nameplate they affixed like a charm to the building's entrance. Dandyish Alexander taught English at the Berlitz School but wore white gloves after hours and drove a fancy Fiat; the sisters were both widely known for their good looks and their glamour.

Their mother, meanwhile, had fallen on harder times, and where she called home in those years is not clear. After 1948, Maria Samptopolo somehow ended up a refugee in the Old City, then Jordan, while her grown children remained on the Israeli side. One longtime resident of the Christian Quarter remembers this formerly wealthy and elegant woman ("very lofty in her ways") impoverished, borrowing money from whoever would loan it—until Clio somehow arranged to cross the border and bring her mother back to the Greek Colony house, where she eventually died.

Long before that, though, and in circumstances that also remain frustratingly hazy, the often unlucky Efklides family had reason once more to celebrate, as pretty Heleni announced that she was engaged to be married—to the architect Spyro Houris.

BOOKS OF SOULS

It's important, of course, to do the math: Heleni Efklides was born in 1896 and her father died in 1916, the month of her twentieth birthday. Had she and Spyro Houris already decided to marry? Or did their wedding plans crystallize in the wake of the doctor's passing?

If Houris had indeed built the Mamilla house in 1912 and had taken the time to study for a degree in Athens, he would have to have been, by my estimate, twenty-three at the very youngest by the time of that first commission, which would make him seven years

Heleni's senior. Perhaps he was older still, born sometime earlier in the 1880s. If he had really built the first houses in the Greek Colony in 1902, this would mean he was appreciably older—born as early as 1879, just a year after Khalil Sakakini and seventeen before Heleni. Could it be? The mustachioed man in that photograph (taken in 1912? 1914?) looks young—though the difference between a poised twenty-three and a baby-faced thirty-five seems negligible from this distance.

Such numerical speculation is maddeningly imprecise, as are the unanswered questions of Houris's initial connection to the Efklides family and the place of the architect's birth. Because of his work, Dr. Photios seems to have moved easily in and out of all categories of Jerusalem society, so that he might have come to know Houris and have hired him to build a house or houses in any number of contexts. But to entrust his oldest daughter's future to Houris (if the doctor had indeed known of the relationship) implies a closer bond. And even if he'd died before Houris and Heleni declared their intentions, the doctor's will had stipulated not only that his children preserve his good name but that his daughters marry of "their own kind." A woman who'd go to the trouble of affixing her late father's nameplate to the wall of her house would also, it seems, take pains to choose a husband she thought he would have approved of. According to this logic, Spyro Houris would have been, like the Turkish-born Photios, an Orthodox Ottoman citizen whose mother tongue was Greek and who called Jerusalem home.

While the emotional and romantic variables of this equation have by now faded to inscrutability, since all those involved are gone, questions of citizenship are another, plainer matter. In search of proof of Spyro Houris's legal status, I make my way to the Israel State Archives, yet another governmental institution that's about to be transferred from its current location to a new facility, as yet unbuilt. The state of the present building is so dismal, though, that those in charge have wisely decided not to wait for construction to take place but to lock up the archive and shift its contents—some forty kilometers' worth of files—to a temporary location in just a few months. The dates are vague (it will be "closed until further notice" according to the official announcement posted on the government-run website), but a palpable sense of panic seems to be propelling this move. Over the course of several months in late 2012 and early 2013, the place was shut down three times—once, as a newspaper report put it, "following the discovery that it lacked a municipal safety permit," as it had for a full nineteen years; again when the Prime Minister's Office, which controls the archives, evacuated the employees without explanation and cordoned off whole parts of the building with tape marked NO ENTRY; and a third time when the staircase at the entryway simply gave out and collapsed after a heavy rain. For some typically mysterious "security" reason, it is forbidden to photograph the building from the outside—though the ironies here are multiple, since the real threats to the structure seem to emanate from within.

But this final summer of its presence here on the third floor of that unphotographable office building, a former car showroom in a semi-industrial, semi-residential part of town, the reading room of the archive is as it's been for all the years that I've had reason to visit—an exhausted-looking and permanently temporary-seeming space filled with fake-wood furniture and dried-out houseplants dying in plastic containers. More reminiscent of a down-on-its-luck insurance agency or struggling accountant's office than the repository of all this allegedly history-proud state's historical treasures, the archive is decamping from this ramshackle place not a moment too soon. As it is, with its flickering fluorescent overhead lights and rickety elevator, its heaps of fraying files and bruised cardboard boxes scattered haphazardly around the reading room, the archive has a way of making these remnants of the recent past seem dangerously vulnerable, almost on the verge of destruction. While ancient Jewish history is treated in this country with the greatest respect, even veneration, the papery remains of the last century (especially those that are Turkish or British, but also the files that pertain to the more recent, less mythic Jewish history of the state) are handled with a careless sort of disregard that borders on abuse. The dingy reading room seems the ultimate embodiment of all that pointed neglect.

Today an especially gloomy air hangs over the Israel State Archives. This summer's war still rages on, and that fact seems to have kept away most of the foreign scholars and local doctoral students who tend to fill the seats in these hot vacation months. This very week the country's only international airport was shut down for several days by rocket fire from Gaza. The reading room is unnaturally hushed, though the ostensible calm is periodically interrupted by the wail of a buzz saw outside or a burst of anxious sound within. A few older men who appear to be researching Holocaust or family history are absorbed in their work, and one of them, wielding a cane and wearing a large bandage around one knee, keeps limping heavily across the room to complain loudly to the melancholic yet somehow sweetly jolly Russian archivist, H., that the Xerox machine has stolen his money. Each time, she hoists herself up from her desk and wearily goes to help him. At a certain point, the younger bureaucrat in charge of this section of the archive swoops in and across the room, then into her corner office. Wearing an even more distracted and sour expression than is her sour and distracted wont, she leaves her door open and, grabbing hold of the telephone, begins to hold forth, so that her voice and its chatty though somehow aggrieved tone pour out across the room. Try as I might to ignore her and concentrate on what I'm doing, her Hebrew words fill the sorry space: "Rockets . . . sirens . . . soldiers . . . *Any OTHER country would just have* . . . Arabs . . . alert . . . *What can we do?* . . . shame . . . Arabs . . . THEY have only been taught how to hate US." She sighs theatrically, and that sigh makes me sigh as well—not because I agree with any of the standard-issue racist pronouncements that she's broadcasting to the entire room but since that sigh, like a yawn, is catching.

I'm also sighing because my search today is proving even steeper than usual. I relish an archival challenge but may have met my match in this particular undertaking, which entails sitting before an aged microfilm machine and attempting to squint my way through the handwritten Palestinian census records from 1875 to 1918. As H., the melancholy/jolly Russian archivist, warned gently and with a slight tinge of pity as she helped me scroll the first film loop through the maze of the infernal machine's rollers, lenses, and feeds, "You know they're in Ottoman Turkish?"

I knew, but thought that being able to read Arabic might give me an orthographic leg up. I was wrong. The lists are incomprehensible to me, microscopically inscrutable scrawls that might as

well not be letters at all but tightly packed hundred-year-old scrib-
bles or chicken scratches, made still harder to decipher by the geri-
atric machine and the white-on-black film itself. For the purposes
of taxation and military conscription, the Ottoman authorities recorded details of the population in a so-called *nüfus defter,* or Book
of Souls—465 of them survive at the archive—with distinct lists of
each town's Jews, Muslims, and Christians, divided further into
some forty categories, from Ashkenazi, Bukharan, Georgian, Moroccan, Sephardi, Kurdish, Yemenite, and Hasidic Jews, to Muslims
defined as Uzbeki, Afghani, Indian, Moroccan, Sudanese, Sudanese
Dervish, Gypsy, Black, and so on, to the Christians—whose de-
nominational divisions are the most elaborately multiple of all and
include Armenian, Armenian Catholic, Coptic, Greek, Greek Orthodox, Maronite, Protestant, Pentecostal, Quaker, Episcopalian,
Syrian Catholic, Assyrian, Ancient Assyrian, Assyrian Catholic, etc.,
etc. Which is to say nothing of the Circassians, the Druze, and the
Baha'i . . . Thanks to the maniacal sectarian specificity of this list, I
have at least some sense of where to begin looking amid the dozens
of spools of microfilm: Jerusalem district, city of Jerusalem, Greek
Orthodox.

But when faced with this tangle of strange signs, such order is of
no use to me at all. I am in fact about to give up after just a few minutes of this charade (Who am I kidding? Why do I bother? This is
work for a scholar, not a writer. Why don't I just ditch all this archival exertion and try my hand at a novel?) when, slouched in front of
the machine and probably projecting my despair through my rotten
posture, I hear a voice:

"*Btikhi 'Arabi?*"

Do you speak Arabic? It is offered softly but distinctly, even as the
chief bureaucrat keeps up her steady stream of high volume anti-
Arab invective just a few feet away.

"*Aywa,*" I answer, in my surprise, *yes.* What is going on? The young
man who has posed this question is bearded and a bit pudgy; he has
green eyes and wears white socks and brown shoes with schoolboy
laces. His neatly clipped beard suggests religious Islam. I'd call it in
fact a "Hamas beard," and though one's facial hair shouldn't necessarily indicate one's politics, I realize that I've gone ahead and read

it that way, unconsciously resorting to the all too legible language of nonverbal signs that one spends much of one's time deciphering in this city. He is perhaps the last person I expected to meet at the Israel State Archives in the middle of this war.

We start in Arabic but quickly switch to Hebrew, and he asks if I need help. Yes! He tells me his name only when I ask, and he is, it seems (he does not announce this but it becomes clear), something of an expert in these Books of Souls and quite comfortable in Ottoman Turkish. Does he work here, I wonder, maybe as the authority on the archive's Ottoman holdings? At first I think it must be so, given the generous way he's wandered over to advise me. But as we continue to talk I understand that N. has come to the reading room today to conduct his own research and is now offering to forfeit some of his work time to help me, not because it's his job but because he wants to. Perhaps he's a doctoral student? I don't ask since he seems not to want to say too much about himself and I don't want to pry. His demeanor is calm and contained. He's a little distant, very correct. There is no element of a come-on or a boast involved in his offer to assist me, a strange Jewish woman, with the work of decoding these difficult Turkish texts; in fact, he seems to want to pitch in not so much because I myself clearly need help but because somehow this history itself does.

I explain briefly about Spyro Houris and what I'm doing. He looks a bit skeptical. This is, he says, a foreign name. . . . Non-Ottoman citizens weren't obliged to register with the authorities, so that Houris may have been here in Jerusalem without his name appearing in the records. But if I'd like, he'll have a look. He can probably do this more quickly than I can, he suggests. I agree.

And with that—though without any fanfare—N. takes my place at the machine and begins to scroll through. With a steady, low-lidded kind of concentration, he spends the next half hour sitting very straight and silently scanning each page of the inky squiggles of the Greek Orthodox registers of the city and district of Jerusalem for some sign of Spyro Houris.

All those names go whizzing by as he turns the knob and the film flies through—as do all those souls. The bureaucrat is still blabbing her racist chitchat into the phone; the old man with the bandage and cane limps across the reading room to complain loudly yet again to sweet, weary H. about that thieving Xerox machine; she hoists herself up once more to help him, as I try to set down in my own barely legible chicken scrawl a few fleeting snatches of this endlessly mutating scene, some record of *these* Jerusalem souls . . . and the war goes on.

MAZES

Spyro Houris isn't here.

N. issues the verdict in the same cool, slightly detached tone with which he's addressed me throughout our conversation. Perhaps he lived in Bethlehem? Beit Jala? That would place his name in a different census book. Have I, he asks, tried the Greek patriarchate? He offers various other suggestions for where else I might look, including the Central Zionist Archives.

The patriarchate is logical—but the Central Zionist Archives? It's a place where I've conducted research before: A few of Erich Mendelsohn's letters are there; Patrick Geddes's plans for Jerusalem Actual and Possible are there. But since that archive serves as the official repository for the historical documents of the World Zionist Organization, the Jewish Agency, the Jewish National Fund, and various other major Jewish institutions, it hadn't, frankly, ever occurred to me to go dowsing there for traces of the decidedly un-Jewish, presumably non-Zionist, possibly Arab, definitely Greek Orthodox Spyro G. Houris, Architecte. But unflappably Palestinian N., with his pious Muslim bearing and beard, seems to think it's worth a shot.

Here our exchange takes a swerve into the realm of the surreal, as, with the bureaucrat's pronouncement that "THEY have only been taught how to hate US" still ringing in my ears, I follow N. to one of the reading room's archaic computers, where he insists on patiently pulling up the site of the Zionist archive and conducting a low-speed Internet search on my behalf, in Hebrew, for the name "SPYRO HOURIS." Once again, this yields a list of similar but somehow overly Jewish names: Shapiro, Sapiro, Spiro . . . none of which seem to have anything to do with my Spyro. When I try to thank N. for all his help, he has already turned away, eyes averted, back to his own work.

And so I turn back to my own.

Though I busy myself with scurrying down various historical trails and documentary footpaths, it takes me several days before I make my way to that other unlikely archive.

At first I'd decided not to pursue it, since N.'s Internet search had brought forth no sign of Houris at all, and it seemed to me just one more in a series of increasingly demoralizing dead ends and false starts. The only "Spiro Khoury" who appeared in the Mandate-era State Archives files turned out to be a grain merchant who lived and worked in Jaffa, had a brother and business partner named Georges, and apparently no connection whatsoever to the architect Spyro Houris.

When I told T., a Palestinian doctor friend, what I was up to, he announced that he knew an architect in Ramallah named Spiro Khoury! It must be a son or a grandson; architecture runs in families . . . and in a flash I pictured a formerly unexamined but fabulously revealing cache of letters, diaries, sketches, photos, site plans, and blueprints emerging from under a neatly made West Bank bed, to say nothing of the hours of fond reminiscences of their late great patriarch that his large, loving, and architecturally savvy family would, I hoped, happily pour forth into my smartphone and its digital voice recorder. But when T. asked this other Spiro Khoury about Spyro Houris, he was told that "it's definitely not me but somebody else with the same name." The Ramallah Khoury (an engineer, it turned out, who often designs buildings) seemed to have no idea of his architectural forebear or nominal doppelgänger, though the same connection keeps suggesting itself. As I continued to ask various knowledgeable people, they all said they'd heard about Spyro Houris but didn't know much more than his name . . . and suggested I consult the architect Spiro Khoury in Ramallah, who must be a son or a grandson; architecture runs in families . . .

An Israeli architect passes on the name of yet another Khoury, in Haifa—a land surveyor the architect has heard might be related to Houris, though when I call and speak to this Khoury's wife, she is sympathetic but says she's never heard of Spyro Houris. He wasn't a relative. Did he live in Haifa? She also points out a fact I already know, one that makes my search much harder. The name Khoury is approximately as unique as Cohen or Smith. The Jerusalem phone book alone lists 151 of them, so that looking for Spyro Houris's possible descendants this way seems futile at best.

A friendly e-mail exchange with the Palestinian American professor of law and political commentator George Bisharat, whose family built and lived in one of the grand ceramic-fronted Talbiyeh mansions regularly attributed to Houris is promising at first. Bisharat has written often and eloquently about his family's loss, after 1948, of their elegant porticoed home, inset with turquoise-and-black tiles that declare it, in English and Arabic, the VILLA HARUN AR-RASHID, 1926. Other Arabic lettering was apparently removed when Golda Meir was an Israeli government minister and lived in the house. As the (apocryphal?) story is often told, she was expecting a visit from Dag Hammarskjöld and ordered the tiles sandblasted off, so the UN secretary-general wouldn't see that she was living in an Arab house.

Although George is unsure of the architectural history of the building, he agrees, across the ten-hour time difference from California to Jerusalem, to ask his uncle Ibrahim. Also known as Fred, Ibrahim was not only born in the villa in 1928—his twin brother, Charles Habib, was three years old when he died of pneumonia within its very walls—but he is, George tells me, a retired architect and the last surviving family member of the generation that lived in the house. And at this news I think once again that I've finally stumbled onto the X that marks the Spyro Houris spot and now all the missing facts about him will come spilling forth like gold coins from a long-buried treasure chest . . . though after several weeks of cybersilence (at our first contact, George tells me he is "in knots" about Gaza: I don't want to push), Fred himself writes me from his home in Palo Alto and sets straight the story of the house's construction.

He knows of Spyro Houris's work from pictures he has seen online but tells me that the architect of the villa named for the justice-loving Abbasid caliph was the Benedictine monk Mauritius Gisler. A Swiss archaeologist, missionary, and church builder who lived for years in Jerusalem and was close to Fred's father—the Jordanian-born, Fribourg-educated businessman Hanna Ibrahim Bisharat, who commissioned the house—Gisler was also involved in the planning and construction of the Dormition Abbey on Mount Zion. The fact immediately clicks when I hear it. Aside from the tiles on its front, the Villa Harun ar-Rashid has always struck me as somehow distinct from the other houses ascribed to Houris: The stonework is too chunky and rusticated; the wide, symmetrical front bears no relation to his other designs; the ceramics are set differently into the façade, more squarely and sparely. Once we've determined the mansion's actual builder, Fred goes on in a darkly wistful way about his uncle's house next door and the family's close friendship with the well-known Jerusalem oud player Wasif al-Jawhariyyeh. "He played duets with Mama on their lutes on our veranda. He played his lute at Jewish weddings also . . ."

There's a mazelike quality to this search—and when I make my way to the Greek patriarchate in the Christian Quarter of the Old City, the sense that I am wandering a labyrinth becomes not just intellectual but physical as well: After convincing the gatekeeper that I have important business within, he (a cheerful, bespectacled man named Alexander who seems glad for something to do besides sitting and watching this war-racked summer's meager groups of tourists straggle by) leads me into a flagstoned courtyard and up an outdoor staircase and around and around, then guides me into a formidable set of chambers. In the first room—an utterly modern office, save the marble floors, long gold drapes, and many paintings of Christ being taken down from the cross—black-cassocked, Greek-speaking monks and nuns in high hats and tight wimples work matter-of-factly at computers and answering telephones, as if this were some sort of ecclesiastical call center or corporate headquarters on high. In the next, still more formidable room, a pair of Palestinian teenagers in miniskirts and lipstick sit surrounded by heavy banquet-hall-styled gold-painted neo-rococo furniture and also answer telephones, check their e-mail and Facebook, and chat with each other in English. One is teaching the other, an American, Arabic. When I enter, they are working out the difference between the word for ice cream in literary Arabic and in Palestinian dialect. They offer me juice and chocolate on an elaborately painted tray.

I sip, we chat. They seem a little bored with their summer jobs at the patriarchate and happy to have someone new and female to talk to, some nonpriestly conversational diversion. Though I'm here at the heart of Palestinian East Jerusalem, the war in Gaza feels light-years away. The girls are trying to pick which movie to go see tonight in Ramat Hasharon, an upscale suburb of Tel Aviv, and at one of the desks, a pretty middle-aged Palestinian woman in jeans and a T-shirt, a sparkly crucifix hanging from her neck, is also giving an Arabic lesson. Her student is a befuddled-seeming young monk, his hair pulled into a disheveled bun, and she keeps teasing him in gentle Greek about his inability to pronounce certain critical guttural sounds. A few gray-haired men with flapping black capes and long beards finally come marching in, and everyone sits up straight. Soon I am ushered by one of the teenagers into the cluttered closet-like office of the chief secretary of the patriarchate, a tiny archbishop with a tall chimney hat, who seems distinctly uninterested in the question of my question. Fascinating as this setting is, no one here has heard of Spyro Houris.

Neither has Father Cornelius, the bishop with the pointed face, wispy beard, and lazy eye at the ecclesiastical court across the alleyway—though at first I think it might be otherwise. After doodling in inscrutable silence for several minutes on the paper where I have written the words "SPYRO HOURIS," he stands very slowly, walks with a certain vague resolve toward a tin cabinet from which he pulls an impressive pile of heavy ledger books and then, without opening any of them, proceeds to return the pile right back to the tin cabinet and close then lock its door, insisting as he does that none of these registers of weddings or deaths could possibly pertain to the years that might include Spyro Houris. *Are you sure? Could I look?* But my powers of archival persuasion are useless here. Father Cornelius has already shuffled back to his desk to doodle.

At the small Greek Cathedral of Mar Yacoub, or Saint James, beside the Church of the Holy Sepulcher—where I've been told that all the community's births have been recorded for years—I'm welcomed much more warmly by a strapping, white-haired, pink-faced man who introduces himself in English as Abraham. "You are from the Khoury family?" he wants to know. "Not exactly," I say, though by now the object of my search almost feels like my long-lost uncle

Spyro. Meanwhile, I'm somehow grateful to Abraham for not taking one look at me and jumping to ethnic conclusions. Greek, Arab, Jewish? Who can really tell? Abraham, too, has a ledger book—table-sized, leather-bound, apparently very old. "These are," he announces, "the families of Jerusalem." He sets it gingerly onto his desk and begins to run his finger down its alphabetized Arabic columns, which he says account for nearly two centuries of Jerusalem births in the Greek Orthodox community: *Said Khoury, Elias Khoury, George Khoury, Anton Khoury, Michel Khoury, Elias Khoury . . . Khoury, Khoury, Khoury . . .* There is, he apologizes as he closes the book, no Spyro here.

My last stop in the maze of the Christian Quarter, several days later, is the Greek consulate, where I pass through a metal detector and sit in the very clean, very empty waiting room, which—aside from the glittering icon propped on one counter—looks like it might be an Israeli bank branch, with its pale new fake-wood office furniture and NO SMOKING sign in English, Hebrew, and Arabic. It is quiet here—too quiet. Depressed. Is the sad hush in the air a function of the rotten economic situation in Greece? The war in Gaza? Summer vacation? I can't say, but I can wonder, as the receptionist answers calls in a near whisper, in Arabic and Greek, and the only people who enter are a young Palestinian father and his three small children. They've come to pick up their Greek passports and dart out as soon as they have the documents in hand, as if heading straight for the airport and away from this place.

Besides the Palestinian receptionist, two lone hassled Greek employees are the only people here, and when I'm finally greeted by one of them—a slight, fair-haired woman with chic glasses and baggy khaki pants—she looks poised to burst into tears. Holding a thick stack of visa applications in one hand, she waves me into her office, even as she blurts that she's overwhelmed. A staff of thirteen has been cut to three in the last month, and she's scrambling just to keep up. She has never heard of Spyro Houris but seems genuinely interested and even makes a point of leading me to a wall of weathered documents and another locked cabinet, which together constitute the consular archive, and where I have a strong sense that there must be some record of him. Much as she'd like to help me, however, she can't. Palestinians desperate for Greek citizenship have, she explains, lately been trying to prove lines of ancestry. These claims may or may not be based in reality, but because of their frequency, and the use of the historical record in making such assertions, the old files have been sealed.

Meanwhile, she can't offer to look through those records on my behalf, since her time is completely consumed with these heaps of urgent visa applications and dire passport requests. "I'm trying," she says softly, "to help people *live*." Which I can't, of course, argue with, and as I make my way back out into the street, her words follow me, challenging me gently. The case of Spyro Houris may not be that kind of now-or-never emergency, but in a way I, too, am trying to help someone live, or live on. Though I've begun to wonder at the odds.

THE JEWISH JUDGE

I've begun to wonder, that is, about Spyro Houris and all the blank looks that his name prompts. If he was once such a major architect, such a force in town, why is there so little trace of him left? Perhaps he's a figment of David Kroyanker's imagination?

This seems highly unlikely. I've seen his name for myself on those cornerstones, and I believe that most of the buildings Kroyanker ascribes to him are indeed his. I've come to think that several other impressive houses around Jerusalem, unmentioned by Kroyanker, may also be his handiwork. Based on community lore, Anastas Damianos and Elias Messinas have both confirmed his role as an important figure within Greek-speaking Jerusalem; several local conservation architects have enthused to me about his work as they've included attributions of certain buildings to him in carefully prepared documentation files that must be presented to the municipality before renovations can take place on a protected structure. When we meet to talk at a café just across the street from the back of Harrison's post office, one of these architects, M.—among the most knowledgeable and engaged of all those currently involved in protecting the new city's historical fabric, a young man with a yarmulke, an encyclopedic knowledge of various neighborhoods, and a host of major preservation projects to his name—describes Houris to me as a long-held fascination and one of his very favorite Jerusalem builders. "I really, really love him," he tells me. "I don't think there was anyone else who dared to do what he did," and he goes on to praise Houris's range, his flexibility, the fine detail and solidity of his construction, and the inventiveness of his exterior designs. "Even if you say the buildings are 'over designed,' the richness he achieved was remarkable." While M. has no biographical particulars to add to my minuscule store, his professional knowledge and informed appreciation of Houris's various creations mean a great deal, and our conversation at least makes me feel I'm not completely deluded.

I'm also relieved to find documentary evidence of his presence in the city—not just as a worn historical remnant but as it once was, in fresh print. Houris's name has bobbed up in various articles from the English-language *Palestine Bulletin* that mention, for instance, the not especially earth-shattering or architectural October 1931 news that "the Palestine Football League has chosen its Disciplinary Committee. Mr. Spyro Houris joins Mr. Halutz and Mr. Sadomsky as well as the chairman Mr. J. Burns."

In June 1932, a room is advertised as "to let" in "Spiro Houris House":

Room

TO LET

Furnished. With or without pension. Apply: Miss Waldes, Spiro Houris House, Queen Melisande's Way, near Immigration Dept., Jerusalem.

This house is or was apparently the elegant building with the Armenian tiles on its side and whose front also faces onto Jaffa Road, opposite Zion Square. He and his eponymous house were well enough known so that this address was sufficient.

And on March 21, 1933, Mr. Spyro Houris is listed among "some 500 persons" who were expected to attend the party being thrown at the King David Hotel to celebrate the sixtieth birthday of one of Mandatory Jerusalem's most prominent citizens, a popular English Jewish teacher and school principal named Annie Landau. Though the headline declares that "Speakers of all Communities Laud Headmistress's Service and Generosity" and the guest list features a few distinguished Arab, Greek, and French names, the invitees are primarily Englishmen and Jews. The most telling thing about Houris's presence on that tony Anglo-Zionist society roster is, then, that he seems to have been welcomed in such circles. Also that he—unlike most others on the list, named by the newspaper in Noah's Ark–like order, in twos (including the ever-elusive M. and Mme. Petassis)—planned to come alone. At press time, no Mrs. Houris was slated to attend. Where, one may wonder, was Heleni Efklides that March afternoon?

But these are just bits and pieces. I'm hungry by now for some real paper proof of his existence as an architect, and it's this slightly starved feeling—together with N.'s suggestion and a rather idle late-night Internet search—that finally drives me to the Central Zionist Archives.

Having knocked on all the doors I can think to open with the password "Spyro Houris," I've taken to hunting down information about the various people who hired him to build. Among these is the man for whom Houris constructed a grand if slightly curious mansion—one of those inscribed with his name—in what appears to be the first new neighborhood established in Jerusalem after the British conquest. Located at what was then the edge of the city and is now the bustling, gritty area of the central bus station, Romema was the site of the Turkish surrender to the British in December 1917. A very English stone cenotaph marks that historic spot.

As the rather wishful-sounding creation story of the neighborhood is told by certain present-day Israelis, the mukhtars of the neighboring Arab villages of Lifta and Sheikh Badr each claimed rights to this piece of land, and when in 1918 a Jewish judge-turned–property lawyer, one Yom-Tov Hamon, was called in to resolve the dispute, he "saw the significance of erecting a Jewish neighborhood near the entrance to the city" and did so by buying the large plot and letting the village chiefs split the proceeds. The story may have some basis in truth (perhaps this genuinely was contested land), though the Zionist nature of the decision to found Romema on this tract seems a later narrative addition. In 1921 a small and unusually mixed group of well-to-do locals—Sephardim, Ashkenazim, together with a few Muslims—planned it as an upscale suburb of some two dozen spacious houses, with gardens and streets that radiated like spokes around the cenotaph.

However the land was acquired, and for whatever reason, the judge's central role in founding the neighborhood is certain. Yom-Tov Hamon, or Amon, was a Turkish Jew from an aristocratic family that traced its roots back to the caliph's physician in Granada; subsequent generations of Hamons included doctors to various sultans. Born and educated in Constantinople, Hamon had arrived in Jerusalem in 1911, at the behest of the Jewish community of Palestine, whose members wanted a judge to represent them before the Ottoman authorities. Though some groused that he didn't know Arabic and wasn't familiar with "the local ways," he was eventually accepted in town. His Turkish and his character were both considered excellent, and there was talk of putting Hamon's name up for the "Jewish seat" in the Ottoman parliament in Constantinople: "Even though he's not a Zionist," one community leader wrote, "he has knowledge of the subject; he's an honest man and a young and well-known judge." Hamon declined that position and stayed in Jerusalem, where he served on the bench for several years before the authorities ordered him to move to Aleppo; he refused and took up work as a lawyer instead. During the war he was exiled back to Constantinople by the Turks for his connection to certain Zionists, and when he returned to Jerusalem in peacetime, he again worked as an attorney and continued to practice there until his death.

Most of this I did not, mind you, read in a late-night haze or online, but by bright July daylight and in several dry Hebrew books about Judges and Lawyers in the Land of Israel and the Jews of the East in the Land of Israel—neither of which would seem a place to turn for clues about a long-lost architect named Spyro Houris. Yet this bibliographic roundabout (and my inability to absorb any more dismal Internet news about Gaza this particular dark night) leads me to a hint that glows back at me from my screen just a few minutes before I'm about to turn off the computer and trundle into bed. Buried in the admittedly questionable context of Yom-Tov Hamon's Hebrew Wikipedia page are the words: "Hamon died in 1952 at age 79. His personal papers, which were recently discovered in the basement of the house where he lived till his death, were passed on to the Central Zionist Archives."

The house where he lived until his death is of course the grand if slightly curious house that Spyro Houris built for Hamon, and which is, as it happens, a five-minute walk from the Central Zionist Archives. The next morning I am there at the archive almost when it opens. Unlike the state archive, this institution is well kept, with a small, pleasant, rosemary-and-lavender-filled garden that somehow manages to serve as a sweet-smelling buffer between the modest building and the grime and traffic all around it. The holdings inside are also far more orderly than their government-controlled counterparts at the state archive, so that when I plant myself before one of the computers in the reading room and type in the words "HAMON, YOM-TOV," I'm glad to see his name and a record group number pop up but surprised by what follows when I click on the link and run headlong into yet another archival stop sign: "NO RESULTS FOUND."

Wikipedia, granted, isn't necessarily a trustworthy source, but Hamon's name and this number do appear in the archive's system, which means his papers must be somewhere in this building. I ask at the desk and am told with a shrug by one of the chronically indifferent clerks that he has no idea. I should go downstairs and talk to S.

Down a floor is where the higher-ups sit, and there I find S., who turns out to be a middle-aged French-Israeli woman in a beret—not, that is, a French beret, but an Orthodox Jewish beret, or maybe it's both? In any event, she has the matter-of-fact and slightly officious bearing of an overworked high school principal who might genuinely like to help but who has a whole hall full of students and teachers waiting outside her door for her to fix their very pressing problems. She looks doubtful as I explain what I'm after, and at first she seems not to know what I'm talking about—though as I keep babbling about Yom-Tov Hamon and Spyro Houris (I realize I probably sound unhinged, like some sort of archival stalker), she loosens slightly, her eyes brighten, and she says in her soft French accent, yes. We do have those papers here. But they are—she shakes her head disapprovingly—in no condition to be examined. They haven't been properly cataloged; there's only a preliminary handlist. They're dirty and need to be cleaned.

However composed and businesslike, a good archivist *gets* it. She appreciates and even vicariously relishes the obsessive nature of such a search, so that when I begin the slightly humiliating act of begging S. to let me at least peek at what's there, she relents quickly—perhaps preferring to spare us both the embarrassment of my pleading—and offers to print out the draft of the list. She is obviously not happy with my request, and, as she attempts to unjam the faulty communal printer behind her desk, keeps repeating that these papers really aren't in any state to be seen. But, like N. at the state archive, committed to the cause of History itself, she goes ahead and clears a space at a table in her office and lets me sit there and read through.

The account of the 114 files that make up Hamon's archive is precise about the Hebrew contents of this trove: "Legal ruling with regard to claim number 4888/28 by the leaders of the Communal Fund against the Warsaw Kolel and Eliezer King in the matter of the occupancy of an apartment on the premises" and "Power of attorney from Yosef Chaim Bason to Attorney Hamon concerning the matter of the distribution of the estate of his parents Meir and Chaviva." But besides being a Hebrew-speaking attorney with extensive legal records that eventually came to clutter his ample basement, Yom-Tov Hamon was also a genuine Levantine cosmopolitan, and his papers range across languages and subjects—and, it seems, well beyond the cataloging capabilities of whoever the intern or volunteer was who drew up this rough initial survey. (S. had, to be fair, warned me.) So it is that the pages she has coaxed from that reluctant printer also include dozens of far vaguer descriptions of "handwritten things in Arabic" (was it Turkish?) and "letters and documents in French and Arabic." English and Ladino also appear on the list. I reason that any trace of Spyro Houris to be found here will likely emerge from the realm of these non-Hebraic mystery items. Though S. may not be pleased with my search, she generously allows me to order up a pile of these files, and I return to my seat in the reading room upstairs to wait.

And there he is—amazingly enough, in the very first file I open.

In three drafts—one scrawled in pencil, one written in a flowing hand and neat browning ink, the third typed and in multiple copies—a French-language contract, dated July 15, 1922, details the agreement between "the undersigned, Mr. Y. Amon, Attorney, local subject, residing in Jerusalem, the party of the first part" and "Mr. Spiros G. Houris, Architect, Greek subject, also residing in Jerusalem, the party of the second part." The two have, the contract states, agreed that Mr. Spiros Houris is committed to build and deliver in full within a period of four months "a house that will be the home of Mr. Y. Amon, situated in Sheikh Badr (the Colony of Mr. Aron Many), according to the plans agreed upon by the two parties," while Mr. Y. Amon has agreed to pay the architect, Mr. Spiros G. Houris, the sum of 2,400 Egyptian pounds according to the plans, etc. A carefully outlined payment scheme follows, with a 200-pound deposit tendered to Houris up front, and subsequent installments due after the foundations and cistern have been completed and the construction "has reached a meter in height"; after the masonry of the ground floor "including ceilings" is done; when the first floor is finished; with the installation "of all the woodwork, doors, windows, etc. etc. etc." and so on, through "painting and trim" till "the completion of the house." Various other technical stipulations follow, as does the guarantee that Houris will fulfill all his responsibilities and hand the house over to Hamon no later than the first of November 1922.

None of the contracts are signed, and it's not clear if this was the final version of the agreement between them, though several other files indicate that the construction didn't go quite as quickly as planned. It wasn't until January 13, 1924, that a representative of the Palestine Building Loan & Saving Association wrote Hamon a letter stating that an inspector had examined the house "and found it to be completely finished." And while few other details of the building process itself exist, another startling document emerges from this pile of papers that have covered my fingers with a thin film of grit. Ordi-

narily this would bother me, but since it has come from the basement of the very house whose foundations and walls are specified in
the contract I've just held in my hands, the grit itself almost feels like
part of the archive.

In the fall of 1923, as construction of the house reached its height,
an urgent communication was dispatched to the honorable Y. Amon
from yet another architect, Eliezer Yellin, scion of a venerable Jerusalem family and himself an important figure in the establishment of
several new neighborhoods, including Rehavia, where he would
build the very first house (his own) the next year. Typing in Hebrew,
on the old-world letterhead of the Council of Jerusalem Jews, Yellin
wrote on behalf of the Committee for Immigration and Labor of the
council, and his tone was sharp:

> *Dear Sir,*
>
> *Nearly a month ago we approached your honor in writing, noting
> that a good many of our working brethren are currently unemployed
> and that our national duty demands of us that we provide work for as
> many of them as possible.*
>
> *To our sorrow, we must approach your honor once more with regard
> to this matter, since our hope that your honor would value what we
> had said in the appropriate way and strive to employ Hebrew workers
> as much as possible <u>has not taken place</u>! In contrast to the number of
> foreign workers employed in our building trade, how small is the num-
> ber of workers among our Jewish brethren.*
>
> *We believe that it is not your honor who has brought this situation
> about, but the contractor who did not grant them work. But we think
> that it is your honor's duty to <u>insist</u> that the contractor increase the
> number of Hebrew workers, and that it is your honor's responsibility to
> make absolutely certain that this takes place.*
>
> *We hope that your honor will heed what we are saying and realize
> the profit that comes to the nation by employing Hebrew workers. We
> are sure that the conclusion of things between us will be better than
> the start . . .*

Though "the contractor" is not named in Yellin's chiding letter,
it would seem to be the non-Jewish architect Spyro Houris who was

taking the rap for the number of "foreign" (no doubt Arab) workers on the building site. The fact that the Constantinople-raised, possibly non-Zionist Hamon himself appears not to have been especially bothered by the ethnic or religious constitution of the construction crew is telling. He had, after all, both hired a non-Jewish architect and ignored the council's first warning about the workers he'd employed. Perhaps his vision of what "the nation" might best profit from differed from that of his peers on the Council of Jerusalem Jews. This is, of course, mere speculation—maybe his preference for Arab labor was a matter of cost and not principle—but it is notable that the employment of Jews (and exclusion of Arabs) was not a pressing priority for the formerly Ottoman judge.

Spyro Houris himself, meanwhile, has begun to emerge—slowly, as a photo in developing fluid—from Yom-Tov Hamon's archive. He was, the files make clear, a Greek citizen. He *did* live in Jerusalem. He earned real money for his designs. (The precise sum is hard to say, but as I'm later told by one in the economic know, 2,400 Egyptian pounds in 1922 could at the very least be the contemporary equivalent of $180,000, and possibly much more. Whatever the figure, a typical wage for a Palestinian construction worker during this period was some 10–20 piastres for an eight-hour day, which is to say that a five-day workweek would earn a hard-toiling laborer a single pound.) French was definitely one of his languages. Houris may have been welcomed warmly by the guests at a grand 1933 birthday party for a Jewish schoolmistress at the King David Hotel, but his involvement in the struggling economy of Jewish Jerusalem in the early years of the Mandate was quietly frowned upon by at least several upstanding members of that community.

And while there's a certain frustration built into the contrast between all that I still don't know about Houris and the rich wash of details about Hamon that come pouring out of the lawyer/judge's papers—which include coquettish if slightly formal letters in French from his wife, Rachel, of the patrician Roditi family ("Mon cher mari, It was with very great pleasure that I received your letter dated June 17, informing me of your good health . . ."), and exhaustive monthly Arabic lists of his private expenses (stamps, a telegram to Istanbul, a can of green peas)—I'm grateful for what I know now about Spyro Houris that I didn't a few hours ago. What else, I wonder, is hidden in these piles of dusty letters and crumpled legal dossiers, those bug-eaten receipts and tattered bank statements? Where did Spyro Houris come from? I wonder. Could he, like Hamon, have started out in Constantinople? Might they already have known each other from the Ottoman old country? To obtain Greek citizenship in the late Ottoman era, I've read, a member of the Orthodox community need only have lived in Greece for three years. No matter where he was born, if Spyro Houris had studied architecture in Athens, he could easily have obtained a passport . . .

I am so absorbed in the files before me and the thoughts they prompt that I don't stand up for hours, except to stoop and snap pictures of the documents with my digital camera. I skip lunch, drink no water, and when the clerk announces that the archive is closing in five minutes, I feel like I'm waking from some strange dream. Slightly dizzy, I stumble out into the still-bright sunlight and find myself walking in a kind of trance toward the house itself.

THE HOUSE ITSELF

At the time Houris and Hamon signed that contract, these hills spilled with orchards and fields. Now one approaches crowded, traffic-clogged Romema from the area of the archive by turning away from the ostentatious non sequitur of a towering white Santiago Calatrava bridge that marks the run-down entrance to the city. One then passes through a dank, Moscowesque underground passageway where a shade-craving old Russian busker with a synthesizer, a cotton cap, and a morose look is almost always playing 1960s Israeli schmaltz, lento.

Behind the massive slab of a central bus station on Jaffa Road, Yom-Tov Hamon's formerly pastoral neighborhood is dilapidated, filthy, and almost entirely ultra-Orthodox. It's hard not to see the derelict condition of this formerly elegant area as an ugly encapsulation of the current state of the city as a whole. The physical neglect here almost seems deliberate, as though the residents of today's Romema believed they might better prove their readiness for the

world to come by abusing the world they live in. Many of the once
gracious mansions here have been enlarged in the most slipshod way,
with mismatched extensions and extra floors slapped on crudely, stone
verandas enclosed with fiberglass or cluttered with laundry, floor rags,
and old appliances. Gardens that decades ago were filled with flower-
ing fruit trees are now strewn with trash.

The surprise, then, is to find—at the corner of streets called
Hamon and, of all things, Haadrichal, or the Architect—the judge's
house looking better (or at least better tended) than it has for decades.
"The Architect" of the street sign is not Spyro Houris but, for some
reason, Richard Kauffmann, who planned many neighborhoods in
Jerusalem and seems to have lived briefly in Romema, but so far as
I know had nothing to do with its design.

Having recently undergone an extensive, even extravagant,
renovation, the house sits oddly in the midst of this diesel-soot-thick
slum. The building's fine pale stones have been thoroughly cleaned,
its slatted wooden shutters and quirky, curving Art Deco doors refurbished, the curlicued metal railings on the side balconies freshly
painted. The building's most notable—and eccentric—feature, its flar-
ing skirt-shaped red copper-plated roof has been carefully restored,
and a lush garden encircles the house, as does a jasmine-covered stone
wall with a heavy new iron gate, a sign advertising the name of the
landscaping company, and several conspicuous security cameras aimed
at all who would think to draw near.

The house has also almost doubled in size. What once was a
spacious but proportional building is now enormous by local standards, steroidal, a Middle Eastern McMansion with substantial additions to the side and the back, and the somewhat jarring presence
of a neatly mowed and very American front lawn, well-watered
Floridian green in the midst of this parched Judean summer. The
effect of the lavish expansion and renovation is peculiar, as the
house—for years a decaying hulk, once more a grand villa—has
certainly been spared the kind of demolition by neglect that is taking place all around it; someone *cares* about the building and
grounds and isn't ashamed to show it. By Jerusalem's admittedly
low standards, the renovation is thoughtful. The architect has taken
pains to match the color of new stones to old, and to build in the
same approximate style that Houris did, with decorative urns and

white balusters along the roof of the extension and ornamental keystones that attempt to mimic the originals. Though there is an ersatz wedding-hall quality to some of these touches, they do at least indicate awareness of what has come before.

On the other hand, the additions have thrown the building's scale and relationship to its setting severely off-kilter. There's something flamboyantly alien about the building now—though Hamon's villa may also have seemed flamboyantly alien when Houris completed it in the early winter of 1924. With its Victorian-styled widow's walk, funny metallic roof, and bulbous neo-Renaissance balustrades, this was never a modest or "typical" Jerusalem abode, and it seems to have been designed to call attention to itself and its owner's fancy foreign tastes. Hamon had clearly wanted to show off with the house—and perhaps Houris had, too. Wherever he started his career, this was one of his first big Jerusalem commissions, and it may be that he felt it best to pull out all the structural and decorative stops for the occasion. It's among the oldest buildings that bear his cornerstone "signature," which the renovation has preserved, and which I must stand at an angle, on tiptoe, to see through the dense fence of newly planted cypress trees.

As I'm attempting to perform this awkward maneuver, a young ultra-Orthodox couple appears, having just descended the staircase that leads to the extensive addition at the back of the house. She wears a wig; he wears a fedora. They are speaking English to each other, and almost without thinking, I blurt the question: "Do you live here?"

A bit suspiciously, the young woman eyes me and my short-sleeved blouse, my cotton slacks, my uncovered head. She did, she says, before she got married . . . As her husband stands off at a pointed distance, she and I talk a bit about the house—"There was a judge who lived here," she tells me—and before long I find myself, still bareheaded and by now almost delirious from dehydration, making my way up that same staircase and into the house's spanking-new addition. There I'm greeted and welcomed with unstinting and to me rather startling warmth by an ultra-Orthodox woman, about my age, in a housecoat and kerchieflike hat. She seems unfazed by my unlikely presence on her doorstep, and when I introduce myself, she hears my accent and switches from Hebrew to American English and ushers me through the foyer, all bright marble floor tiles and clean white walls, and up a few steps into her spotless kitchen. In what seems a single, uninterrupted movement, she pours me a plastic cup of water, pulls out a chair for me, darts into the next room to find a neatly wrapped folder that holds several Xeroxes of old photographs of the house and the judge and his children, and plunks herself down to talk animatedly about the building and what she knows of its history, its purchase from Hamon's heirs, the renovations, how they closed up the cistern because "there are children here," and so on. She insists on giving me one of the photographs to keep, and lets me snap a picture of the other.

While she can't, unfortunately, let me see the inside of the original house, where her in-laws live (it has, I've read, been gutted and completely redesigned), she can and does show me yet another part of this town I've never seen before. She doesn't know she's doing this, of course, but for all my years here and all I think I know about Jerusalem, I've never once been inside an ultra-Orthodox house in this city, let alone sat and chatted so easily at one of its kitchen tables. And I have rarely met a Jerusalemite so very proud of her home. While she knows little about Spyro Houris—for her, the Jewish judge is the hero of the story—he has led me here, as he keeps leading me into the most unlikely places and spaces, up staircases, down corridors, and into rooms I never realized were there.

WHO'S WHO

The Hamon house doesn't look quite like any other building in Jerusalem . . . save one—at what was once the other edge of Sheikh Badr, and is now the fringe of Rehavia, on a street named for the Russian-born Zionist leader Menachem Ussishkin—which was constructed with the same strange kind of red copper roof, grand Italianate sweep, and offbeat relation to ornament, and which may or may not have been planned by Spyro Houris. Kroyanker dates that building to 1927 and ascribes it to someone else, though other Jerusalem historians and architects speculate that it was indeed Houris's handiwork.

The confusion is understandable: "Houris's style was not consistent," writes Kroyanker, in a stiff Hebrew, "and many of his buildings are different from one another, but many are distinguished by their stylized character, their decorative colored ceramics, their ornate railings, and crenellated parapets." He applies the loose architectural term "eclectic" to Houris's mix-and-match approach—though here it's perhaps worth stopping to consider the ties that *do* bind the grab bag assortment of structures that Houris appears to have built. Not all of those ties are visible to the naked eye, but—once recognized— they indicate the complex web of *human* connection that characterized Jerusalem in these years. The fact that Spyro Houris's identity (like Khalil Sakakini's, like Photios Efklides's, like Yom-Tov Hamon's) may well have been composed of multiple shifting, even contradictory elements—Was he born in Greece? Was he Arab? Ottoman? Palestinian? Local? Foreign? Was he all these things at once?—seems only to underscore that the city he was helping to build was itself content to be eclectic, ethnically, politically, religiously, aesthetically. One didn't always have to take sides, and in fact the petrified binaries that would soon come to dominate the conversation, or shouting match, about the city would probably have seemed strange to its residents in those late Ottoman and early Mandate days. Houris built for Greeks and Jews and Catholics and Muslims. At the very same time he was overseeing the construction of that stately Italianate mansion for the Sephardi Jewish judge in the northwestern neighborhood of Romema, he was also overseeing the construction of a stately Ottoman-style villa for the Muslim poet, essayist, and educator Is'af al-Nashashibi in the northeastern neighborhood of Sheikh Jarrah, on a rise leading up to Mount Scopus. Both of these buildings are "signed" by Houris and their foundations were poured in 1922. That one has a singular slanting metal roof and the other is flat-topped and fronted with ornamental Armenian tiles seems not to indicate some sort of stylistic wobbliness on Houris's part so much as his fluid and highly adaptable awareness of context, and of the various cultures that swirled around him.

And for all their differences, Houris's buildings themselves offer visual clues to the social ties that cut across the city in those years. When, for instance, that other impressive Italianate house in Sheikh Badr/Rehavia was conceived nearly ninety years ago, it was meant to be the home of yet another Constantinople-born Jewish property lawyer, Elihu Fraji, who arrived in Jerusalem just a few years after Hamon (and who took private Arabic lessons with Khalil Sakakini three days a week). Perhaps they both hired Houris to build them grand houses with odd metal roofs? Or maybe the younger Fraji had paid a contractor to copy the mansion built by Houris for his esteemed senior colleague? In either event, the two homeowners must have known each other well. Of the forty-nine attorneys who received the first licenses to practice law in British Palestine in 1921, only four were Jews: Hamon, Fraji, Hamon's brother-in-law and sometime law partner Tawfik Adas, and Hamon's Romema neighbor, Aharon Mani.

And from here the game of architectural connect the dots begins, as Aharon Mani (whose name appears on the Houris-Hamon contract as being the owner or initiator of the "colony" where the house would be built in Sheikh Badr) not only lived next door to Hamon but would also soon hire Houris to build one of those elegant pink-stoned commercial/residential buildings on Jaffa Road, across from

Zion Square, past which I can't stop walking this summer. Born to a distinguished Iraqi Jewish family in the old Jewish community of Hebron, Mani was a well-respected property lawyer as well as an expert in the Arabic language, Islamic law, and traditional Jewish sources. In later years, he would go on to write multiple books on these subjects and to translate Maimonides's *Guide for the Perplexed* from Judeo-Arabic into Hebrew.

Not only did Hamon and Mani have a profession, a neighborhood, and an architect in common, they seem also to have shared ideas about the city's various communities and how they might (literally) work together. As Hamon had been scolded for his employment of "foreign workers" by Eliezer Yellin, so Mani was attacked in the Hebrew press for doing the same. In an article from early May 1925, the author of the "Jerusalem Day to Day" column in the Hebrew newspaper *Doar Hayom* describes how "in recent weeks, the pace of building has picked up appreciably, and there is hardly a street or neighborhood where construction isn't taking place." After listing several of the more notable and impressive projects, the anonymous writer goes on to complain: "On Jaffa Road, between the Zion Cinema and the Solel Building [on what is now Havatzelet Street], Mr. Aharon Mani is building a row of stores with apartments upstairs. It should be said that most all of the aforementioned work is being done by Jewish laborers—except for that of Mr. Mani, who has given the job to a non-Jewish contractor and as a result all the work is in the hands of non-Jews, and the Hebrew worker won't be seen or mentioned."

In the very same issue of the newspaper, a letter to the editor appears under the heading "ON HEBREW LABOR." Signed by sixteen Jewish "builders, stone cutters, laborers," the letter declares the authors' "deepest dismay at the actions of Mr. Aharon Mani . . . for having given the work on his building on Jaffa Road to a non-Jewish contractor who is employing his own workers . . . We are the heads of families who make our living solely from building work provided by Jewish contractors, and from others we never have and never will earn a single penny . . ." They accuse him of having initially hired a Jewish contractor whom he abandoned for a non-Jew "because of a difference [in cost] of less than 5 percent." The fact that Mani is, they write, an important employee of the Zionist Palestine Land Development Company makes this unacceptable. They demand that the public judge "what our high-ranking officials do with The People's money . . . Is this any way to build a National Home?"

It took several days for Mani to respond, but when he did he registered in quietly irate terms his disgust at the numerous errors contained in this letter: He is not and never has been an employee of the Palestine Land Development Company; he has never needed nor taken The People's money; the Jewish contractor he'd originally hired had turned out to be slow, unreliable, and financially irresponsible; some of the workers are in fact Jews, though among them were those who simply walked away from the job when the foundation digging began. "It is to be hoped," he offers, with a sarcastic jab, "that this will not be the case when the less difficult work of building commences." And more strongly still, he registers his belief that one should treat others as one would like to be treated. If, he writes, someone behaved in this (discriminatory) way "toward me or towards one of my brothers anywhere in the world, I would send up a cry that would reach the heavens."

He also makes a point of stating that "the current contractor is not completely Arab. There are two contractors, an Arab and a Jew."

"Not completely Arab" is a curious way to describe Spyro Houris, though by that Mani doesn't seem to mean "Greek" so much as "working with a Jew." Who his Jewish partner was on this project we do not know—though we do know that links like the ones that yoked Houris to Hamon to Fraji to Mani were not at all unusual in this context. Similar sorts of social ties and commercial connections (among friends, across ethnic and religious lines) brought Houris much of his work during these years, and as he adjusted himself to each commission and the preferences of his diverse range of clients, his architectural style shifted—though not always in obvious relation to his employers' ethnicity. The row of Jaffa Road buildings that it seems Houris designed (with Petassis?) alongside the Mani building and opposite the Zion Cinema in the late 1920s and early '30s blends together easily, as an organic whole—and these structures were commissioned, respectively, by Saba al-Araj, a wealthy Palestinian Christian from Beit Jala; Yosef Aminof, a Persian Jewish business-man who'd recently immigrated from Mashhad; and another myste-rious investor named Khoury (whose initials "CK" are still inscribed on a grille above that building's doorway). The fifth building in this block, sometimes also ascribed to Houris and Petassis, was con-structed for a pair of entrepreneurial Sephardi brothers whose fam-ily had arrived in Palestine from Georgia in the 1870s and shortened their name from Kukashvili to Kukia. Houris's own office is said to have been located in the building marked "CK," as was, for some time, the Egyptian consulate.

While from this distance we can't trace all the lines that led from one of these commissions to another, certain chains of transmission and relation seem plain. Another business associate of Hamon's and Mani's, for instance, was a well-to-do Muslim quarry owner from

nearby Lifta who went by the name of Hajj Mahmud and who it appears hired Houris to plan a substantial apartment building at the edge of Romema in 1925. Built right on Jaffa Road and now standing beside the looming bus station, this imposing three-and-a-half-story edifice was designed in that more floridly orientalist style that Kroyanker describes, with its red-and-white-striped trim, its point-arched windows, vaguely Mamluk crenellations, richly colored and patterned floor tiles, and blue-and-white ceramic panels set into the façade, complete with swirling Koranic quotations: *"Put in the heart of men kindness towards them, and provide them with the earth's fruits so that they may give thanks."* Its occupants were both Arabs and Jews.

And the dot-connecting game goes on . . . as Hajj Mahmud's business partner was none other than the wealthy Jerusalem-born Arab Catholic aristocrat Elias Thomas Gelat, for whom Houris would build one of his most spectacular villas, in the neighborhood of Talbiyeh in 1926, the same year that Gelat married a pretty, dark-eyed young woman named Catherine and the British foreign office approved Gelat's appointment as honorary consul of Hungary to Palestine. From their office on Mamilla Road, the firm of Gelat & Hajj Mahmud provided all kinds of serious services. That same 1937–1938 *Directory of Arab Trade, Industries, Crafts and Professions* where I could find no trace of Spyro Houris lists them as "Suppliers of all Grades and Gauges of Crushed Stone & Dust" and "Building & Road-Making Contractors." Gelat's own stationery from the 1920s, meanwhile, surfaces in the midst of yet another late-night Internet search. A digitized cache of bills, letters, and contracts concerning the supply of stones and construction of the American School of Oriental Research in Jerusalem, now known as the Albright Institute, features Gelat's name prominently. There he is described as a "Building & Public Works Contractor, Housing & Land Agent, Real Estate Transfer Agent," and "Joint Owner of Stone Crushing Plant of Gelat & Hadj-Mahmoud," and at one point his already crowded letterhead expands still farther to make room for a picture of a darkly luxurious, now vintage, then state-of-the-art automobile, together with the words CHRYSLER AGENCY. Not only did they make the roads, they sold the cars that drove on them.

If the apartment house that Houris built for Hajj Mahmud on Jaffa Road combined a whole pattern book's worth of Eastern touches in what seems a slightly cut-rate and even gaudy way (the building was meant as an investment, not the quarry owner's home), the Gelat house in Talbiyeh was and remains a much more refined variation on a theme. The villa features many of the same external elements as Hajj Mahmud's building—striped *ablaq* trim, joggle-arched windows, jagged crenellation, and vivid ceramic panels set into the façade—but it had then and still has a unity, elegance, control, and sense of ornamental play that Hajj Mahmud's building lacks. Much closer to the villa Houris built for Is'af al-Nashashibi in its architectural particulars, its interior combines in unusual hybrid fashion the floor plan of a typical Syrian/Palestinian urban mansion, with a cavernous central reception hall known as a *liwan*, and a more "European" arrangement of rooms along a corridor. It seems the *liwan* was meant as a public space, for entertaining, while the other parts of the house were intended just for the family and servants. Both inside and out, Houris took pains to array the Gelat house with a host of precisely wrought touches, from gray-and-black Carrara marble floors, colorfully patterned tiles, and arched wooden doors within to carefully and often surprisingly inventive inset ceramic medallions of various shapes and sizes without. The house's exacting design also includes prismatically carved capitals and several striking and sui generis diamond-shaped stone posts that frame the rooftop veranda.

Whatever we do or don't know about Spyro Houris—and, once again, it's bewildering to encounter the relative paucity of available details about him, compared to the glut of biographical information about those for whom he built—it seems safe to say that while he didn't discriminate on the basis of race or religion, he designed buildings only for those who stood at the top of the city's social and economic ladder. A member of the chamber of commerce, later president of the Rotary Club, and frequent guest at Government House, Elias Gelat was one of the richest and most powerful men in town and, as he must have conveyed to Houris when he commissioned the house, he wanted only the best for his new bride and the family they were planning. Soon after moving into the house, they had four children in

rapid succession. Antoine, Gloria, Vivian, and Norma would attend French schools, have a German nanny, and be waited on by a cook, two servants, and a chauffeur who drove one of those darkly luxurious, now vintage, once state-of-the-art Chryslers. Catherine, it was said, bought her dresses at the very best shops in Cairo and Paris, and the family spoke English and French together but knew Arabic, German, Italian, and Spanish as well; for reasons now obscure, Elias also commanded Magyar.

Linguistic and diplomatic talent seemed to run in the family, which had lived in Palestine for centuries, and whose members considered themselves descended from Crusaders. Elias Gelat's father, Antoine, had made his name in the late nineteenth century as the first interpreter of the American consulate in Jerusalem, and had become a trusted adviser to the archaeologists at the American School of Oriental Research. (Hence his son's eventual commission to construct its new buildings and the appearance of his crowded letterhead on that website.) The American archaeologists later credited Gelat senior with protecting much of their property during the difficult days of the First World War, when the Turkish authorities were busy requisitioning whatever foreign holdings they could. He also managed to safeguard the "valuable treasures and jewels" that had been "deposited as votive offerings" at the French, Italian, and Russian churches throughout the city.

For his pains, and for his friendliness with the representatives of an enemy power, Antoine and his family—including Elias, who was already in his late twenties and had by then become the second interpreter and clerk to the American consulate, and his father's right-hand dragoman—were exiled and sent on a grueling odyssey throughout Syria and Turkey, where they suffered. Illness plagued them as they wandered, Elias was forcibly conscripted into a non-Muslim military work brigade, and one of his younger brothers died of typhus before the war ended and they managed to make their mournful way home.

Strangely enough, on the morning I'd sat in the reading room at the Central Zionist Archives, waiting for Yom-Tov Hamon's files to arrive from storage and rather idly searching the computerized catalog, I'd stumbled on yet another document I'd never expected to find in such a place. In this moving, twenty-two-page typed English-language report dated March 1919 and titled "Experiences of A. Thos. Gelat and Family During Period of Exile in Asia Minor and Causes Which Led Up to Same," and signed by the older Gelat, he describes how "in that strange land . . . where the cold attains 25 degrees Centigrade below the zero mark . . . we endured loneliness, discomforts, sickness and privations of all kinds together with heavy loss in health and wealth, and above all we will ever . . . regret the bereavement caused to the family."

The war had been over for eight years, and his father had already been dead for two when Elias Gelat hired Spyro Houris to build him and Catherine that lavish villa in Talbiyeh. One may wonder, though, if the younger Gelat's desire to shelter his own family in such an impressive, even palatial, structure didn't somehow have its unconscious and possibly compensatory roots in the memory of that cold, that deprivation, that exile.

And where was Spyro Houris during the war? Did he wander? Did he suffer? Did he grieve? Wherever he was, it's clear that the wartime deprivation, cold, and exile of several others played a further—central—role in shaping both his plans for this house and his architectural vocabulary in a broader sense, as they shaped critical aspects of the way Jerusalem looks today.

The ceramics: They are *the* element that marks the Gelat house most clearly as one of Houris's buildings, emblems not just of this particular provincial city but of a far wider cosmopolitan web . . . And though the presence in Jerusalem of those intricately inlaid bone-and-blue, ruby-and-turquoise tiles has by now become a souvenir shop commonplace—it was not always so. In fact, before Spyro Houris made them his trademark when he embedded them in the façades of the Nashashibi Villa in Sheikh Jarrah and Hajj Mahmud's building on Jaffa Road, it seems no one else had thought to bring this most regal Ottoman element to bear on the scrappy old-new Palestinian town's domestic spaces.

But when grappling with the presence of these luminous ceramics on the exterior of, for instance, the Gelat mansion, it's not enough to search for Spyro Houris's fading fingerprints. To fathom how those tiles landed on the walls of this Arab Catholic family's elegant home—and ultimately on the doorposts of so many of the city's twenty-first-century Jewish residents—it's crucial to grasp how this now almost-forgotten Greek architect took inspiration from the arrival on the scene of an Armenian refugee ceramicist, brought from afar by a group of aesthetically alert British officials intent on repairing the façade of the most iconic building in the entire city, and a structure sacred to Muslims everywhere.

It's crucial, that is, to keep connecting the dots, to see how, in this city of all cities, this summer of all summers—a hundred years since the start of the Great War, in the midst of yet another petty but punishing war—one thing leads to another.

SPOLIA

The first winter the British controlled Palestine, 1917–1918, had been wet and stormy in the extreme, and these drastic conditions had, as the preening but prescient military governor of Jerusalem, Ronald Storrs, would later write, "a deplorable effect upon the wind-racked north-west façade of that utmost fulfillment of colour, rhythm and geometry, the Dome of the Rock." The vibrant tiles of this major seventh-century Islamic monument, which sits at the highest point of the Haram al-Sharif—the Noble Sanctuary or Temple Mount—

and has come to stand for Jerusalem in the mind of the world, were "constantly falling from the walls" and turning up for sale in the city's markets. As such, one of the governor's first and highest priorities had been to take emergency action to prevent the ruin of this most spectacular building—the oldest Muslim shrine in existence, built over the so-called foundation stone, a slab pierced by a mysterious hole and smeared with a thickly mixed potion of history and myth.

Considered by the Talmud's rabbis to be the spot from which the world was created, that stone, they said, sealed off the waters of the abyss. Adam's tomb allegedly lay in the rock's approximate vicinity. Certain early Muslim traditions held, and still hold, that, after inventing the universe, Allah had gone up to heaven from this very rock, leaving a footprint. The Jewish and Christian faithful also view that overburdened boulder as the setting for Abraham's near sacrifice of Isaac, and devout Muslims believe that from this same spot Muhammad ascended to heaven on the back of his winged steed, al-Buraq, after venturing from "the sacred mosque" in Mecca to "the farthest mosque," al-Aqsa, on his Night Journey.

Over the millennia, multiple sacred buildings had been raised then razed on or right near this very spot: the two Jewish Temples stood within this compound. So, according to legend, did Solomon's sumptuously secular palace, with its cryptic crystal pools and golden, jewel-studded throne. Later, Hadrian built a Roman temple here, complete with statues of Jupiter and the emperor himself on a horse. By the early seventh century—in the years immediately preceding the start of the Dome of the Rock's construction by the fifth Umayyad caliph, Abd el-Malik, around 692—the esplanade was strewn with columns, capitals, and decorative friezes and served no particular religious or social function. It had, according to one leading modern expert on this sacred zone, "become a messy space. Its mounds of architectural fragments represented either debris dumped haphazardly from all over the city or else ruins of some earlier glorious building, now gone." And once it was erected, the Dome of the Rock itself took shape as the most magnificent hodgepodge—apparently the handiwork of foreign craftsmen working under two native-born Muslim supervisors who built according to an approximately Byzantine floor plan with materials salvaged from churches demolished during the Persian occupation of the city.

Which is to say that this small but pregnant patch of earth had—like the city as a whole—almost always been associated with both monumental building and monumental destruction. That fact was keenly appreciated by the nameless British officer who, in a secret dispatch posted in March 1918 from General Headquarters in Egypt to the War Office in London, warned of the dire condition of the Dome of the Rock, known mistakenly to the English as the Mosque of Omar. (Although it sits right beside the al-Aqsa Mosque—a major Islamic pilgrimage site—the Dome itself is not a mosque and has nothing to do with the caliph Omar ibn al-Khattab, Muslim conqueror of Jerusalem.) Whatever one called it, the structure was in desperate need of repair, "which if deferred may give rise to a dangerous condition." Whether the danger was physical or political was not specified.

It was just like the self-satisfied and ostentatiously Anglocentric Ronald Storrs to start his story of the Dome's decay with the stormy weather that accompanied the arrival of the British in Palestine, as if all watches had stopped and calendars reverted to day one with General Edmund Allenby's entrance on foot through the Jaffa Gate in anno Domini 1917. A lifelong member of the British foreign service, the thirty-six-year-old Storrs was "the most brilliant Englishman in the Near East" in the probably hyperbolic estimation of his friend and colleague T. E. Lawrence; if nothing else, Storrs certainly enjoyed playing that role and was a proud connoisseur of his own connoisseurship. His self-declared "interest in the physical presentment of a lost world" led him to begin collecting objects as a young man—Byzantine icons, Persian rugs, statuary. But Storrs's curatorial ethos went beyond his interest in the accumulation of Eastern knickknacks. He encouraged struggling sculptors and painters (he would become one of David Bomberg's most enthusiastic patrons during the artist's Jerusalem years), read widely, wrote opera reviews, spoke several languages well and flaunted the few words he knew in many others. As he moved from commission to commission, he threw himself into the cultural life of the various cities where he was posted, hosting regular exhibits, parties, and "musicales." He was known for his social skills, and for his snobbery; one Jerusalem acquaintance described him as "the most entertaining talker here . . . especially if one doesn't mind what he says."

Since coming to Jerusalem in late 1917, Storrs had made the city's physical conservation his pet project and had pledged to protect it "by an aesthetic, as well as a liturgical and political *Status Quo*." There was, to be sure, something highly selective in the governor's notion of the Status Quo. A blue-blooded Oxbridge orientalist and believing Christian, Storrs had no qualms about altering the landscape to correspond to his idea of what Jerusalem *should* be. To Storrs's purist and undeniably patronizing eyes, Jerusalem's chief value lay in its quaintly picturesque Old City—or, again, in his *idea* of its quaintly picturesque Old City. As he'd later lament, "The fifty previous years of unchecked religious exploitation had already hidden or thrown out of scale most of the ancient northern and western walls, by the building hard against them of colossal and hideous convents and monasteries."

Now that the Turks had decamped and the British taken over and returned life in the war-battered city to something like normal, Storrs understood that a compulsion to hurriedly bulldoze and build "on a large scale" might soon seize the populace. This was his chance to stop that from happening, and, blithely likening the role he'd assumed to that of "Aristotle's Beneficent Despot"—"my word," he boasted, "was law"—he immediately issued several sweeping proclamations, including one whose flat legalistic tone belied the profound effect it would have on the town for years to come as it banned the use of stucco and corrugated iron within the Old City walls. These were "inexcusable materials," according to Storrs, and this ban would later evolve into a series of ordinances that made it illegal throughout all of Jerusalem, old and new, to build of any material but stone.

Although the municipal boundaries have since expanded beyond recognition, and though the building codes have mutated dramatically over the years—with the solid load-bearing blocks prescribed in the early period giving way to thinner and thinner stone cladding affixed to concrete—Storrs's basic vision still holds today, and in some ways has done more to determine how the modern city looks than any other single legal or architectural gesture made over the course of the whole century. Whatever one thinks of the governor's imperious tone, his downright dictatorial approach to power, and his fundamentalist attitude toward building materials, one can—and I do—look out at the crowded contemporary Jerusalem landscape and silently thank the aspiring potentate Ronald Storrs for having anticipated that this most aggressively fractious town would need, desperately, some semblance of unity, of visual coherence. Latter-day Jerusalem may appear an increasingly cluttered construction site, but without the foresight of the military governor, operating under emergency regulations and within the early months of a now far-off British occupation, it would probably long ago have devolved into utter architectural chaos.

The edict banning stucco and tin entailed singular intuition on Storrs's part. More widespread was the realization that the condition of the Dome of the Rock had become dire. In various classified communications, the men of the British Foreign Office argued about how best to handle the situation, with the Anglo-Catholic diplomat, traveler, and conservative member of parliament Mark Sykes cautioning that the repair of the Dome and al-Aqsa Mosque was "dangerous ground." It was critical that "any Europeans employed should be employed by authorities of Mosque, and we should have no responsibility." (As one of the authors of the highly controversial Sykes-Picot Agreement of 1916, which proposed carving up the former Ottoman lands and apportioning them variously to British and French control, Sykes knew a thing or two about the dangers of rocky Middle Eastern terrain.) Foreign Secretary Lord Balfour himself weighed in on the

subject of the renovations at the Haram, agreeing that "every endeavor should be made to conciliate possible Muslim susceptibilities."
Storrs for his part had lobbied hard for the involvement in the restoration of his former roommate from his years in Cairo, the architect
Ernest Tatham Richmond.

The man who would later become Palestine's director of antiquities and tussle politely with Austen Harrison about the height of the
tower of the archaeological museum was the son of the celebrated
portrait painter William Blake Richmond. As his father's middle
name indicates, a very British vision of Jerusalem ran thick in Richmond's blood; so did visual talent. The grandson of the artist George
Richmond—who'd closed his Jerusalem-obsessed friend William
Blake's eyes on his deathbed—he was also the great-grandson of the
miniature painter Thomas Richmond. Before the Great War, E. T.
Richmond had spent sixteen years in Egypt, working as a British
army and government architect and immersing himself in the history and practice of Islamic building, as well as the Arabic language.
Because of this experience, his services were now deemed "urgently
required" in Jerusalem. Once the mufti had given his blessing for the
"loan of a British expert," Richmond was ordered to proceed to Palestine, "in uniform please," and asked to assess the current state of
the Dome as he offered a scheme for "the works of preservation that
had long been needed."

Richmond had a gimp leg and ice-blue eyes that would later be
remembered for their "penetrating, fiery quality," which "made you
feel a little uncomfortable. You were never quite sure when he fixed
them on you whether the look they gave you was a friendly one or
not." Many years after his death, one of his nieces would recall his
"rather bitter mouth, with a slight twist to it, which somehow matched,
and was not unconnected with, the stiff leg with which he had had
to cope since youth." She also noted that he had "great charm of the
sort that can be turned on and off" as well as "a cruel streak" and
admitted that "much as I liked and appreciated—was perhaps flat-
tered by his attention—I was glad to be his niece rather than his wife
or daughter."

Forced to close his London architectural office during the war,
Richmond was now nursing various wounds. By his own account
he'd been too lame for active service but had, ironically, suffered a

severe injury when he'd worked for the Ministry of Munitions in the Trench Warfare Department and had been responsible for the supply of grenades. While he was demonstrating one of these devices for a visiting officer, it had exploded in his left hand, leaving him permanently maimed and often in pain. (Another acquaintance remembered him as being "thin, like a knife, always ill . . . [with] aesthetically cadaverous cheeks and nervous fingers.") Jerusalem represented a fresh start of sorts for him, and on arriving there in early 1918, he again moved in with Storrs and a third Englishman, who were living in a sprawling arcaded house, a former Lutheran parsonage that Storrs had rented on the Street of the Prophets.

Richmond then got down to the business of carefully assessing the state of the Dome and preparing to write a report on its condition, which had, he insisted (pace his roommate Ronald), degraded gradually: "During more than twelve hundred years," he wrote, "the building has been exposed to the destructive attacks of winter storms, of summer suns, of earthquakes, of fire, and of 'souvenir' seekers. Repairs have been many, but at distinct intervals; little or nothing being done between those intervals; for the workers had gone." Those

"workers" were the foreign craftsmen, the Persians and Armenians who'd been imported over the centuries, together with materials, to refurbish the Dome. This process had probably begun in the sixteenth century, with a complete—and flamboyant—restoration of the building by the Ottoman Sultan Suleiman, who brought expert potters from Turkey to resurface the mosaic-covered outer walls with an exquisite array of thick turquoise, green, white, yellow, black, and blue tiles, ornamented with a mesmerizingly kinetic profusion of floral and geometric patterns and Koranic inscriptions.

As Richmond was studying the piers, drum, and "interesting rain water gargoyles of baked and glazed clay" of the early medieval structure, he was joined in Jerusalem—and eventually in a small office on the grounds of the Haram al-Sharif—by yet another English aesthete invited to Jerusalem by Storrs to write an official report, this one on the improbable-sounding subject of "the Arts, Crafts & Industry of the Holy City in connection with the new civic plans." As a student in England years before, Storrs had heard a lecture by the architect, designer, and passionate proponent of the Arts and Crafts, Charles Robert Ashbee, and had been impressed, and now it seems he meant to add the employment of this energetic devotee of William Morris to his gallery of artful achievements. Even as the governor struggled with severe food shortages, rampant unemployment, the threat of both typhus and meningitis epidemics, and, as he put it, "restraining the two and twenty jarring sects," he was eager to hear Ashbee's thoughts on, of all things, the state of Jerusalem's cabinet-making and masonry, its landscape gardening, wood turning, tin-smithing, printing, and calligraphy. He also meant, it seems, for one of England's most acclaimed artisans to help devise a means of restoring to its former glory the great monument perched at the axis mundi. A newly refurbished Dome of the Rock would be an excellent addition to the empire's—and Ronald Storrs's—collection.

GREAT CITY

Of all the complex and contradictory personalities who have left their mark on Jerusalem's own complex and contradictory personality,

C. R. Ashbee seems one of the least likely. A half-Jewish, Anglican, bisexual, married, Socialist, conservationist, romantic, rebel, fop, and self-described "practical idealist," Ashbee never planned to come to Jerusalem or to the Middle East. He hadn't really given the place much thought, in fact, and had been happily ensconced in England before, as he put it, "the Great War scattered us artists to the winds." In 1916, he, like Richmond, had been forced to close his London architectural office, a painful move that followed on the heels of another, still more painful one. In 1907 the enterprise to which he'd devoted the first several decades of his working life—the radical adventure in creative production known as the Guild of Handicraft—had gone into liquidation.

Before it foundered, the Guild had been for Ashbee the concrete and often joyful realization of all the lofty ideas about art and society that had fascinated him since he was a student at Cambridge. A workshop-based craft collective that lasted nearly twenty years, the Guild had produced a remarkable array of objects, many designed by Ashbee himself. These ranged from inlaid-ebony-and-holly-wood writing cabinets to delicately painted semigrand pianos and handsomely vellum-bound books, produced by the printers and with the equipment inherited from the late William Morris's shuttered Kelmscott Press.

But more important to Ashbee than the fabrication of any one of these pretty things was the Guild's creation of a fellowship of artisans, working closely together and with what appears to have been a sense of common pride and delight in their craft. It was an embodiment of his own most cherished belief that "the imaginative things are the real things." This was not some dainty, ingrown notion of art for art's sake, and Ashbee railed against the image of the Guild as "a nursery for luxuries, a hothouse for the production of mere trivialities and useless things for the rich." Rather, his was a dynamic vision of a world in which the working class would engage in meaningful labor, and the craftsman's creations would express not just his technical skill but his singular being and the bonds that connected him to others. The human being must, he wrote, "leave his stamp on the material, his mark on something." And he must do this freely and with his own two hands. According to Ashbee, the Arts and Crafts movement, as embodied by the Guild, "assume[d] through its contacts with the realities of life, an ethical significance of the greatest moment."

Although the Guild experiment had fizzled, Ashbee remained an unreconstructed utopian and so turned his attentions to a new field—town planning, believing as he had come to that "through the city we focus civilization." During this time he designed a substantial manor estate on the outskirts of London and, more ambitiously, submitted a detailed seventy-two-page scheme to a high-profile international competition (organized by an old hero of his, Patrick Geddes) for the redesign of crowded, impoverished downtown Dublin.

For all the talk of "focus," though, Ashbee seemed during this time to have lost his own. Among other things, his design for the manor estate—a centripetally arrayed garden city on a grand Renaissance model—was passed over and the competition won by "an entirely unknown man in a suburb." While Geddes called Ashbee's Dublin scheme "remarkably able" and preferred it to all the others submitted, it was eventually rejected, since the judges considered his plan of greater sociological than spatial value. And when the war came, Ashbee's sense of drift was only compounded. It gave way, sometimes, to despair: "I woke up this morning sobbing," he reported to his journal in August 1914. "All we have worked for, all we have hoped for the last 25 years . . . is to go by the board." Soon after, he would declare in a letter to a friend that the Arts and Crafts were "practically defunct."

Perhaps as a means of countering this crisis—or maybe as a way to keep himself busy in the absence of the Guild and his architectural work—he answered an ad in *The Times Literary Supplement* for a job at an English-language teachers' training college in Cairo; the younger staff members had been drafted, and men of Ashbee's postconscription age called upon to take up the slack. He was then a gangly, youthful fifty-three years old. Leaving his pregnant wife, Janet, and their three small daughters behind in their drafty, snowbound Campden home, he set sail for Alexandria in February 1917 and soon found himself reeling at his first brush with the East and a very different kind of town. The slums of Cairo in particular excited him, not least for the living presence he found there of medieval-styled crafts guilds and of the traditional crafts themselves.

Besides relishing the "constant sun and open air," which he

described in letters to Janet as a "kind of quinine or tonic," Ashbee continued to gather his thoughts about what he termed "the new civics" and had begun work on the book he would call *Where the Great City Stands*, after a line from Whitman's celebratory "Song of the Broad-Axe." This slim volume would serve as his urban ars poetica, at the heart of which lay a vision of the metropolis as a unified and vibrantly democratic space, where "beauty and history are a common heritage," neither "nationality nor religion . . . is where we touch our fellow men," and each citizen takes willing and engaged part in something greater than himself: "Though the individual creates," Ashbee declared, "it is the continuous and unfolding life of the community that finds the individual his place."

Meanwhile, in the actual city where Ashbee now found *his* place, the English and Egyptian authorities looked on his presence with barely muted alarm. The pleasure Ashbee took in his Egyptian male students, with whom he staged Shakespeare plays and set out for long lazy picnics by the Nile, seems to have especially distressed them. Within a month of his arrival in Cairo, in fact, a confidential memo, sent by MI5 to the director general of public security at Egypt's Ministry of the Interior, warned of his presence on the scene. It was reported that the police back in Gloucestershire considered Ashbee "a crank, and a strange fellow, the object of suspicion of some of his neighbors: of Socialist tendencies." This was "not at all a man it is desirable to have loose among the Egyptian students."

By the time Storrs requested Ashbee's presence in Jerusalem, MI5 was very glad to see him go. And Storrs was eager to have him. William McLean, the Alexandria city engineer and town planner of Khartoum, who had been invited by Storrs to provide a preliminary scheme for the development of Jerusalem, had read and appreciated *Where the Great City Stands* and apparently recommended the book and its author to Storrs, who also remembered that inspiring lecture he'd heard as a teenager. Ashbee's expenses would be paid, Storrs informed him, his rations provided; he should alert his department forthwith and hold himself "in readiness to start."

Ashbee declared it, a bit vaguely, "all very romantic & wonderful & exciting," while Janet for her part was thrilled: "all your deliberations have been nullified by your <u>going</u> to Jerusalem after all," she wrote as soon as she received his news. "How much better to rebuild it nearer to the Heart's Desire out there than in England's green & pleasant land—to mix Omar & Blake . . . It sounds the sort of job created & begotten for you by some God of Architecture before ever man was."

Inviting such an inveterate iconoclast to fill this official role had been, meanwhile, audacious on Ronald Storrs's part. As Ashbee recounted one exchange with the governor, Storrs said, " 'Well I've fixed it all up & you're to come, but I've had the greatest difficulty— three generals afraid of you—so you will promise me to say nothing about "socialism" or "nationalism" or "despotism" or any other ism— but stick closely to the point!'

"I promised."

SKIN AND BONES

Whichever winter had done the damage to the Dome of the Rock, by the summer of 1918, when Richmond and Ashbee set up their office in a small domed room at the northern end of the Haram, the formerly grand monument looked battered in the extreme.

In the section dedicated to "Clay, Pottery, Glass, and Mosaic" in his detailed, ninety-six-page report on Jerusalem's Arts and Crafts, Ashbee would describe "slabs of tile work . . . that have already become slabs of grey cement, their form and color gone," and in his own account of the building's condition, Richmond wrote of the "roots of wild plants which, owing to the damp conditions, have been able to establish themselves between the tiles." The once gilded dome that gave the structure its name was now covered with dull lead; the windowsills were encrusted with hundreds of years' worth of what Richmond termed "bird dirt," which soaked up water during the rainy season and penetrated the tile backing in the messiest way. Though he ventured that the building was structurally solid, its surfaces—the shell of the dome and its outer tiles—were decaying. "The bones of the building are sound," he wrote, like a kind of monument doctor, having performed an extensive physical exam and found the patient ailing. "Its outer skin, however, is in need of extensive renewal and repair." This should happen, he urged, immediately. "Every delay increases both the extent of the dilapidation and the rate at which it progresses."

Ashbee referred to his and Richmond's work as being "interlaced," and this was never more the case than over the course of the scalding summer months when they shared that office and, in Ashbee's words, "plan our reports & scheme & discuss details of administration & what is to happen to the future of this country."

The two also often ventured together out into the field. In the case of Richmond's survey of the Dome, that "field" lay just beyond the windows of their small room on the Haram. As they explored the wide, stony expanse of the sanctuary, with its multiple Mamluk and Ottoman shrines, schools, and covered ablution fountains, they found a small building known as the Najara, or Carpentry Shop, which Richmond supposed "of twelfth-century Frank construction." It contained the lead needed for roof repairs and what seemed to be the original crescent-moon finial of the Dome of the Rock. Located above the area known as Solomon's Stables, the Najara also held numerous tiles "of varying quality," in Richmond's skeptical estimation, and—most exciting for Ashbee—a set of old kilns, which apparently had been used by earlier potters who had worked on the Dome. Clearly, these had once been functioning ovens, since the Englishmen found fragments and tiles "spoilt in the baking," as well as intact tiles made there.

Their patron, Storrs, would later somewhat fancifully characterize these as "the original furnaces and kilns in which the Mosque [*sic*] tiles had been fired"—in the process linking his own rule to Suleiman's and maybe even to Solomon's—though it seems more likely that the ovens dated from the time of the last Dome renovation in 1874. But the historical particulars hardly mattered to Ashbee, for whom the presence of the furnaces meant one plain and enticing thing: A precedent existed in Jerusalem for the craft of tile making. He meant now to do all he could to revive it, in the spirit of what he called "our Dome"—"that great pagan, oriental, imaginative building," which to him represented Jerusalem itself. For Christians, Muslims, and Jews, he asserted, it was "the symbol that keys them together" though it "transmutes and transcends" any single tradition.

"There is," he insisted, "nothing Jewish in it. It has nothing of the Christian Church, and it is not a Moslem building, for Greek workmen built it in the seventh century, setting it together with consummate skill out of the materials of a crumbling civilization." Pious Muslims and learned art historians would no doubt strongly disagree, as did the more tightly coiled and devout Richmond. The soon-to-be Catholic convert and expert in Islamic building viewed the Dome as "of a living Faith, the living symbol, striving, by the strength of the Faith it represents, to survive in the face of many and great difficulties."

But in his own earnest if eccentric and politically obtuse way, Ashbee was declaring that he, too, was a believer—if not in holy writ then in the more universal, aesthetic faith that gave rise to the Dome of the Rock. The building stands, he wrote, "for a serene continuity, the everlasting optimism of the creative artist who knows that beauty does not die." The structure was, he enthused, borrowing Richmond's dermatological vocabulary, "a serpent ever renewing its skin . . . Every decade or so the skin changes. To keep our Dome alive you must keep alive its pelt of glittering blue and green and white and gold; and unless you have a school of craftsmen always at work and studying you cannot do this and retain the life."

If not Jehovah, Jesus, or Allah, in other words, C. R. Ashbee worshipped the gods of the Arts and Crafts. And while he stood in obvious awe of the Dome, the structure on the Haram most sacred to him may have been that humble little Frankish Najara with its ash-filled old ovens that he longed to fill again with clay and roaring fire.

TURKISH ROOMS, ARMENIAN TILES

How many people does it take to build a house? A neighborhood? A city? How many characters can a city's story bear?

Chasing Spyro Houris's ghost, I keep being pulled along by different spirits—all these others who were central to or who infused his biography or his buildings with some critical element, as they did the city's own buildings, its biography. And as I delve into the diaries and letters, the photos and sketches of these "characters," about whom, in almost every case, I know far more than I know about Houris, often in juicy if irrelevant detail (I could but won't write pages, for instance, about Ashbee's complicated sex life and Richmond's creeping fascism), I begin to wonder at the centrifugal nature of this hunt. Instead of leading me to Houris's inner world—as most biographical undertakings do—the search for him and his traces keeps sending me outward, and outward . . .

. . . into other provinces and, in this case, to the small Anatolian city of Kütahya where before the war the young Tavit Ohannessian, as he was then known, was one of the owners and the manager of the main pottery workshop in town. The village-born son of a once well-off, later down-at-his-heels itinerant fabric dyer with a drinking problem, he had been the best student in his provincial school and had mastered French as a boy. From the outset, though, he'd been restless, curious, and, it seems, had felt himself destined for something more. After leaving school at fourteen to support his family, he'd traveled to Izmir and Constantinople and eventually apprenticed himself to potters in Kütahya. Having immersed himself in the craft for which the town was renowned, he'd formed a partnership with several Armenians and a Turk, and had, together with them, bought the atelier in which he worked. He quickly established himself as a superior potter—as well as a man so enterprising and imaginative he could, it was said, "draw bread out of stone." Ohannessian was well connected to the Ottoman authorities and had executed various important commissions—from the façade of the governorate in Kü-tahya to Constantinople's main post office and the shrine of a sultan in that city to the dome of the Mevlevihane Mosque in Konya (home of the whirling dervishes), to the entrance and mosque of Prince Muhammad Ali's sumptuous Manial Palace on the island of Rhoda in Cairo.

These impressively regal credentials no doubt endeared him to the sixth baronet of Sledmere, with whom Ohannessian had a fateful encounter in Kütahya sometime in 1911. The baronet was none other than the same Mark Sykes who would later both mastermind the borders of the modern Middle East and sternly warn the Foreign Office about the politics of Jerusalem mosque repair. As avid adventurer and colonial emissary, Sykes had wandered widely throughout the Middle East, and that year, just a few months after his family's grand Yorkshire manor house had been reduced in a blaze to four ash-covered walls and a single fireplace, he had embarked on one of his many trips to Turkey. Intent on rebuilding the family manse to his own exacting tastes, Sir Mark had discovered on this trip a tile factory in Kütahya that impressed him greatly. Although he sneered at what he saw around him in this town "of mud and ruins, the poor shriveled mummy . . . of history," he could not stop enthusing about the local pottery and immediately began to draw up sketches for the singular "Turkish room" he imagined for the risen-from-the-ashes version of his Chippendale-filled Georgian mansion. He wanted nothing less than a replica of the apartments of the sultan's mother in Constantinople's Yeni Mosque. Linked to a complicated set of tubs and showers in the basement of the manor house, it was meant to serve as the "drying room" after a very English "Turkish" bath.

As Sykes was impressed by Ohannessian's lofty Ottoman connections and his obvious talent, so Sykes's interest in the local ceramics probably suggested to Ohannessian the possibility of a whole world of plush foreign commissions, and the two came to an agreement about the twenty-six hundred tiles needed for the "Turkish room." When Sykes was in Kütahya again several years later, the ambitious Armenian potter even invited the aristocratic Englishman to his home to eat a meal and meet his family, and showed him various test colors for the Sledmere commission. Both were difficult and discriminating men, and though they argued over some of the specifics, the room began to take shape in their collective imagination and in the ceramicist's actual workshop.

Mark Sykes would soon have the luxurious Turkish bath of which he'd dreamed. Ohannessian's dreams, meanwhile, gave way to nightmares, as trainloads of Armenian exiles passed through Kütahya on the way to forced marches across the Syrian desert and toward the killing fields of Der Zor. In the early days of these transports, the Muslim governor of Kütahya was still relatively sympathetic to his Armenian subjects, but before long their luck flickered out, and the Ohannessians soon found themselves, together with thousands of their countrymen, stumbling toward the desert—and very probable death.

Weak, thirsty, and terrified, the family was fortunate enough to have had a mule and a cart for part of the journey. Tavit's wife, Victoria, had sewn gold coins into the hem of her skirt, so she could bribe the gendarme who guarded their caravan. She'd also packed lentils, rice, and other supplies, and managed to pick wild greens along the route. She saw to it, in other words, that they didn't starve, but the situation was extremely grim. At a certain point Ohannessian became delirious with typhus, and the family somehow (How? Details are scant) peeled away from the convoy near Aleppo, where they rented a room and found themselves surrounded by almost unspeakable sorrow and horror, not unlike what the Gelat family had experienced in their own wartime exile. Though they'd escaped the death camps in the desert, death itself had come to camp in the city streets. Refugees were collapsing of exposure and hunger right and left; corpses lay all around.

Nothing, in short, must have seemed farther from Tavit Ohannessian than the light clay, bright paints, and quartz glazes that had filled his days in Kütahya. Recovered from his typhus but cut off from his craft, he first circled the outdoor market of Aleppo, selling the pocket bread that Victoria had baked and stuffed with dried apricots. Later he found work at the train station. Somehow the family managed to survive, and somehow—these particulars, too, have slipped away—when the British army entered Aleppo in the autumn of 1918, the former master potter of Kütahya was reunited with his old patron and friend, the diplomat Mark Sykes, and with that encounter Jerusalem's face began subtly to shift.

FIRINGS

As usual, Ronald Storrs condescended horribly and took all the credit—though as so often when he did that he also managed to get something good done. After the discovery of the Haram kilns, he claimed years later in his memoirs, "I remembered the name of Mark Sykes' Armenian, David Ohanessian [*sic*], who had created the Persian bath-room at Sledmere, and summoned him from Damascus with another expert from Kutáhia to report upon the possibilities of designing, painting, glazing, and firing the new tiles in the ancient furnaces."

The misrepresentations here are so multiple, Storrs's reminiscences start to seem a fantasy, if not deliberate obfuscation. The urbane and accomplished Ohannessian (who'd be known in English-speaking circles from now on as David) was certainly not the private property of Sir Mark Sykes; the sultan-worthy chamber that he had so lovingly designed for the new-and-improved Sledmere was no mere WC (neither was it Persian); and in inviting Ohannessian to Jerusalem, the governor had hardly "summoned" a lowly subject to bow before the throne of the king. Ohannessian had been living in Aleppo and not in Damascus. The furnaces were not ancient. But so the legend was printed. The thirty-nine-year-old Sykes would die of influenza within a few months of his Aleppo reunion with Ohannessian and so didn't have the chance to check Storrs's facts. Richmond, for his part, would later remember that "it was at Sykes's suggestion that he [Ohannessian] came to Jerusalem and started a pottery in the hope of ultimately producing glazed tiles of good enough quality to justify their use in repairing the tile decoration of the Dome of the Rock." And even Storrs, in a draft of a 1920 lecture, admitted that he'd brought Ohannessian to the city "with the help of my friend, the late Mark Sykes"—but later crossed that out.

In any event, Ohannessian and his family were soon installed in a warren of rooms in the *vank*, or gated convent-compound that is the core of the Armenian Quarter, a miniature walled city within the walled Old City. Although David was not an actively practicing Christian (it was whispered in the family that he might secretly be a Sufi), Victoria was quite devout. And living over the cleanly swept courtyard attached to the nine-hundred-year old Cathedral of St. James, whose walls were covered with perhaps the world's most extensive array of eighteenth-century Kütahya tiles, its ceilings hung with delicate egg-shaped ornaments from the town, and its cabinets bursting with votive pottery offerings brought to Jerusalem by Armenian pilgrims, they must have felt weirdly at home. The city wasn't just a haven from the miseries they'd recently experienced. It was in a peculiar way the most natural place for David Ohannessian to devote himself once more to the alchemical transformations of clay and paint into shimmering planes of color and light—here, in close proximity to all those ceramic totems of that lost world.

But before anything like alchemy could be achieved, he and Ashbee and Richmond had painstaking work to do as they prepared to see if the kilns on the Haram al-Sharif were even functional. Ashbee had by now been appointed Jerusalem's first ever civic adviser and was busy planting parks all over town, clearing the Old City ramparts to make way for a dramatic promenade, and drawing up plans to revive various local arts and crafts—weaving, glassblowing, and (he hoped) ceramics. But those first firings were, he declared, "a dismal failure," though neither Ohannessian nor a Damascene potter who was also consulted could agree to the reasons for this. The Pro-Jerusalem Society—a group of dignitaries from the city's various communities that Storrs and Ashbee had convened to oversee certain municipal projects—had already invested several hundred pounds in these experiments and now decided to cut its losses by dismissing both Ohannessian and the other potter and planning to shut down the fledgling operation. Maybe tiles for repair of the Dome could be imported from Europe.

Having come this far and already sacrificed so much, Ohannessian was not, though, easily dissuaded. He must have felt he had little left to lose. So at this point he stepped forward with, as Ashbee described it, "an offer of partly capitalizing the industry." He asked only that he be allowed to continue to use the Haram kilns and—

more audaciously—that he be granted the means of traveling *back* to Kütahya, to gather materials, tools, and skilled help. Ashbee and Storrs agreed to this, and though there is no record of the conversations surrounding this startling chapter in the history of Jerusalem's saturated modern surfaces, one imagines that Ashbee in particular would have thrilled at the thought of the aesthetic and social dimensions of this act. Not only were they rescuing a doomed art from extinction, they were delivering a group of human beings from mortal danger. The Armenian potters whom Ohannessian meant to bring back with him had somehow survived or avoided the massacres, but their future in Turkey was tenuous at best. That these survivors were *craftsmen* was not secondary; neither was the fact that they would, if all went well, apply themselves to establishing a time-honored art at the very heart of the heart of the Great City.

Armed with nothing more than a train ticket and a letter of safe passage, Ohannessian made what must have been a fairly traumatic voyage—and traveled alone, back to the land from which he and his family had been forced out just a few years before. Although Kütahya had been home to some thirty-five hundred Armenians at the start of the war, by the time of his return to Turkey, the town had been, according to one witness, "totally emptied" of Armenians. Yet somehow, according to Ashbee, Ohannessian was able to "convey a body of his workpeople—men, women, and children" from Kütahya to Jerusalem, to-  gether with ample quantities of the excellent white, kaolin-rich clay, oxide pigments, sand glazes, and borax that gave their pottery its special earthy glow. The group soon got down to business and, "after some four months of fresh experiment and hard work," in Ashbee's words, "tiles were produced which compared very favourably with some of the early tile-work on the Dome, and certainly exceeded in beauty and skill the later European factory production with which for the last fifty years the Dome has been repaired."

Expert craftsmen now assembled and kilns fired, the project

seemed poised to thrive, as everyone involved pitched in: Ohannessian signed a contract with the Waqf, or religious endowment responsible for the care of Jerusalem's Muslim monuments, pledging himself to "the permanent establishment of the industry," and the Pro-Jerusalem Society put up a guarantee of his financial stability. The Waqf paid back the society's original loan and invested funds in Ohannessian's materials. Anticipating the dwindling of their supplies from Kütahya, he and his fellow potters experimented with local substitutes as they continued their tests of the Haram kilns. And Ashbee enthused, in terms at once practical and idealistic, "Yes, it will take David Ohannessian and his Armenians a long time yet before they bring their tiles to the standard set by Suleiman the Magnificent. But," he wrote, "have patience and bear in mind the Arab proverb: 'Hold by the old, for in any case thou shalt lose the new.'" And in the same breath he continued to ask, rhetorically, "Can't you see, our Dome stands for unity and peace as does no other building?"

He was perhaps protesting too much, maybe aware of the fact that the cooperation that had marked the early stages of this project was about to grind to a permanent and most unceremonious halt. For reasons that remain murky, the fires at the Haram were doused almost as quickly as they had been lit. According to one account, the money ran out; another version maintained that the kilns were faulty and couldn't produce steady heat. Storrs related that the mufti was uneasy with the idea of a commercial enterprise on the Haram. Yet another explanation had it that the work of Christian ceramicists at so holy a Muslim site was not welcomed by the faithful.

The true reason for the cooling of the kilns probably lay well beyond the precincts of the Haram. This was the beginning of the end of what Ashbee would later dub "a very plastic period in the social history of Palestine." Nationalist tensions had been mounting on all sides, and "in politics Jerusalem was growing more difficult and less agreeable," as Storrs rather peevishly put it, sounding somehow irritated that the citizens had evinced the gall to break up his private party. It was, he wrote, "the difference perhaps between the beginning of a picnic and the end." But really this was no picnic at all, despite Storrs's attempts to make it sound so. "In 1920," he wrote, "the air was full of rumours and of that nervous quality to which the altitude of Jerusalem undoubtedly contributes." Several violent incidents—most notably a deadly riot that erupted around the traditional Nebi Musa pilgrimage festival in April 1920—brought things to a boiling point and, according to Storrs, "all the carefully built relations of mutual understanding between British, Arabs, and Jews seemed to flare away in an agony of fear and hatred."

Back on the Haram itself, the air pressure had also changed. Soon after the British military authorities ceded control to a civil administration and the first high commissioner of Palestine, Herbert Samuel, arrived that same year, he turned over responsibility for the restorations there to the newly formed Supreme Muslim Council, a body he'd established to manage local Islamic affairs. As both fair-minded English liberal and self-conscious Jew, Samuel was well aware of the need to somehow involve—or conciliate—Palestine's Arabs, and this transfer of architectural power seemed one obvious way to achieve that.

There were darker reasons, too, for wanting to let a respected group of Muslim Jerusalemites take control of the site. On the eve of the extremely contentious election for a new mufti in April 1921, Arabic signs had appeared around the Old City blaring WAKE UP MUS-LIMS and warning that certain candidates for the highest Islamic office in the land planned "to help in handing over to the Jews the Haram ash-Sharif, the Dome of the Rock, and al-Aqsa, that they may pull them down and build in their place the Temple." Now, under the leadership of the wide-awake new mufti, Hajj Amin al-Husseini, the members of the Supreme Muslim Council devoted themselves to "preserving and safeguarding" the Haram. They were urged along in this case by Richmond, who had left Palestine when he'd finished his report and recently returned not in an architectural role but as assistant political secretary to Samuel, officially serving as intermediary between the government and the country's Arab population and unofficially as one of the most outspoken and bitterly anti-Zionist members of the British administration.

That his legitimate political critique of Zionism often gave way to full-blown anti-Semitic ranting surely did his cause no good, as he fixated on "the Bolshevik type of imported Jew" he believed was taking over the country, helped along by a hazy, omnipresent force he called the "International Money Power." Richmond's hostility was rooted in his conviction that the English government was working at the behest of a shadowy gang of Fagins and Shylocks. With a sneer, he referred privately to "our Jew-beridden administration" and warned that "the Jewish race is altogether differently constructed mentally and morally from ourselves." The "Jewish quality" he identified all around him was "sneaking, round-the-corner, rat-in-a-trap, timid, often shockingly arrogant, never level, never based on any principle except that, since God made their carnal ancestors the Chosen People, therefore what the Jews contend is true and what Jews want they ought to get. Means do not matter, however base, however oblique. They <u>will</u> be clever and that is so fatal . . ." He also had no qualms about stoking Muslim fears of a Jewish plot to rebuild the Temple in place of the buildings now standing on the Haram al-Sharif: "Astonishing as it may seem," he would write in the published version of his report, "there are those who, for reasons best known to themselves, would wish to see the Dome of the Rock discredited in the eyes of the world and regarded as a building that has been so ill treated by time, so neglected by its guardians, as to have lost any value it may once have possessed: a building that might well be left to a natural and rapid decay, culminating in its early demolition and replacement by a worthier shrine built perhaps to the honour of some other Faith."

The Supreme Muslim Council itself now cranked up the pan-Islamic volume by placing the site in the hands of the prominent German-trained Turkish architect Ahmet Kemalettin, whose work was known for its strongly patriotic flavor and who saw himself as heir to the great tradition of imperial Ottoman architecture. (He would also go on to render plans for the apartment building that would eventually be reconceived as the council's luxurious Palace Hotel in Mamilla.) For Kemalettin, it was only during Suleiman's reign that "the art of Islamic architecture and decoration reached its peak" and the Byzantine-inspired Dome of the Rock was redecorated "along lines more suitable to the spirit of Islam." The melding of cultures and visual styles that so delighted Ashbee was for the Ankara-based architect the worst kind of bastardization. "Thank God," he wrote, sometime around 1922, "the Islamic sanctity of the Haram has been protected from the multi-religious superstitions of Jerusalem by its surrounding walls . . . Oh God, how incredible is the beauty with which You have endowed these holy premises and how great is the power of creativity You have inspired in the masterbuilders of Islam . . ." and so on. There was, it would seem, little room in this—very Ottoman, very Islamic, very grandiose—vision for a rather ragtag group of Armenian Christian refugee potters (secret Sufis or no), to say nothing of a half-Jewish, bisexual bohemian Brit and Ruskin-quoting promoter of the most homespun arts and crafts.

With so much combative praying and propagandizing crowding the area of the Haram, David Ohannessian and his potters would clearly need to find another place to work. And given the creeping

tension on all sides, it is in many ways remarkable that he and Ashbee and Storrs didn't just give up in disgust at this point but managed instead to transform their initial high-flown plan to manufacture nearly thirty thousand tiles for the Dome of the Rock into something more feasible and grounded. Within months of the closure of the Haram kilns, the Pro-Jerusalem Society arranged for Ohannessian to build a furnace and open a workshop in a cavernous old set of rooms near the third Station of the Cross along the Via Dolorosa.
Dubbed the Dome of the Rock Tiles, this new enterprise kept the great shrine's name but dispensed with the ferment surrounding the building itself, allowing Ohannessian to engage in the practical business of training craftsmen—many of them Armenian orphans, survivors of the Turkish massacres. He taught the young men to work the wheel and to draw or trace patterns from lacy stencils onto the clay's surfaces, while he instructed the girls and women how most

effectively to fill in colors with brushes made of donkey or cat hair. Besides managing the workshop, he supervised every aspect of the work itself—mixing glazes and paints by hand and according to his own formulas, as he fired the kiln with olive and pinewood and baked the pottery in a deep pit in the workshop's second-story courtyard.

Abandoning the idea of tiling the massive expanse of the Dome itself, Ohannessian now set his sights on beautifying smaller domestic and civic spaces. By 1921, he and his craftsmen were already scrambling to meet the demand for the lushly colored bowls, vases, plates, ashtrays, beer mugs, and candlesticks that bore on their bottoms the small ocher signature of the Dome of the Rock Tiles. Many of these pieces were exported to sideboards in Europe, the United States, and across the Middle East, while among local Arab aristocrats, British officials, Jewish collectors, and tourists alike, the pottery quickly took on a kind of emblematic status as if—like the mysterious building that had inspired its transplantation to this place—the Armenian faience of Kütahya somehow embodied Jerusalem itself. Storrs and Ashbee worked to further accentuate the near-talismanic connection between Ohannessian's ceramics and the city when in the early 1920s the Pro-Jerusalem Society commissioned his workshop to create street signs in English, Arabic, and Hebrew. If the three languages couldn't coexist harmoniously in real life, then at least they could in tile. Ever the verbal jeweler, Storrs imagined the trilingual names of Jerusalem's alleys and boulevards "gleaming against the sober texture of her walls like chrysoprase and lapis lazuli." And in what was perhaps the ultimate linkage of the city, its symbols, and this colorful tile, on the occasion of the 1922 wedding of the British Princess Mary, Storrs commissioned, Ashbee designed, Ohannessian fashioned, and "the Palestine Moslems" presented to Her Highness and Her groom a miniature ceramic model of the Dome of the Rock—its famously rounded golden roof replaced with the potter's trademark peacock greenish-blue.

And at some time right around this very year—When? How? Once again, the questions are far more abundant than the answers— Spyro Houris first commissioned David Ohannessian to mold, paint, and fire the large floral panels and small inset ornaments that would adorn the first-ever building in the new city of Jerusalem to feature those tiles on its façade, along with Houris's own name on its cornerstone: Is'af al-Nashashibi's villa, perhaps the very grandest house in town. Could it be that Nashashibi himself—son of a distinguished old Jerusalem family, deeply learned student of Arab civilization, proud cultural nationalist— had been the one to make the connection between the history of the Dome of the Rock's decoration, the Armenian potter, the Greek architect, and the walls of his own home, known around town as his *qasr*, his castle?

Ronald Storrs

One of Nashashibi's closest confidants was Khalil Sakakini, who wrote regularly in his diary of Richmond, "my trusted friend." (At around this time, Sakakini and his family were living in the windmill that Erich and Luise Mendelsohn would later call home.) Sakakini also noted in his journal each time he gave Ashbee an Arabic lesson, as he had when he taught Elihu Fraji, another client, it seems, of Spyro Houris. Does one of these strands join them?

Or could it be that Ohannessian and Houris already knew each other from some other time and place? Perhaps Houris's idea of ornamenting his buildings with the Kütahyan's tiles derived not from the Dome of the Rock but from a childhood spent playing in the shadow of such elaborate, ceramic-fronted Ottoman buildings. Though I've still found no proof of the architect's birthplace, so many of his commissions point back to Constantinople and its environs, I wonder if his roots reach there.

And keep wondering. The summer is rapidly drawing to a close. The latest round of fighting has ended. More than twenty-one hundred Palestinians and seventy-two Israelis are dead, whole Gazan neighborhoods lie in rubble, thousands are homeless there, and in Israel the events of the summer have been hastily buried. Life in Jewish Jerusalem has slipped unnervingly back to humdrum routine. In Zion Square, the protesters have vanished and been replaced by gaggles of noisy American Jewish teenagers. Next to the bright yellow bloodmobile with a Magen David painted on its side, a yarmulke-wearing electric guitarist plays "Stairway to Heaven" off-key at all hours of the day. This scene unfolds right across from the row of pinkish Jaffa Road buildings that it seems Spyro Houris built, just outside the window of the office where he once sat and worked—but he remains a ghost.

ROCK PAPER SCISSORS:
AN EPILOGUE

IN THE CHILDREN'S GAME OF OUTSTRETCHED FISTS AND FINGERS, rock always beats scissors, scissors trump paper, and paper inevitably vanquishes rock—but when it comes to the history of Jerusalem, paper and rock, or in fact, *stone*, seem locked in a never-ending struggle to determine who'll be the biggest loser.

Some paper, of course, endures: Luise Mendelsohn held on to nearly every one of the more than three thousand letters she and Erich wrote each other over the years, complete with decades-old pressed flowers; despite all their wanderings, she saved most every sketch he rendered—on notepaper, tracing paper, concert programs— and after he died, she wrote her memoir of their lives together and

retained it in multiple drafts. Salman Schocken left Rehavia and Palestine before the Mendelsohns did, but soon after his departure his
papers were filed in impeccable, almost parodically Germanic order
by various learned Eastern and Central European–born émigrés and
are now tended by an equally learned, conscientious Russian émigré;
these files remain locked in lemonwood cabinets in the Jerusalem library Erich Mendelsohn built for his patron. While Austen Harrison
took pains to burn certain evidence, he stashed away "Some Letters,"
and various friends and employers preserved other words in his hand.
Yom-Tov Hamon's archive somehow survived the damp and the dirt
of Spyro Houris's carefully constructed cistern. And the English
officials who once ruled Jerusalem made a point of keeping diaries in
solidly bound notebooks. They wrote letters and saved copies, or
sent them to correspondents who would. Aware of posterity's gaze,
they too wrote memoirs. Although C. R. Ashbee, for instance, lasted
only four years in Jerusalem, his impressions of the place live on after
almost a century: "The city belongs to us all," he proclaimed in a
cheerful 1920 letter. "Let us focus on the creative present, forget the
old Jahweh and Elohim, and the Byzantine Gods who promised this
land to so many people. There is no room any more for an exclusive
religious nationalism or a chosen race, certainly not in Palestine."

That was, as he'd later come to acknowledge, wishful thinking.
By the time he left in 1922, both political and personal disillusion-
ment had clouded his earlier sunny view, and when the next year
he published a scathing account of his time in Jerusalem, *A Palestine
Notebook*, he made clear his belief that "Zionism as understood and as
sometimes practiced in Palestine is based upon a fundamental injus-
tice and therefore dangerous both to civilization and to Jewry." But
such dark views about the place didn't keep him from recording for
later generations his shifting thoughts on the subject. If anything,
they seemed only to prompt him to fill more pages, and more. Apart
from what he called "the reports, plans, new street alignments, the
park and garden system, the civic ordinances and by-laws, and the
thousands of minutes scattered up and down hundreds of more or
less futile files," his scrapbook-like diaries and letters, watercolors
and lantern slides of Jerusalem make up multiple volumes and rest on
neat shelves at his Cambridge college, King's.

When Ashbee fled the Middle East, he took all his journals and jottings with him. But even those Englishmen like Ronald Storrs who stayed on in the region and whose written legacy was subject to local political violence managed to leave behind a prodigious paper trail. After his Jerusalem posting, Storrs was named governor of Cyprus and there, in approximately ten minutes one October night in 1931, rioters burned Government House and all its contents to the ground. That fire claimed much of his correspondence, his journals, his books—along with his by-then substantial collection of art and artifacts, including an especially valuable David Bomberg painting, rendered from Austen Harrison's garden. But lucky for Storrs, his doting mother had saved all his weekly letters home to England, together with "a few diaries of special missions or journeys during the war," so that he had enough first-hand documentation to compose the self-serving memoir he had been preparing his whole life to write.

Harrison left, and the Mendelsohns left, as did Ashbee and Storrs. David Ohannessian left in 1948, for Egypt and then for Beirut, where he died a few years later. Richmond left and came back and left again. Not only did he write in exquisite longhand a furious retrospective memoir of his years in Palestine, *Mammon in the Holy Land* ("a description of how we 'built up Zion with blood and Jerusalem with iniquity'"), he also kept a scrawled diary for one year of his work as political secretary under High Commissioner Herbert Samuel, 1922, "an important one in the gloomy history of the Holy Land under 'British' auspices." This screed he titled *An Administrative Cesspool.*

As all these archives made their way to safe holding places in libraries or family attics elsewhere, the papers of others who stayed met far dimmer fates. The villa that Spyro Houris built for Is'af al-Nashashibi on the way to Mount Scopus was meant to serve as a home for both the highly learned bachelor intellectual and his enormous library. His collection is estimated to have held between thirty thousand and fifty thousand books as well as hundreds of medieval manuscripts; given what a prolific writer he was, his drafts and letters and scribblings must also have taken up many shelves and drawers throughout the large house. Stories are told of how he'd stay inside his *qasr* for months on end, content just to read and to write.

Nashashibi's vast library, copious writings, and personal papers should, in other words, constitute one of the most important Palestinian archives anywhere—except that, after his sudden death on a trip to Cairo in early 1948, looters broke into the mansion and ravaged his possessions, emptying those cavernous rooms of their contents. (The culprits have never been identified, though latter-day rumor has it this wasn't part of the political violence of that cataclysmic year but a robbery by people who knew that no one was home.) Some of these treasures may have been sold to libraries or book dealers, though one eyewitness later reported that for months after Nashashibi's death and this wholesale pillaging of the house that Spyro Houris built, certain neighborhood grocers could be seen using pages of Nashashibi's most valuable books to wrap cones of sugar and salt.

That said, the house itself still stands, gracious and sturdy as ever, the only known building of Spyro Houris's located in what is now Palestinian East Jerusalem. Though Ohannessian's original tiles have been replaced with brighter, less distinctive reproductions, the villa—one of Houris's finest—has recently been restored to its former grandeur with care and intelligence by a Jerusalem-born and raised, British-trained Palestinian civil engineer working for a local charitable organization. After years of mild neglect, its rich pink masonry, black and white marble floors, and point-arched windows have been returned lovingly to their former state. The building now serves as a Palestinian cultural center and library, and the rooms that once held Nashashibi's books are being slowly filled with other books, carefully cataloged and kept.

This building is, then, part of Spyro Houris's archive. If he didn't leave a trove of letters and journals, he built solidly—he meant his creations to last—and he had the foresight to carve those spare words SPYRO G. HOURIS, ARCHITECTE into the cornerstone of the Nashashibi Villa, the Hamon mansion, and one last building, in the Greek Colony.

Directly across the street from the low blocky house in which the Efklides siblings lived rests one of Houris's most elegantly understated dwellings. Known as the "red house" for the glowing color of its stone (not really red so much as a warm pink), the building boasts no colorful ceramics that announce it as Houris's, and it doesn't have a fancy roof like the Hamon or Fraji houses—but it does command the graceful proportions and thoughtful structural details that mark it as one of his designs. And his cornerstone "signature" makes that definitive. According to David Kroyanker, the building was constructed in 1928 as the home of Shauki Sa'ad, an Arab detective in the Criminal Investigation Department of the Palestine Police. But another story is also told by certain contemporary Jerusalemites: that Houris built the house to be his own home. Although the evidence here is strictly circumstantial, I have come to suspect—given its very close proximity to the Efklides house—that in fact he planned it for himself and the girl next door, his bride-to-be, Heleni.

In the late 1920s, Houris was busy with building. As he finished work on the Gelat Villa, he was, it appears, planning and overseeing construction of those various major Jaffa Road structures, as well as designing an impressively tiled commercial and residential building for the Christian Arab Masu family right in the middle of the German Colony, on the Beit Safafa Road (now Emek Refaim Street, where it still stands today, its colored tiles chipping but present); he had also built an elegant home in the neighborhood of Ba'qa—complete with intricate inset ceramic medallions by Ohannessian and a large glass-enclosed porch—for a man named Shukri Dib, the most important car dealer in town. And he was, we know, planning to marry.

But as these various buildings took solid shape, his private life, it seems, began to crumble. As always here, the specifics are sketchy, though we do know that on a Wednesday in mid-October 1930, a rather ominous notice appeared in small print on the last page of *The Palestine Bulletin*, declaring: "ARCHITECT CLEARED." The article was short and bittersweet:

> We are pleased to learn that Mr. Spiro Houris, the well known Jerusalem architect, was discharged by the Attorney General of the false accusation preferred against him, some fourteen months ago.
>
> The innocence of Mr. Spiro Houris being fully proved, an official letter staying the proceedings has been sent to his counsel . . .

Another article from around the same time doesn't mention Houris but offers a tersely sensational account of the extremely messy situation, which involved the bribery trial of "a well-known rich man of Beit Jala village," accused of paying another man to murder his two brothers who "seduced his wife." The accused had, it seems, tried to bribe a judge who himself was later charged with subornation. According to another account, Houris was also accused of attempting to bribe the magistrate on behalf of the "well-known rich man," though he "denied that he had done such thing."

Confusing as the case was—and innocent as Spyro Houris appears to have been—the charge and its frequent mention in the press can't have been good for his mood, or his impending marriage. Once again, the emotional details have long since disappeared from view, but certain dryer facts are a matter of record, as, on the very first day of January 1933, a tiny notice appeared in *The Palestine Post* announcing the wedding of Miss H. Photios Efklides and one Mr. L. Caumeau.

Heleni Efklides was—it's said by those who remember her as an old woman—extremely concerned with appearances, especially her own. And though we will never know for sure why she turned her back on Spyro Houris and chose instead to marry Lucien Caumeau, assistant to the French consul general, we can at least suspect that she preferred a life of evening gowns and canapés to one lived with even the hint of criminal suspicion, no matter how gravely mistaken. And for a brief period, M. and Mme. Caumeau's names surfaced regularly in the society pages of *The Palestine Post*: now they were giving a dinner at the King David Hotel in honor of the acting French high commissioner in Syria and the Lebanon; now they were dining with His Excellency the high commissioner at Government House, together with the mayor, his wife, and various other dignitaries . . .

Heleni seems to have been quite fickle. Within a few years she'd divorced the French diplomat and returned to live with her sister and brother in the small house that Spyro Houris built, where the three remained into very old age. None of them married; there were no children. Clio and Heleni shared a bedroom, and Alexander was forced by his rather spoiled sisters to sleep in the fancy white-tiled sauna that then took up one of the house's three small rooms. "Heleni liked," I am told, "fine things." The sauna was one of those fine things.

As Anastas Damianos and I sit on heavy stuffed chairs in the

Efklides family's refurbished living room, he tells me in a low voice about the siblings' final days. Clio and Alexander died first, and then Heleni. They had no one but each other, and the West Jerusalem Greek community was already too small and poor to own a hearse, so, in each instance, Anastas himself had been forced to perform the grim task of loading their bodies into his car and driving them to the Greek Orthodox cemetery on Mount Zion.

Besides Heleni's pretty painted sewing chest—filled to this day with her thread and lace and needles—none of the furniture that's here now belonged to them, since this house, too, was broken into and pillaged after its owners were gone. When the community decided to turn the place into a museum, Anastas and a few others came to clean up the mess, and one day as he was sweeping, he found, he says, Dr. Photios Efklides's firman from the sultan crumpled on the floor. Now it hangs here alongside several ghostly pictures of the lovely young Heleni Efklides, still dressed up for some long-forgotten party.

Next to her, in his own frame but on the same wall, Spyro Houris is still sitting in that elaborately carved throne of a chair, silently staring out.

⊕

As things seem to end, though, they're also beginning.

One morning, I open my e-mail: "Here are some links regarding Houris." The message comes from Silvia K., the big-hearted Argentinean Israeli archivist responsible for bringing the bulk of Austen St. Barbe Harrison's papers from Athens to Jerusalem. In the course of my work with his letters and sketch pads, his photographs and gardening notebooks at the Rockefeller Museum, she and I have become friends of a strangely single-minded sort. It's as if "Austen," as she calls him, were a mutual friend who'd introduced us and whose architectural and personal exploits still provide the fodder for most of our conversation. That said, I've told her about my search for Spyro Houris and, unbeknownst to me, she has asked for help on my behalf from an Israeli conservation architect she thought might know something of the elusive Jerusalem builder. He doesn't, but he has found these links, two of which I've already discovered, while one is unfamiliar. Under pictures of an Israeli flag and an architect's golden square and compass, it provides page 12 of a quirky, bare-bones twenty-four-page French-language history of *La Franc Maçonnerie en Israel*, the Freemasons in Israel, and lists the dignitaries and officers elected to the newly formed Grand Lodge of Palestine at a special meeting on December 1, 1932. A scramble of Jewish and Arab names follows (Gorodissky, Nazha, Sandberg, Khouri, Bouzaglou, Tamari, Yellin, El Far, etc.), including the grand secrétaire—none other than Spyro G. Houris.

When I first consider it, Houris's affiliation with the world's most famous secret society seems an elaborate inside joke. Not only was he a builder in actual stone and mortar, he built in the very city that provides the Masons the hub of their complex mythological system. According to Masonic lore, King Solomon gathered stoneworkers of all races together to build his Temple in Jerusalem, and this act gave rise to the founding of the fraternity which, in the words of one nineteenth-century manual for initiates, "unites men of every country, sect and opinion; and conciliates true friendship among those who might otherwise have remained at a perpetual distance." In this architectural and geographical force field, Houris's ties to Ohannes-

sian and the Dome of the Rock potters—whose ceramics were initially meant to adorn the mysterious Islamic shrine that occupies the
space where it seems that Temple once stood—also seems too ab-
surdly appropriate to be true. Across the globe, Masonic lodges are
modeled on Solomon's Temple, which members of the guild venerate
as a symbol of loss, as well as an ideal. And when the Masons were
still hands-on, practicing masons, special honor was paid to the
workmen who completed a lodge by covering it with, yes, tiles. Now,
more metaphorically, the "tilers" are those appointed to guard the
door during meetings, keep the guild's secrets, and prevent the entry
of intruders.

On second thought, however, and once I begin to investigate just
what being a Freemason might have meant to Spyro Houris, I realize the serious cultural and historical implications of this discovery.
The legends surrounding the Masons may be shadowy and even
slightly sinister, with the suggestion of weird initiation rites, secret
handshakes, and plots to rebuild the Temple hovering in the conspiracy theory–charged Palestinian air. (In their notoriously ranting
charter, Hamas, for example, denounces as their enemies those who
were "behind the French Revolution, the Communist revolution
and most of the revolutions we heard and hear about" as well as those
who used their money to form "secret societies, such as Freemasons,
Rotary Clubs, the Lions and others . . . for the purpose of sabotaging
societies and achieving Zionist interests.") But in actuality, the organization has existed in the Middle East as a rather matter-of-fact
men's club since sometime in the early 1700s. With Napoleon's invasion of Egypt, it spread widely throughout the region, and by the late
nineteenth century, it had evolved into a well-established philan-
thropic and communal entity, "one of the most influential social
institutions in the Ottoman Empire," according to the American
historian Michelle Campos, who's written extensively about the Masons in this context. During this period, nearly every city and large
town in the empire had a lodge or lodges, and despite the suspicions
surrounding their motives and rituals, these lodges proved strong
social magnets. As Campos explains, the society promoted modern
Enlightenment ideals while also providing its members a powerful
economic and political network—access to a formidable subterranean

who's who. French revolutionary principles had indeed been central to the beliefs of Ottoman masons, and (lunatic as their charter sounds, Hamas isn't entirely wrong) various progressive social movements had used the underground society as an organizing base. The 1882 anticolonialist Egyptian revolution had been propelled by Masons, as were the sultan-toppling Young Turks of 1908. In early twentieth-century Palestine, Masonic lodges drew young professional men of the middle and upper classes from all the different communities, with Muslims and Christians, Sephardi Jews and Ashkenazi Jews, Armenians, Greeks, Englishmen, Frenchmen, and Americans all calling themselves brothers.

And what of Spyro Houris? If he was elected to such a lofty office as grand secrétaire in 1932, he must have been a Mason for much longer—maybe even under Ottoman rule. Although we've never met, Campos happens to be the friend of a friend, which gives me an excuse to write her an e-mail and ask if by any chance she's heard of him. By now I've bumped into a footnote in one of her scholarly articles that mentions Yom-Tov Amon (aka Hamon) as having been a member of Jerusalem's Moriah Lodge in 1913. Could it be that Houris met the Jewish judge through the Masons? Were other "brothers" his clients?

"Happily," this generous stranger writes me, from a University of Florida e-mail address, "I can tell you that Spyro Houris was indeed a Mason before World War I." Based on records she has examined at the Bibliothèque Nationale in Paris—where she wasn't looking for Houris at all but for a whole range of material about Ottoman Palestine's many Masons—she knows the answers to various riddles I've spent months trying to solve. And now I, too, know that Spyro Houris was born on December 25, 1883, in Alexandria.

Before I have a chance to fully absorb the implications of this discovery or to consider the irony of the fact that these details have been lying for years in something like plain sight within the open files of an ostensibly secret society, Campos offers more information. Houris pledged as an apprentice, she writes, at the Italia lodge in that Egyptian city in April 1910, and graduated to the second level, a companion, in September 1910. On April 29, 1914, he was promoted to the third level—master mason—at the Moriah lodge in Jerusalem, which is to say that he had apparently left Alexandria and arrived in Palestine sometime in the course of those three and a half years. She relates, too, the intriguing if perplexing fact that his Jerusalem lodge records describe his professional affiliation as an "architect of the Imperial Russian Society." I've found no hint of his relationship to this charitable Russian organization, or, for that matter, to anything or anyone Russian at all. During these years—at least as the history books tell it—the tensions between the Greek and Russian Orthodox in Jerusalem were extremely high. Given Houris's clear connection to the Greek patriarchate, this detail is confusing.

Campos also sends along a list of the other members of his Jerusalem lodge, which was mostly made up of Sephardi Jews and both local and foreign Christians, Arab and otherwise. (The Moriah lodge held its meetings in French and caused something of a scandal when in 1913 it broke away from the other Jerusalem lodge, the Arabic-speaking Temple of Solomon.) Moriah's Masons included bankers, merchants, teachers, clerks, a doctor, a soldier, a dentist, two railroad employees, a souvenir merchant, an accountant, the Christian Arab head of the railway station, the Jewish director of the liberal Alliance Israélite Universelle school, one Greek member of the holy synod, a French electrician, the director of the Italian post office, and the Latvian-born Jewish painter Abel Pann, listed simply as a "teacher at the Bezalel School." Besides Hamon, no names associated with Houris's buildings surface in these records, but the range of people and professions there does indicate whole complex webs—if not of conspiracy, then of *connection*, which seem to have persisted well into the Mandate period, when Houris was elected to that grand secretarial post in the national lodge, whose emblem was a crown of laurel leaves encircling the usual masonic compass, along with a Star of David, a cross, and a Muslim crescent.

But all of this has, it seems to me, far less to do with Freemasonry than with Jerusalem itself, as it confirms what I've already come to see—that Spyro Houris lived and built in a time and place where one's own identity could be multiple, and where the bonds that stretched across what are now considered nearly impassable ethnic, national, and religious borders were not only conceivable, they were critical to what made the city the city. Whether or not its twenty-first-century residents care to admit it, that multiplicity and those bonds—imperfect and often tense as they may sometimes have been—created modern Jerusalem. The dynamic "eclecticism" that distinguishes Houris's buildings was an expression of the city's own dynamic eclecticism, which still lingers, though these days it's severely endangered. In a way the discovery that Houris was a son of that other quintessentially polyglot and polymorphous Levantine town, Alexandria, is also a confirmation of something I've unconsciously been circling around for some time now. (Long before I learned where Spyro Houris's life began, I chose as this book's epigraph those lines from "The City" by Constantine Cavafy, the great modern Greek poet of Alexandria.) It also seems a kind of warning. Once the epitome of the most vibrant sort of pluralism and cosmopolitanism, Alexandria is for all intents and purposes now a monolingual, monocultural, monoreligious city, and one that's far less for that. If Jerusalem's rulers have their way, this city faces a similar grimly monolithic future. The near-disappearance of Spyro Houris's traces—to say nothing of the scenes I witnessed the cruel summer of 2014 in Zion Square—makes clear that this process is well under way.

For now, though, I'm still trying to follow out the traces that *do* exist, and, at Campos's suggestion, I contact a Greek historian named Angelos Dalachanis whom she's met only once but who she thinks may know something more about Spyro Houris. He, too, responds quickly and warmly by e-mail, and—wonder of archival wonders— he forwards a digital photograph of a handwritten Greek-language document dated January 19, 1925. Under the seal of the Jerusalem patriarchate, this is a marriage certificate that just happens to exist in his computer's hard drive and that lists Spyridon Houris, architect, as the best man at the Jerusalem wedding of one Maria Houris, age thirty-five, to Nikephoros Petassis, age forty-five, architect, Jerusalem. Spyridon is Maria's older brother (he is forty-two at the time of the wedding), Petassis his sometime architectural partner. Spyro and Maria's father Gavriil (or Gabriel) is deceased, their mother, Amalia, a housewife. The ceremony is registered as taking place at the Grand New Hotel, the elegant, column-fronted structure that the archimandrite Efthimios built in 1882, just inside the Jaffa Gate.

I ask Dalachanis how he understands the name "Spyro Houris,"

and he muses on the fluidity and meaning of names in this setting.
He suggests that perhaps the architect's father had been a Christian
Arab from Jerusalem who moved to Alexandria and married there,
Hellenizing the spelling of an Arabic surname. The father's own
name—Gavriil—sounds to him more appropriate for a Christian Arab
than for a Greek, though he can't say for sure and wonders if Gavriil,
too, had been born a Houris. Amalia was the Bavarian first queen
of Greece, and in the nineteenth century, this German name was
common for Greek women; among Alexandrians, it often indicated a "connection to the motherland." Greek boys of the time
were, he says, usually named for their grandfathers, though he points
out that Spyro Houris's December 25 birthday wasn't Christmas for
the Orthodox but the name day of Saint Spyridon, for whom it seems
Amalia and Gavriil chose to name their firstborn.

Now that Houris's Alexandrian origins have been established, the
question of his alleged time in Athens also suddenly cracks wide
open. While Kroyanker writes that the architect studied there, no
solid evidence of this exists. Kindly offering to make enquiries on
this front, Dalachanis asks the chief librarian of the National Technical University of Athens to check the records of the local institutions
granting architectural degrees during this period. She obliges, and
combing through the rosters of all the graduates from 1890 to 1949,
she finds no sign of a Spyro Houris—or, in fact, any Houris at all. I
wonder if he might have obtained Greek citizenship in Egypt, without ever setting foot in Greece, which was possible during these
years. But where, then, did he study architecture? Did he study it
at all? Perhaps he'd learned on the job. Where? In Alexandria? In
Jerusalem? Elsewhere? And why, in fact, did he set forth from his
hometown? What did he hope to find in Jerusalem? Did he find it?
The various documents that Silvia K. and the Israeli conservation
architect and Campos and Dalachanis and I have unearthed provide
answers to certain questions, though each answer only prompts more
questions.

There is, however, one further mystery that I've managed to solve
with the help of yellowing paper, the Internet, and a generous stranger.

When N. at the State Archive had made various suggestions of
where I might follow the trail of Houris after we hadn't found him in

the Books of Souls, he'd mentioned *The Palestine Gazette,* the official record of Mandate laws and declarations, where he thought architects needed to register their licenses. I find no sign of such a license there, but a single telling entry surfaces just a few seconds after I type his name into the digitized searchable version of the heavy Mandatory tome:

IN THE DISTRICT COURT OF JERUSALEM

In the matter of the succession of SPYRO GABRIEL HOURIS, deceased.

Petitioner: MRS. MARICA PETASSIS (née HOURIS).

Let all persons take notice that MRS. MARICA PETASSIS (née HOURIS) of Jerusalem, the only sister and heir of the said deceased SPYRO HOURIS, has applied to the District Court of Jerusalem for an order declaring the succession to SPYRO HOURIS, deceased, who died at Jerusalem on the 17th February 1936 and that the said application will be heard at the District Court, Jerusalem, on the 19th day of February, 1937.

All persons claiming any interest must appear at the said place and time, otherwise such order will be made as to the Court seems right.

Dated this 23rd day of January, 1937.

D. SHAMI
Chief Clerk, District Court, Jerusalem

With no other heirs, with no wife and no children, Spyro Houris had, in other words, very good reason to carve his name into those Jerusalem cornerstones. He wanted both to announce his pride and his presence as his buildings went up, and for the memory of his pride and his presence to linger on the sides of those buildings long after his colleagues and patrons, his friends and his enemies, his "brothers" and his sister were gone, after his city had evolved into another. How else would we know he was here?

All summer long—before I learn of Houris's birth in one profoundly mixed Middle Eastern city and his premature death in another—I've made my way repeatedly not just past the revenge-demanding protestors in Zion Square but also onto Mount Zion itself, where the Greek Orthodox cemetery abuts the Armenian, the Protestant, the Roman Catholic, and where, nearby, Jewish and Muslim graves spill steeply down the city's slopes. In a death-filled season, it may seem perverse to go hunting for yet another grave, but as the war has raged, I've been looking for Spyro Houris's—returning again and again to this oddly hushed, somehow peaceful enclosure.

Munir, the wiry, tattooed, chain-smoking Greek- and Arabic-speaking keeper of the cemetery, has been helping me, but as we wander out in different directions across the chaotic plot of crowded, cracked, and jumbled tombs, we find no sign of him or of his grave. So many of these stones, though, are shattered or faded or covered with lichen, we could well be walking right past, or over, him. Who knows? Jerusalem is an almost endless set of buried layers, and there are whole cities here of the forgotten dead. Dr. Photios Efklides's gravestone once stood inside this compound but now is nowhere to be found; Sultana Sakakini, beloved wife of Khalil, who died in 1939 and was laid to rest within these walls, has also disappeared. Where are Alexander and Clio and Heleni? Where is Spyro Houris? Now fall has come, bringing the first rains, and as I pick my way among the thistles, the trash, and the broken stones, I'm still looking.

NOTES

ABBREVIATIONS

AH	Austen Harrison
Beinecke	Beinecke Rare Book & Manuscript Library, Yale University, New Haven
CEG	Collection on Eric Gill, Clark Library, University of California, Los Angeles
CO	Colonial Office, National Archives, Kew, England
CRA	Charles Robert Ashbee
CRA KC	Papers of Charles Robert Ashbee, King's College, Cambridge, England
CZA	Central Zionist Archives, Jerusalem
EM	Erich Mendelsohn
EM: D & F	Regina Stephan, ed., *Erich Mendelsohn: Dynamics and Function, Realized Visions of a Cosmopolitan Architect* (Ostfildern-Ruit, 1998)
EM/LM	Erich and Luise Mendelsohn Papers, Getty Research Institute, Los Angeles
ETR	Ernest Tatham Richmond
FO	Foreign Office, National Archives, Kew, England
FS	Freya Stark Collection, Harry Ransom Center, University of Texas, Austin
Had.	Hadassah Medical Organization Papers, American Jewish Historical Society, New York
HUA	Hebrew University Archive, Jerusalem
IAA	Israel Antiquities Authority Archive, Jerusalem
JMA	Jerusalem Municipal Archives, Jerusalem
LM	Luise Mendelsohn
MECA	Middle East Centre Archive, St. Antony's College, Oxford, England
NYT	*The New York Times*
OI	Oriental Institute Research Archives, University of Chicago
PB	*The Palestine Bulletin*
PN	C. R. Ashbee, *A Palestine Notebook, 1918–1923* (Garden City, NY, 1923)

PP   *The Palestine Post*
RAC   Rockefeller Archive Center (Rockefeller Family Collection), Sleepy
                Hollow, NY
RIBA   Royal Institute of British Architects
RIC   E. T. Richmond Papers, Durham University, Durham, England
RS   Ronald Storrs Papers, Pembroke College, Cambridge, England
SA   Salman Schocken Archive, the Schocken Institute, Jerusalem
SS   Salman Schocken
TGDB   David Bomberg Papers, Tate Gallery Archive, London

BEYOND JAFFA GATE: AN OPENING

The history of Jaffa Road is drawn from Yehoshua Ben-Arieh, *Jerusalem in the 19th Century: Emergence of the New City* (Jerusalem, 1986); David Kroyanker, *Jaffa Road: Biography of a Street—Story of a City* [Heb.] (Jerusalem, 2005); Ruth Kark and Michal Oren-Nordheim, *Jerusalem and Its Environs: Quarters, Neighborhoods, Villages, 1800–1948* (Jerusalem, 2001). Melville's notes come from *Journals*, ed. Howard C. Horsford with Lynn Horth (Evanston, 1989), 86–87. Further details of the scene just beyond the gate appear in George Hintlian, "The Commercial Life of Ottoman Jerusalem," in *Ottoman Jerusalem: The Living City, 1517–1917*, ed. Sylvia Auld and Robert Hillenbrand (London, 2000); Abigail Jacobson, *From Empire to Empire: Jerusalem Between Ottoman and British Rule* (Syracuse, 2011), 53–60. She quotes native son Yaakov Yehoshua, 56.

Details about the Ottoman and British clock towers come from *The Storyteller of Jerusalem: The Life and Times of Wasif Jawhariyyeh, 1904–1948*, ed. Salim Tamari and Issam Nassar, trans. Nada Elzeer (Northampton, MA, 2014), 139–40 (Jawhariyyeh likens the former to a lighthouse); Salim Tamari, *Year of the Locust: A Soldier's Diary and the Erasure of Palestine's Ottoman Past* (Berkeley, 2011), 36–38; Ron Fuchs and Gilbert Herbert, "A Colonial Portrait of Jerusalem: British Architecture in Mandate-Era Palestine," in *Hybrid Urbanism: On the Identity Discourse and the Built Environment*, ed. Nezar AlSayyad (Westport, CT, 2001); Beatrice St. Laurent and András Riedlmayer, "Restorations of Jerusalem and the Dome of the Rock and Their Political Significance, 1537–1928," *Muqarnas* 10 (1993). The estimate of the number of times the city has been captured and recaptured is Eric H. Cline's, in *Jerusalem Besieged: From Ancient Canaan to Modern Israel* (Ann Arbor, 2004), 2. For more on the various civilizations that have built the city, see Simon Goldhill, *Jerusalem: City of Longing* (Cambridge, MA, 2008). Quotes are as follows: "What I see," Joseph Roth, "Going for a Walk," in *What I Saw: Reports from Berlin, 1920–1933*, trans. Michael Hofmann (NY, 2003); "on 60, 80, or even 100," George St. Clair, *The Buried City of Jerusalem and Geographical Survey of Palestine* (London, 1887), 11; "disfigured," Storrs in *Jerusalem, 1920–1922*, ed. C. R. Ashbee (London, 1924), vi; "the dilapidated structures," Aryeh Sharon, *Planning Jerusalem: The Old City and Its Environs* (Jerusalem, 1973), 128, 130; "It is . . . a city unique," Ashbee, *Jerusalem 1920–1922*, 4.

JERUSALEMSTRASSE, 1934

All of Mendelsohn's letters come from Eric Mendelsohn: Letters of an Architect, *ed. Oskar Beyer, trans. Geoffrey Strachan (London, 1967) unless otherwise noted.*

NO ROCOCO PALACE

Mendelsohn's views of Palestine's modern architecture are drawn from EM/LM 31/1, 39, and the following sources: "wild, tropical vegetation," "The New Architecture in Palestine: An Interview with Mr. Erich Mendelsohn," *Palestine Review*, Aug. 20, 1937; LM, "a little heap . . . the impression," "My Life in a Changing World," typescript (Museum of Modern Art, special collections), 127; "pariah existence," "The New Architecture"; "tear jug," EM to LM, July 2, 1947; "brutal disregard," EM/LM 31/1, 39; "Palestine is not a virgin," "The New Architecture"; "bastard buildings . . . wholly unsuitable . . . pestilence," EM, "Twenty Years of Building," *PP*, Dec. 29, 1940.

Luise's descriptions of Erich appear in drafts of her memoir, held at the Getty, and the finished version, "My Life in a Changing World": "arrogant, impatient . . . humble," EM/LM 31/2, 1–3. His account of the trip to Mount Scopus and of the view come from EM to LM, Dec. 12, 1934. Jerusalem's evolving demography is described in Rochelle Davis, "Ottoman Jerusalem: The Growth of the City Outside the Walls" and "The Growth of the Western Communities, 1917–1948," in *Jerusalem 1948: The Arab Neighbourhoods and Their Fate in the War*, ed. Salim Tamari (Jerusalem, Bethlehem, 2002). Population figures from various sources are compiled in Kark and Oren-Nordheim, *Jerusalem and Its Environs*, 28.

Details of the Mount Scopus plans derive from the minutes of endless meetings in Had. 2/20/52; "Mount Scopus Hospital Ceremony" and "America Listens In," *PP*, Oct. 17, 1934; Marlin Levin, *It Takes a Dream: The Story of Hadassah* (Jerusalem, 1997), 184–85. Quotations are as follows: "cosmopolitan city of Jerusalem . . . foster," Chaim Yassky memo, Aug. 15, 1933, Had. 2/21/53; "an entirely new master plan," EM to LM, Dec. 12, 1934; "like a proper organism," EM, "Building on Mount Scopus," *PP*, May 9, 1939; "executed by one hand," EM to LM, July 30, 1936; "House of Life," from Chaim Nahman Bialik's inauguration address, reprinted in *The Hebrew University of Jerusalem, 1925–1950* (Jerusalem, 1950).

General background about EM's German work comes from Regina Stephan, ed., *EM: D & F*; Bruno Zevi, *Erich Mendelsohn: Complete Works*, trans. Lucinda Byatt (Boston, 1999); Bruno Zevi, *Erich Mendelsohn* (NY, 1985); Kathleen James, *Erich Mendelsohn and the Architecture of German Modernism* (Cambridge, 1997); Arnt Cobbers, *Erich Mendelsohn* (Köln, 2007); Wolf Von Eckardt, *Eric Mendelsohn* (NY, 1960); *Erich Mendelsohn, Complete Works of the Architect* (NY, 1992); Arnold Whittick, *Eric Mendelsohn* (London, 1956); Susan King, *The Drawings of Eric Mendelsohn* (Berkeley, 1969); Regina Stephan's German notations to the Getty Research Institute and Kunstbibliothek Staatliche Museen zu Berlin's recently digitized Erich Mendelsohn Archive.

EM's own view of his work at this time and details of his American trip are from the following sources: "The primary element," EM to LM, Aug. 19, 1923 (translation altered slightly); Jan Wollner, "The Architecture of *Metropolis*," *Umělec*, 2012; "everything. The worst strata," EM, *Erich Mendelsohn's "Amerika"* (NY, 1993), xi; "Motion is life!" quoted in Cobbers, *Mendelsohn*, 50.

The opinions of his potential patrons and peers are as follows: "great artists," Kurt Blumenfeld to SS, Sept. 3, 1924, quoted in Ita Heinze-Mühleib, *Erich Mendelsohn: Bauten und Projekte in Palästina (1934–1941)* (Munich, 1986); "one of the outstanding," Chaim Yassky to J. A. Ketzive, Nov. 26, 1946, Had. 2/50/88; "ultra-modern style . . . not suitable," minutes of building committee meeting, Dec. 20, 1934, and the complaints of Mr. Green, Had. 2/20/52; "not an easy man . . . capable . . . This is not," minutes, Dec. 20, 1934, Had. 2/20/52; "must come here," EM to LM, Dec. 30, 1934.

The account of the Mendelsohns' 1923 trip, his early attempts to build in Palestine, and the aftermath of that encounter is woven from Gilbert Herbert and Silvina Sosnovsky, *Bauhaus on the Carmel and the Crossroads of Empire: Architecture and Planning in Haifa During the British Mandate* (Jerusalem, 1993), 98–121; Gilbert Herbert and Ita Heinze-Greenberg, *The Beginnings of Modern Architecture in Israel: The First Power Stations, 1921–1932* (Haifa, 1997), E9–E12; Heinze-Greenberg, "Travels to Holland, Palestine, the United States, and Russia," in *EM: D & F*, 60–65; Gilbert Herbert and Liliane Richter, *Through a Clouded Glass: Mendelsohn, Wijdeveld, and the Jewish Connection* (Tübingen, 2008), 78–92; LM, "My Life," 59–61; Alona Nitzan-Shiftan, "Erich Mendelsohn: From Berlin to Jerusalem" (master's thesis, MIT, 1993). Quotes are as follows: "I . . . call myself its true child," quoted in Heinze-Greenberg, "The Mediterranean Academy Project and Mendelsohn's Emigration," in *EM: D & F*, 189, letter dated July 11, 1933; "engineers willing," "Verzeichnis derjenigen Ingenieure . . . ," March 23, 1920, CZA L3\608; "too European," EM, "My Own Contribution to the Development of Contemporary Architecture," UCLA School of Architecture lecture, March 27, 1948, EM/LM 9/10; "too Oriental," Ita Heinze-Mühleib, *Erich Mendelsohn in Palestine* (Haifa, 1987), 7–8; EM, "My Own Work, Liverpool 1933, Cambridge 1934," RIBA, Arnold Whittick archive, 1/3; "take time to settle," EM to Oskar Beyer, March 9, 1923; "cycles of emotion . . . No Jew," quoted in Herbert and Sisnovsky, *Bauhaus*, 106; "entirely unprepared," EM/LM 33/1, 105; "Although I see my work," quoted in Herbert and Richter, *Through a Clouded Glass*, 122; "Reflections kept . . ." EM to LM, Jan. 16, 1925.

The description of Am Rupenhorn comes from EM, *Neues Haus, Neue Welt* (Berlin, 1932); Heinze-Greenberg, "Success, House, and Home," in *EM: D & F*, 170–81; LM, "My Life," 91–98. Quotes: "what I am particularly anxious," Ozenfant's essay is excerpted (in a different translation, used here) in Beyer, *Letters*; "machine for living in," Le Corbusier, *Towards a New Architecture*, trans. Frederick Etchells (NY, 1986), 4.

EM's views of the Mediterranean emerge from the following sources: "little rectangles," EM, "Overland to Athens," *Berliner Tageblatt*, May 1931, translated in *Letters*; "Heavens, water, the distant islands," EM to LM, June 3, 1933, *Briefe eines Architekten*, ed. Oskar Beyer (Munich, 1961); "its fullness, its tranquility . . . the Mediterranean contemplates," EM to LM, Oct. 29, 1931, quoted in Heinze-Greenberg, "Success, House, and Home," 184; "eternal creative force," EM to LM, Dec. 10, 1934.

Details of the Weissenhof exhibition are drawn from James, *Erich Mendelsohn*, 201–209; Richard Pommer and Christian F. Otto, *Weissenhof 1927 and the Modern Movement in Architecture* (Chicago, 1991); Karin Kirsch, *The Weissenhofsiedlung: Experimental Housing Built for the Deutscher Werkbund, Stuttgart, 1927* (NY, 1989); Richard Pommer, "The Flat Roof: A Modernist Controversy in Germany," *Art Journal* 43, no. 2 (1983). All quotes from the exhibit's detractors come from Pommer's article about flat roofs. Of the sixteen architects, it seems only one—Josef Frank—was Jewish; Adolf Rading was married to a Jew and eventually made his way to Palestine.

The description of the Mendelsohns' last days in Berlin is derived primarily from LM's "My Life." Quotes are as follows: "three days in Berlin," letter from EM to LM,

Nov. 10, 1931, quoted in Ita Heinze-Greenberg, "An Artistic European Utopia at the Abyss of Time: The Mediterranean Academy Project, 1931–34," *Architectural History* 45 (2002), 448 (translation adjusted); "free myself, which is to say *us*," EM to LM, Feb. 23, 1933, EM/LM 2/1; "Germany awake . . . shattering blow," LM, "My Life," 105.

For details of the Mediterranean Academy project and the Mendelsohns' arrival in England, see Heinze-Greenberg, "An Artistic European Utopia"; Heinze-Greenberg, "The Mediterranean Academy Project," 182–89; LM, "My Life," 109–15; C. H. Reilly, *Scaffolding in the Sky: A Semi-Architectural Autobiography* (London, 1938), 291–93. Quotes: "young architect into," in Heinze-Greenberg, "An Artistic European Utopia," 186; "interrupted warmly," "Mr. Mendelsohn: German Architect's Lecture: Great Reception," *The Manchester Guardian*, Nov. 18, 1933; "I do not feel very happy," quoted in Charlotte Benton, "Building in England and the Partnership with Serge Chermayeff," in *EM: D & F*, 202–203; "Why not directly," letter, July 11, 1933, quoted in Herbert and Richter, *Through a Clouded Glass*, 122, and, in part, in Heinze-Greenberg, "The Mediterranean Academy Project," 189. This version combines the translations.

EM's account of his early days in Jerusalem comes from his letters to LM: "The hotel is filling . . . I am completely absorbed," Dec. 7, 1934, EM/LM 2/2; "The Mediterranean . . . is a first step," May 30, 1933. Details of the cold shoulder EM got from various former colleagues and should-be supporters are as follows: "collegial greetings," Herbert and Richter, *Through a Clouded Glass*, 123; "no special friend," quoted in James, *Erich Mendelsohn*, 246; "bizarre Expressionist," Alfred H. Barr Jr., "Preface," Henry-Russell Hitchcock and Philip Johnson, *The International Style* (NY, 1997), 28; "a poor imitation," quoted in Franz Schulze, *Philip Johnson: Life and Work* (NY, 1994), 73. Johnson's Nazi sympathies emerged fully the next year, when he attended a Hitler rally near Potsdam and reported that "you simply could not fail to be caught up in the excitement of it." He was especially thrilled by "all those blond boys in black leather." See Schulze, 89–90; EM's hanging up is recounted in James, *Erich Mendelsohn*, 245.

Further impressions of these early Jerusalem days are drawn from Erich's December 1934 letters to LM and her memoir: "crackle of drawing paper," LM, "My Life," 129; "a mystical image," Dec. 7, 1934, EM/LM 2/1; "What obliges us . . . I am resolved," Dec. 10, 1934; "eye—food of the soul," Dec. 19, 1934; "I have visited all the buildings," Dec. 27, 1934. The words *"self-complacency"* are in English in the original German letter.

VISIONS, VERNACULARS

Luise's account of first meeting Erich and Erich's of his visions are found in her memoirs and his letters to her: "uneasy but captivated . . . trousers . . . energetic chin . . . Everything," LM, "My Life," 14; "as something of fundamental," EM/LM 31/2, 10–11; "among incessant," June 17, 1917; "the visions are once more," Aug. 11, 1917; "my architectural dreams," EM, "My Contribution to the Development," 5; "Although my pessimism," September 29, 1938, *Briefe*.

EM's take on this period is drawn from his letters to LM (unless otherwise noted): "If possible . . . it will be," March 30, 1935; "In Berlin," EM to Oskar Beyer, April 30, 1935; "the rush begins," April 8, 1935, EM/LM 2/2; "The Orient . . .

resists," EM to Beyer, April 30, 1935; "a life between poles," April 11, 1935, EM/ LM 2/2.

Descriptions of the windmill come from LM, "My Life," 131–33; EM/LM 33/3, 284; 31/1, 43–44; EM to LM, April 8, 1935, EM/LM 2/2. See also Hala Sakakini, *Jerusalem and I: A Personal Record* (Jerusalem, 1987), 4–5, for a description of the mill as it was when her family lived there. For historical background on the mill, see David Kroyanker, *Jerusalem Architecture—Periods and Styles: The Period of the British Mandate, 1918–1948* [Heb.] (Jerusalem, 1989), 307–309. Further background on Rehavia comes from Amnon Rimon, *Rehavia: A Neighborhood in Jerusalem* [Heb.] (Jerusalem, 1998). Names of EM's employees appear in Ita Heinze-Greenberg, "Architecture in Palestine, 1934–1941," in *EM: D & F*, 214, and other details about the office are drawn from Gabriel Epstein's German-language remembrances of the Jerusalem office, in Regina Stephan, ed., *Erich Mendelsohn: Wesen, Werk, Wirkung* (Ostfildern, 2006). Further details of their life and his work in the mill: "came with the mill," EM/LM 31/7, 42; "to dress her in such a way . . . perfect," LM, "My Life," 131; "were not able to understand," EM/LM 33/3, 308–309; "I am . . . building the country," EM to LM, sometime in 1935, quoted in Bruno Zevi, *EM* (1999), 235; "dark and dirty . . . dangerously deteriorated," EM/LM 33/3, 320–21. LM describes how the music made the whole mill sing in a draft of her memoir, EM/LM 3/1, 44.

The story of Julius Posener and EM and their exchange is told in Ita Heinze-Greenberg, ". . . This Once Gold-Diggingly Created City: Eric Mendelsohn and Tel Aviv," *Docomomo* 40 (March 2009); I've adjusted the translations of Posener's words. Further details of EM's ideas about building in the Mediterranean come from: "the lighthearted character," Hans Schiller to Whittick, Feb. 28, 1955, EM/LM 11/3; "No one . . . ought to build," EM to Posener, March 30, 1937; "Will Palestine develop," "An Era of New Building in the Land of Israel: An Interview with Dr. [*sic*] Erich Mendelsohn," *The Jewish Chronicle, Palestine Supplement*, May 1, 1936.

Particulars about "the Circle," Sharon, and EM's relationship to this group are found in Aryeh Sharon, *Kibbutz + Bauhaus: An Architect's Way in a New Land* (Stuttgart, 1976); Zvi Efrat, "Modernism and Zionism as Reflected in the Lifework of Arieh Sharon," *Bezalel Papers on Architecture* 7, no. 11 (2009); Myra Warhaftig, *They Laid the Foundation*, trans. Andrea Lerner (Tübingen, 2007), 122–25; Michael Levin, *White City: International Style Architecture in Israel* (Tel Aviv, 1984), 31–32; Alona Nitzan-Shiftan, "Contested Zionism—Alternative Zionism: Erich Mendelsohn and the Tel Aviv Chug in Mandate Palestine," *Architectural History* 39 (1996); Eric Zakim, *To Build and Be Built: Landscape, Literature and the Construction of Zionist Identity* (Philadelphia, 2006), 152–69; Sharon Rotbard, *White City, Black City: Architecture and War in Tel Aviv and Jaffa*, trans. Orit Gat (Cambridge, MA, 2015). "Brigade of planners" is Efrat, playing on Hannes Meyer. Quotes are as follows: "architectural revolt . . . a courageous fighter . . . infiltrating . . . primitive," Sharon, *Kibbutz + Bauhaus*, 47–48; "Oriental," Ratner, quoted in Nitzan-Shiftan, "Contested Zionism," 150; "freeing their dwellings," Julius Posener, "One-Family Houses in Palestine" [Heb.], *Habinyan* 2 (Nov. 1937), 1; "an *English* architect," EM to Beyer, April 30, 1935; "The principal hope of the Jewish people," *Habinyan*, Feb. 1935, English supplement, 3; "We have . . . a lot of rethinking," EM to Posener, March 30, 1937.

HOMING

The quotes by and about EM and his personality are as follows: "towns and villages in oneness," EM/LM 31/1, 27–28; "Oriental from East Prussia," EM to LM, August 26, 1923 (translated as "East Prussian Oriental"); "mercilessly in the pursuit . . . Every detail . . . exuberant vitality," EM/LM 34/1, 602–605; "authoritarian," Julius Posener, quoted in Regina Stephan, "Mendelsohn and His Assistants in the 1920s and Early 1930s," in *EM: D & F*, 156, "almost painful meticulousness," 153. The details of the daily functioning of the office are related by Posener in this article.

On his interactions with various female clients: "interior desecrators," Von Eckardt, *Eric Mendelsohn*, 16; "But you will ruin everything," Vera Weizmann, *The Impossible Takes Longer* (NY, 1967), 139; "more unforgettable," Heinze-Greenberg, "Architecture in Palestine," 217.

Background on the early plans for the Schocken Villa comes from Heinze-Mühleib, *Bauten*, 118–50; Heinze-Greenberg, "Architecture in Palestine," 214–20. The patron and architect's international correspondence on the subject is found in letters, July 17 and 24, Aug. 4 and 17, 1934, SA 844/182. Particulars of SS's land purchases are in SA 823/11. Quotes are as follows: "decision," letter, July 17, 1934, SA 844/182; "It's strange," May 20, 1934, SA 844/182; "I am . . . a force," quoted in Heinze-Mühleib, *Bauten*, 120; "free and light," EM to LM, Dec. 19, 1934; "very beautiful," EM to LM, Dec. 27, 1934; "delighted," Dec. 15, 1934, quoted in Heinze-Greenberg, "Architecture in Palestine," 216.

The Mendelsohns' newly frugal life is described in LM, "My Life," 133; EM/LM 33/3, 308–309. Details of SS's art collection are found in SA 871/52 (II). EM's specifications for the house come from, among multiple files, SA 823/58/1, SA 823/126. Quotes are as follows: "The materials," SA 823/56/2; "The trees to be chosen," EM to SS, March 6, 1935, SA 823/126. For details about the Ha'avarah, see Yehuda Bauer, *Jews for Sale? Nazi-Jewish Negotiations, 1933–1945* (New Haven, 1994), 5–29; Heinze-Mühleib, *Bauten*, 127–28; Tom Segev, *The Seventh Million: The Israelis and the Holocaust* (NY, 1991), 18–34.

The involvement of Jellicoe and Page in the garden is clear from plans (stamped with the firm's name and address and initialed "RP") held at the SA. See also the letter from EM to SS, Nov. 20, 1936 (SA 823/126), in which he explains that the plans "have been done by the expert landscape architect Mr. Russell Page." The saga of the carpet is drawn from EM/LM 31/7, 68–69. Quotes: "It brings the same," EM to SS, June 12, 1937; "fill the house," EM to SS, July 8, 1937; "not suitable," SS to EM, July 15, 1937, all cited in Heinze-Mühleib, *Bauten*, 131. Further quotes in this chapter: "Jewish Bismarck," Elisabeth Young-Bruehl, *Hannah Arendt: For Love of the World* (New Haven, 1982), 189; "follow his rhythms and swirls," EM/LM 31/2, 10; "when I am rested," LM translates him in EM/LM 33/3, 301; "very good," EM to LM, July 9, 1936.

BAUMEISTERS

Background on the Schocken Library comes from Heinze-Mühleib, *Bauten*, 151–65; Heinze-Greenberg, "Architecture in Palestine," 218–20; Zilka Shefer, "The History of Salman Schocken's Book Collection" [Heb.] (master's thesis, the Hebrew University, 1995). For more on the Institute for the Study of Hebrew Poetry, see Adina Hoffman and Peter Cole, *Sacred Trash: The Lost and Found World of the Cairo Geniza* (NY, 2011), 113–25. SS's vision for the library is articulated in his speech at EM's party, March 15,

1937, SA 8/842. Further details of the building and the SS–EM bond are as follows: "absurd . . . spirit and something," EM to LM, Dec. 7, 1934; "be an extension of the great," quoted in Anthony David, *The Patron: A Life of Salman Schocken, 1877–1959* (NY, 2003), 262.

Background on the Aghion House comes from Kroyanker, *Jerusalem Architecture . . . Mandate*, 314–15; Moshe Hananel, *The Jerusalemites: A Journey through the British Mandate Telephone Book* [Heb.] (Jerusalem, 2007), 29–30. EM is quoted as writing to LM that the Aghions are "enthusiastic . . . but too careful," in Heinze-Greenberg "Architecture in Palestine," 273, n39; "our common experiences," quoted in David, *The Patron*, 242; "I know that you value," EM to SS, Feb. 26, 1936, SA 844/2; "Suddenly she asked me," EM/LM 31/1, 4–5. Details of the financial disagreements between patron and architect are drawn from the voluminous correspondence in SA 823/11; EM to LM, July 13, 1936; "Here every act is a struggle," EM to LM, Dec. 19, 1934, EM/LM 2/2.

The disagreement about Hadassah hiring EM is detailed in letters and minutes of meetings: "dangerous at this time . . . are there any," Dec. 20, 1934, Had. 2/20/52; "not really Palestinians," Jan. 24, 1935, Had. 2/20/52; "too modernistic," undated, Had. 2/20/52; "functional procedure of the institution," Robert Kohn to Mrs. De Sola Pool, Feb. 20, 1935, Had. 2/21/53; "I tried to emphasize," "Excerpts of Mrs. Jacobs's letter of July 19[, 1935]," Had. 2/21/53; "must . . . be built," an article from *Opinion* magazine, quoted in a letter to the editor, *PP*, Sept. 30, 1937; "In his opinion," "Memorandum of a Meeting between Mr. Schocken, Dr. Golub and Dr. Yassky, Jan. 21, 1936," Had. 2/48/86.

For the cost-cutting measures EM was forced to take, see Had. 2/20/52 and 2/21/53, in particular: "rather aggrieved . . . not first rate," "Memorandum on a conference between Yassky, Mendelsohn and Golub"; "Even my enemies'," EM to LM, Aug. 17, 1936; "all is one turbulent," EM to LM, Jan. 21, 1936.

UPRISINGS

Population figures and background to the revolt come from ed. Itamar Rabinovich and Jehuda Reinharz, *Israel in the Middle East: Documents and Readings on Society, Politics, and Foreign Relations, Pre-1948 to the Present* (Waltham, MA, 2008), 571; *Palestine Royal Commission Report*, July 1937, esp. 82–83, 96. For descriptions of the city's division: "Disturbances in Country, Jerusalem, May 15, 1936," Had. 2/23/55; A. J. Sherman, *Mandate Days: British Lives in Palestine, 1918–1948* (London, 1997), 96–97.

The accounts of the field-hospital conditions at Hadassah are taken from "Reports Concerning Disturbances" in Had. 2/23/55/5 and 6, and Yassky's diary from this time, found in Had. 2/23/55/6. "Owing to the lack," Yassky diary, June 18. Quotes are as follows: "nerves . . . drawn tight," Rose Halprin to Mrs. Robert Szold, April 28, 1936, Had. 2/23/55; "caused by eating decayed foods," Yassky diary, July 3–July 6; "horrible . . . Part of the brain," Yassky diary, Aug. 21. The murdered professor was Levi Billig. See also Gershom Scholem's letter to Walter Benjamin about his killing and the ensuing "uproar," Aug. 26, 1936, *Correspondence of Walter Benjamin and Gershom Scholem, 1932–1940* (NY, 1989), trans. Gary Smith and Andre Lefevere.

For details of the charged mood surrounding the violence, see "sooth[ing] the seething," *Haaretz* article by Herman Swet, June 4, 1936, trans. in Had. 2/23/55; "Despite my objections," Yassky diary, Aug. 21, 1936. Accounts of the attack at the Edison and the funeral come from Yassky's diary, May 16; "Jerusalem Gangs Curbed by Curfew," *NYT*, May 18, 1936. Further quotes: "hysterical weeping," "Jerusalem Buries Its Dead," *PP*, May 18, 1936; "unwittingly become the depot," Swet, *Haaretz*; "Purposely," "Disturbances in Country, Jerusalem, May 15, 1936," Had. 2/23/55; "news with regard," Swet, *Haaretz*; "I need hardly attempt," Rose Halprin to Mrs. Robert Szold, May 26, 1936, Had. 2/23/55.

EM's work and mood during this time are detailed in "Report on the period May 1–15, 1936," May 18, 1936, Had. 2/21/53; EM to LM, July 23, 1936, Aug. 1, 1936; "Scopus Medical Center," *PP*, Oct. 20, 1936. Quotes: "fresh and delicious," EM to LM, July 6, 1936, EM/LM 2/2; "Schocken is in a good temper," EM to LM, July 9, 1936; "still a naked babe," EM to LM, July 23, 1936 (translation tweaked); "The chief building seems," EM to LM, July 27, 1936; "exciting days," EM to LM, July 30, 1936; "lean and uncertain," EM to LM, July 13, 1936; "certain elements of Jewry," Sept. 2, 1936, meeting of Yassky, Magnes, and Halperin, Had. 2/20/52; "We thought that after," EM to LM, Aug. 15, 1936, *Briefe*. Details of the hospital's construction are drawn from "Hadassah Hospital Medical Centre," *PP*, Oct. 21, 1936; minutes of meeting at EM's office, Jan. 15, 1937, Had. 2/20/52.

Background about the Palace Hotel is drawn from Yildirim Yavuz, "The Influence of Late Ottoman Architecture in the Arab Provinces: The Case of the Palace Hotel in Jerusalem," *Proceedings of the 11th International Congress of Turkish Art, Utrecht, Aug. 23–28, 1999*; Daniella Ohad Smith, "Hotel Design in Zionist Palestine: Modernism, Tourism, and Nationalism, 1917–1948" (Ph.D. diss., Bard Graduate Center, 2006), 196–204; Uri M. Kupferschmidt, *The Supreme Muslim Council: Islam under the British Mandate for Palestine* (Leiden, 1987), 136–37; Baruch Katinka, *From Then till Now* [Heb.] (Jerusalem, 1961), 257–63; Kroyanker, *Jerusalem Architecture . . . Mandate*, 216–17; Kroyanker, "Palace Hotel: Recycling Plan—From Offices to Hotel" [Heb.], Jerusalem Municipality Planning Department, June 1981; "Jerusalem's New Hotel," *PB*, Dec. 22, 1929; "Hotelkeeper a Voluntary Bankrupt," *PB*, March 7, 1932; "Where the Commission Will Sit," *PP*, Nov. 12, 1936. The seventh-century lines inscribed on the hotel's façade are by the Umayyad poet al-Mutawakkil al-Laythi. Details about the King David come from Ohad Smith, "Hotel Design," 185–96; she quotes Vogt, 190. For the description of "the great meeting place," see Sherman, *Mandate Days*, 165. The commission's doings are detailed in the *Palestine Royal Commission Report* and the *Palestine Royal Commission, Minutes of Evidence Heard at Public Sessions* (London, 1937).

The labor strife surrounding the hospital's construction is recounted in "Labour Quarrel on Mount Scopus," *PP*, Dec. 8, 1936; "Further Revisionist Disturbances," *PP*, Dec. 10, 1936; "Police Arrest Three for Attack on Hadassah Jerusalem Offices," *The Chicago Sentinel*, Dec. 17, 1936. Quotes are as follows: "the Socialist . . . groups," League for Jewish National Labor to Mrs. Jacobs, Dec. 9, 1936, and "VIOLENT DEMONSTRATIONS," Yassky to Szold, Dec. 11, 1936, both in Had. 2/21/53.

The progress of the hospital is charted in various documents in Had. 2/20/52: building committee meetings, Sept. 1, 1936, March 1, 1937; the accounts of meetings at EM's office, Feb. 9, 1937, Jan. 15, 1937. Quotes: "Mr. Mendelsohn pointed out," meeting at EM's office, Feb. 9, 1937; "There can be no thought," meeting March 1, 1937. The quarry's incompetence is discussed in minutes of many meetings, including Nov. 9 and 13, 1936; Jan. 15, 1937. In a letter from EM to Yassky, April 3, 1940 (Had. 2/64/104), he mentions "the machine-cut stone" as "a personal invention of mine that saved Hadassah several thousand pounds." Further quotes: "apart from the question of the expense" and "the appearance of a long building . . . Stone," meeting March 1, 1937, Had. 2/20/52. All the quotes about composite stone come from the minutes of this meeting. Rose Jacobs's threat to halt building is mentioned in a memo, April 6, 1937, and EM's insistence on the stone's porousness in minutes from March 1, 1937. The quarry's "permanent difficulties" are described in "Report for the Period of Nov. 16, 1937 to July 31st, 1938," by EM, Had. 2/21/53; "unfaced for some time," May 13, 1938, Had. 2/20/52.

Further quotes: "it seems probable," *Palestine Royal Commission Report*, 372; "peculiarly English proverb," *PRCR*, 394; "There is little moral value," *PRCR*, 375; "dream of a socialist state," EM to LM, May 16, 1937, *Briefe*; "the grand scope," EM to LM, May 25, 1937; "express . . . freedom," EM to LM, Aug. 10, 1937; "deeply moved . . . a mood of reverence," EM/LM 33/3, 289.

ACTUAL AND POSSIBLE

EM's sense of his "special mission" is conveyed in EM to SS, July 27, 1936. For the vision of the university as "a holy place," see David N. Myers, *Re-Inventing the Jewish Past: European Jewish Intellectuals and the Zionist Return to History* (Oxford, 1995), 40; Arthur A. Goren, "Sanctifying Scopus: Locating the Hebrew University on Mount Scopus," in *Jewish History and Jewish Memory: Essays in Honor of Yosef Hayim Yerushalmi*, ed. Elisheva Carlebach, John M. Efron, David N. Myers (Hanover, NH, 1998). The question "What is Judaism?" is quoted in Norman Bentwich, *Judah L. Magnes* (London, 1949), 156. The buildup continues: "already waiting," EM to LM, Dec. 7, 1934; "an entirely new master plan," EM to LM, Dec. 12, 1934; "to profit from the presence of," quoted in "Rosenbloom Building," Feb. 22, 1935, HUA 027; "he . . . is going to give us," Magnes to Warburg, Jan. 11, 1935, HUA 027; "a new epoch," the words are Nahum Sokolow's, quoted in Goren, "Sanctifying Scopus," 331.

Details about the buildings then standing on Mount Scopus are drawn from Diana Dolev, "Architecture and Nationalist Identity: The Case of the Architectural Master Plans for the Hebrew University in Jerusalem (1919–1974) and Their Connections with Nationalist Ideology" (Ph.D. diss., University College London, 2000); Kroyanker, *Jerusalem Architecture: . . . Mandate*, 100–104; *The History of the Hebrew University of Jerusalem, Origins and Beginnings*, ed. Shaul Katz and Michael Heyd [Heb.] (Jerusalem, 2000), 1:163–280; Warhaftig, *They Laid*, 44–47; Bentwich, *Judah L. Magnes*, 159.

Geddes and Mears's plans (and quotes from them) come from Patrick Geddes, "The Proposed Hebrew University of Jerusalem: A Preliminary Report by Professor P. Geddes assisted by Captain Frank C. Mears," CZA L12\75. For the conversation surrounding these plans, see: "something more than . . . a spacious City," Mears to Eder, Oct. 15, 1924, CZA L12\39; "there has not been a single person," quoted in Dolev, "Architecture and Nationalist Identity," 152; "the intellectual masterpiece," Lewis Mumford, "The Hebrew University: The Vision of the Architect," *Menorah Journal* 8, no. 1 (Feb. 1922); "I have the impression," quoted in Diana Dolev and Haim Gordon, "The Architectural Challenge of a Jewish Studies House at the Hebrew University: A Lost Opportunity," *Shofar* 11, no. 1 (Fall 1992), 2; "unscrupulously 'chunked,'" from a 1930 letter to Mumford, quoted in Dolev, "Architecture and Nationalist Identity," 163. Dolev quotes Geddes as writing a letter to Lewis Mumford in 1925: "There is an active endeavor among various important Zionists to have separate competitions . . . among *Jewish* architects—and thus get rid of me—and Mears too," "Architecture and Nationalist Identity," 155.

Background to EM's plans for the campus comes from Heinze-Mühleib, *Bauten,* 179–80; Heinze-Greenberg, "Architecture in Palestine," 220–23; Dolev, "Architecture and Nationalist Identity," 173–90. Quotes: "I am . . . bewitched," EM to LM, Jan. 3, 1935; "the cooling west winds . . . 'Look,'" EM, "Building on Mount Scopus," *PP,* May 9, 1939.

The Rosenbloom gift is outlined in "$500,000 Gift for Hebrew University Announced by Mrs. Sol Rosenbloom," *Jewish Daily Bulletin,* Feb. 18, 1926. In the end (according to the archives of the Hebrew University), the actual amount was closer to $100,000. The dispute surrounding the building is described in Dolev, "Architecture and Nationalist Identity," 167–72. Details of the conflict are as follows: "stands at the head of a school," Dec. 20, 1934, meeting of the building committee, Had. 2/20/52; "a long narrow one story," Feb. 22, 1935, "Rosenbloom Building," HUA 027 (all the following quotes are from the same HUA file); "unsatisfactory . . . as the Library building," Feb. 22, 1935; "We are very much dissatisfied," Charles Rosenbloom to Magnes, May 14, 1935; "a splendid, practical, and beautiful conception," Magnes to S. Ginzberg, Aug. 22, 1935; "completely opposed," Mack to Weizmann, June 30, 1936. SS's letter to Celia Rosenbloom is dated Aug. 26, 1936, and to Weiss, Oct. 20, 1936; EM's furious response is written to SS, July 27, 1936 (in the *Letters*).

For EM's turn to the English authorities and Wauchope's patronage, see: "called in the Romans . . . secret agreement . . . integrated town planning," EM to LM, July 30, 1936; "in view of the unique site . . . to form one harmonious," "Extract of Minutes of the Last Meeting of the Jerusalem Town Planning Commission," Aug. 19, 1936, SA 042/61; "he would not like to lose me," EM to LM, Aug. 7, 1936; "I imagine he stands . . . In the National Homeland," Wauchope to Parkinson, March 11, 1936, CO 733/307/7; "he said the National Home," EM to LM, Aug. 7, 1936; "it would be one of the few joys . . . one of the most friendly," EM to LM, Aug. 13, 1936. Further quotes: "must carry the blame," EM to SS, July 27, 1936; "the layout and architecture," EM, "Building on Mount Scopus." Alterman's poem is "The Orient's Enchantments," which first appeared in *Haaretz,* Oct. 20, 1936, reprinted in *Moments* [Heb.] (Tel Aviv, 1975), vol. 1.

Progress on the hospital is evident from a photo album compiled by Arie Gorodetsky, a junior engineer on the project; this chronicles the building of the whole medical center and shows a picture labeled "Medical School. The first day of work. May 24, 1937." Lack of progress on the campus is evident from the following: "sheer fancy," "Notes on the Proposed Agreement with Mr. Mendelsohn," May 6, 1938, HUA 027 (all HUA items from this file); "a singularly unsuccessful," Magnes to SS, May 8, 1938; "absolutely opposed," Magnes to "the Administrator," Feb. 2, 1938; "strikes ever so many . . . has been sound . . . I do not think," Magnes to SS, May 8, 1938; "bomb of a very . . . we must envisage," Yassky to Szold, Oct. 14, 1938, Had. 2/21/53. EM describes to LM his gloom about political events in a letter dated Sept. 29, 1938, *Briefe.*

CITY OF REFUGEES

The chapter's title comes from George Seferis's poem "Stratis Thalassinos at the Dead Sea," written in 1942 and translated by Roderick Beaton in *A Levant Journal* (Jerusalem, 2007): "Jerusalem, unruled city, city adrift, / Jerusalem, city of refugees."

The account of Jerusalem, London, and the Mendelsohns' place in both during this period is drawn largely from LM, "My Life"; EM/LM 31/7; EM/LM 33/4. Quotes: "Instead of praying," EM to LM, Oct. 6, 1938. The second part of the same letter is untranslated in the English letters; see *Briefe*, 112. "Rehavia is full," EM to LM, May 2, 1938, *Briefe*; "You need . . . to choose," Blumenfeld to EM, Feb. 8, 1939, quoted in *Bauten*, 53; "every effort," Yassky to EM, quoted in Herbert and Richter, *Through a Clouded Glass*, 128. Their British naturalization certificates were issued August 20, 1938, Home Office 334/150/12373. On EM's election by RIBA see Herbert and Richter, *Through a Clouded Glass*, 128.

Quotes about the White Paper are as follows: "within ten years," from *The Israel-Arab Reader: A Documentary History of the Middle East Conflict*, ed. Walter Laqueur and Barry Rubin (NY, 1984), 46; "Black Paper," "Day of Visitation," *PP*, May 18, 1939; "liquidation of the National Home," "Jews' Day of Protest Ends with Rioting in Jerusalem," *PP*, May 18, 1939.

LM describes Else Lasker-Schüler in EM/LM 33/4, 380–81. Hans W. Cohn quotes Benn in *Else Lasker-Schüler, The Broken World* (Cambridge, 1974), 29. Other quotes about and by the poet: "the whole of her seemed," Heinz Politzer, "The Blue Piano of Else Lasker-Schueler," *Commentary* 9 (Jan.–June 1950); "to the building of Palestine," quoted in the introduction to Lasker-Schüler, *Hebrew Ballads and Other Poems*, trans. Audri Durschlag and Jeanette Litman-Demeestère (Philadelphia, 1980), xix; "a really bewildering figure," Scholem to Benjamin, April 11, 1934, *Correspondence*; "a ruin, more haunted," Scholem to Benjamin, April 19, 1934, *Correspondence*.

For the poet's vision of Middle East peace, see: "Arab children play," Else Lasker-Schüler, *Das Hebraerland, Werke und Briefe*, ed. Karl Jürgen Skrodzki and Itta Shedletzky (Frankfurt am Main, 2002), 5:107; "Every guest who enters," Durschlag and Litman-Demeestère, *Hebrew Ballads*, 51, translation adjusted. For others' views of her take on the East: "a terrifying muddle," Politzer, "The Blue Piano," 336; "wonderful fairy city . . . a pity," "Fairy Lands," *PP*, Jan. 26, 1940; "She lived entirely," EM/LM 31/7, 22. And for more of her own (conflicted) vision: "throw away all the books . . . we'll reconcile," Lasker-Schüler to SS, July 27, 1939, *Briefe, Werke und Briefe*, 10:236; "solve the Arab-Jewish problem," Schalom Ben-Chorin, quoted in Durschlag and Litman-Demeestère, *Hebrew Ballads*, xx; "the healing bath . . . God's chosen bride," Durschlag and Litman-Demeestère, *Hebrew Ballads*, 51; "I can no longer maintain," quoted in Betty Falkenberg, *Else Lasker-Schüler: A Life* (Jefferson, NC, 2003), 151; "The Dimdumim begin," Lasker-Schüler to SS, Dec. 6, 1939, *Briefe*, 10:266.

Further descriptions of Lasker-Schüler include Yehuda Amichai's account of having laughed at her as a boy, "Preface," Durschlag and Litman-Demeestère, *Hebrew Ballads*, ix. In *Else Lasker-Schüler—A Poet Who Paints* (Haifa, 2006) Irit Salmon quotes the artist Yigal Tumarkin as saying she looked like "a witch with a weird hat talking to birds." Her likeness to a bird is emphasized by others, including Maron Sima, quoted in the same catalog, 12. Politzer describes her as a "solitary, exotic night bird," "The Blue Piano," 336.

The account of her reading is drawn from EM/LM 33/4, 342; Lasker-Schüler to Fredy Berlowitz, June 26, 1939, *Briefe*, 10:230; "Social and Personal," *PP*, June 27, 1939. Further information on the poet in this context appears in Ita Heinze-Greenberg's lecture, "Erich Mendelsohn, Salman Schocken und Else Lasker-Schüler in Jerusalem," delivered at a conference in Schocken's honor in Chemnitz, Germany, October 9, 2013. For a description of the rite-like nature of the event at the Schocken Library, see also Schalom Ben-Chorin in *Jüdische Welt-Rundschau*, July 7, 1939.

PALESTINE AND THE WORLD OF TOMORROW

The Haifa hospital is described in Heinze-Greenberg, "Architecture in Palestine," 228–35, and Gilbert and Sosnovsky, *Bauhaus on the Carmel*, 152–55. Its building is called "A Record of Speed," in the *PP*, Dec. 25, 1938. EM says it "follows the sweep" in "My Own Contribution." The report "as, under present circumstances" is "Journalists on Hadassah Medical Centre Tour," *PP*, May 4, 1939.

The various parties, concerts, and explosions are recounted in the following *PP* stories: "Hadassah University Centre Reception," May 16, 1939; "Orchestra's Future," July 7, 1939; "Scherchen Conducts," May 11, 1939; "Youth, Enthusiasm and Fire," May 11, 1939; "Bombs and Fire at Immigration Offices," May 18, 1939; "Let There Be Light," May 30, 1939; "Another Jewish Protest in Jerusalem," May 22, 1939; "Five Thousand Jewish Women Demonstrate in Jerusalem," May 23, 1939; "Eighteen Injured by Bombs in Jerusalem Cinema House," May 30, 1939; "Wreckage at the Rex," June 2, 1939; "Ban on Jerusalem Buses to Be Lifted on Sunday," June 2, 1939; "Rachel Ohev-Ami Sentenced to Life Imprisonment," June 13, 1939; "Five Injured Main Hall Damaged," June 10, 1939. The "wanton sabotage and tragic loss" are described in "Armourer Killed by Third Bomb in G.P.O.," June 12, 1939. See also "Twenty-five Hurt in Palestine Riot," *NYT*, May 18, 1939; "12 Die as Palestine Terror Rages; Bomb Kills 5 Arabs in Jerusalem," *NYT*, June 3, 1939.

For descriptions of the bank building, see Gail Hoffman, "Jerusalem's Newest Landmark," *PP*, June 16, 1939; EM, "The Anglo-Palestine Bank," *PP*, June 17, 1939. Details of the post office come from Gail Hoffman, "The New G.P.O. Opens Its Doors," *PP*, June 17, 1938. EM's letter to AH is dated Jan. 10, 1938, AH archive, IAA. Edward Keith-Roach describes MacMichael's hobbies in *Pasha of Jerusalem: Memoirs of a District Commissioner Under the British Mandate* (London, 1994), 195. SS's complaint is registered by Shmuel Hugo Bergmann in his *Tagebücher & Briefe*, ed. Miriam Sambursky (Königstein, 1985), 1:540. "We are still in the midst," is EM to Arnold Whittick, quoted in Whittick, *EM*, 130.

"Palestine and the World of Tomorrow" appears in EM/LM 9/7 and is reprinted in *Erich Mendelsohn in Palestine* and Heinze-Mühleib, *Bauten*. EM's letter to Mumford, April 12, 1939, is quoted in Heinze-Greenberg, "Architecture in Palestine," 241. For details of EM's dispute with Hadassah, see EM to Yassky, April 3, 1940; Yassky's letter to Halprin, April 28, 1940; Halprin to EM, Sept. 16, 1941; EM to Halprin, Oct. 2, 1941, all in Had. 2/64/104. Other quotes: "collection of unrealized projects," EM is quoted in a letter to SS from Ch. Raphael of the Friends of the Hebrew University, July 20, 1938, and "SORRY HEAR," Weizmann to SS, Feb. 6, 1941, both in SA 042/6; "He made himself very unpopular . . . It seemed clear," EM/LM 33/4, 345–46; "It is up to you," Yassky to EM, and "I left Palestine," Mendelsohn to Yassky, quoted in Gilbert Herbert, *EM in Palestine*, 15.

On Lasker-Schüler's death, see "Poetess Buried on Mount of Olives," *PP*, Jan. 23, 1945. "If I had the chance," EM to Oskar Beyer, March 27, 1953, *Letters*, 180. This translation comes from Bruno Zevi, *EM* (1999), 201. EM's ashes were scattered in "an unrecorded place" according to Whittick, *EM*, 177.

BEAUTIFUL THINGS ARE DIFFICULT, 1923

Unless otherwise noted, all quotations from Harrison's letters come from his own typed and bound "Some Letters of Mine," in his personal archive, held at the Israel Antiquities Authority Archive, Jerusalem.

IN THE GARDEN

For background on Harrison, I've relied on the comprehensive and very thoughtful dissertation by Ron Fuchs, "Austen St. Barbe Harrison: A British Architect in the Holy Land" [Heb.] (D.Sc. thesis, the Technion, 1992). This appears in truncated form, in English, as Fuchs and Gilbert Herbert, "Representing Mandatory Palestine: Austen St. Barbe Harrison and the Representational Building of the British Mandate in Palestine, 1922–37," *Architectural History* 43 (2000). Further context came from an interview (Feb. 5, 2013) and multiple e-mails exchanged with Yani Papadimos, Harrison's adopted grandson; Julie Williams's written recollections of the architect (from 1961 to 1973); and an ongoing conversation with IAA archivist Silvia Krapiwko.

Descriptions of the Abu Tor house are drawn from Fuchs, "Austen St. Barbe Harrison"; Helena Harrison's Journal of a Visit to Palestine, GB165-0136, MECA, entry dated March 18, 1925; AH to his mother, Jan. 22, 1941; AH to Catherine Harrison (n.d.), 1923; AH also describes the house in a letter to Freya Stark, April 12, 1949, FS 14/8. The quote "most grudgingly" is AH to Ena Harrison, Oct. 21, 1923. For details of AH's friendship with Freya Stark, see Freya Stark, *Letters*, vols. 4 and 5, ed. Lucy Moorehead (Salisbury, 1977). See also AH's letters to Stark, FS 14/8. AH's own descriptions of his social life are: "rather an Ermetical," AH to Lilian Bomberg, Oct. 16, 1960, TGDB 873/3/3; "I am really a sociable," AH to Markus Reiner, Aug. 12, 1947. LM describes "a very sensitive artist . . . He did not like," in EM/LM 33/3, 294–95. Durrell's descriptions all come from *Bitter Lemons* (London, 1957), 98–101. For more on the friendship between AH and Durrell, see "Letters of Lawrence Durrell to Austen Harrison," ed. David Roessel, *Deus Loci* 3 (1994), and Durrell, *Spirit of Place: Letters and Essays on Travel* (London, 1969). AH's description of "a particular kind of rubble" appears in "Government House Plans," Aug. 24, 1927, CO 733/145/1A.

Details of AH's pre-Palestine doings come from his letters; his CV (CO 733/145/1A); a handwritten "Candidate's Separate Statement" submitted to RIBA, July 1927 (AH archive, IAA); Samuel's telegram is dated Dec. 9, 1921, CO 733/8. Quotes about the Nuffield commission appear in Howard Colvin, *Unbuilt Oxford* (New Haven, 1983), 174. Quotes from AH's letters are as follows: "I admire English people," AH to Markus Reiner, Aug. 23, 1948; "How can I be happy," AH to his mother, Jan. 13, 1942; "the only job . . . whether I would not have been," AH to his mother, Dec. 18, 1916; "abject desolation . . . Everywhere were," AH to his father, Sept. 15, 1917; "the awful silence," AH to his father, Dec. 19, 1919; "among the massive walls," AH to his father, Sept. 28, 1919; "Curiously enough," AH to his father, Dec. 19, 1919; "crawl[ing] up and down," AH to his mother, Oct. (n.d.), 1919; "never . . . in all my life been so consciously," AH to his father, Sept. 28, 1919; "irregularities of Byzantine construction," AH to his father, Oct. 19, 1919; "a wonder," AH to his father, Jan. 2, 1920. He describes the shattered vases and gold leaf in a letter to his father, Nov. 29, 1919, and "calcined and wrecked" mosaics to his father, Nov. (n.d.), 1919; AH refers to the "destroyed cities" in a letter to his mother, Feb. 25, 1921, and says he wants to find further work in the East in a letter to his mother, (n.d.), 1920. "I had become a little tired," AH to his father, Nov. 11, 1920.

Fuchs and Herbert characterize him as "almost the sole author," "Representing," 287. Other Israeli architectural historians, including David Kroyanker and Ada Karmi-Melamede, refer to him in similar terms. AH's description of "descend[ing] the stepped suk," comes from "The Dome of the Rock," *The Sphinx*, 1946, in a "Press Cuttings" notebook in his archive. His first surviving letter written in Jerusalem is dated July 21, 1922.

FALLEN WALLS

The various statements about AH's capability are all reiterations of earlier assessments, copied into his file, Sept. 1928, CO 733/145/1A. The different jobs dangled before him are recounted in AH to his father, June 18, and Dec. 12, 1925. He describes the "vague rumours" and his supervisor's irritating manner to Ena, Oct. 21, 1923. Further quotes: "pure humbug . . . A general feeling of uncertainty," AH to his father, (n.d.), 1923; "This will bring," AH to Ena, Oct. 21, 1923; "little overawed," AH to his father, Nov. 2, 1923; "Herculean," AH to his father, (n.d.), 1923; "shows patches of damp," AH to his father, Nov. 2, 1923. AH's account of the pre-Jebusite wall, school, and police station come from AH to his mother, Oct. 22, 1924; AH to his father, Dec. (n.d.), 1925. He describes it as "hack work," AH to his mother, Oct. 20, 1926.

Background about the Palestine Pavilion and British Empire Exhibition come from *Palestine Pavilion Handbook and Tourist Guide* (London, 1924); *The British Empire Exhibition, 1924, Official Guide* (London); "A Festival of Empire: Impressions at Wembley" and "At the Stadium: Grand Spectacle in the Amphitheatre," both in *The Times*, April 24, 1924; Nicholas E. Roberts, "Palestine on Display: The Palestine Pavilion at the British Empire Exhibition of 1924," *Arab Studies Journal* 15, no. 1 (2007); Fuchs, "Austen St. Barbe Harrison," 80–85; the minutes of committee meetings, CZA S25\10980 and 10981. AH's own assessment of the pavilion are: "ruined by a committee . . . two terminal," AH to Ena, Oct. 21, 1923; "so modified it," AH to his father, Nov. 2, 1923. Virginia Woolf's description comes from her essay "Thunder at Wembley," *Selected Essays* (NY, 2008).

AH's account of his work in this period derives from letters: "I don't relish," AH to his father, Nov. 26, 1925; "Mr. Harrison's austerity," AH to Ena, Aug. 27, 1926; "reason to believe is horrid," AH to his mother, Oct. 20, 1927. The "schedule of accommodations" for the Amman house appears in Fuchs and Herbert, "Representing," 289. AH's opinion that "the house must be as habitable" is from a CO file, quoted in Fuchs and Herbert, "Representing," 290. Fuchs and Herbert suggest AH took inspiration from the kiosk at Topkapi Palace in "Representing," 291, and Fuchs, "Austen St. Barbe Harrison," 87. Architectural details of the Çinili Kiosk come from Gülru Necipoğlu, *Architecture, Ceremonial, and Power: The Topkapi Palace in the Fifteenth and Sixteenth Centuries* (Cambridge, MA, 1991), 210–18. AH's account of the progress on the residence and the wife of the representative's response is from AH to his mother, Jan. 27, 1927, and AH to his mother, July 7, 1927 (apparently misdated, since he mentions the earthquake that took place a week later).

His explorations of the country are recounted in AH to David Bomberg, July 11, 1932, TGDB 878/2/2; AH to his mother, Oct. 16, 1931; to his father, Nov. 2, 1923; to his father, Saturday (?) 22, 1923; to his mother July 17, 1923; Helena Harrison, Journal. Quotes: "A clever modest fellow," AH to his father, March 8, 1926; "a glorious ten days . . . after a motor run," to his mother, July 24, 1925; "graves of nomads . . . a wide-mouthed well," to his mother, Oct. 26, 1926.

Biographical information about David Bomberg is drawn from Richard Cork, *David Bomberg* (New Haven, 1987); Richard Cork, *David Bomberg* (London, 1988); *David Bomberg in Palestine, 1923–1927* (Jerusalem, 1983); Alice Mayes, "The Young Bomberg," TGDB 7312; William Lipke, *David Bomberg: A Critical Study of His Life and Work* (London, 1967). Jonathan Wilson's novel *A Palestine Affair* (NY, 2003) is an intriguing fictionalized version of Bomberg's Jerusalem years. AH describes learning "certainly much more than from anyone else" to Lilian Bomberg, Oct. 16, 1960, TGDB 873/3/3. His account of mistaking the painter for a chimney comes from the same letter. Alice Mayes (Bomberg's first wife) also writes that Harrison "saw David painting by moonlight one night and could not believe his eyes at first," Mayes, "The Young Bomberg," 45. AH says he descends from "undistinguished country gentry" in a file marked "Ancestors," AH papers, IAA; he describes his lessons and servant in a letter to his sister Catherine, (n.d.), 1923. The account of the Bombergs' fighting comes from Helena Harrison's journal. "Pugnacious is too mild" are the words of Joseph Leftwich, quoted in Cork, *David Bomberg* (1987), 19.

Muirhead Bone's attempts to help Bomberg are detailed in "Memorandum on the Suggested Employment of an Artist by the Zionist Organisation in Palestine," TGDB 8/5/5. Alice writes that "David got no inspiration" in "The Young Bomberg"; the term "heroic pictures" is Bomberg's own, from untitled notes for a talk, "Palestine, as Seen through the Eyes of an Artist," TGDB 878/4/7. AH dubs DB "the most intense painter" in Lipke, *David Bomberg*, 57. Bomberg's call for "a *Sense of Form*" is quoted in Cork, *David Bomberg* (1987), 78. AH writes to Lilian Bomberg that "We talked of everything," Oct. 16, 1960, TGDB 873/3/3. Bomberg insists that he learned from AH when he tells AH that a certain set of paintings were the result of the architect "goading [him] on," AH to DB, July 14, 1944, TGDB 878/2/2. Bomberg's long days and nights spent in Harrison's garden are described in Bomberg's letters to Alice, Oct. 21, Nov. 12, and Dec. 23, 1926, TGDB 878/1/1.

AH describes DB's paintings as "void of propaganda value" to Lilian Bomberg, Oct. 16, 1960, TGDB 873/3/3. Further quotes: "as I expect I shall find it less easy," AH to his mother, July 24, 1925; "hates the house," AH to his father, Jan. 18, 1926; "no personal policy," quoted in Bernard Wasserstein, *The British in Palestine: The Mandatory Government and the Arab-Jewish Conflict, 1917–1929* (London, 1978), 151; "There is no political situation," Horace B. Samuel, *Unholy Memories of the Holy Land* (London, 1930), 91; "Everything is propaganda," AH to his father, June 18, 1925; "that unappreciated genius," AH to his mother, Oct. 7, 1935; "everything is now settled," AH to his mother, Oct. 20, 1926; "I have always heard," handwritten note in file CO 733/129/8, dated Nov. 4, 1926; "To cap it all . . . important buildings," AH to his mother, Oct. 20, 1926.

TECTONICS

Descriptions of the quake are as follows: "a tremendous noise," AH to his mother, July 13, 1927; "a heavy rumble," Keith-Roach, *Pasha*, 104; "was awakened by the door," Mayes, "The Young Bomberg," 60. Details of the devastation come from D. H. Kallner-Amiran, "A Revised Earthquake-Catalogue of Palestine," *Israel Exploration Journal* 1, no. 4 (1950–1951); "Quake Caused Avalanche of Melons," AP, July 13, 1927; "$1,250,000 Damage in Palestine Quake," *NYT*, July 14, 1927. Quotes as follows: "the appearance of having passed," "Serious Damage in Jerusalem," Jewish Telegraphic Agency, July 12, 1927; "I suppose in the world's view," AH to James H. Breasted,

July 25, 1927, Government of Palestine, 1927, OI; "and then he got the shock," Mayes, "The Young Bomberg," 60; "The earthquake has," AH to his mother, July 7, 1927 (misdated?); "The rabbis of Jerusalem," "Palestine Quake Toll Set at 670 Dead," *SF Chronicle*, July 15, 1927; "destroying a picture," "Stone Destroys Ex-Kaiser's Picture," AP, July 14, 1927; "huge stone . . . burst," "Palestine Portents," *Time*, July 25, 1927; "a German Institution," notes dated June 29, 1926, in CO 733/129/8.

Details of the plans for Government House are: "almost no precedent," AH to his mother, July 7, 1927 (misdated?); "it would be well worth while," notes dated Sept. 19, 1928, in CO 733/145/1A; "suited to its environment . . . undesirable . . . sensible use . . . avoid flouting," AH to Pudsey, Sept. 21, 1926, quoted in Fuchs and Herbert, "Representing," 287–88. Fuchs and Herbert say he designed five different versions of the building, of which the first two remain obscure though the initial plan may date to Samuel's time in office. Further quotes: "financial and religious considerations," memorandum from Plumer, April 19, 1926, CO 733/129/8; "If the H.C.'s house is too large," note by A. J. Harding, June 1, 1927, CO 733/137/12; "conceived on monumental," HM Office of Works to Harding, May 16, 1927, and "no reflection," Shuckburgh to Symes, June 15, 1927, both in CO 733/137/12; "rotten in every respect," AH to his mother, July 3, 1927; "I believe based on a misunderstanding," "Director of Public Works, Subject: Government House Plans," Aug. 24, 1927, CO 733/145/1A. For details on the quarry and sewage drain, see extensive correspondence in CO 733/137/12; "after mature consideration," "Report," (n.d.), CO 733/137/12.

The anecdote about "*mizzi Harrison*" appears in Fuchs and Herbert, "Representing," 331. Though this was at first a nickname, it seems to have quickly become the official way of referring to this sort of stone: see A. Arnstein, "Palestine Building Stones," *Palestine & Middle East Economic Magazine* 7–8 (1933), in which the author lists Mizzi Ahmer, Mizzi Heloueh, Mizzi Yehudi, Mizzi Harrison, and other stones, without comment. AH's "a house is not like a factory" is quoted in Fuchs and Herbert, "Representing," 305; the "radical defects" are mentioned in Fuchs and Herbert, "Representing," 293. AH's quotes about his vision of the furniture and décor come from "Notes by the Architect on the Choice of Furniture for the Principal Rooms of the New Government House in Jerusalem," CO 733/194/1. Chancellor's sense that "there is reason to think" is quoted in Wasserstein, *The British in Palestine*, 156.

Background about the events of 1929 comes from Wasserstein, *The British in Palestine*, 155–59, 217–35; Sherman, *Mandate Days*, 77–82; Hillel Cohen, *Tarpat: Year Zero in the Jewish-Arab Conflict* [Heb.] (Jerusalem, 2013). Humphrey Bowman is quoted in Sherman, *Mandate Days*, 82; "a seismic effect," Wasserstein, *The British*, 156. "A Crusaders' Castle of To-Day," by Christopher Hussey, appears in *Country Life*, Oct. 31, 1931; the article that describes the laborers working "in harmony on this building" is "The New Jerusalem Government House," *Architectural Review* 70 (Oct. 1931), and the piece that says "The solid building stands out" is "Palestine's New Government House," *The Near East and India*, April 9, 1931.

ABOVE, BELOW

The basic history of the museum is recounted in Fawzi Ibrahim, *West Meets East: The Story of the Rockefeller Museum* (Jerusalem, 2006). AH describes "a real secret" in a letter to his mother, Jan. 27, 1927, and warns it's "highly confidential" in another, July 7, 1927 (misdated?). He tells Markus Reiner "How heartily sick I am," March 10, 1947.

Background about the Breasted-Rockefeller dealings comes from Charles Breasted, *Pioneer to the Past* (Chicago, 2009), 376–402; Jeffrey Abt, "Toward a Historian's Laboratory: The Breasted-Rockefeller Museum Projects in Egypt, Palestine, and America," *Journal of the American Research Center in Egypt* 33 (1996), and Abt, *American Egyptologist: The Life of James Henry Breasted and the Creation of His Oriental Institute* (Chicago, 2011), 317–44; "The past of Palestine," is described in the draft of a letter from Rockefeller to Plumer, July 27, 1927, RAC 2/E/25/263. The conditions at the previous Palestine museum are recounted in Breasted, *Pioneer*, 392, and J. H. Iliffe, "The Palestine Archaeological Museum, Jerusalem," *The Museums Journal* 38, no. 1 (April 1938). Quotes are as follows: "historical laboratory," Abt, "Toward a Historian's Laboratory," 174; "Origin and Development of Civilization," quoted in Abt, *American Egyptologist*, 228–29. Breasted uses the term "Fertile Crescent" and describes the "earliest home of men" in *Ancient Times: A History of the Early World* (Boston, 1916).

Details of the plans for (and quotes about) the Egyptian museum come from the glossy booklet "The New Museum and Research Institute at Cairo," RAC 2/6/25/258A. Quotes: "absolutely unacceptable," Breasted, *Pioneer*, 396; "human development," "The New Museum and Research Institute," 26; "a vain and self-conscious . . . to intoxicate . . . give him such a pipe-dream," Breasted to George Ellery Hale, July 20, 1925, quoted in Abt, "Toward a Historian's Laboratory," 186.

Early plans for the Palestine museum appear in the copious correspondence on the subject in OI, Government of Palestine, 1926, 1927 (all OI files cited are labeled "Government of Palestine"), RAC 2/E/25/263 and IAA ATQ 202, first jacket. Quotes: "fundamental matters of circulation," Breasted to Raymond Fosdick, July 27, 1927, RAC 2/E/25/263; "the Romanesque such as one finds," AH to Breasted, April 26, 1927, OI, 1927; "how pleased I am," AH to Breasted, July 25, 1927, OI, 1927; "I am writing this letter, in order that you," AH to Breasted, Sept. 16, 1927, OI, 1927. The terms of the agreement with the Palestine government are detailed in a letter from Breasted to Plumer, Aug. 9, 1927, OI, 1927; see also Abt, *American Egyptologist*, 333, quoting Fosdick: "We are treating the Palestine Government far more liberally than we offered to treat the Egyptian Government." The secret and confidential letter is Breasted to Plumer, Aug. 9, 1927, OI, 1927, and the gleeful note is written by Fosdick to Rockefeller, Jan. 18, 1927, quoted in Abt, "Toward a Historian's Laboratory," 189. Breasted declares to AH that "The man who has the courage," Oct. 5, 1927, OI, 1927.

AH describes the "howl and suggestions . . . despite the clause . . . Without any prejudice" in a letter to his mother, Nov. 16, 1927. Richmond says he "happily gained the confidence" in a handwritten note, "Proposed Palestine Museum," n.d., IAA ATQ 202, first jacket. AH recounts "a rather vicious campaign . . . They say I was sent," AH to his mother, June 1928, labeled "(before 24th)." Richmond's complaint about the tower appears in a letter to Breasted, Jan. 21, 1928, OI, 1928. Background on the YMCA comes from Kroyanker, *Jerusalem Architecture . . . Mandate*, 228–32, and Inbal Ben-Asher Gitler, "Reconstructing Religions: Jewish Place and Space in the Jerusalem YMCA Building, 1919–1933," *Zeitschrift für Religions und Geistesgeschichte* 60, no. 1 (2008). Further quotes: "fighting the local committee . . . They don't like," AH to his mother, Feb. 5, 1928; "the self consistency," Breasted to ETR, Jan. 28, 1928, OI, 1928; "all the pleasant things," AH to Breasted, Feb. 9, 1928, OI, 1928.

The history of Qasr ash-Sheikh comes from A. S. Khalidi's letter dated June 1, 1942,

IAA ATQ 18/203; the same file holds "Endowment Deed of Karm ash-Sheikh" (see also IAA SRF 104). The pine's age and Rockefeller's "special request" are described by Iliffe in "The Palestine Archaeological Museum," 3. In an Aug. 7, 1926, letter from John Garstang to Breasted, he describes the site and its "ancient Crusader building which can be adapted as a special feature," OI, 1926. Breasted writes to AH, July 6, 1927, and calls it a Crusader Castle, OI, 1927. AH writes to Breasted, "I do feel that it would be easy" on Sept. 16, 1927, OI, 1927. Correspondence about the graves appears in ATQ 1/202 toward the end of June 1928 and AH's letter to Breasted, July 4, 1928, OI, 1928. Clermont-Ganneau's mention of the graves appears in "Letters from M. Clermont-Ganneau," *PEF Quarterly Statement*, April 1874, 95–96, and they're mentioned, for instance, in P.L.O. Guy to Breasted, April 27, 1927, IAA ATQ 1/202. Quotes: "found a grave," AH to ETR, June 29, 1929, IAA ATQ 1/202; "skulls and many human bones," unsigned, undated typed report, Dept. of Antiquities, IAA SRF 104; "pending further investigations," AH to ETR, July 30, 1928, IAA ATQ 1/202; "the foundations of the Museum," AH to his mother, Dec. 5, 1929.

RELATIVE RELICS

The wording of the inscription is found in "Note on the Proposed Inscription for a Foundation Stone for the New Museum" from IAA ATQ 202, first jacket, together with the "Order of Procedure at Laying of Foundation Stone of the Palestine Archaeological Museum." Mention of the lead box filled with "Palestine coins" comes from a caption on the back of one of the photos in the OI file "Palestine: Jerusalem— Rockefeller Museum." (Although I've found no correspondence about this—and the stone is now buried—it seems Eric Gill may have played a role in carving the inscription, since his papers at the Clark contain a rough sketch of the same, see CEG 320.) Rockefeller's telegram is dated June 5, 1930, RAC 2/E/25/263. The "List of invitations issued by Department of Antiquities for the laying of the Foundation Stone for the New Museum," surfaces in IAA ATQ 202, first jacket, along with "Remarks of the High Commissioner at Laying of the Foundation Stone of the Archaeological Museum" (also in OI, 1930).

AH describes the museum as "the one work in Palestine" to his mother, Jan. 1, 1938. For an excellent description of the building and its "reinterpretation of the townscape of Jerusalem," see Fuchs and Herbert, "Representing," 311–24; see also Fuchs and Herbert, "A Colonial Portrait of Jerusalem," 97. For details of the delays and Rockefeller's extensions of his grant, see various correspondence in RAC 2/E/25/263 and 269, and ATQ 202, first jacket. Quotes: "in no way whatever to blame," "File— Jerusalem Museum (Conversation with Dr. Breasted) From: Mr. Packard," Sept. 19, 1932, RAC 2/E/25/263; "outbreak . . . wherein the Arabs," Breasted to Packard, May 4, 1933, RAC 2/E/26/269. AH's wariness about Wauchope is detailed in a letter to his mother, Oct 16, 1931. The description of the high commissioner as Dr. Jekyll and Mr. Hyde is from Keith-Roach, *Pasha*, 132–33.

The problems with the stone supply and the museum's progress are described in "Palestine Archaeological Museum: Report on Progress—June 30, 1932," RAC 2/E/26/269. (Breasted's quotes come from the same file, as do the reports on the finishing trades and Syrian walnut.) The account of "the basic fear in the Arab mind" is in Joseph M. Levy, "Arabs Riot Again; Unrest Spreads," *NYT*, Oct. 29, 1933. AH's letter to his mother, "there is no cause at all," is dated Nov. 16, 1933. AH writes to Ena:

"as usual, he gives me credit," Sept. 3, 1935. Details about the contractors and furnishing come from Kroyanker, *Jerusalem Architecture . . . Mandate*, 76–77; "The Palestine Archaeological Museum, Jerusalem," *The Architect & Building News*, Sept. 6, 1935; Iliffe, "The Palestine Archaeological Museum." *The Hippias Major* quote is 285d, *Plato in Twelve Volumes*, vol. 9, trans. W.K.M. Lamb (London, 1925).

Background about Gill is drawn from *Eric Gill, Autobiography* (London, 1992), Fiona MacCarthy, *Eric Gill: A Lover's Quest for Art and God* (NY, 1989), Malcolm Yorke, *Eric Gill: Man of Flesh and Spirit* (London, 1981). A note at the start of *From the Palestine Diary of Eric Gill* (London, 1949) mentions "the various civilizations." The list of "ancient nations" is included in Gill's letter to Rev. John O'Connor, Oct. 1, 1933 (this seems to be misdated, since Gill and AH were corresponding about the carvings in early Oct. 1934), *Letters of Eric Gill*, ed. Walter Shewring (London, 1947). Gill's notion that "art embraces all making" appears in his introduction to O'Connor's translation of Jacques Maritain's *The Philosophy of Art* (Ditchling, UK, 1923). Jones's comments on Gill are drawn from an interview, "Recollections of Eric Gill," April 9, 1961, transcript in CEG, box 5, folder 2.

Gill's consultation with Horsfield and use of Hoptonwood stone are mentioned in Judith Collins, *Eric Gill: The Sculpture* (London, 1998), 187. Gill writes AH, "I hope . . . you won't think," Feb. 2, 1934, Beinecke, Gen mss 1263. All the captions appear on the sketches that are held at the Clark, CEG 320–65. Gill's descriptions derive from the following letters to his wife (these appear in edited form in *From the Palestine Diary of Eric Gill*. The originals are in CEG, box 106): "Suffice it to say . . . Clean shaven," April 5, 1934; "We've started the job," March 24, 1934; "all is well," March 29, 1934; "a lot of bother," April 5, 1934; "Up to the present," started April 22, 1934 (he writes this letter over several days); "a half circle representing MAN," April 8, 1934. Gill writes to AH, "I am . . . v. miserable," on Aug. 17, 1934, Beinecke, Gen mss 1263. Gill's glowing descriptions of Jerusalem are all from his *Autobiography*, 251–56, while his confession to his wife that it is "impossible to convey Jerusalem" is from a letter April 19 (?), 1934. He tells her "The city is fundamentally depressing" on April 8, 1934.

AH tells his mother "To have almost finished," quotes Frank Mears, and says that it "would take a lot to turn my head" on Oct. 7, 1935. AH refers to Lotte Baerwald's article in a letter to Ena, Sept. 3, 1935. The article (from *Jüdische Rundschau*, August 23, 1935) and its translation appear in a collection of press clippings in AH's archive at IAA. The "terrible rows" are described by Eunice Holliday—wife of the British architect Clifford Holliday, then working in Jerusalem—in a letter from Feb. 13, 1934, in Eunice Holliday, *Letters from Jerusalem: During the Palestine Mandate*, ed. John Holliday (London, 1997). Horsfield's letter to Mrs. Harrison is dated Nov. 25, 1936, and turns up in AH's "Some Letters of Mine." Wauchope's comments appear in a letter to Parkinson, March 11, 1936, CO 733/307/7. AH's letter saying "I am very, very tired" is written to C. R. Ashbee, Aug. 25, 1937, CRA KC 1/54.

AH tells Ena he has "escaped" in a letter marked November (?), 1938 (the date in the typed version of the letter is crossed out and possibly incorrect, since he left in late December 1937). The fact that his furnishings were put up for sale in his absence was related to me by Julie Williams, and AH mentions "the sale of my effects after my departure" in a letter to his mother from Cairo, Jan. 22, 1941. The farewells from various friends are quoted in a letter from AH to his mother, Jan. 1, 1938; the original

Gill letter is dated Dec. 30, 1937, and is at the Beinecke. The description of Starkey's murder appears in "Palestine Treasures," *The Times*, Jan. 13, 1938. The article about the government compound is "Government Offices in Jerusalem," *The Architects' Journal*, May 13, 1948. AH writes "I am expecting to hear" to Markus Reiner, Nov. 16, 1948.

The transfer of the museum's Jewish employees is described in "Informal Talk on the Rockefeller Museum given by Hanna Katzenstein for Volunteer Guides of the Israel Museum," Sept. 19, 1983, IAA. For more on the post-1948 state of the building, see Raz Kletter, *Just Past? The Making of Israeli Archaeology* (London, 2006). AH's later, unbuilt designs for Palestine are described in Fuchs, "Austen St. Barbe Harrison," 244–49. AH's quip that "I am . . . extremely busy" appears in a letter to Markus Reiner, Dec. 2, 1946.

The fate of AH's personal papers is recounted in Fuchs and Herbert, "Representing," 329, and was confirmed by Yani Papadimos, who also had a hand in saving much of this archive from the fire. In recent years Papadimos has donated the valuable remains of Harrison's correspondence and notebooks to the IAA.

WHERE THE GREAT CITY STANDS, 2014 / 1914
The future plans for EM's bank are related in Keshet Rosenbloom, "A Visionary's Unfinished Contribution to Jerusalem's Skyline," *Haaretz*, Dec. 27, 2012. Kroyanker's assessments of Houris are: "one of the best known," David Kroyanker, *Talbiyeh, Katamon, and the Greek Colony* [Heb.] (Jerusalem, 2005), 284; "among the most outstanding," Kroyanker, *Jerusalem Architecture: Arab Building Outside the Old City Walls* [Heb.] (Jerusalem, 1985), 41. In his book on Arab building, Kroyanker ascribes Jaffa 36, 38, 40, and 42 to Houris and his partner Petassis, 11, 314–15, though in the same book and in *Jerusalem: A Guide to Neighborhoods and Buildings: An Architectural View* [Heb.] (Jerusalem, 1996), he says Houris alone was responsible for 36. In *Jaffa Road*, he says Petassis was responsible for 40 and that "it seems" they were both responsible for 44 as well. In his *Jerusalem Architecture . . . Mandate*, he says they both built 40. Others have various versions of this: In *The New Jewish City of Jerusalem During the British Mandate Period* [Heb.] (Jerusalem, 2011), 2:924–25, Yehoshua Ben-Arieh ascribes 38 to Houris, and in their article "The Shaping and Development of Jaffa Road in Jerusalem" [Heb.], *Cathedra* 121 (Sept. 2006), Dana Tsoar and Ran Aaronsohn say he alone built 36 and 40.

Kroyanker describes "the ethnic aspect of architecture" in "Jerusalem's Built Heritage: The City's Architecture—Periods and Styles," Passia lecture, June 15, 2000, and writes about the absence of documentary material in *Jerusalem Architecture . . . Arab Building*, 14. His archive is described by Yuval Hamon in "Even Kroyanker's Leaving Jerusalem, Why?" [Heb], *Maariv NRG*, May 20, 2012. His departure is reported in Nir Hasson, "Jerusalem's Leading Lights Bolt for the Tel Aviv Coast in a Flight of Cultural Freedom," *Haaretz*, June 29, 2012; he calls Jerusalem "a ragged city" in Noam Dvir, "A Yearning Free of Illusions," *Haaretz*, Oct. 19, 2011, and says, "I don't believe that anywhere," in Neri Livneh, "With Jerusalem, It's Love-Hate," *Haaretz*, Sept. 8, 2005. Kroyanker dubs EM "among the greatest architects" in *Jerusalem Architecture . . . Mandate*, 442. While Kroyanker has written only admiringly of EM in his books, he was the author of a preservation report about the Schocken Villa in which he recommended tearing it down. *Haaretz* architecture critic Esther Zandberg points out—as have others in relation to various projects with which Kroyanker has been involved—that the survey was carried out at the behest of the developers who wanted to construct a new residential building over the ruins of EM's building. See Zandberg, "Not a Word About the Light Railway," *Haaretz*, Aug. 14, 2003. The history book that provides Petassis's first name is Kark and Oren-Nordheim, *Jerusalem and Its Environs*, 184.

For background about Sakakini, see Salim Tamari, "The Vagabond Café and Jerusalem's Prince of Idleness" and "Sultana and Khalil," in *Mountain Against the Sea: Essays on Palestinian Society and Culture* (Berkeley, 2009) and Sakakini, *Jerusalem and I.* I've also relied on the new Arabic edition of the diaries (Ramallah, 2003–2010), ed. Akram Musallam, with introductions by Faisal Daraj, Adel Manna, and Yusef Ayub Haddad among others, as well as Gideon Shilo's introduction to his Hebrew translation of the abridged version, *Such Am I, Oh World!* (Mivaseret Tzion, 2007). For more on the various readings of Sakakini's work, see Nadim Bawalsa, "Sakakini Defrocked," *Jerusalem Quarterly* 42 (Summer 2010). The idea that Sakakini's diary is typical of his class and community is put forth by Elie Kadourie in "Religion and Politics: The Diaries of Khalil Sakakini," *St. Antony's Papers* 4, no. 1 (1958). His calling card is described in *The Storyteller of Jerusalem*, 152 (translation tweaked). For information about the Acre-born Achille Seikaly, who was also an editor, translator, and high-ranking member of Egypt's nationalist Wafd party, I'm grateful to May Seikaly and Ramez Hakim.

Sakakini's relationship to the Greek Orthodox Church is described in Tamari, "The Vagabond Café"; Laura Robson, "Communalism and Nationalism in the Mandate: The Greek Orthodox Controversy and the National Movement," *Journal of Palestine Studies* 41, no. 1 (2011), 15–16; his desire to replace the Lord's Prayer with Imru' al-Qays is related by Tamari in *Mountain Against the Sea*, 116. The dominance of the Orthodox community is described in Michelle Campos, *Ottoman Brothers: Muslims, Christians, and Jews in Early Twentieth-Century Palestine* (Stanford, 2011), 20–21, 84–85. "My aim" is quoted in Tamari, "The Vagabond Café," 185. He announces, "I can't be a part of this denomination" in *Diaries*, vol. 2, Dec. 12 and 20, 1914; "Greek of the Greeks," quoted in Bawalsa, "Sakakini Defrocked," 21; "I'm neither Christian nor Buddhist," *Diaries*, vol. 2, March 12, 1915. For a nuanced account of the layered nature of Palestinian identity during this period, see Rashid Khalidi, *Palestinian Identity: The Construction of Modern National Consciousness* (NY, 1997).

Details about the founding of the Greek Colony come from John H. Melkon Rose, *Armenians of Jerusalem: Memories of Life in Palestine* (London, 1993), 84–96; Kroyanker, *Talbiyeh, Katamon*, 279–81. Kark and Oren-Nordheim give a slightly different version in *Jerusalem and Its Environs*, 173–75, as does Gideon Biger, "The Development of Jerusalem's Built-Up Area During the First Decade of the British Mandate, 1920–1930," in *Jerusalem in the Modern Period* [Heb.], ed. E. Shaltiel, (Jerusalem, 1981), 271. (They say the land was bought privately.) Anastas Damianos has confirmed that the version Melkon Rose and Kroyanker offer is accurate. Kark and Oren-Nordheim also ascribe the buildings there to Houris, without qualification. For more on the Greek Church's real estate holdings and the recent related scandals, see Itamar Katz and Ruth Kark, "The Church and Landed Property: The Greek Orthodox Patriarch of Jerusalem," *Middle Eastern Studies* 43, no. 3 (May 2007); Dan McDermott,

"Shaping the Church, Shaping the City," *NIMEP Insights* 2 (Spring 2006); Chris Mc-Greal, "Greek Orthodox Church Mired in Jerusalem Land Row," *The Guardian*, March 22, 2005; "Ousted Patriarch Behind Locked Doors in Jerusalem," AP, January 7, 2011.

Background about Efklides and the municipal hospital comes from Zalman Greenberg, "The Turkish Municipal Hospital in Jerusalem" [Heb.], *Cathedra* 78 (Dec. 1995); Yaakov Yehoshua, *Neighborhoods in Jerusalem*, vol. 4 [Heb.] (Jerusalem, 1971); Helena Kagan, *The Beginning of My Way in Jerusalem* [Heb.] (Tel Aviv, 1982); Kroyanker, *Jaffa Road*, 296–98; interviews with Anastas Damianos (July 15 and 29, 2014), John Tleel (July 30, 2014), and Zalman Greenberg (Sept. 21, 2014). Kagan relates the first version of the legend about the hospital. The story of the necrophiliac wedding comes from Bertha Spafford Vester, *Our Jerusalem: An American Family in the Holy City, 1881–1949* (Jerusalem, 1950). In *To Be Governor of Jerusalem: The City and District During the Times of Ali Ekrem Bey, 1906–1908* (Istanbul, 2005), David Kushner writes that the governor gave various honors "to officials and public figures whom he believed gave exemplary service to the state . . . [among them to] the chief doctor of the municipal hospital, Doctor Photios, for his good services," 125. The firman is reproduced and translated in Greenberg, "Turkish Municipal Hospital," 58–59. It was Greenberg who interviewed Heleni Efklides on her ninetieth birthday.

For details about Mamilla's recent development, see Kroyanker, *Jerusalem: Mamilla—Prosperity, Decay and Renewal* [Heb.] (Jerusalem, 2009); Gil Zohar, "Long-Awaited Luxury," *The Jerusalem Post*, May 24, 2007. Esther Zandberg's comments come from "Too Grandiose for Its Own Good," *Haaretz*, July 27, 2003. Quotes from American rabbi Marvin Hier appear in Bradley Burston, "Visit Jerusalem's New Museum of Tolerance. Feel Your Blood Boil," *Haaretz*, June 7, 2012. For further details on the museum's presence over Muslim graves, see, for instance, Rashid Khalidi's explanation of the situation in "Tolerance of Whom?," The Daily Beast, April 10, 2012, and his subsequent responses to the Wiesenthal Center's defenders, as well as Saree Makdisi's "The Architecture of Erasure," *Critical Inquiry* 36 (Spring 2010). For a full history of the site, see also Yehoshua Ben-Arieh, "The Tolerance Museum and the Mamilla Cemetery: Plain Facts" (copy provided by the author), and Khalidi's Edward Said London Lecture, presented at the British Museum on May 31, 2011, and reprinted on the *Jadaliyya* website as "Human Dignity in Jerusalem." Details of (and quotes about) Gehry's design are drawn from Makdisi, "Architecture of Erasure." Gehry's official statement appears on the Wiesenthal Center website.

Efklides's death and funeral are described as "truly a demonstration of sorrow" by Conde de Ballobar in *Jerusalem in World War I*, ed. Eduardo Manzano Moreno and Roberto Mazza (London, 2011), 95; Kagan, *The Beginning*, 56. The article announcing "The Doctor Is Dead" [Heb.] is from *Haherut*, May 7, 1916. The German air force picture is B. Jerusalem, Teilbilder der Stadt mit weiterem Vorgelände: Rephaim-Ebene, Tempel-Kolonie, Ophel-Sion, Birket-es-Sultan, Laufzeit: 28 Juli 1918; Signatur: BayHStA, BS-Palästina 783. The first map I've been able to find in which the house appears is the "Plan of Jerusalem and Environs by E. F. Beaumont," 1929. In an interview (July 30, 2014), John Tleel described Maria Samptopolo as "very lofty in her ways." Kroyanker writes of the engagement in *Talbiyeh, Katamon*, 290. Anastas Damianos and others in the Greek community have confirmed this story.

Details about the Israel State Archives and their sorry state are drawn from Ofer

Aderet, "Israel State Archives Close Again, This Time Due to a Collapsed Staircase," *Haaretz*, Jan. 14, 2013; Nir Hasson, "Israel State Archives Close Due to Lack of Safety Permits," *Haaretz*, Oct. 31, 2012; Liel Kyzer, "Archives Building Low Key, but Material Inside Is Anything But," *Haaretz*, Oct. 7, 2010. Information about the Books of Souls comes from Yonatan Pagis, *Ottoman Population Registers in the Land of Israel, 1875–1918* [Heb.] (Jerusalem, 1997), and Kemal H. Karpat, "Ottoman Population Records and the Census of 1881/82–1893," *International Journal of Middle East Studies* 9, no. 3 (Oct. 1978).

The history of the Villa Harun ar-Rashid is recounted by George Bisharat in "Talbiyeh Days: At Villa Harun ar-Rashid," *Jerusalem Quarterly* 30 (Spring 2007). See also his "Origins of the Middle East Crisis: Who Caused the Palestinian Diaspora?" in *The Electronic Intifada*, Dec. 3, 2003, and "Right of Return to a Palestinian Home," *SF Chronicle*, May 18, 2003. For an essayistic riff on the house and what its loss represents, see Suad Amiry's *Golda Slept Here* (New Delhi, 2014).

Background about Romema comes from Shabtai Zacharia, *Neighborhoods in Jerusalem: Romema* [Heb.] (Jerusalem, 1999); Kark and Oren-Nordheim, *Jerusalem and Its Environs*, 164–66; Yehoshua Ben-Arieh, *The New Jewish City of Jerusalem*, 2:533–51. The quote "saw the significance" is from Ehud Menachem Zvi Keene, *Chaikins* (Jerusalem, 2000), 57. Biographical details about Hamon come from Nathan Brun, *Judges and Lawyers in Eretz Israel: Between Constantinople and Jerusalem, 1900–1930* [Heb.] (Jerusalem, 2008), 61–64; M. R. Gaon, *The Jews of the East in the Land of Israel* [Heb.] (Jerusalem, 1982), 2:719–20; Ben-Arieh, *The New Jewish City*, 2:536. The quotes about Hamon are from Brun, 63. Hamon's papers pertaining to the house are in CZA A541\32 and 36. The wages for a construction worker are drawn from Zachary Lockman, *Comrades and Enemies: Arab and Jewish Workers in Palestine, 1906–1948* (Berkeley, 1996), 85–86. The requirements for Greek citizenship are described in Campos, *Ottoman Brothers*, 63. Kroyanker's words about the inconsistency of Houris's style appear in his *Jerusalem Architecture . . . Arab Building*, 417. For a subtle take on the city's earlier "eclecticism," see "Jerusalem, Between Urban Area and Apparition: From a Multiethnic City to Nationalism? Jerusalem in the Early Twentieth Century," a conversation between Meron Benvenisti and Salim Tamari in *City of Collision: Jerusalem and the Principles of Conflict Urbanism*, ed. Philipp Misselwitz and Tim Rieniets (Basel, 2006).

Biographical details about Fraji derive from Gad Frumkin, *The Way of a Judge in Jerusalem* [Heb.] (Tel Aviv, 1954), 1, and Brun, *Judges and Lawyers*, 61–64. (He also lists the first four Jewish lawyers licensed by the British.) Sakakini mentions teaching Fraji Arabic throughout vol. 2 of his diaries. See also Adel Manna's introduction to that volume. Aharon Mani's particulars are drawn from D. Tidhar, *Encyclopedia of the Pioneers of the Yishuv and Its Builders* [Heb.] (Tel Aviv, 1947), 1:473; Kroyanker, *Jaffa Road*, 216, 222. The account of the controversy surrounding Mani comes from *Doar Hayom*, "Jerusalem Day to Day," May 20, 1925; Mani's response is "On Hebrew Labor," May 22, 1925 [both in Hebrew]. Details about Hajj Mahmud and his building come from Kroyanker, *Jaffa Road*, 332, and *Jerusalem Architecture . . . Arab Building*, 318; Ben-Arieh, *The New Jewish City*, 2:547–49.

The portrait of the Gelat family is drawn from Kroyanker, *Talbiyeh, Katamon*, 90–91; George A. Barton, "Antoine Thomas Gelat, an Appreciation," *Bulletin of the American Schools of Oriental Research* 13 (Feb. 1924); Rachel Hallote, "Before Albright:

Charles Torrey, James Montgomery, and American Biblical Archaeology 1907–1922," *Near Eastern Archaeology* 74, no. 3 (Sept. 2011); W. F. Albright, "Report of the Director of the School in Jerusalem 1921–1922," *Bulletin of the American Schools of Oriental Research* 8 (1922). In "Palestine from Day to Day: Chamber of Commerce Meeting," *PB*, June 6, 1926, it says "the Hon. President was asked to send a letter to Mr. Elias T. Gelat, member of the Committee, on the occasion of his marriage." The younger Gelat's appointment as honorary consul is mentioned in "Hungarian Consul in Palestine," *PB*, Dec. 12, 1926. The various documents concerning the supply of stones appear online: BU American School of Oriental Research Archive, Jerusalem School Collection, box 2, folder 37. Antoine Gelat's account of their wartime travails is contained in CZA K13\35.

Storrs's description of the state of the Dome is from Ronald Storrs, *Orientations* (Middlesex, 1940), 313. Background about the legends and history surrounding the Dome of the Rock comes from Oleg Grabar, "The Umayyad Dome of the Rock in Jerusalem," *Ars Orientalis* 3 (1959); Grabar, *The Shape of the Holy: Early Islamic Jerusalem* (Princeton, 1996); Grabar, *The Dome of the Rock* (Cambridge, 2006); Julian Raby and Jeremy Johns, *Bayt al-Maqdis: 'Abd el-Malik's Jerusalem* (Oxford, 1992); Nasser Rabbat, "The Meaning of the Umayyad Dome of the Rock," *Muqarnas* 6 (1989); Grabar, "The Haram al-Sharif: An Essay in Interpretation," *BRIIFS* 2, no. 2 (Autumn 2000), 3. Grabar says it had "become a messy space," *Dome of the Rock*, 35. The secret dispatch is dated March 9, 1918, FO 371/3401/46315. For more on the background of the Dome's twentieth-century state, see John Carswell, "The Deconstruction of the Dome of the Rock," in Auld and Hillenbrand, *Ottoman Jerusalem*.

Lawrence's characterization of Storrs comes from his *Seven Pillars of Wisdom* (NY, 1962), 56. Storrs describes his "interest in the physical presentment" in *Orientations*, 96. Helen Bentwich calls him "the most entertaining talker" in *Tidings from Zion: Helen Bentwich's Letters from Jerusalem, 1919–1931*, ed. Jenifer Glynn (NY, 2000), 16. Further background about Storrs is drawn from *The First Governor: Sir Ronald Storrs, Governor of Jerusalem, 1918–1926*, ed. Nirit Shalev-Khalifa (Tel Aviv, 2010). Quotes: "protect Jerusalem by an aesthetic . . . The fifty previous," Storrs, *Orientations*, 310; "on a large scale," W. H. McLean, *Regional and Town Planning: In Principle and Practice* (London, 1930), 65; "Aristotle's Beneficent Despot . . . my word," Storrs, *Orientations*, 317; "inexcusable materials," Storrs, *Orientations*, 310.

For the earlier rule about stone, see "Town Planning Ordinance, 1936," *The Palestine Gazette*, 1939, 874–75. For the evolution of the policy—and a critical take on its political implications—see Eyal Weizman, *Hollow Land: Israel's Architecture of Occupation* (London, 2007), 27–33. The "dangerous ground" is mentioned in "Repairs to Mosques in Jerusalem," March 21, 1918, FO 371/3401/46315; Balfour insists that "every endeavour should be made" in the same file, March 21, 1918. For background on the politics of the renovations, see Daniel Bertrand Monk, *An Aesthetic Occupation: The Immediacy of Architecture and the Palestine Conflict* (Durham, 2002).

Biographical details about Richmond (ETR) are drawn from his papers held at Durham University and from the privately held *Liber Maiorum*. Quotes: "urgently required . . . in uniform," Clayton to (?), June 6, 1918, FO 371/3401/181716; "loan of British expert," GH in Egypt, March 21, 1918, FO 371/3401/87708; "the works of preservation," ETR, *The Dome of the Rock in Jerusalem* (Oxford, 1924), 1; "penetrating, fiery quality," Felicity Ashbee, *Child in Jerusalem* (Syracuse, 2008), 135; "rather bitter mouth," Susanna Richmond, "Memories of Uncle Ernest," enclosed in a letter to Sally Morphet, dated July 10, 2000. ETR discusses his injury in "Mammon in the Holy Land," 1–2, RIC 5/1/6, and Thomas Hodgkin describes ETR as "thin, like a knife" in *Letters from Palestine, 1932–36*, ed. E. C. Hodgkin (London, 1986), Feb. 14, 1933. ETR's description of the "more than twelve hundred years" comes from ETR, *Dome*, 3, and "interesting rain water gargoyles" in "Summary Report upon the Condition of the Dome of the Rock and of the Aksa Mosque," FO 371/3401/46325.

CRA describes his mission in Jerusalem to Janet Ashbee, June 9, 1918, CRA KC 1/42. Much of the biographical material about CRA is drawn from Alan Crawford, *C. R. Ashbee: Architect, Designer and Romantic Socialist* (New Haven, 1985); Fiona Mac-Carthy, *The Simple Life: C. R. Ashbee in the Cotswolds* (Berkeley, 1981); Felicity Ashbee, *Child in Jerusalem*; Felicity Ashbee, *Janet Ashbee: Love, Marriage and the Arts and Crafts Movement* (Syracuse, 2002). See also CRA's own *An Endeavor Towards the Teaching of John Ruskin and William Morris* (London, 1901). CRA speaks of "the imaginative things" and "a nursery for luxuries" in *Craftsmanship in Competitive Industry* (Campden, 1908), 9. He talks of how the human being must "leave his stamp" and how "through the city we focus civilization" in *Where the Great City Stands: A Study in the New Civics* (London, 1917), 113 and 3, respectively. His Dublin scheme is discussed in Michael J. Bannon, "Dublin Town Planning Competition: Ashbee and Chettle's 'New Dublin'—A Study in Civics," *Planning Perspectives* 14, no. 2 (1999), and "Dublin Town Planning Competition," *Town Planning Review* 7, no. 2 (April 1917); Noah Hysler-Rubin, "Arts & Crafts and the Great City: Charles Robert Ashbee in Jerusalem," *Planning Perspectives* 21, no. 4 (Oct. 2006). Crawford quotes him: "I woke up this morning sobbing," 162, and "practically defunct," 163. Further quotes: "constant sun," March 25, 1917, CRA KC 1/40; "beauty and history," CRA, *Where the Great City*, 58; "Though the individual creates," CRA, *Where the Great City*, 57; "a crank, and a strange fellow," memo dated March 7, 1917, FO 141/669/4394; "not at all a man," undated letter from C. F. Ryder, FO 141/669/4394/8; "in readiness . . . all very romantic," June 9, 1918, CRA KC 1/42; "all your deliberations," June 18, 1918, CRA KC 1/42; "Well, I've fixed it all up," June 21, 1918, CRA KC 1/42.

Quotes about the Dome are as follows: "slabs of tile work," CRA, "Report on the Arts and Crafts," 21, JMA box 362; "roots of wild plants . . . The bones," "Summary Report"; see also ETR's description in *Jerusalem, 1918–20*, ed. C. R. Ashbee (London, 1921), 8–9. CRA quotes: "interlaced," Aug. 14, 1918, CRA KC 1/43; "plan our reports," Aug. 29, 1918, CRA KC 1/43. The saga of the Najara and the kilns is recounted in ETR's *Dome* and "Summary Report," CRA, "Report on the Arts and Crafts," and *Jerusalem 1918–20*, 31–32. Storrs calls them "the original furnaces" in *Orientations*, 314. Quotes are as follows: "that great pagan," CRA, *PN*, 7; "transmutes and transcends . . . serene continuity," CRA, *PN*, 240; "of a living Faith," ETR, *Dome*, 4–5; "a serpent," CRA, *PN*, 243.

Biographical information about David Ohannessian is drawn from Pheme Alice Ohannessian Moughalian, *The Families of Tavit and Victoria Ohannessian* (privately published, 1992); Sato Moughalian, "David Ohannessian and the Armenian Ceramics of Jerusalem," in *A la découverte de la Jérusalem des Arméniens*, ed. Patrick Donabédian, Dickran Kouymjian, and Claude Mutafian (Paris, forthcoming); "David Ohannessian, Ceramicist," apparently written by Ohannessian's daughter Sirarpi, with her father's help, in May 1952, Beirut. I've also drawn from various Ohannessian family papers, as well as extended conversations with Sato Moughalian and an interview with Anahid Ohannessian (Aug. 18, 2014). Additional background comes from Garo Kürkman, *The Magic of Clay and Fire: A History of Kütahya Pottery and Potters* (Istanbul, 2006), 194–200; Yael Olenik, *The Armenian Pottery of Jerusalem* (Tel Aviv, 1986); Nirit Shalev-Khalifa, "David Ohannessian—Founder of the Armenian Ceramics in Jerusalem," in *The Armenian Ceramics of Jerusalem*, ed. Nurith Kenaan-Kedar (Jerusalem, 2003).

Background about Mark Sykes and Sledmere derives from Christopher Simon Sykes, *The Big House* (NY, 2005); Roger Adelson, *Mark Sykes: Portrait of an Amateur* (London, 1975); Shane Leslie, *Mark Sykes, His Life and Letters* (London, 1923). Sykes's description of the town appears in *The Caliph's Last Heritage* (London, 1915), 519. The number of tiles and particulars of Sykes's conversations with Ohannessian appear in Moughalian, "David Ohannessian."

Details about the Armenian population of Kütahya and its fate are drawn from Raymond Kevorkian, *The Armenian Genocide* (NY, 2011), 273, 564–65, and Grigoris Balakian, *Armenian Golgotha*, trans. Peter Balakian with Aris Sevag (NY, 2009), 406. Storrs takes all the credit in *Orientations*, 314. ETR says "it was at Sykes's suggestion" in *Lieber Maiorum*, 77, and Storrs's confession that he had "the help of my friend" is quoted in Shalev-Khalifa, *The First Governor*, 32e. CRA calls the first firings a "dismal failure" and describes Ohannessian's trip to Constantinople in *Jerusalem 1918–20*, 31–32. The "kaolin-rich clay" of Kütahya is described in John Carswell, *Kütahya Tiles and Pottery from the Armenian Cathedral of St. James, Jerusalem* (Oxford, 1972), 41, and Olenik, *The Armenian Pottery of Jerusalem*, 16, 19. CRA's "Yes, it will take" is from *PN*, 244. The various explanations for the failure of the Haram kiln project come from Shalev-Khalifa, "David Ohannessian," 30; interview with Neshan Balian (grandson of Ohannessian's potter, Neshan Balian, and current owner of the Palestinian Pottery on Nablus Road, Jerusalem, Aug. 29, 2012); Storrs, *Orientations*, 314; Beatrice St. Laurent, "The Dome of the Rock and the Politics of Restoration," *The Bridgewater Review*, December 1998; St. Laurent and András Riedlemayer, "Restorations of Jerusalem."

Quotes about the political situation are as follows: "a very plastic period," CRA, *Jerusalem 1920–22*, 2; "in politics . . . In 1920 . . . all the carefully," Storrs, *Orientations*, 329–30; "WAKE UP," quoted in Wasserstein, *The British in Palestine*, 99; "preserving and safeguarding," quoted in Kupferschmidt, *Supreme*, 130. ETR's quotes are as follows: "the Bolshevik type," ETR to Storrs, June 16, 1920, RS III/2; "Jew-beridden," ETR, "Mammon," 54, RIC 5/1/49; "the Jewish race . . . Jewish quality . . . sneaking, round-the-corner," "Mammon," 185–86, RIC 5/1/114; "Astonishing," ETR, *Dome*, 5.

Information about (and quotations from) Kemalettin are drawn from Yildirim Yavuz, "The Restoration Project of the Masjid Al-Aqsa by Mimar Kemalettin (1922–26)," *Muqarnas* 13 (1996). Details about the Ohannessian workshop come from Ohannessian Moughalian, *The Families*, and from "The Man in the Furnace," *PP*, July 28, 1944. Storrs's accounts of the tiles "gleaming against the sober texture" and the miniature Dome for the princess are from *Orientations*, 314–15. Sakakini calls ETR "my trusted friend" in his diaries, vol. 3, March 2, 1919.

ROCK PAPER SCISSORS: AN EPILOGUE

CRA quotes: "The city belongs to us all," CRA to Samuels, April 8, 1920, CRA KC 1/45; "Zionism as understood," CRA, *PN*, 267; "the reports, plans," *PN*, viii. The description of the fire at the Cyprus Government House is drawn from a Reuters account, "How Sir Ronald Storrs Escaped Mob with Burning Torches, Valuable Art Treasures Destroyed," RS IV/3; Storrs, *Orientations*, xv, 507–509. Austen Harrison writes Lilian Bomberg on Oct. 16, 1960, about one of his own Bomberg paintings: "You realize of course that the painting of Siloam hanging over my sister's mantelpiece was . . . a study for that remarkable picture which Storrs got burned" (TGDB 873/3/3).

Details about Nashashibi, his library, and the pillaging of his house come from Basheer Barakat, "The Castle of Is'af al-Nashashibi," *Studies on Jerusalem* [Arabic] (Kuwait, 2014); "Muhammad Isaaf Nashashibi," *This Week in Palestine*, August 2014; Radi Saduq, *Palestinian Poets of the Twentieth Century* [Arabic] (Amman, 2000); multiple references in Sakakini's journals, where Nashashibi is called "Abu al-Fadl"; interviews with Khaled Khatib (Sept. 11, 2014) and Basheer Barakat (Sept. 27, 2014).

The newspaper references to Spyro Houris (all from *PB*) are as follows: "Architect Cleared," Oct. 15, 1930; "Bribes Murderer to Put Away His Brothers," Nov. 28, 1928; "Jerusalem Perjury Case," Nov. 23, 1931. For further background on the case, see "Bribery Charge Against Magistrate," Dec. 22, 1931. Heleni's wedding announcement appears in *PP*, Jan. 1, 1933.

Background about the Masons in the Middle East comes from "Freemasons," *Encyclopedia of Religion*, 2nd ed. (New York, 2004); "Farmasuniyya," *Encyclopedia of Islam*, 2nd ed. (New York, 1960–2005); "Freemasons," *Encyclopedia of the Modern Middle East and North Africa* (New York, 2004); Jacob M. Landau, "Prolegomena to a Study of Secret Societies in Modern Egypt," *Middle Eastern Studies* 1, no. 2 (January 1965); Elie Kedourie, "Young Turks, Freemasons and Jews," *Middle Eastern Studies* 7, no. 1 (January 1971). The manual quoted is Alfred F. Chapman, *Master's Manual* (Boston, 1874), 19; the quote from the Hamas Covenant of 1988 is article 17; the Masons were "one of the most influential," according to Michelle Campos, "Freemasonry in Ottoman Palestine," *Jerusalem Quarterly* 22/23 (Fall/Winter, 2005). See also her *Ottoman Brothers*, 183–96. The Bibliothèque Nationale file in which she found mention of Spyro Houris is BN-FM2/142. Houris's death notice appears in *The Palestine Gazette*, Feb. 4, 1937.

ACKNOWLEDGMENTS

It takes a city to write certain books. In this case, it took many. As I've researched, written, and revised, I've had the help of people far and wide—from Jerusalem to New Haven, London to Los Angeles, Athens to Zurich, and points beyond.

I'm indebted first of all to the grandchildren of my "characters." Francis Ames-Lewis, Racheli Edelman, Daria Joseph, the late Sally Morphet, Sato Moughalian, Anahid Ohannessian, Yani Papadimos, the late Sam Richmond, Sophie Richmond, and Emma Shackle have graciously entrusted me with invaluable materials and memories as they've also granted me permission to quote from the papers of their gifted forebears. Emma, Sophie, and Sato have been especially involved and passionate in working with me to try to solve various mysteries surrounding their talented, difficult grandfathers, and I'm thankful to them for their willingness to put up with my numerous and nosy questions. Further assistance on the family front came from Richard Morphet, Liz Richmond, and the estate of David Bomberg. Nicholas Vester's wisdom and infectious good humor have served as a tonic throughout the book's composition.

My entry into the multiple Jerusalems that I've wandered through here has been eased and enriched by several experts who shared their substantial learning with me. Venturing into Mendelsohn's Palestine, I've been lucky to have as a guide Ita Heinze-Greenberg, who knows the main boulevards and backstreets of this subject better than anyone.

I'm likewise obliged to Stefanie Mahrer for pointers in navigating the labyrinth of Salman Schocken's archive. Ron Fuchs shed welcome light on Harrison's accomplishment and Houris's architectural context. Julie Williams's reminiscences of Harrison were vital to my attempts to render a portrait of him here. Busy as they each are, Khaled Khatib and Moshe Shapira were both unstinting with their time and hands-on familiarity with Houris's buildings. I'm also beholden to Eli Wardi, who has been a canny adviser on matters of architectural conservation and the built facts on Jerusalem's ground. Salim Tamari's knowledge of Palestinian cultural history is prodigious, as is his generosity. Michelle Campos and Angelos Dalachanis each played a significant, last-minute role in the emergence of the book's closing section, and their openness, intelligence, and willingness to share with me their startling archival discoveries were a serious boon at a crucial point.

Baruch Yonin of Jerusalem's Schocken Institute has been indispensable to the making of this book. His enthusiasm and understanding of the Schocken Library (from the hinges of its doors to the files in its cabinets) were in large part what first sparked my curiosity about Mendelsohn; his patience and magnanimity are key to what has sustained my interest. So, too, Silvia Krapiwko, of the Israel Antiquities Authority, has been an utter delight to work with. Her devotion to Austen St. Barbe Harrison's archive—and her largesse with its contents—made writing the second section possible. My debt to her is huge. As should be clear from the book's final parts, Anastas Damianos brought me into the past and present of Jerusalem's Greek community with grace, warmth, and tact.

Kostas Giorgiadis, Yahya Hijazi, Gabriel Levin, Robert Schine, George Syrimis, and Moira Weigel helped me translate from a range of languages, while a number of architects and architectural historians have rendered valuable assistance as I set out to hear what Jerusalem's stones might be saying. My thanks go out especially to Suad Amiry, Marian Cohen, Dolores Hayden, Elias Messinas, Theo Metropoulos, Jennifer Siegal, Yildirim Yavuz, and to David Kroyanker. For important contributions of all sizes and sorts, my gratitude to Neshan Balian, Basheer Barakat, Yehoshua Ben-Arieh, Fred Bisharat, George Bisharat, Robert Blecher, Varda Brief, Hillel Cohen,

Julie Cohen, Alex Corfiatis, Elina Dai, Sister Monika Dullmann, Rafi Greenberg, Zalman Greenberg, Ramez Hakim, Verity Harte, Hannan Hever, Adam Hinds, George Hintlian, Fawzi Ibrahim, Baha Ju'beh, Ruth Kark, Asher Kaufman, Nancy Kuhl, Richard Laster, Emily Levine, Nathan Marcus, Amir Mohtashemi, Cathy Nichols, Alan Paris, Du'a Qirresh, Tarik Ramahi, May Seikaly, Nirit Shalev-Khalifa, Itta Shedletzky, Karl Jürgen Skrodzki, Barbara and Philip Spectre, Michael Stöneberg, John Tleel, Katie Trumpener, Dror Wahrman, Christian Weller, and Lenny Wolfe. Raphael Gorodetsky allowed me to make use of an album of photos shot in the late 1930s by his father, Arie Gorodetsky, who served as a junior engineer on Mendelsohn's Hadassah project. One of those photographs appears on the book's jacket. For various forms of behind-the-scenes aid, I'm obliged to Megan Mangum, Joe Florentino, and John Donatich.

My documentary explorations were made possible by the dozens of dedicated archivists and librarians who work at the institutions whose holdings I've mined. A complete list of those institutions appears in the notes. Special acknowledgment is due to Kathryn James of the Beinecke Library, who acted as a kind of archival fairy godmother at one important juncture. A Guggenheim Fellowship and a Windham Campbell Prize provided support both monetary and moral, and my sincere thanks are due to those who administer both.

For manifold forms of friendship and focus, critical encouragement, and encouraging criticism proffered as this book took shape, I'm deeply grateful to Deborah Baker, Jeanne and Harold Bloom, Lisa Cohen, Amitav Ghosh, Judy Heiblum, Phillip Lopate, Jorge Martin, Elana and Jim Ponet, Corey Robin, Claudia Roden, Phyllis Rose, Michael Sells, the late A. J. Sherman, Nathan Thrall, and Eliot Weinberger.

I'm happily beholden to Miriam Altshuler for her calm and her savvy. At FSG, John Knight has been a constant and gracious help, while numerous others have also been essential to building this book about building. As always, working with Ileene Smith has been a source of tremendous gratification. I'm fortunate to be able to call her my editor.

And finally, firstly, Peter Cole is with me inside every word—here, there, and everywhere.

INDEX

ILLUSTRATION CREDITS

Frontispiece: Corridor, south wing, Palestine Archaeological Museum, from a photo album compiled by Austen St. Barbe Harrison: Israel Antiquities Authority Archive, SRF 104.

4 Turkish clock tower, Jaffa Gate: American Colony Photographers, from the G. Eric and Edith Matson Collection, Library of Congress, Prints and Photographs Division.

6 British clock tower, Allenby Square: Matson Collection.

7 "The Jaffa Road as it is": Papers of Charles Robert Ashbee, King's College, Cambridge, England 21/4/11, by permission of the Ashbee estate.

8 "The Jaffa Road Market as I want it to be": CRA KC 21/4/11, by permission of the Ashbee estate.

13 Erich Mendelsohn at one of the Schocken sites, Rehavia: photographer unknown, by permission of the Getty Research Institute, Los Angeles.

20 Construction site of the Einstein Tower, Potsdam, 1921: bpk, Berlin/Staatliche Museen zu Berlin—Preussischer Kulturbesitz, Kunstbibliothek/© Heddenhausen & Wieß/Art Resource, NY.

21 Universum Cinema: Arthur Köster, "Erich Mendelsohn: Universum-Kino (Woga Komplex), Kurfürstendamm/Lehniner Platz, Berlin-Charlottenburg, 1928/ © 2015 Artists Rights Society, New York/VG Bild-Kunst, Bonn.

22 Schocken department store, Stuttgart: © Landesmedienzentrum, Baden-Württemberg.

26 Am Rupenhorn interior, with mural by Amédée Ozenfant: Arthur Köster, *Neues Haus, Neue Welt* (Berlin, 1932)/© 2015 ARS, NY/VG Bild-Kunst, Bonn.

28 Erich Mendelsohn at Karnak: from Regina Stephan, ed., *Erich Mendelsohn: Wesen Werk Wirkung* (Ostfildern, 2006).

29 Nazi postcard of the Weissenhofsiedlung as an Arab village: published in *Schwäbisches Heimatbuch*, reproduced in Richard Pommer and Christian F. Otto, *Weissenhof 1927 and the Modern Movement in Architecture* (Chicago, 1991).

33 Envelope addressed by Erich Mendelsohn in Jerusalem to Luise in Cairo, December 15, 1934: bpk, Berlin/Kunstbibliothek/© Daria Joseph/Art Resource, NY.

38 Imaginary sketch from the Russian Front, 1917: bpk, Berlin/Kunstbibliothek/ © Daria Joseph/Art Resource, NY.

40 Windmill, Ramban Street, Rehavia: photographer unknown, by permission of the Getty Research Institute.

43 Luise at the windmill: from "Three Photos of Luise Mendelsohn," Getty Research Institute © Daria Joseph.

58 Schocken Villa, aerial view: courtesy of the Schocken Institute, Jerusalem.

59 "Rembrandt window," Schocken Library: courtesy of the Schocken Institute.

65 Staircase at the Schocken Library: courtesy of the Schocken Institute.

73 The Mendelsohns' Jerusalem curfew pass, issued July 9, 1936: by permission of the Getty Research Institute.

76 Hadassah Medical Complex construction sign: courtesy of the Hebrew University Archive.

78 Palace Hotel, Mamilla: Matson Collection.

82 Erich Mendelsohn, sketch of mortuary chapel, Hadassah Hospital: bpk, Berlin/ Kunstbibliothek/reproduction photo by Deitmar Katz/© Daria Joseph/Art Resource, NY.

85 "The breasts of the building" (Hadassah) in progress: Matson Collection.

89 Geddes and Mears's design for the Hebrew University's Great Hall, on a postcard with Einstein and Weizmann, and a quote from Isaiah 11:9: "The earth will be full of knowledge": from David Kroyanker, ed., Dreamscapes: Unbuilt Jerusalem (Jerusalem, 1992).

97 Erich Mendelsohn's university clubhouse: courtesy of the Hebrew University Archive.

112 Erich Mendelsohn's Anglo-Palestine Bank, Jaffa Road: Matson Collection.

114 Harrison's post office and Mendelsohn's bank (under construction), Jaffa Road, c. 1938: Matson Collection.

123 Hadassah Hospital, Mount Scopus, completed: courtesy of the Hebrew University Archive.

125 The Archaeological Advisory meeting room, Palestine Archaeological Museum: courtesy of the Israel Antiquities Authority Archive. (All other photos from this collection are labeled IAA.)

130 Austen Harrison with his dog, Bogie, in Jerusalem: IAA.

138 Palestine Pavilion, Wembley: supplement to The Palestine Weekly, September 5, 1924.

145 David Bomberg on the roof of the Banco di Roma, Jerusalem: unknown photographer, reproduction © Tate, London, 2015.

146 David Bomberg's Mount Zion with the Church of the Dormition: Moonlight, 1923: courtesy of the Ben Uri Gallery, London © 2015 ARS/DACS, London.

156 Government House ballroom: IAA.

158 Government House door with ornaments: IAA.

158 Government House fireplace: IAA.

160 Government House drawing room from above: IAA.

162 Government House with Union Jack: IAA.

169 Austen Harrison, letter to James Henry Breasted, September 16, 1927, with sketch of the museum: courtesy of the Oriental Institute of the University of Chicago (OI).

174 Sketch and photo of a tomb at Karm ash-Sheikh: IAA.

176 "The Scrollery" at the museum: IAA.

178 Crowd at the ceremony of the laying of the museum's foundation stone, June 19, 1930: OI, photographed by the American Colony Photographers, by permission of the American Colony.

179 Austen Harrison looking miserable at the ceremony. In the foreground are the high commissioner, John Chancellor, and his wife, Elsie; E. T. Richmond is speaking; Edward Keith-Roach, the district commissioner, is holding his hat. Harrison is sitting in the back corner, looking down: OI, photographed by the American Colony Photographers, by permission of the American Colony.

181 Ceramic model of the museum: IAA.

183 Columns of the museum's library, in progress: IAA.

187 Eric Gill's preliminary sketch of the Roman bas-relief for the museum courtyard: courtesy of the Williams Andrews Clark Memorial Library, University of California, Los Angeles.

188 Eric Gill carving at the museum; the caption is Harrison's: IAA.

189 Finished Gill panels: Assyria, Greece, Phoenicia: IAA.

190 Gill's "Mind the Step" from the museum's central court: photographed by the author, August 2014.

192 Finished museum and field: IAA.

196 Palestine Department of Antiquities, Arabic, English, Hebrew: photographed by the author, August 2014.

199 Jerusalem street sign, made by David Ohannessian: from the exhibition catalog *The First Governor*, ed. Nirit Shalev-Khalifa (Tel Aviv, 2010), by permission of a private collector. Reproduction photo Leonid Padrul © Eretz Israel Museum, Tel Aviv.

203 The al-Araj House, on what was Queen Melisande Way and is now Heleni Hamalka Street: photographed by the author, November 2012.

211 Spyro G. Houris stone signature: photographed by the author, July 2014.

214 Ad from *Doar Hayom*: November 17, 1919.

215 Spyro Houris: from David Kroyanker, *Talbiyeh, Katamon, and the Greek Colony* (Jerusalem, 2002).

216 The Vagabonds, *sitting*: Khalil Sakakini, Achille Seikaly, Adel Jaber; *standing*: George Khamees, Hanna Hamameh, Musa Alami, Anton Elias Muchabek. Photographed by Khalil Raad: courtesy of the Institute for Palestine Studies, Ramallah, Theodorie Collection.

223 Dr. Photios with Heleni and Clio: courtesy of Zalman Greenberg.

241 Ad from *Doar Hayom*: June 14, 1932.

251 The Hamon House, Romema, soon after it was built.

252 Judge Yom-Tov Hamon and his children, on the porch of the house that Spyro Houris built for them in Romema.

255 The Khoury House (site of Houris's office?), with the Aminof House under construction in the background, Jaffa Road: Matson Collection.

257 The Hajj Mahmud House, Jaffa Road 222, as it was soon after its construction: Matson Collection.

257 The Hajj Mahmud House: photographed by the author, July 2014.

260 The Gelat Villa, Talbiyeh: photographed by the author, August 2014.

263 Dome of the Rock: Matson Collection.

268 E. T. Richmond, pages from his memoir *Liber Maiorum*: courtesy of Emma Shackle and Sophie Richmond.

273 C. R. Ashbee in Jerusalem, 1919: CRA KC 1/44/356, by permission of the Ashbee estate.

281 David Ohannessian: IAA.

285 Armenian girls painting at the Dome of the Rock Pottery: Matson Collection.

287 Ronald Storrs and an Ohannessian Dome of the Rock; the inscription is Ashbee's: CRA KC 1/47/043, by permission of the Ashbee estate.

289 The al-Araj House and sky: photographed by the author, November 2012.

295 Heleni Efklides, Talbiyeh, 1930s: courtesy of Alex Corfiatis, Anastos Damianos, and the Greek community of West Jerusalem.

CPSIA information can be obtained
at www.ICGtesting.com
Printed in the USA
FFOW03n1945120417
34482FF

9 780374 536787